SUB-MODALITIES:

GOING META

Cinematic Frames for Semantic Magic

L. Michael Hall, Ph.D.

With
Bobby G. Bodenhamer, D.Min.

Foreword by Robert B. Dilts

© **1999** *The Structure of Excellence* (original title), **L. Michael Hall**
  2005 Second Edition, re-titled: *Sub-Modalities Going Meta*

Washington D.C.
Copyright Number: TXU 809-143
ISBN Number: 1-890001-17-1

Publishing Company: **NSP**: **Neuro-Semantic Publications**
                        P.O. Box 8
                        Clifton, CO. 815120—0008 USA
                        (970) 523-7877

Printing Company: **Action Printing**
                        Jerry Kucera, Owner
                        516 Fruitvale Court, Unit C
                        Grand Jct. Co. 81504
                        (970) 434-7701
                        Actionpres@aol.com

Special Thanks to—
  Fred Tapella of *Meta Publications* who granted permission for us to quote extensively from Robert Dilts' series, *"Strategies of Genius."*

  Vicky McCreary who carefully did the proof-reading of this text.

Neuro-Semantics® is the trademark name for the ISNS —International Society of Neuro-Semantics. See the many websites around the world for more than 3000 pages of free information:
                    www.neurosemantics.com
                    www.runyourownbrain.com

SUB-MODALITIES:
GOING META

APPENDICES

FOREWORD

By Robert Dilts

In this recent collaboration, Michael Hall and Bob Bodenhamer take the reader on an in-depth exploration into one of the key characteristics of personal excellence and genius: *the ability to shift levels of perception, or "go meta."* The term *meta* is a Greek word meaning "over," "between" or "above." In English it is also used to mean "about." A "meta model," for example, is a model *about* other models.

"Meta-cognition" is the awareness of one's own cognitive processes, i.e., cognition about cognition. *"Meta messages* are messages about other messages, which provide frames or context markers that influence the meaning of messages. *"Meta leadership"* involves leading leaders.

The ability to go *meta* is a key capability in NLP. It is one of the basic ways in which we are able to get a "double description" of a particular event or interaction. In conflict situations, achieving a "meta position" is essential for a successful resolution. A "meta position" would be a position "above and between" the two in conflict, which includes and acknowledges both conflicting perspectives to create something new. The new perspective either synthesizes the conflicting positions or allows them to co-exist in harmony.

Taking a meta position is also essential to effectively model ourselves or others, and to reflect on our own actions or relationships in difficult situations. From a "meta" position it is easier to look past the content of an action or situation and see its formal characteristics or deeper structure. The ability to go "meta" to one's own model of the world is a fundamental feature of introspection, self-reflection, and wisdom.

In this book, Michael and Bob apply this fundamental ability in the form of *the Meta-States model,* and through a new perspective on the mechanism and influence of "sub-modalities." In NLP, "sub-modalities" are the particular perceptual qualities that may be registered by each of the five primary sensory modalities. Each representational system is designed to perceive certain basic features of the experiences it senses. Our visual modality, for instance, can perceive such qualities as color, brightness, shape, depth, etc.; our auditory modality is capable of registering volume, pitch, tempo, etc.; our kinesthetic system perceives such qualities as pressure, temperature, texture, etc., and so on. These qualities are called "sub-modalities" since they are sub-components of each of the representational systems.

Hall and Bodenhamer assert that "sub-modalities" are not *"sub"* at all; but are rather meta-level phenomena—akin to Aristotle's idea of "common sensibles." According to Aristotle, the process of finding *patterns* from particular sense-perceptions takes place through the "common sense"—the place in our "psyche" where all of our senses meet and integrate their perceptions.

Aristotle believed that one of the functions of the "common sense" was to register something which was repeated in a number of experiences as a pattern. *Patterns or "universals"* were perceived in terms of a set of content-free qualities that Aristotle called the "common sensibles," the discriminations shared by all the senses. *Common sensibles* are movement, rest, number, figure, magnitude, unity; these are not peculiar to any one sense but are common to all. *Aristotle's common sensibles* are not a function of any particular sensory modality. They are on a different level than the so-called "sub-modalities" in NLP, which are perceived by the individual senses.

For example, "intensity" is something you can register in any sense. You can have intensity of color, sound, taste, smell or touch. It is the same with "number;" you can see three things, hear three things, feel three things, etc. Location and movement are also perceptible via all the senses. You can see, hear, feel or smell that something coming from a particular location or moving in a particular direction. These qualities are not a function of only one sense. They are something that can be shared by all the senses and facilitate the transfer of information between the senses. According to Aristotle, *common sensibles* allowed us to do our higher level mental processing.

Hall and Bodenhamer contend that all "sub-modalities" have the qualities that Aristotle associated with the "common sensibles." The traditional view of NLP tends to "objectify" or "nominalize" "sub-modalities," perceiving colors, smells and sounds as "things." (Many NLP techniques treat "sub-modalities" as if they are a checklist of "things" rather than higher level qualities.)

For instance, people talk about an internal image being *bright* or *distant* as if it were a "thing" associated with that particular image. To determine if an image is "bright," however, it is necessary to first determine, *bright compared to what?* An image is neither inherently "bright" nor "dim," "colorful" nor "dull," "distant" nor "close;" it is distant, colorful or bright compared to something else such as its background or another image. Hence, *distance, color, location* etc., are not things they can be put in a wheelbarrow; instead, they are *distinctions at a higher logical level.*

In the first part of the book, the authors explore this shift in perspective to update and extend the traditional NLP model, introducing the distinction of *Meta-Detailing* as an alternative to the typical view of "sub-modalities." They describe meta-detailing as a process which "operates on details from a meta-frame perspective." The authors say that meta-detailing represents a bridge between a global perspective and attention to specific details ... thus eliminating the conflict between the two as if an *either/or* choice.

The second part of the book has six sub-models constructed around six meta-level phenomena: believing, valuing, negating, foregrounding, understanding, and reframing. The authors give practical applications for these phenomena, including how they apply to belief change (the *Meta-Yes-ing* pattern) and value transformation. They have a chapter on Negation—with a list of eight kinds of negations. The authors take this approach to "sub-modalities" and the notion of meta-detailing as an explanation for the ability of many geniuses to move back and forth between different chunk sizes and levels of thinking.

One key characteristic of genius is the capacity to move easily between the broader vision and specific actions required to manifest the bigger picture. Geniuses can work with the little pieces and yet not become caught up in all of the details. They are also able to see the big picture without losing sight of the little pieces. The word *genius* comes from a Latin term meaning, "the superior or divine nature which is innate in everything." I like to point out that excellence comes from a passionate commitment to a single perspective. In order to become good at something, one must stay associated in one's own first position and focus. This is an important way to learn and progress, but it is not necessarily wise. Sometimes it produces unecological repercussions.

Genius comes from a passionate commitment to the integration of multiple perspectives. J. Bronowski (*The Ascent of Man*, 1973) claimed that *a genius* is a person who has not one, but *two great ideas,* and spends the rest of his or her life trying to get them to fit together. The implication is that when one has become excellent in several different areas and is able to synthesize them, one begins to approach genius.

Hall and Bodenhamer argue that this comes from the ability to *go meta*. We could also say that wisdom comes from a passionate commitment to the constant process of taking multiple perspectives. Since the world is in constant change, we cannot rely on yesterday's answers as being true for tomorrow. Wisdom is not something you do or get, it is something you participate in—in an ongoing way. In the words of Gregory Bateson: "[Wisdom comes from] sitting together and truthfully discussing our differences—without the intent to change them."

Michael and Bob have done NLP a great service by refocusing on its theoretical roots in the work of Bateson and Korzybski, and by re-placing its attention on the important and seminal notion of the ability to *go meta*. I am grateful to both of them for having brought so much insight about the nature of excellence, genius and wisdom into a single volume.

Robert Dilts
Co-Founder of NLP
Santa Cruz, CA.

PREFACE

With permission from the control tower to depart on this adventure, the Captain is making the final preparations for departure, so as you put your tray tables in their upright and secure position and secure your seat-belts ... take a moment to put yourself in a state of joyful and playful anticipation of the journey before us as we soar to new and greater heights of mind and meaning in search for the distinctions of genius within our mind-body-emotion Matrix..

Sub-Modalities Going Meta has to be one of the all-time strangest book titles, doesn't it? It's so full of esoteric terms and ideas:
*   What in the world are "sub-modalities?"
*   What does it mean to "go meta?"
*   How do "sub-modalities" go meta?
*   What difference does it make if our "sub-modalities" go meta?

Let me see if I can de-mystify some of that. This book deals with the *movies* that we make in our minds as we think. In fact, that's *how* we "think." We think by *representing* sights, sounds, sensations, even smells in our mind to create snapshots and movies. These "languages of mind" make up our *movie-mind*. Yet there's more. We have the ability to step back from our inner movies and *edit* them.

Do that right now. Think about a time and situation when someone was ugly and critical of you. Someone criticized you, called you names, acted stupid in your presence. Got a memory of that? Good. Did you notice how quickly images and perhaps sounds (words) popped in and out of your awareness? Did you see the person or the place? Did you have a sound track in your mind of his or her tone of voice and specific words? Did you step into the movie so that you were there or did you watch the movie as if from a distance?

Okay you've got a mental movie. Now make it all green, bright green. No, change that to pink, soft delicate pink. No orange, brilliantly bright orange. And are there some purple monkeys jumping around making monkey grunts as they throw banana peels on the ground or are you watching the critical person slipping and falling on his or her ass? And what if the person began complaining with a voice like Elmer Fudd, no Bugs Bunny, no Elvis Presley. Now, with all of that in mind, try to feel really bad (mad, sad, stressed, etc.) about that movie. How bad do you now feel?

Congratulations! You just played *Editor* to your own movie. You have just played around with a few of the cinematic frames to alter the sights, sounds, and sensations of one of your inner movies. And in doing so, you have probably changed your state, even your attitude. You have begun to "run your own brain" and to take charge of your inner self-communications so that you can respond to things rather than react.

Would you like more? Then that's what this book is all about. As the editor of your own movies, you can take charge of the dials or the cinematic features that frame your movies. These are called "sub-modalities" in NLP. And when you know how to play with them effectively, you can take your self-management, self-awareness, and emotional intelligence to a new level.

Re-Modeling NLP

Technically this book is about how we represent and encode information using "sub-modalities." Yet "sub-modalities" are not actually "sub-"—they are meta (which is the big secret in this book). So in this book we re-model NLP. Here we examine the finer distinctions of our representations (the so-called "sub-modalities") and *unmask* them. Doing so will *reveal* that they are actually higher to the modalities and so "meta-modalities." But that's still too much jargon, so we will call them the cinematic features of our movies.

This re-modeling creates lots of changes. It challenges the old structural understanding of "beliefs," understandings, negation, etc. It offers new structural models, and it opens up a whole new view of the cinematic features of our movies.

This book explores in some depth the NLP model and introduces facets of Neuro-Semantics. With these models that offer practical descriptions of human functioning and communicating, we explore afresh the idea of *modeling excellence.*

In the first part of this book we challenge and present several new refinements to the NLP model. Through the exploring and questioning of NLP, we offer some new developments that enriches and expands the model. What's our motive for this bold audacious assault on "sub-modalities?" We want to make the NLP model more consistent, elegant, effective, and useful. While we presuppose the reader is familiar with NLP, we also believe that an astute and careful reader will have little problem understanding these distinctions.

The second part of the book is more practical and dynamic. With the re-modeling that unmasks the true nature of "sub-modalities," and that fully integrates the pervasive role of *meta-levels* (meta-states, cinematic frames, etc.) into NLP, we present six new mental models for working with the meta-level experiences of beliefs, values, negations, knowledge, backgrounding /

foregrounding, and meaning.

Next we re-format several NLP patterns to create some new techniques
—processes which are now a part of the field of *Neuro-Semantics*. Using the
Meta-States model, we recast these meta-level phenomena and introduce
processes that have been proven in clinical experience that give people much
more control over their minds and states and therefore over their emotions,
behaviors, and lives.

Modeling the Structure of Excellence
What is the heart and passion for modeling? It is to *find the structure of
excellence* (of some expertise or genius) *and replicate it.* The exciting thing
about this is that it accelerates our learning and development. It puts us a fast
track to mastery.

One significant problem with the "sub-modality" model is that it failed to map
the way to greater quality of experience in the NLP community. Something was
missing. Do you know what? Here we identify that missing ingredient and
chart out how to use it to model excellence.

The idea of excellence drives our interest in genius and the structure of
achieving peak experiences. The adventure begins with *the structure* of
excellence. Actually, to detect excellence is easy. If we have eyes to see, we
can recognize it all around us. The challenge is to *unpack its form* so that we
can replicate it in our own lives—that's where the tough part comes in. Yet the
ultimate adventure in modeling is to map the structure of an expertise so that we
can replicate it and make it part of our experience.
* Can *genius* or mastery be modeled?
* What *skills* do we need in order to detect and unpack the patterns of
genius?
* What *distinguishes* mastery from non-mastery?
* What separates a genius in his or her *thinking*?
* What *factors* play a determining role in formatting our thinking and
feeling for excellence?
* How does the experience of *genius* work in human personality?
* What mechanisms and processes govern peak performances?
* How can we more efficiently handle with our intra-psychic processes
of thinking, emoting, understanding, remembering, valuing, etc. so that
we can cultivate more of our own *genius*?
* How do "sub-modalities" (the representational distinctions or cinematic
features of our inner movies) affect genius?
* How does genius or excellence relate to the features and components
of the representation systems?
* What is *meta-detailing* and what role does it play in excellence?

Behind the Scenes

After Bob and I collaborated on several books, the subject of the effectiveness of various "sub-modality" patterns repeatedly surfaced. Over the years, we both noted that many of *the "sub-modality" patterns* simply do not work consistently or dependably. Well, that's how I explained it. Bob said that he thought that it must be him, that *he* did not know how to work some of the patterns. That began our exploration. We began asking other practitioners and trainers about their experience with "sub-modality" patterns.

- What has been your experience with "sub-modality" patterns?
- Do you generally get the response that you expected and wanted?
- How does the "Doubt to Belief" pattern work for you?
- How does the "Confusion to Understanding" pattern work for you?

At the same time, I was traveling on a full-time basis conducting *Meta-States Trainings.* This gave me additional opportunities to ask such questions and to explore the relationship between meta-levels and "sub-modalities." From those experiences, I published several articles on the subject. That's when we teamed up to more intensively research these questions which led to unmasking "sub-modalities" and discovering their true nature.

In collaborating, we first wrestled with the ideas and then I formulated them in writing. The following pages primarily reflect my writing style even though *the ideas* and *the design* emerged from the synthesis of our interactions. In person and in cyberspace, our style is to bounce ideas back and forth until a joint synergy arises. Without Bob's creativity, insights, and practical wisdom which comes from his experience in teaching and consulting, I would not have half the "thought-balls" bouncing around in my head.

In this work, as in most of our projects, Bob provided more case study stories than I could possibly include. This is his expertise. He *actually* takes what we talk about and applies the discoveries directly and immediately with the people he consults. It's amazing! He has a marvelous *go for it* attitude that leads him to continuously delight his students and colleagues as he tries out the latest patterns we come up with. That then gives us more feedback for refining our models.

When I began researching this work, my intention and focus was on one thing—to map *the distinctions of excellence using "sub-modalities."* So when I first began to collaborate with Bob, we simply intended to write a book about "sub-modalities." Initially we set a simple intention—to write about the latest developments in "sub-modalities." We had no intention of challenging the "sub-modality" model, let alone re-modeling it. At that time we fully accepted the "sub-modality" model as we had received it from our elders. We only wanted to explore the limits of that model and see what else we could do with it and to perhaps chart out some new uses. It was in the process of working with "sub-modalities" as a model that we found it lacking and severely problematic. In the end, we discovered that the classic model was simply wrong. That began our heresy!

As we tweaked the "sub-modality" model, we found to our surprise that we were able to add some of the latest insights and developments from *the Meta-States model*. And as we did, we happened upon many new applications, patterns, techniques, and processes. We found a new way to change beliefs based upon a structural analysis of "beliefs."

Then Neuro-Semantics Emerged

This re-modeling and discovery of new patterns offers numerous thinks that extend and enrich the meta-discipline of NLP. At first we thought that our discoveries "introduced another meta-domain to NLP." That's what we wrote in the first edition. But we were wrong. The meta-domain of "sub-modalities" had been there all along, we only identified it as a *meta*-domain and showed its value and importance.

What did emerge was *Neuro-Semantics*®. With hindsight we can now see that the first edition, which we entitled *The Structure of Excellence* (1999), allowed Neuro-Semantics to emerge as a new model and field. Unknowingly we actually began developing Neuro-Semantics with the writing of *Mind-Lines: Lines For Changing Minds*. That book examined "the structure of meaning" and its expressions in our conversational frames about the world. So in *Mind-Lines* we used *Meta-States* to remodel the reframing and persuasion models of NLP.

Because this book explores and challenges NLP, several people encouraged us to write with an eye on those new to the field of NLP. So to make the work understandable, we present a simple description of the NLP model as a model (Ch. 1-3). The new reader will there discover the modeling or structural approach to human experience and the patterns that make up the form of our mental processing (our neuro-linguistics). These describe how we use our neurology (physiology) and linguistics to create our "programs" for functioning and operating in the world. These mapping processes contribute to make us the persons we are. Best of all, these descriptions enable us to actually do something about how we run our own brains and create our behavioral patterns.

The two terms, *neuro-semantics* and *neuro-linguistics* originated with Alfred Korzybski, founder of General Semantics. *Neuro-Semantics* refers to how we use our nervous system and brain to construct layers of *meaning* from our experiences. Doing this profoundly affects our physical experiences (neurology, body, health) as well as our psychological experiences (thinking, emoting, etc.).

A experience is *neuro-semantic* when we get our ideas and meanings so much into our body that we *feel* them in our body and can experience *semantic reactions*.

In the process of re-modeling NLP, we have honed, refined, and expanded many "sub-modality" patterns. This has given rise to an entirely new methodology that we call *meta-detailing*.

Is this still NLP? Or is this Neuro-Semantics? It is *enriched NLP*. The entire focus of everything here continues with the original passion of NLP—*modeling the structure of excellence*. So exploring what enables us to be at our best, to achieve peak performance, and to access our own genius, we continue the original passion that initiated NLP.

By exploring and re-modeling meta-level phenomena such as foregrounding and backgrounding, negating, believing, valuing, understanding conceptual knowledge, and reframing, we get a close-up look at the crucial role of *meta-level* structures as prerequisites for mastery.

It is these structural formatting of our internal knowings-and-feelings that either makes genius or undermines it. As excellence has structure, so does prevention-of-excellence. The new *meta-level patterns* for foregrounding, negating, believing, understanding, valuing, etc. enables us to clear out the things that prevent genius—limiting beliefs, traumas, and old programs and habits that hang on.

On the practical side this book refines the models and patterns that we use in *Accessing Personal Genius* (APG) training. The material in the book, *Secrets of Personal Mastery*, serves as a sequel to the patterns in this book.

Unmasking the Secrets of "Sub-modality"
In this book you will discover lots of new things in the domain of "sub-modalities." These new patterns offer practical uses for detecting and playing around with cinematic frames so that you will be able to perform marvelous and magical incantations for growth and persuasion.

Although we began with a desire to simply push the boundaries of "sub-modalities" in creating some new applications, a detour along the way sent us in an entirely different direction. That caused us to spend lots of time scratching our heads. Eventually we began re-thinking *the model* itself. That is when we discovered something pretty incredible— *there is no **sub-** in "sub-modalities."*

This came as a tremendous shock. After all, we had written about such in previous works (*Adventures with Time-Lines, Patterns for Renewing the Mind*).

It wasn't long before we discovered that the term itself misled.   It was a "linguistic fraud." Perhaps the idea of "finer" distinctions tricked someone and seduced them to associate *"sub"* with *"finer."* (Thank goodness they did not do the same thing with the *"finer"* distinctions of the *meta*-programs!) Shortly, you will get the first-hand scoop on these discoveries about the so-called ""sub-modalities" so that you will no longer be duped.

If you feel that we challenge too much of the NLP model about "sub-modalities," wait until you see the new refinements that it leads to and how the refinements revolutionize working with frames and meta-frames. This new approach will put into your hands some new and powerful ways to think about "sub-modalities," thereby enriching your ability to run your own brain.

- Do you want to know more explicitly *how* "sub-modalities" actually work?
- Do you want to discover how "sub-modalities" actually work magic at higher levels?
- Would you like to see the unmasking of the *sub* of "sub-modalities?"
- Would you like to work more elegantly and powerfully using these distinctions?
- Do you want greater ability to leverage a mind-body-emotion system?

Meta-States and "Sub-Modalities"
One of the *secrets of magic* you will discover here is that if a "sub-modality" shift works, it works because it activates a meta-level structure (or frame).

When we work with primary states, we can get by with mapping across the "sub-modalities" of one primary experience (feeling highly motivated) to another primary experience (feeling tired, fatigued, bored, unmotivated, etc.). We can *map across* the qualities and distinctions that make up strong and intense motivation (close, 3-D, movie, in color) to replace the old representational codings of the state of low motivation (far off, flat, slide, black-and-white or faded colors).

This will typically not work with meta-states. When it comes to layered states-about-states, we need to map across the meta-level structures or frames as well. You will also discover that the representational distinctions *take on more symbolic and semantic functions.* [If primary and meta-states are new distinctions, we will define these shortly.]

How do you represent high self-esteem and low self-esteem? Where do you *feel* these states kinesthetically in your body? These differ, do they not, from a primary state like anger, fear, joy, lust, relaxation, tension, etc.?

The "difference that makes a difference" does not occur inside the "sub-modality" features (our cinematic frames). It occurs at the level of frames. *Frames* comprise "the difference that make the difference." If you happened upon a "*sub*-modality" that just so happens to function as the see-hear-feel referent symbol, then you can get the frame to change. [Chapter 4 will make this clear.]

From where do we make "*sub*-modality" shifts anyway? You'll discover that it is from a higher level. By *going meta,* by stepping back from the structure of our subjective experience and from the modalities that format that structure, from *there* we do the contrastive analysis and shift the representational distinctions.

You'll also discover that this re-modeling of "sub-modalities" chases out the false attribution that "the difference that makes the difference" occurs at the "sub-modality" level. Today we know better. It does not. The difference that makes a difference in subjective human experiences occurs at meta-levels. It lies in the frames-of-references within which we find the experience embedded.

True elegance and skill in working with representations and representational distinctions ("sub-modalities") arise from the skill and recognition that higher frames-of-reference always govern, organize, and modulate lower levels. As you recognize them, and learn how to utilize this secret of magic, your work with "sub-modalities" will become much more magical. You will become a neuro-linguistic magician. You will recognize the very mechanisms and structures that govern thinking, emoting, speaking, and behaving. And it will give you more predictive powers about what shifts to make to obtain more efficient leverage in transforming a system.

Here you will discover a multitude of things about the structure of excellence.
- How to think about, and work with, "sub-modalities" as attractors in a self-organizing system.
- How to view them as *meta-level* structures.
- The explanatory principles that govern *why* "sub-modality" shifts sometimes work and sometimes do not.
- How to determine which ones will work and which ones will not with a given person.
- How to decide on which "sub-modality" shift to use when working with someone.
- How to more accurately predict which representational quality or feature to shift to reach the desired change.
- How to read "sub-modalities" in a person's external expressions and how to externalize them.
- How to use meta-level structures (frames, beliefs, values, domains of knowledge, meta-states, etc.) to amplify the effect of representational

distinctions.

- How to outframe "sub-modalities" that create internal misery as in trauma, phobia, and other painful states.
- How to linguistically communicate "sub-modality" codings to increase sales, influence, persuasion, etc.
- How meta-level understanding of "sub-modalities" expands and extends NLP, making it more elegant and powerful.
- How to correct the inadequacy and problems of "sub-modality" patterns by meta-level frames.
- Why certain failures with "sub-modalities" patterns do not implicate the practitioner as "an inept NLP-er" (as some have expressed their fears). It implicates the model as inadequate.

We know that we have given *the term* "sub-modalities" a really hard time in this book. We recognize that it may seem that we have taken it into a back room and pummeled it right and left leaving it black and blue and doubled over in pain. But don't worry. We do that mostly for effect. We really have no intention of putting a gun to its head and blowing out its brains.

Given that the term has become deeply entrenched in NLP, our intention is not to retire it. We will continue to use it but with this difference—we will put it in quotes. *Quotes,* as a Korzybskian device, alerts the discerning reader that there are problems with the term. Handle it with care or it will bite you.

The re-modeling of "sub-modalities" here does not fault the original NLP model. It rather refines the model that we consider a stroke of genius. Here we build upon it, fully aware that we have a privilege and opportunity that the original developers did not—namely, thirty years of hindsight!

Going for It

If you want to discover more about the structure of excellence, or in running your own brain more powerfully and elegantly, this is the book for you! We have loaded it with all kinds of goodies for your consumption. And you can even now begin to wonder about just how sumptuous you will find these goodies as you anticipate turning page after page to get bigger and brighter pictures about all the possibilities before you ... and as you hear an ever-increasing resonant voice arising within you compelling you into a more ferocious state of discovery, of learning, and excitement ... as you feel a sense of warmth and lightness arising making you more alert, more creative, more joyful than you have ever been before now ... but only the beginning of the kind of playfulness that you will see and hear in yourself and others as you sense your future getting clearer and brighter about accessing your own personal genius ... as you look up in that direction now ... because that inner voice allows you to know that you can.

PART I

UNMASKING

"SUB-MODALITIES"

THE *META* OF *SUB*-MODALITIES

Re-modeling "Sub-Modalities"

By Identifying the Meta-Levels

Formerly Mapped as "Sub-"

Chapter 1

BRIEF OVERVIEW OF NLP

"NLP is an attitude,
backed up by a methodology,
that leaves behind a trail of techniques."
(Richard Bandler)

When NLP began in 1975, it opened up a whole new understanding regarding human functioning and human potential. As a science of human excellence, it showed how to precisely take charge of our lives by discovering the magic of "running our own brains."

Co-founded by two most unlikely creators of this new domain, NLP struggled for credibility among the academicians and theorists because the founders did not have a psychology background. And yet, as two creative geniuses outside the paradigm, they saw and developed things that those within the psychological paradigms did not see. This tremendously contributed to the richness and creativeness of the model.

Mr. Linguistics Meets Mr. Computer Mathematician
It all began when a student of computer programming and mathematics (Richard Bandler) discovered that he could hear and replicate the language patterns of the world renown psychotherapist, Fritz Perls (founder of Gestalt Therapy) and the equally famous Family Therapist, Virginia Satir. What enabled Bandler to detect and replicate *the excellence* of such psychotherapeutic mastery? He didn't know.

Enter his linguistics professor, Dr. John Grinder. Using the tools of Transformational Grammar, his speciality field, Grinder unpacked the structure of the magic that Perls and Satir demonstrated and which Bandler's genius could so easily mimic.

Together, they designed a model that modeled the structure of "the magic" that the therapeutic wizards so skillfully manifested. This first appeared as the books, *The Structure of Magic* (1975, 1976). They then met another genius, Milton Erickson, M.D., founder of Ericksonian hypnosis. Modeling his "magic" with hypnotic language they produced the books, *Patterns of the Hypnotic Techniques of Milton H. Erickson, M.D.* (1975, 1977). This officially gave birth to the field of NLP.

Programs For Running Your Own Brain

When it comes to *running your own brain*, we first have to have a bit of understanding regarding how brains operate or "run."

- How do brains operate?
- What do brains *process* in order to create our sense of reality?
- What comprises the "software" of consciousness?
- How can we take charge of our own brain so that it cooperates with our highest values and goals?
- How do we install new and better software programs?
- What mechanisms govern how this works?
- What principles or laws govern these mechanisms?

Somewhere at the beginning, Grinder and Bandler stumbled upon the idea of *reducing* consciousness or mind to a most surprising and yet un-profound element, and yet this led to a most astonishing discovery. What did they discover? They discovered that they could use *the human senses* (i.e., the sensory systems of sight, sound, sensations, smells, and tastes) as the very *components* out of which "thought," consciousness, and "mind" arise. This discovery proved both simple and yet profound.

Profound because it revolutionized the field of psychology and communication. Others key figures in psychology (Wilheim Wundt, Tichner, Williams James, etc.) had come so close to this very thing, and yet they never quite put it together. It took two men outside the paradigm to do that. Coding mental phenomena in terms of the senses enabled Bandler and Grinder to formulate the foundations our human neuro-linguistics. Next, they specified several key *mechanisms* by which we use the sensory representational systems to effect and take charge of our everyday experiences. This initiated the field of NLP.

To run our own brain, we first need to become aware of the *modes* of awareness—our visual images, auditory sounds, kinesthetic sensations, the smells and tastes. As a shorthand, we call this *the VAK* (an acronym for Visual, Auditory, and Kinesthetic, this stands for all sensory representations). We also have another *mode* of awareness—words, the words we say to ourselves, and which we use, as mental representations. These comprise yet another *modality*. Together, all of these pictures, sounds, voices, and feelings in our head run our internal communication or signaling system to the rest of our nervous system (i.e., our neurology, body, emotions) which creates our states, moods and attitudes.

> Is this discovery that important?
> If it is important, in what way?
> What makes it important?

What happens when we reduce something as complex as all of our mental phenomena—thinking, mind, consciousness, etc., to something as simple as the *sensory elements* of sights, sounds, sensations, smells, tastes, and words? It puts into our hands the controls for running our own brain. Now we can use these communication processes and mechanisms to take charge of the signals we send to our own mind-body system.

Tony Robins (1989) calls this "representational power." By using these *modes* of awareness and taking control of our own internal world, we take ownership of our mind-brain system. Practically, this means that we no longer have to wait until we're "in the mood" to take charge, feel resourceful, or take effective action to respond in a way that will build up personal excellence. *We can create the mood.*

We do not have to wait until we get into the state or attitude of mind to where we feel motivated, confident, loving, joyful, or whatever. We can induce ourselves into the best states. We can even design engineer (Korzybski's 1921 terminology) our own states of mind-and-emotion. This gives us some pretty powerful *choice points* as it puts us in a place where we can truly take charge of our mind and life. This is the foundation of excellence.

Understanding this platform about the structure and distinctions of excellence, we can choose to keep entertaining the same old sights, sounds, sensations, words, etc., and keep getting the same old results we have always gotten.

> Keep doing what you've always done and you'll keep getting what you've always gotten.

But why do that? If we want to do something new, even revolutionary, we can choose to edit some of the internal movies in our heads for an entirely different effect. We can entertain ourselves with a whole new virtual reality on a Star Trek™ holodeck of our mind, and then step into it.[1] Just think of the possibilities!

What we *do* inside our minds via the *control knobs* of our internal sense representations (visual images, auditory sounds, kinesthetic sensations, words, etc.) creates (or constructs) what we experience as "reality." Given the kind of bodies that we have, we operate as pattern detectors. The functioning of our nervous system "abstracts" or *maps* our sense of reality. What we remember of the past and what we imagine in the future—we *construct* using our sensory tools. These are the things that run our brains. Picturing, hearing, sensing, smelling, and saying words—are the *processes* by which we "think" and "encode" information.

Virtual Reality Center— An Internal Holodeck

Suppose that you became aware that an old B-rated movie continues to play in your head which makes you feel like crap. Remembering those horrible scenes from the past then undermines your resourcefulness. That would certainly put a dent in accessing your personal genius. Let's further suppose that you not only have been playing that old horror movie over and over, but that you continue to do so. Would that be a fun way to live?

As strange as it may seem, some people actually run their brain that way. And, they keep on doing it year after year. Why? Probably because it's a habit and on automatic. Or, they may simply not know any better. Or, they may not know *how* to stop it. Or, they may believe that they *have to* do that.

But no longer. Now, you can sit back in the theater of your mind and play that B-rated movie while *just observing* it and wonder what resources that younger you needed back then, can you not? You can *just watch* it like a spectator. When you finish it, you can fast forward it to a happy time. Then you can step into that scene of pleasure and just for the hell of it, rewind the movie in one second. You can freeze-frame it, turn it into a black-and-white snapshot, and then let it fade out, if you know what I mean. You can see your resourceful adult self walk into that old movie and kick butt, can you not? Now, as you do these kinds of things—just inside your head, of course—you can munch on your popcorn and enjoy the process.

In fact, you can do all kinds of things, things in your world of mind that would make Steve Spielberg drool, can you not? And best of all, the Mind Police will not arrest you for it. In that world of mind, you are the lord and master. And why not? It's *your* virtual reality. It is not the territory. It merely represents a mapping of the territory. And *you* created it. It represents *your* neuro-linguistic construction, your model of the world. And sure enough, you can create any kind of wild and crazy world you want. But remember, you also have to use it to navigate the outside territory. (Yes, I know, "What a bummer!") This explains how some people create totally bizarre and schizophrenic maps *and* attempt to use them for real-world navigation. They just prefer the Virtual Reality World of their Matrix to the stuff on the outside.

As mental mapping, the way we construct our sights, sounds, and sensations, our internal movies of memories and imaginations, set the stage for our Virtual Reality World. Now, if it provides you an intelligent way for taking effective action and navigating your ship to the places you want to go, then, by all means, keep it. Set it as your story, your blueprint, your frame. Let it keep serving you well. But if it fools you, if it map things falsely and not true-to-fact; if it sends you down dead-end alleys, and makes your life a living hell, then by all means close down that holodeck, exit the Matrix, clear the slate, and program something that will enhance your life.[1]

Our power of representing the world and constructing mental maps is our ultimate power and freedom. As a map-maker, you have the ability to represent things in any way you choose. Richard Bandler says repeatedly, "Hey, it's your brain! It's *you* doing it!"

Consider this kind of magic which governs the inner landscapes of our mind and how we language our realities into existence. With this kind of magic, we can even go so far as to custom design and engineer our map of reality. But, do you dare? Do you have a map for such daring?

Do you want to feel loved and valued, curious and resilient, full of hope and trust? Do you want to operate from a mental map of assertiveness, thoughtfulness, authenticity, gentleness, forgiving and yet decisive? Do you want to dream wild and wonderful dreams like Disney and Einstein? Do you want to turn visions of the future into realistic tools and products for today like Leonardo de Vinci and Nikola Tesla? Would you like to develop the excellence of negotiating, selling, persuading, teaching, parenting, staying fit, or experiencing a caring relationship? All of these states and experiences arise from *the way we structure our thoughts* as we use the movies in our mind. These create our strategies, whether strategies of genius or of pathology.

The Original Driving Model
NLP began with the Meta-Model as its foundational model—a linguistic model that enables us to pull apart and understand the structure of experience. Recognizing that the maps we build at the linguistic levels activate sensory-based representations at the neurological levels—the founders used to track from surface sentence structures the to deep structures as their central methodology. Transformational Grammar endowed NLP the basic orientation of the Meta-Model: "Look behind and within terms themselves. Question them until you get a full and well-formed linguistic mapping that can be represented or mapped as a VAK movie in your mind."[2]

Strategies first, then "Sub-modalities"
Richard Bandler and John Grinder soon discovered that they could use the sensory modalities of the representational systems (our VAK mental movies) to map the structure of experience. This mental mapping uses our internal pictures (visual), sounds (auditory), sensations and feelings in the body (kinesthetics), smells (olfactory), tastes (gustatory), and words (language) to construct and

represent ideas. Words in the movies could be the sound-track or a higher or meta-representation. In this, language operates as a higher level or system of representation about the movie, a *meta-representational system.*[3]

These pieces describe the component variables of the NLP model. With them, we can put together the structure and sequence of an experience using the template of a stimulus-response flow chart. This lets us track a person's responses from original **S**timulus to final **R**esponse (S-R). The cognitive psychologists, Miller, Pribram, and Gallanter (1960) developed this model to create the TOTE— the **T**est-**O**perate-**T**est-**E**xit model. Into this Bandler and Grinder put the representational steps. They created the strategy model out of the feedback-loop TOTE model.

Dilts, *et al.* (1980) formulated the strategy model in the first Volume of *Neuro-Linguistic Programming* by taking the linear stimulus-response model, updated as the TOTE Model (Miller, Pribram, and Gallanter, 1960) and introduced the discrete sensory representations into it.

From strategies, the modelers then identified the features of the representation modalities. As they listed dozens of "finer" distinctions, they designated the characteristics, qualities, and variables in each sensory system *"sub-modalities."*

Actually, it was Todd Epstein who first designated these distinctions by name. He called them *Pragmagraphics.* This term focused on the *graphics* in the visual, auditory, kinesthetic systems and their *pragmatic* effects. In this, the term is more accurate than "sub-modalities." The features of our VAK movies —the graphic characteristics lead to action tendencies in the body.

Now the story or myth that I heard about this is that Richard Bandler didn't like that term pragmagraphics because it was too big. So, wanting something simpler, he changed it to "sub-modalities." (Like that really helped!) Yet this introduced the misleading idea that somehow the cinematic features of our mental movies were *"sub"* to our representations. So with this term several unuseful assumptions to modeling the structure of experience were introduced into the NLP model—the subject of chapter four.

David Gordon's (1976) book *Therapeutic Metaphors* was the first book to mention the term "sub-modalities." Actually David devoted an entire section of the book to "sub-modalities" and showed their power and effectiveness. Then something very surprising happened. After that work, not another book even mentioned "sub-modalities" for the next eight years. It was as if the idea of "sub-modalities" didn't even exist in NLP. None of the original "seminar"books that Steve Andreas edited from Bandler and Grinder even mentioned "sub-modalities" (*Frogs into Princes*, 1979, *Tranceformations,* 1981,

Reframing, 1982).

Then a revolutionary discovery was announced—"Sub-Modalities" has been found! In 1984-1985 several books suddenly discovered "sub-modalities." 1985 was the date on the first "NLP history chart" that I received in my NLP trainings with Bandler—the date they found "sub-modalities!" Suddenly "sub-modalities" was front and center in NLP literature, books, and trainings.

> *Magic In Action* (1984).
>
> *Using Your Brain—For A Change* (1985) transcripts of Bandler's edited by Connirae and Steve Andreas.
>
> *An Insider's Guide to "Sub-modalities"* (1988) by Bandler and McDonald.
>
> *Change Your Mind and Keep the Change* (1989)by Steve and Connirae Andreas
>
> *The Heart of the Mind* (1990) by Steve and Connirae Andreas

These classic NLP books wonderfully presented the magic of the structure of experience. In them are many of the most practical "sub-modalities" patterns that we have in NLP. Some of the "sub-modality" patterns by the Andreases and Bandler present highly powerful distinctions that convey the magic to alter experiences. These patterns include the movie rewind pattern to cure phobias and neutralize traumatic memories, effective grieving and pre-grieving, using "time" codes to effectively manage our sense of past, present, and future, the encoding of empowering decisions, the meta-level phenomenon of "understanding" versus all the ways we can feel confused, the structure of feeling criticized, how to take criticism effectively, motivation, etc.

Focusing on this realm as "*sub*-modalities" meant making the subterranean dimension or the sub-molecular level of consciousness the secret within the secret of NLP. It totally captured the attention and interest of Richard Bandler. With the passing of time, he became completely lost in making every model operate from "sub-modalities." As he increasingly relied on this model, he seemed to forget about (or discount) meta-functions and meta-patterns. Perhaps that's why he doesn't use the Neuro-Logical Levels of Dilts or the Meta-States of Hall. In the DHE (*Design Human Engineering.*™) approach he builds imaginary structures or metaphors like grids and globes, and uses trance states to get people to project these structures out onto the territory. You will find this approach in his works on time patterns (*Time for a Change*, 1993) and persuasion (*Persuasion Engineering*, 1996).[4]

Then Came The Patterns
With the elements of our mental mapping (the sensory modes and the meta-representation system of words) and a process flow chart for ordering and structuring the syntax of mind (the TOTE model / strategies model), the

modelers only needed to invent various processes that would provide us specific techniques for running our own brain. And this they did.

Joined by Leslie Cameron-Bandler, Robert Dilts, and Judith DeLozier, the team of co-founders began specifying human technologies that we call *patterns*. Using the patterns of excellence that they found in their original models, as well as in others, along with those that they invented or stumbled onto, they began generating a whole list of patterns.

These patterns as tools or technologies provided ways to create instant rapport, to de-energize old phobic patterns, to frame meanings, to re-align unconscious conflicting programs, to change limiting beliefs, to alter memories of personal history, etc. For a list of 77 of the most central NLP Patterns see *The Source Book of Magic*.

When the Magic Failed— Discovering Meta-Programs

It wasn't long into the NLP experience that Leslie Cameron-Bandler began noticing that the classic NLP patterns sometimes did not work. Taking this as the doorway to new valuable information rather than "failure," she and Richard began questioning, wondering, and exploring. Out of the spirit of unquenchable curiosity they discovered the second meta-domain of NLP—*Meta-Programs*.

They discovered an incredible feat that humans could perform. They discovered that every one of the most powerful NLP processes could be stopped dead in its tracks if a person *filtered it* in just the right way. Imagine that! Perceptual filtering styles and thinking patterns can sabotage the best technology for creating health, sanity, and excellence!.

What does this mean? It means that at *a meta-level,* a person can have a *program* running (a meta-program) that can nullify the most advanced technology of excellence. Incredible, don't you think? *Meta-programs* must be incredibly powerful filters.

At first they only had eight or nine meta-programs. Eventually by the time Roger Bailey and Ross Stewart found them and organized them into the LAB profile, the number of meta-programs grew to fourteen. Sometime later, Wyatt Woodsmall and Tad James (1988) formalized and expanded them. After that, we (Hall and Bodenhamer, 1997) extended the Meta-Programs model to 51 meta-programs as a basis for understanding "personality." This is found in the encyclopedic formatting in *Figuring Out People* (1997) and then used in *The Structure of Personality* (2001).

Discovering the Third Meta-Domain—Meta-States

From the beginning NLP has been a *meta*-domain. The first model, the Meta-Model, mapped out how language works in our neurology to create our experiences. Bateson gave Bandler and Grinder the phrase *"going meta"* which they used prolifically. They talked about meta-parts, meta-positions, meta-persons, meta-communication, meta-representation system, the meta-function, etc.

The terminology of "going meta" and its concept originated with one of the foundational sources of NLP, Gregory Bateson. In one of the most challenging yet rewarding books, *Steps To An Ecology of Mind*, Bateson (1972) introduced the *meta function*. This then led to the use of the *meta-position* in modeling the structure of experience. He and his associates incorporated it into their Double-Bind Theory as they asserted that it as an absolutely essential component in modeling the structure of schizophrenia. Bateson also used it explicitly in his Levels of Learning model.

It was from Bateson that I constructed the Meta-States model, Bateson and Korzybski. Yet I wasn't the first to use the phrase. Woodsmall (1989) listed "meta states" in an appendix his workbook on Meta-Programs describing other possible meta-programs. However, Meta-States® *as a model* found its first explicit expression in 1994, and so became the third meta-domain. Yet, as with Meta-Programs, Meta-States arose when I found the strategy model inadequate for modeling a complex and layered state like resilience. I came up with Meta-States to track the meta-levels of resilience (Hall, 1995).

Meta-States as a model built on, and enriched, the two discrete NLP models for working with and modeling subjective experience: strategy and state. The model about "states" formatted subjective experiences in terms of our states mind-body-emotion states: our states of mind, states of body, and states of emotion. These facets (i.e., mind, body, emotion) comprise what Bandler and Grinder designated as a *neuro-linguistic* state (a term shanghaied from Korzybski).

What drives these dynamic mind-body states? Sensory-specific representations which make up the movies we play in our minds and their distinctive *cinematic features* (what we call "sub-modalities") as well as higher level mental constructions (i.e., the meta phenomena of ideas, understandings, beliefs, values, decisions, etc.)—encoded in language, the meta-representation system.

In Meta-States I identified and distinguished three kinds of states: *primary, meta, and gestalt.* In a primary state, our thoughts-and-feelings and full somatic experience, go out to reference an object "out there." In primary states, our state is *about* things out beyond our nervous system.

> "I think he's a jerk because he seems angry and I feel threatened by his behavior."

By way of contrast, in a meta-state we experience our thoughts-and-feelings *reflecting back* onto ourselves.

> "I wonder if I look afraid of him; I hope not. Why do I have to wimp out just because someone else is having a bad day?"

The meta-states here are *wondering* about self-image and self-questioning. A meta-state involves what has been termed *self-reflexive consciousness.* Thinking-about-thinking generates thoughts-and-feelings at a higher logical level and creates a state about another state. In this way, meta-states reference previous states—either in part (a thought, a feeling, a somatic experience) or in full. Rather than referring to something "out there" in the world, a meta-state refers to something about or regarding some previous thought, emotion, concept, understanding, etc.

Korzybski described this phenomenon. He talked about meta-states as an abstraction about an abstraction—as a second-order abstraction, a third-order abstraction, etc. He noted that this ability of self-reflexivity goes on and on and on without end. In animals, the process always ends. In human consciousness it does not. Whatever thought or emotion we entertain, we can then experience another thought or feeling (state) about it. This describes a crucial difference between humans and animals. At some point, every animal stops abstracting. Both Korzybski and Bateson noted that we may find animals abstracting two and three levels. Both also noted that *at some point* they quit abstracting.

But not us humans. We never quit. Feed us a thought—and you can count on a human mind coming up with a thought or a feeling *about* that one. Then one about that one. This creates the looping and spiraling of the mind.

As *a symbolic and semantic-class of life,* we inevitably live our lives at meta-levels. In fact, our most unique human experiences occur, not at the primary level, but at the meta-levels. At these levels we experience all sorts of higher level phenomena: beliefs, values, domains of understandings or background knowledge, concepts, expectations, decisions, permissions, identity, intentionality, etc. It's not surprising, then, that to model human excellence (or pathology), we have to *go meta* and specify the layering of our states and frames. We have to recognize the meta-levels because they play a role in the systemic nature of consciousness. This phrase, by the way, refers to how these higher levels of awareness operate reflexively and recursively. They go around and around. They loop. They utilize feedback and feed forward loops.

A meta-state refers to what we all experience every day of our lives —*states about states*. Fear of our anger. Hesitation about our fear. Procrastination about our impulsiveness. Guilt about our fear of our anger. Joy about our learning. Calmness about our anger. Willingness to face our fear in the anticipation of obtaining a desired outcome that we value. Take any state of mind-emotion-body and apply it to any other state, and presto—you create a meta-state.

The active process of meta-stating refers to the process of *bringing* a state to bear upon another state, *applying* one state to another, or referencing one state in terms of another. When we do this, we *set* a frame-of-reference at a higher level.

To bring calmness and relaxation to bear upon our anger sets a frame so that we feel anger calmly. This generates a new structure: *calm* anger. Calm thoughts-feelings-soma (body) now layers the consciousness of anger. Once a higher frame gets set, then we think, feel, perceive, and respond from within that frame. This stabilizes the experience. Our everyday experiences are then *embedded* in that context.

By meta-stating we construct higher level constructs—paradigms, concepts, understandings, and models of the world. These then govern the lower level thoughts. Such frames (or meta-states) will then operate as *attractors* in a self-organizing system. As such the system (i.e., a human organism with a nervous system that abstracts) now experiences the *organizing influence* of the frame. So, in the mind (in the neuro-linguistic system of mind-body) the higher levels of mind, constructed by mind as it utilizes feed-back and feed-forward energies, become a dynamic self-organizing energy itself.

Bateson described this as the higher levels organizing, driving, and modulating the lower levels. Dilts described this as part of the operational definition of a higher "logical level." As we do this, the higher meta-states formulate our larger and ultimate model of the world or paradigm, or what Dennis Chong calls our "Hierarchy of Paradigms."

In our ongoing mission for exploring our internal virtual realty, we use our layered meta-states as our reference system for "making sense" of things. This ever moving upward to process higher levels (and the frames it generates) *frames* our meanings, evaluations, or semantics. It creates our *neuro-semantic* levels.

What's the point? The point is that these higher frames explain and format our experiences. It all began with simple representing, then it got complicated. We represent our representations. We reflect back on our thoughts with more thoughts and in the end, we build up a complex internal world full of paradigms and higher level frames, our Matrix. This *structures* our understandings, beliefs, values, and meanings.[5]

Then, as we move through the world in our everyday lives, we have all kinds of ready-made *programs* from which we give meanings to things. We don't have to think about it. It just happens. We are primed to bring our virtual reality constructions to bear on all kinds of things out there. We first meta-state ourselves, then we meta-state others. The structure of excellence resides in these systemic processes, as also does the structure of psychosis.

We can also *outframe*. That is the ultimate meta-move. We can go above and beyond all of our frames and think-and-feel about our frames. What a rush that is. Talk about transcendence! We can step back or move up a level to get some distance and then as we think about our states, we can reality test them, evaluate their usefulness (the ecology check), and blast out those that are not ecological. Talk about choice. Talk about the possibility of setting entirely new frames. And here, we also can engage in serious meta-magic that can re-set our whole reality strategy.

NLP as a Model
As a *model,* NLP has all of the parts which make it an operational model.

1) A theory. We have theory in the NLP presuppositions and principles. These summarize the theoretical foundation and background of the model. These presuppositions point us to Korzybski's map/territory model, the linguistic model in Transformational Grammar, the systems theories in cybernetics and computer programming, the cognitive psychology model in Miller's TOTE, etc.

2) Variables and elements: A model has a structure or formula that contains and holds various elements and variables. In NLP, we have the sensory-systems, the representation systems, the language model, strategies, and meta-programs.

3) Operational principles or guidelines: The specific instructions about how we can use the model and patterns to run our own brain, manage our states, and create new resources and options.

4) Patterns: The step-by-step processes that we can use to achieve new levels of performance and pleasure, and to actualize our potentials.

These are the parts of the model that enable us to organize our perceptions and understandings about experience and how it works. Whether we focus on pathological experience (dysfunction, limiting beliefs, disordering of personality, etc.) or on excellence and genius (peak experiences, flow, or being "in the zone") we now have a way to model the structure of excellence.

Summary

*   NLP provides many models for taking charge of your life. So far we have three meta-domains: a model for language elegance (the Meta-Model), a model for perceptual refinement (the Meta-Programs), and a state management model (Meta-States). The fourth one will soon be revealed.

*   The primary *neuro-linguistic mechanisms* that put mastery into our hands include the sensory model of the representation systems and their distinctive features ("sub-modalities"), the language model about the mapping we do with words, and the patterns for achieving particular mind renewal.

*   Overall the NLP model enables us to run our own brain to create new resources for activating our potentials.

*   As a model with a theory, a structure, and guiding principles, NLP gives us practical technologies for enhancing our communications, empowering our state management skills, and understanding the maps we are using as we move through life.

*   *Excellence* has a structure that we can model and replicate in our own lives.

*   This overview of NLP now allows us to explore it in more depth with an eye on the structure of excellence and how we can use it to access our own personal genius.

End Notes:

1. If *holodeck* is unfamiliar to you, it refers to a room on the starship Enterprise in the movie and TV series, StarTreck where the crew spends leisure time for rest and relaxation. This invention of the twenty-third century enables me to use the computer to generate any kind of environment or world that they want. The *holodeck* is a fantasy world for fun and pleasure, or for learning and discovery.

2. See *Communication Magic* (2000) for an updated and expanded version of the Meta-Model.

3. *Meta* is a relational term that refers to something *above* or *beyond* something else. Language enables us to encode and symbolize meanings at a higher level *about* the sensory representations. A term like "strawberry" summarizes all of the sights, sounds, smells, sensations, and tastes of the juicy red fruit.

4. Chapter 4 will radically challenge the theory that drives DHE and "sub-modalities" and explain why it only occasionally works and when it does, it works semantically at meta-levels.

5. For more about the Matrix, see *The Matrix Model* (2003).

Chapter 2

MAPPING THE STRUCTURE
OF EXPERIENCE

Although we have all grown up confusing the two,
it still remains that—
"The map is not the territory."
(Korzybski, 1933)

"Subjectivity is unavoidable which makes it reality."
(Joseph Yeager, 1985)

•   Can human *experience* be mapped?
•   Can the structure of the experience be mapped in such a way that we can use it as a blueprint?

Richard Bandler and John Grinder initiated the field of NLP by originally mapping the cognitive strategies of three exceptionally talented "therapeutic wizards" *(Virginia Satir, Fritz Perls, and Milton Erickson)*. They then made an explicit model of the implied one used by those geniuses—from that arose the formal discipline known as NLP.

This gave birth to the idea that we can map the structure of any experience, even that of genius. Later Robert Dilts explored in depth numerous geniuses in various fields. He then documented this in his extensive study of three volumes, *The Strategies of Genius*. His research made salient the idea that although geniuses experience similar human conditions and limitations, they have an advantage. What is that advantage?

> *They use their neurology, linguistics, and semantics in such a way that they create inner movies and frames that support their new creative and innovative approaches.*

Robert examined in varying levels of detail the lives and genius of *Aristotle, Sir Arthur Conan Doyle's Sherlock Homes, Walt Disney, Wolfgang Amadeus*

Mozart, Albert Einstein, Sigmund Freud, Leonardo da Vinci, and Nikola Tesla. He tracked down the cognitive strategies and states which allowed them to create such rich maps of the world which, in turn, empowered them to do things and go places that excelled others.

Geniuses operate from a different paradigm, a different way of perceptually filtering and sorting things, from a different conceptual reality, and from a more advanced way of using his or her nervous system. The individuals who perform *excellence* at higher levels and in new ways also use different mental-and-emotional strategies. And now we have the tools and processes for *mapping the structure of experience.* This is the excellent adventure of NLP that we'll explore in this chapter.

The "Excellent" Adventure of NLP
The NLP model launches us into an adventure. By it, we move into the wild and wonderful adventure of exploring human subjective experiences. In this fluid world, the structure that we explore is dynamic and systemic. Doing this leads us to explore the central questions about how we function as mind-and-body humans living within multiple layered internal and external environments.
*   How does our mind-and-body system operate to create our experiences?
*   What neuro-linguistic processes run these operations?
*   How does our mind-body-emotions system work?
*   What are the "building blocks" of subjective experiences?
*   What factors make the most difference for long-term success?
*   How can we run our own brain more efficiently at all levels?

To organize this adventure, NLP sequences the three most influential components that govern everyday experiences:
*   *Neurology*: The human body, nervous system, physiology.
*   *Language:* Symbols, symbolic systems, words, mathematics, music, metaphors, gestures, etc.
*   *Programming*: Processes, habits, patterns.

Holistically, these facets of the human experience combine to create our "reality" (our sense of what's real). And because of this, we can use them to describe how our neuro-linguistic system operates in terms of the processes and dynamics which make up what we call "personality."

As a cognitive model, NLP starts from the General Semantics principle that distinguishes map and territory. Structurally we do not deal directly with the world. We deal with it as filtered throughout our neurology and linguistics. We relate to the world via our maps, frames, paradigms, and models. Whether we like it or not, we live by models, not relaity. Modeling is our way of life. It is the adventure of life as we create maps to navigate life.

Modeling—Mapping to Chart the Territory

Three modeling processes describe how we create our internal maps of the world: *deleting, generalizing,* and *distorting.* By these processes we translate the energy manifestations "out there" in the world and transform them into neurological and mental maps inside ourselves—maps that we use to guide our thinking, feeling, and acting.

Deletion. We delete because we cannot possibly process all of the billions of bits of information that impinge upon us at any given moment. That would overwhelm us. Nor do we even have the sensory apparatus to input all available data. Our eyes scan only a very narrow part of the light spectrum. Our ears receive only a very narrow band of sound wave frequencies. That's why we do not deal with reality directly, but indirectly. We only register a small portion of the sights, sounds, sensations, smells and tastes that we do input. As we do this, our brain protects us by selectively attending. Deleting only becomes problematic when we eliminate critically essential information.

Writing about our brain and nervous system, Huxley (1954) notes:

> "... to protect us from being overwhelmed and confused by this mass of largely useless and irrelevant knowledge, by shutting out most of what we should otherwise perceive or remember at any moment ... To make biological survival possible, Mind at Large has to be funneled through *the reducing valve of the brain and nervous system.* What comes out at the other end is a measly trickle of the kind of consciousness which will help us to stay alive on the surface of this particular planet." (p. 23 *italics* added)

Writing about our mapping of reality, Dilts, Bandler, Cameron-Bandler, Grinder, and DeLozier (1980) wrote:

> "Rather, we operate through coded interpretations of the environment as received and experienced in our sensory representational systems—through sights, sound, smell, taste and feeling. Information about our internal universe (as well as our internal states) is received, organized, consolidated and transmitted through an internal system of neural pathways that culminate in the brain—our central processing bio-computer. This information is then transformed through internal processing strategies that each individual has learned." (pp. 3-4)

In a classic paper, Miller (1956) established $7^{+/-2}$ chunks of information as the typical range for consciousness. This severely limits our learnings. It also explains why we have to habitualize perception and learnings so that they become unconscious and automatic frames. Habitually repeating any response of mind, emotion, or body causes that information to drop out of conscious awareness. Then it runs like an *outside-of-*conscious awareness program.

Generalization. With the over-abundance of data, we generalize to summarize patterns. We create generalizations to simplify the world. This shows up through categorizing, organizing, abstracting, and making higher level learnings. We generalize by putting items of similar function, structure, nature, etc. into categories. We look for gestalts of meaning, configurations of significance, and synthesis of information so as to build generalizations. Doing so enables us to put vast amounts of experience into very small packages. Yet in doing so, we inevitably not only generalize, but distort: "Women are emotional." "Men are insensitive."

In detecting and describing patterns, we generalize. It's built in. When we discover an experience repeating a time or two, we often jump to the conclusion that we have a pattern. Doing this saves us time and trouble so we do not have to constantly face the world anew. Sometimes we jump to false conclusions and create erroneous maps. This is how we attribute to the world of infinite variety *order and meaning.*

By generalizing we engage in what Korzybski called *time-binding.* This means that we *bind* into ourselves (our nervous system and brain) the learnings and understandings mapped by people in previous times. This allows each generation to move beyond re-inventing the computer. Ideally, each generation can begin where the previous generalization ended.

Distortion. Via deleting and generalizing data, we inevitably build models of the world *altered* in form and structure. This is not necessarily a "bad" thing. Sometimes, it enables us to create totally new and wonderful things. We distort positively when we dream, fantasize, see possibilities, etc. When we impose meaning or value on an event, person, experience—we distort. Distorting simply describes how we organize data. "Color" does not exist "out there" in the world. It emerges from the interaction of the energy manifestations of the light spectrum on our rods and cones. Yet while our experience of "color" distorts the world, it creates a richer internal subjective experience.

The sculptor who looks at a piece of block stone and sees within it an angel or soldier on a horse and then chisels away the stone from that image, is using the power of visual distortion. The same process occurs with every architect, musician, urban designer, etc.

Every distortion that we create via our beliefs, values, and perceptions *organizes* us. The format of the distortion, over time, will psychologically organize us (i.e., the way we think, perceive, feel, value, believe, and act). How does this work? It springs from the self-organizing nature of our reflexivity and belief maps. Every belief forms us after its image. The beliefs and values that result from our map-making induce us into states which define, identify, motivate, and order us. This creates our "personality."[1]   Every belief operates as a self-fulfilling prophecy. That's why the paranoid person, believing that others are out to get him, continually gathers more and more supporting evidence which makes it increasingly real for him.

From all of our deleting, generalizing, and distorting we create our unique model of the world for navigating the territory. This explains how very intelligent people sometimes engage in very stupid behavior. Their mental maps create it and predict it. It governs their perceptions, behaviors, communications, skills, states, etc. If their mapping deletes something essential, generalizes a principle, rule, belief, decision too quickly, or distorts too much, it organizes and motivates them to engage in unproductive responses.

These processes are *strategies*. We sequence the way we use our brain's building blocks of the sensory systems in structured and organized ways. Eventually these becomes a routine in our mind-body system. As we repeatedly run the programs we habituate the process and create our habits.

Three Levels of Mapping
The fact that all of our neuro-linguistic mapping does *not* occur at the same level adds tremendous complexity to the modeling of experience. We not only deal with the world through our neurological and linguistics maps about it, but we make more than one map. We actually make a great many mental maps and many maps on many levels. Three of the most important *levels of mapping* include the following:

1) Perceptual Maps
Our first mapping grows out of our neurological equipment. From our sense-receptors (i.e., eyes, ears, nose, mouth, skin, etc.) we *construct* a map (a neurological map) of the world. Why? Because we do not actually "see" with our eyes or "hear" with our ears. These sense-receptors simply give us access to the energies "out there," to the electro-magnetic continuum. We actually see in our cortex—not our eyeball. The eye only reacts to the light manifestations, interacts with it via the rods and cones, and then transforms the data into bio-electrical impulses along the neuro-pathways to the brain where it then transforms it into neurological activity.

What we perceive certainly seems and feels "real." And inside the nervous system and brain, it has a level of actuality. But what we actually see exists as a *construct* from the interaction of the territory upon the particular structure of our eyes and all of the other neurological components that abstract the energies.

2) Representational Maps
From our perceptual maps, we construct representational maps. We no longer

have to open our eyes or ears to receive information. We can generate the sights sounds, and sensations *from the inside.* We can present what we have seen, heard, or felt to ourselves again (i.e., re-present). We can also imagine what we could see, hear, or feel. We encode data via our sensory-based codes and language. This mapping creates our neuro-linguistic states.

3) Conceptual Maps
Nor do we stop there. We develop thoughts about our thoughts, ideas about our ideas, representations of our representations, etc. This enables us to step up yet another level to construct our conceptual maps. We include in this category of mapping all of our learnings, concepts, understandings, beliefs, values, decisions, paradigms, and other higher level symbolizations. This goes on without end. As we keep constructing concepts about concepts into ever higher levels of abstraction, this generates our neuro-semantic states.

The Maps we use in Mediating Reality
What Korzybski, Kant, and others discovered about our mental maps still comes as news. To many it comes as surprising or shocking news. Common sense does not reveal this. This occurs due to the very nature of our neuro-linguistic maps. We do not operate on the world with a flat, 2-dimensional map of pictures, sounds, or sensations in our heads. Nor do we even operate with merely a 3-dimensional map of the world. Rather, we operate with a holographic 3-D map that completely surrounds us. With every step we take, we do so *inside* of the matrix of a hologram, or so it seems.

Actually, we construct layers and levels of maps. Our first map at "the unspeakable level" (Korzybski) of neurology refers to what we colloquially call "perception." This primary level state depends almost entirely upon our sense receptors and neurological health (lack of brain tumors, lesions, etc.). As we grow up with our sensory perceptions, it becomes easy to assume that what we see with our eyes is real—is the territory. Even when we have a head full of knowledge that informs us about rods and cones, the electromagnetic spectrum of energy, etc., most of us readily forget this. We go about daily living, acting, and feeling *as if* what we see (perception) is the reality. This confuses our perceptual map with the territory. When we do this, we *identify* the territory with our perception which creates "unsanity" (Korzybski).

Visual and sensory illusions arise because of such confusions and identifications. Failing to remember and recognize the limitations and restraints of our senses and sense receptors sets us up to visually perceive and hear things that do not exist in the world of physics.

A good illustration of this is seeing a fan. When we turn the fan on, we see what appears to be a disk. But when we turn the fan off, we see three or four fan blades. When turned on, we cannot see fast enough to see the individual blades. To this our nervous system with its eye receptors generalizes and sees what does not exist—a disk.

Our perceptual mapping sees the moving of the blades of a fan as a disk. We cannot see the four blades that actually exist. Although that information is there and available, our sense receptors cannot discern it. Our nervous system abstracts according to its natural limits with regard to how fast it can process external speed. As the fans begin to move faster and faster, we *see* a disk because we *construct* a disk. Even though there is no actual disk, our sense of the disk exists in our brain, in the world of communication. We could say that we hallucinate it. Yet because we all engage in the same hallucination, we share it with the entire human race. Actually, this involves something more complicated than a mere hallucination. After all, even a camera can *see* and record a disk.

If we turn the fan off and continue to watch, we will again see a rush of blades, and then two blades, and then three, and then four—we see four turning blades. If we turn it back on, again *the speed* of the fan will exceed the ability of our eyes to process that quickly. And so we will not see the individual blades, in generalizing a distortion arises.

Recently, while waiting for a plane at the Phoenix airport, I stood at one of the gates and watched a propeller prop plane start up and take off. As the four blades began turning, I noticed the appearance of a "disk" as the speed increased. Then something else happened. Suddenly, the disk disappeared completely and as I looked at where the blades used to be —I then saw *nothing*. They moved so fast that for all purposes of seeing they had become *invisible*. I felt utterly amazed at this sight that I had undoubtedly seen many times before. But now, I was watching and scanning and reflecting on this.

Then, when the plane pivoted about and turned to move out onto a runway, I saw the "sides" of the invisible blades. I could see the big and heavy and bulky metal structures that supported the blades and I could see the disk again. All this is perpetual seeing.

After our perceptual maps come our *representational maps,* and after these our *conceptual maps.* Our ability to reflect back onto our perceptions and representations enables us to create higher level "perceptions" (i.e., a perception of our perception), a *mental* perception. We can re-present to ourselves what we have perceived (i.e., a day at a beach). And as we re-perceive it, now just in our mind, and so label it with words (i.e., a pleasant time, relaxing, beautiful), we can reflect back onto these ideas and entertain thoughts-and-feelings about them (i.e., the purpose of life, how to rejuvenate my energies, a reward for some hard work, a time to build memories for the kids, etc.).

In the world of communication a perception of a perception begins the wondrous human experience of *conceptual* thinking. It enables us to construct higher level awarenesses about the world, others, ourselves, etc. As this self-reflexive process continues, we create more and more abstract concepts as part of our model of the world. Yet these maps transcend the qualities of sensory perceptual mapping. We find that they have fewer and fewer sensory qualities and more mental and conceptual qualities.

The Mapping Difference
The use of these multiple level maps explains the differences between the experiences we have and those of others. We differ from one another because we construct different maps. We use different maps as we navigate the challenges and adventures of life.

Why does *criticism* devastate one person, energize another for better performance, and hardly get noticed by another? Each person maps "criticism" differently. One person maps it as "a terrible personal insult." One maps it as "information and feedback" and "a stimulus for greater effort." Another maps it as "nothing." "Not worth my trouble to respond to; someone else's stupid opinion."

How can one person see an available member of the opposite sex at a party, and feel excited, and walk over and say, "Hello, my name is Jim." Yet another person begins to feel nervous and self-conscious. He or she begins to sweat, takes a step toward the person, then begins to feel foolish. An internal dialogue explodes about how the other person will hate them, think they're a fool, and laugh in their face. Another person responds by playing an internal dialogue of wishing. "I wish I could meet her (or him)." "I wish I wasn't such a loser."

The answer does not lie merely in past experiences. Mere experiences do not *cause* us to think, feel, or act the way we do. We are a class of life that has to take an experience and use it in a limiting or hurtful way. It lies in the very nature of our nervous system and brain that we create internal maps about our experiences. The ultimate mechanism that governs our experiences (emotions, skills, behaviors, etc.) rests in and with our framing that we use to navigate life.

The Building Blocks For Engineering Human Excellence
In modeling the meaning-making (or mapping) process itself, we begin with how we internally *represent* the territory using the sensory representation systems. This makes explicit as we think using our internal "sense" of sights (images, pictures), sounds, sensations, smells, and tastes to create a mental movie in our mind. As we input data from the outside we track things onto our

inner cinema.

These sensory modalities are our basic modes of awareness. We cannot think without these awareness modes. These components make up the form of our inner cinema.

> Do you know what a *strawberry* is? Have you ever seen one? Tasted one? Have you ever smelled a strawberry? Have you ever eaten a bowl of ripe, juice strawberries covered with cream? Have you ever crunched down on a strawberry as you bit into it or felt its texture in your fingers?

While these are just questions, notice how you represent such and what happens in your inner cinema? We use the following for notational purposes in modeling for the basic building blocks of experience.

> **V** — Visual (images, pictures)
> **A** — Auditory (sounds)
> **A$_t$** — Auditory tonal (tones)
> **K** — Kinesthetics (tactile and internal sensations of the body)
> **0** — Olfactory (smell)
> **G** — Gustatory (taste)
> **M** — Motor movements
> **V** — Vestibular (inner ear balance, dizzy, disoriented or stability)

We use these representational systems to process information both from *external* sources and *internal* sources. In notation language, we add an *e* or *i* as a superscript (e.g. V^i for visual internal, internally seeing pictures). We can also either remember information (r) or construct it in our imagination (c).

> r — Remembered information
> c — Constructed information
> i — Internal source of information
> e — External source of information from sensory awareness

The internal cinema we play in our mind represents the world we have externally experienced. Within the movie may be words and language which supplies data for the sound track. Yet as a *meta*-representational system, we use words and language as information about the movie. At this higher level we represent the movie, interpret it, classify it, and frame it with multiple meta-levels. NLP uses the following notation to designate auditory-digital which refers to words:

> **A$_d$** — auditory digital: the language system, words.

All of these basic building blocks of consciousness make up the structures which we then use to map the world. As the building blocks of experience, we use them to encode our matrix of our movie and movie frames to make distinctions about our internal and external environment in our ongoing experience.

Engineering Specialities

Most of us favor one system for representing. We may favor the visual sensory system, the auditory, the kinesthetic, or the language system. This results in our preferences for learning styles. Some people operate primarily as visual learners, auditory learners, experiential learners, or learners through words and conceptual framing. Specializing in any system endows a person with special skills and powers in that intelligence. Howard Gardner (1983, 1991, 1993) developed a *Multiple Intelligence* model around eight key intelligences. Specializing in any given system typically means neglecting the other systems and inevitably creates limitations.

Figure 2:1
Simple Model of Neuro-Linguistic Levels

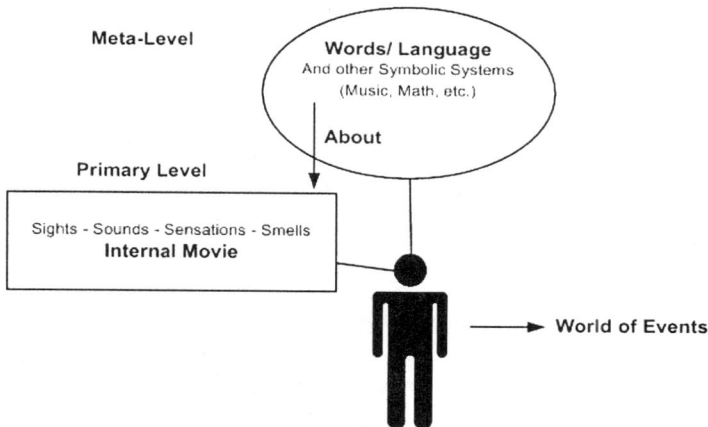

Distinctions Within the Sensory Systems

Refinement does not end with just the sensory representational systems model of our inner cinema. We can make even finer distinctions.

For example, as we could represent a *strawberry* in the various see, hear, feel, smell, taste systems—we can also use the many variations in each system to make more extensive distinctions. In the visual system, we can talk about *a big, bright red* (visual) *strawberry* that looks very *ripe and juicy* (language). These finer cinematic distinctions have traditionally been called *"sub-modalities."*

Figure 2:2

"Sub-modality" Chart
The Distinctions and Qualities of the Sense Modalities

Visual	*Auditory*	*Kinesthetic*
__ Brightness	_ _ Pitch (low/ high)	__ Pressure
(from dull to bright)	__ Location of sounds	__ What sensations
__ Focus	__Continuous/Interrupted	__ Location
__ Color (degree)	_ _ Tone	__ Extent
__ Color/Black-&-white	__ Number of sources	__ Moisture
__ Size	__ Associated/Dissociated	__ Shape
__ Distance	__ Tempo	__ Texture
__ Contrast	__ Volume (low/high)	__ Temperature
__ Movement	__ Rhythm	__ Movement
(Still/ moving)		
__ Direction	__ Duration	__ Duration
__ Foreground/Background	__ Distance	__ Intensity
__ Location	__ Clarity	__ Frequency
__ Snapshot - movie	__ Whose voice	__ Rhythm
(Still — Moving)	__ Music, noise, voice	
__ Number of images	__ Clarity, intelligibility	
__ Bordered/ Panoramic	__ Melody	
__ Shape, form		
__ Horizontal & Vertical perspective		
__ Associated/ Dissociated		
__ 3D or Flat (2D)		

Language (or the Auditory Digital) System
__ Location of Words
__ Sensory based/ Evaluative
__ Simple/ complex
__ Self/ others
__ Current/ dated

Other Systems
__ Smells
__ Tastes
__ Balance (Vestibular: dizzy, disoriented, etc.)

In so designating these cinematic qualities, the architect of the term *assumed* and presupposed that these cinematic features comprise a lower level. Where did that come from? My guess is that it grew out of the molecular metaphor. Just as physicists first discovered physical elements, and then later discovered the molecule, and then even later the sub-molecular parts, the atoms, and the sub-atomic parts, so early NLP developers pictured modalities and then *"sub-modalities."* They then applied this way of thinking to the representational modes. Inside these modes, they said, we find even smaller discriminations or finer distinctions about the qualities and properties of pictures, sounds, sensations, etc. So they called them "sub-modalities"." Shortly we will show the inadequacies of this *building block theory*.

In this way the term "sub-modality" came to refer to those elements within each sensory modality—their specific qualities or properties. By these finer distinctions of these *"sub-modality"* features, we signal our brain-body system more precisely in terms of coding experience.

Engineering With "Sub-Modalities"

Suppose you remember an experience when someone hurt your feelings by saying something unkind and insulting. How do you represent that memory? Typically, we encode it by seeing the person again as if we are again in the experience. Then we zoom in on the person's face, see the muscular tension there, and hear the cutting words in a loud and unpleasant tonality.

Yet how different this experience becomes if we remember the same thing as if it is on the screen in a theater. From that position, we can see our younger self being spoken to by the other person who seems upset or angry, and we can see it as a black-and-white snapshot. Imagine seeing it while sitting back in the 100th row of a theater eating popcorn, and having to strain to hear the dialogue because it sounds so faint... processing it *that way* will create a different set of responses, will it not?

What does this mean? It means something incredibly powerful and important for resourcefulness:

> *The kind and quality of cinematic features that we edit into our internal representations cue our brains and bodies about how to feel, perceive, and respond. The cinematic features of our movies frame the quality of our movies and of the states that we experience.*

This describes the power and importance of the cinematic features or "sub-modalities." Change the critical "sub-modality" *feature*—and the whole experience will change.

"Sub-Modality" Contrastive Analysis

If we make maps, and every map we construct elicits and formats an experience, then every experience has a sensory blueprint. This means that if we contrast and compare *the structural blueprints* of similar experiences we are likely to identify the structural difference that makes a difference.

A *contrastive analysis* is the process of comparing structural elements to identify "the difference that makes the difference." For example:

> Think about a time when you felt hesitant and fearful of speaking up for yourself. Notice the movie that plays in your mind with that awareness. ... Now think about a time when you felt assertive and forthright and spoke up for yourself as you assertively presented your ideas and made your voice heard without becoming aggressive. Notice that movie.

From the eliciting of the two movies we can now examine *the differences* in the movies and in the cinematic features of the movies. Contrasting these differences can then inform us about what makes the difference between each experience. What sights, sounds, sensations, etc. and what cinematic features determine each experience?

The idea behind this is that at the *"sub*-modality" level we will find the secret of subjectivity. Yet, is that true? Does "the difference that makes a difference" really lie there? Is it that simple or are there some other considerations? This is what we'll explore in chapter four.

Experiencing The Distinctions
The following *thought experiment* provides a way to experience and demonstrate these distinctions.

> For a minute or two, let yourself to recall *a pleasant experience* from your past or imagine a pleasant experience...

As you do this, various things will pop into your mind. Whatever pops up into your mind, just allow yourself to go with them. If you do not seem to find a sufficient memory, then allow yourself to simply imagine a pleasant experience, one that you would like to have. If closing your eyes assists you in this process, do that. Once you have this pleasant experience, just enjoy it as you feel it fully for a few minutes.

Good. Now with this pleasant thought in mind, notice its visual aspects. What is the movie you see? If you do not visualize well, then imagine what the pleasant experience *feels* like. Or, allow yourself to just *listen* to some pleasant sounds— words or music and enjoy that kind of an internal pleasant experience. Whether you begin with the sound track, the video track, or the feeling of the movie, let it enable you to create a richer cinema.

Now with the image of the pleasantness, make the picture larger. Let it double in size... and then let that picture double... Notice what happens. When you made the picture bigger, what happened to your feelings of that experience? Did they intensify?

Let's now experiment with it the other way. Let the picture shrink in size. Make it smaller and smaller. Allow it to become so small that you can hardly see it ... Stay with that for a minute. ... Does the intensity of the feelings decrease? Experiment now with making the movie bigger, and then smaller. Oscillate back and forth in your comparisons. When you make it smaller, do your feelings decrease? And when you make it larger, do your feelings increase? What happens when yhou alter these key facets of your inner movie?

Next, put the *pleasant* picture back in a format where you find it most resourceful for you, and let the picture move closer to you. Just imagine that the picture begins to move closer and closer to you, and notice that it will. What happens to your feelings as it does? ... Move the picture farther away. What happens when you move the picture farther away? Do your feelings intensify when you move the picture closer? Do your feelings decrease when you move the picture farther away?

Suppose you experiment with the brightness of the picture? As you look at the movie, do you see it in color or black-and-white? If your movie has color, make it black-and-white, and vice versa if you have it coded as black-and-white. When you do this, did your feelings change?

Consider the focus of your images: in focus or out of focus? Do you see an image of yourself in the picture or do you experience the scene as if looking out of your own eyes? What about the quality of your images: in three dimensional (3D) form or flat (2D)? Does it have a frame around it or do you experience it as panoramic? Experiment by changing *how* you represent the experience. Change the location of the picture. If you have it coded as on your right, then move it to your left.

Debriefing The Experience

Before considering your thinking as an internal movie, it probably never occurred to you that we can change our feelings by altering *how* we internally code our mental movies. We only have to change the map —the blueprint.

The fascination and excitement of this model lies in these very *processes*. NLP works primarily with such structures and processes of encoding rather than with content. Here we have played with *the structure* of the experience, rather than its content. Leaving the content the same, we have changed how we feel about an experience by changing the cinematic distinctions of the movie or structure. Without altering the content at all, we only made changes at the structural level.

- What would happen to us if we made all of our *unpleasant pictures* big, bright, and up close?
- What would happen if we made all of our *pleasant experiences* small, dim, and far away?
- Would we not become an expert at feeling depressed, miserable and unresourceful?
- On the other hand, consider what would happen if we coded our *pleasant experiences* as big, bright, and up close... would that not create a more positive outlook on life for us?
- What if we made our *unpleasant experiences* small, dim, and far away? Wouldn't the negative experience have less influence on our lives?

Mapping Components

What are these maps or models of the world made out of? We construct them out of the simplest of materials: the sensory sights, sounds, sensations, smells and words. These are the mental building blocks of our "thoughts," knowledge, memory, imagination, beliefs, values, understandings, emotion, motivation, etc. There's a problem with these common terms though. They lack sufficient precision and clarity. Merely telling someone to "think positive" typically fails to provide enough precise information to remap.

In chapter one we enumerated the factors that comprise the elements of subjective experience, the components of the neuro-linguistic model. These components, as mapping variables, put into our hands the *processes* that control or govern our experience. These control mechanisms enable us to take charge of our mind, emotions, and choices. They enable us to develop patterns for transforming our personal development, effectively communicating and relating to others, developing expert skills in our careers, and modeling the expertise and excellence in others.

In chapter four we will *unmask* the "sub-modalities" and reveal their key secrets. This will open up new territory for exploration. And because this unmasking will reveal the governing mechanisms regarding the functioning of "sub-modalities," learning these secrets will enable us to work with much more elegance, confidence, and power.

Mapping the Structure

How does it work? is the beginning point and the modeling attitude. This is the attitude that drove the original work of John Grinder and Richard Bandler. In their experiment of modeling the structure of excellence in the three communication "wizards," they looked at the quality skills of Perls, Satir, and Erickson. Asking, "How does this work?" enabled them to construct the first NLP model, the Meta-Model. As the two modelers kept asking, exploring, and applying their linguistic, mathematical, and computer tools to the communication excellence of their exemplars, they created the linguistic model.

From modeling Perls' and Satir's language patterns, Bandler and Grinder (1975) created *a basic model* about language. This *meta*-model made explicit the unarticulated paradigm which Perls and Satir intuitively used to perform their "magic." It guided their responses, behavior, and language. Consequently the *meta*-model gives us a more advanced set of tools for the next level of modeling.

These men came to the modeling task with backgrounds that uniquely equipped them to think in terms of breaking down complex behaviors and linguistic patterns into smaller and smaller chunks while simultaneously looking for larger level patterns (meta-detailing). Adopting this perspective, they began to look for *the components* of "mind" and experience. Eventually they stumbled upon the see-hear-feel senses and used the sensory representational systems (the VAK movie) as the basis for mind and consciousness. They took the sensory modes of awareness for "knowing" and "representing" and turned them into the very building-block components of human map-making.

Next, they asked a series of modeling questions which drove these discoveries. The heart of this exploration lies in *how* questions:

*   *Process:* How do you do this? (i.e., depression, schizophrenia, expert skiing, etc.)
*   What do you do in your thinking, emoting, representing, physiology, etc. that creates this result?
*   How do you know that you know how to do this?
*   *Representation:* How do you represent this?
*   *Sequence:* What goes first, then second, then third?
*   How do you know what to do next?

As they asked such questions, they reflected on how to *sequence* these elements. If our neuro-linguistic "bio-computer" (the information processing unit of brain-body) gets programmed so that we can perform high level behaviors of excellence, then what is the internal structure of these sequences of representational sensory systems?

This central attitude continues today to empower NLP and Neuro-Semantic research as we explore mental and neurological mapping processes. It allows us to move past external behavior and emotions as we explore *the structures* of the mental-emotional-somatic mapping that gives rise to the experiences of states, emotions, and behaviors. We can now explore *the neuro-linguistic* and *neuro-semantic formats* that people use in navigating life.

Originating with Alfred Korzybski, this engineering attitude actualizes the idea succinctly put in his famous quote: "The map is not the territory." Korzybski based this terse statement on a negation; the map is *not* the territory. Map and territory represent different dimensions of reality. In human experience, we have no choice but to create maps. Korzybski showed how the responsive nature of protoplasm and our nervous system initiates this mapping. Because we never immediately experience the territory we can only deal with "reality" through our maps.

What exists "out there" beyond our nervous system? A whole world of energy manifestations. So what gets "in" or "on" our maps? What actually enters into our minds and emotions by way of our sense receptors? Our coding of differences. This is the world of communication.

Korzybski used the term *abstractions* to refer to how our nervous system constructs our maps.

> "*Abstracting* implies 'selecting', 'picking out', 'separating', 'summarizing', 'deducting', 'removing', 'omitting', 'disengaging', 'taking away', 'stripping' ... 'abstracting' implies structurally and semantically the activities characteristic of the nervous system and so serves as an excellent *functional physiological* term." (p. 379)

Prior to consciousness, our nervous system *abstracts*. It summarizes and creates an information coding about the electromagnetic energies out there. These abstractions provide us our first sense of the outside world (the perceptual map). From there, we create abstractions of those abstractions which give us a *consciousness* of the world. We register this as our sensory representations (representational map). We then generate even more abstractions and do so until we have an internal "sense" of sights, sounds, sensations, smells, and tastes. Next, we create linguistic maps about the sensory representational maps —thoughts about thoughts, feelings about feelings (conceptual maps).

What we know and experience in the inner world of communication differs radically from the external world of physics. Our inner communications is our map. It represents the territory, reflects it, symbolizes it, but it is not the territory. The phenomena of map and territory exist on different levels. They refer to different dimensions of reality.

While we do not operate directly on the world, we do operate directly on our *maps* of the world. The models that we build to cope with the world involve a set of structural elements and then a syntax. These elements are the building blocks and the syntax, the set of rules or directions about how we can put the building blocks together.

Engineering New Refinements

On the surface, this may seem to imply that "the difference that makes the difference" occurs at the lower level, the "sub" level. Yet as you will soon discover, it does not. Even though we have drawn that premature conclusion, jumping to that unfounded concept will not stand the light of reason, experience, or experimentation. Yet NLP modeled the so-called "sub-modalities" in this way. Yet as with every theoretical model, if it doesn't hold up over time or does not lead to producing the results we would have predicted, then we need to update—even remodel it.

True enough, the "sub-modality" distinctions often does give us "the switch" (so to speak) to changing emotions and transforming behaviors. Yet how does it provide the switch? What mechanism explains this? It does so *not* because "the difference that makes a difference" occurs at a level *below* our sensory representations. Instead, it does so because the distinctions that we call "sub-modalities" set frames at meta-levels.

Typically we do *not* experience "sub-modalities" consciously. Usually we do not notice the qualities or cinematic features of our internal movies.
- Is that picture in color or coded as black-and-white?
- Do I see it as close or far?
- Does the image appear fuzzy or clear?
- What about the qualities of the auditory sounds?
- Are they soft or loud? Clear or muffled?
- What is the tonality? The tempo?

We can easily make these cinematic features conscious. How? By paying attention to them. By simply taking note of these cinematic features, we bring them into our awareness for detection.

Running with the molecular metaphor, numerous writers have suggested that "sub-modalities" operate, metaphorically, as the DNA coding of the mind. Yet this metaphor brought with it certain entailments. *Entailment,* from the field of Cognitive Linguistics, means "to impose, involve, or imply as a necessary accompaniment or result." Lakoff and Johnson (1980) use it as a key concept in *Metaphors We Live By*.

Starting with the analogy of "mental DNA," it is easy to assume that in the programming of human neurology for feelings, reflexes, behaviors, speech and skills, "sub-modalities" operated at some *sub*-level or substrate, a lower "logical level." This *building block* metaphor invested "sub-modalities" with suggestive ideas similar to the periodic chart of the chemical elements. It suggested that if we simply change a "sub-modality" coding, it alters the structure of an experience. It's upon all of this that Design Human Engineering™ was formatted.

Others ran with the same idea, but used a computer metaphor. This led to the entailment of assuming that "sub-modalities" function in the mind like off/on (0,1 digits) function in a computer. This would make such qualities and characteristics of the sensory modalities the programming language of experience.

The digital distinctions of some cinematic features does seem to operate as Off/On switches. Consider the "sub-modality" distinction in every sensory system: *Association / Dissociation*. In associative processing, we think, feel, and act *as if* inside an experience, inside the movie. In dissociative processing, we step out of an experience or movie and only think, feel, and act *about* it. In using this language, we *conceptually* step in and out, rather than actually.

This operates digitally. Either we code a thought, memory, or imagination as *inside* the movie or *outside* of it. So this *"sub-modality"* (and simultaneously meta-program) operates like an Off/On distinction. One moment we experience things as if *inside* an event; the next moment we experience it as if *outside*. We step in, we step out. When we step inside, we go through the trauma again. When we step out, we take another perceptual position, and can feel resourceful about it.

This shows the power and magic of detecting and recognizing the representational distinctions or "sub-modalities." This knowledge empowers us to run our own brain and neurology. It endows us with the ability to make distinctions between closely related, but different experiences. What codes the difference, for example, between thinking about a fearful event and experiencing it as fearful?

Traditional psychology spent more than a century inventing all kinds of "explanations." Unfinished traumatic memories, weak ego strength, too many dysfunctional defense mechanisms, undeveloped psycho-sexual or psycho-social stage, fixation at some developmental stage, etc.

Because NLP and Neuro-Semantics ask a different question. *"How* do these experiences work?" we are led to different conclusions. To merely think about an experience, we only need to code it from another perceptual position. We can move to a spectator's point of view and witness it as if watching a movie. To *freak out and go into hysterical emotional reactions,* we would need to step into the movie and cue our brain to "be there." Step out and it changes. Step in and it changes again. Off. On. The secret lies in the coding (and something else, i.e., the frame). We do not need "explanations" only a description of the process and that's what this adventure is all about.

Summary

- Human experience is all about mapping or engineering a model of the world which enables us to move, act, and respond more resourcefully.
- The *quality* of our life depends entirely upon *the quality* of our mapping. If we have a limited, unproductive, or toxic map—it affects the way we think, feel, speak, and act. If we have an enhancing, empowering, and productive map—we feel great, utilize our innate gifts, get things done, manage our emotions, and feel on top of the world.
- To model neuro-linguistic *processes* we have to explore *how* the operations work. "How do you do that?" "How does that work?"
- Our mapping occurs at many different levels: perceptual, representational, and conceptual. Because this introduces *levels* and *layers* into "mind" and experience, we have to sort out and distinguish

levels (meta-states) in modeling excellence.

- To find the structure of excellence, we begin with the sensory systems, move to the linguistic model, reckon with the *qualifying distinctions* in these, and consider the meta-levels model.
- What we call "sub-modalities" make a big difference in the structure of experience— but not because they occur at a *"sub"* level.

End Notes:

1: See *Figuring Out People* (1997) and *The Structure of Personality* (2001) for an extended application of NLP and Neuro-Semantics to the subject of "personality."

Chapter 3

LEVELS
IN THE STRUCTURE
OF EXCELLENCE

"Our thinking creates problems
that the same type of thinking will not solve."
Albert Einstein

As there are levels in experiences—there are levels in genius or mastery. All human excellence grows out of the *layering of mind* in ever ascending levels of complexity. Why is this? Because it's the layering of thoughts-and-emotions that create our richer and more complex states. When we speak of "mind," we do not have just one singular monolithic consciousness. We have an ever-developing mind and a mind that operates at various psycho-logical levels simultaneously.

The primitive minds that we all start out with as infants simply engage in perception. Soon in human development, we develop representational skills, and then simple concepts. Later, brain chemistry goes into over-drive and we move from the concrete thinking stage, to formal and post-formal stages where we can entertain ideas of ideas about ideas. We describe this development as the emergence of *self-reflexive consciousness*—a key player in the structure of excellence.

Primary and Meta Levels

In chapter two we offered a simple model of neuro-linguistic levels (Figure 2:1) containing two levels: *primary and meta.* This model dates back to the beginning of NLP when Bandler and Grinder (1975, 1976) separated out the primary representation systems from the meta-representational system of language. Since that development, numerous other NLP theorists and developers have contributed to the understanding of meta-levels, most notably myself and Robert Dilts. I have documented some of this history in *NLP: Going Meta—Advanced Modeling Using Meta-Levels* (Hall, 2001).

Figure 3:1 uses the *Levels of Abstraction model,* developed by engineer-turned-semanticist, Alfred Korzybski. This diagrams the *levels* of "thought" or mental mapping. Note that the meta-modality of language occurs above the sensory systems and so operates as another kind of "sense." By language, we talk about our senses (sense awareness). Language enables us to encode higher level meanings which we then attribute to what we see, hear, and feel.

Figure 3:1
Levels of Processing or Abstractions

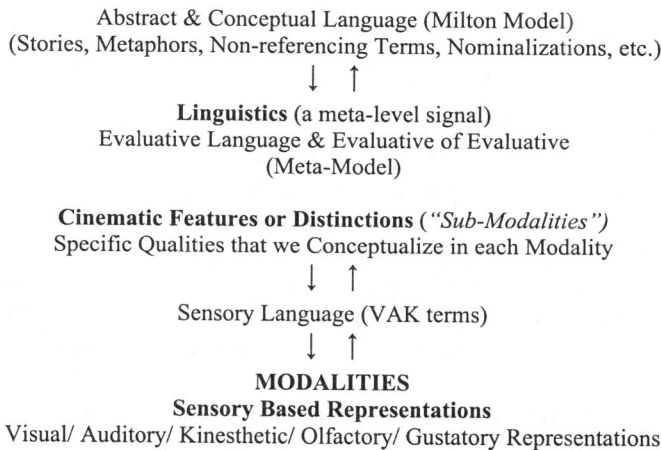

Abstract & Conceptual Language (Milton Model)
(Stories, Metaphors, Non-referencing Terms, Nominalizations, etc.)
↓ ↑

Linguistics (a meta-level signal)
Evaluative Language & Evaluative of Evaluative
(Meta-Model)

Cinematic Features or Distinctions (*"Sub-Modalities"*)
Specific Qualities that we Conceptualize in each Modality
↓ ↑

Sensory Language (VAK terms)
↓ ↑

MODALITIES
Sensory Based Representations
Visual/ Auditory/ Kinesthetic/ Olfactory/ Gustatory Representations

We first map things neurologically using non-language representations using neurological representations. These establishes the primary level of consciousness. Later, when we think about these internal sights and sounds, we map at a higher or meta-level. When we linguistically map by using words, symbols, metaphors, etc., we use language as a meta-system to create meta-relationships between states.

Where do we have the level of distinctions that we call *"sub*-modalities?" Are these *below, within, or above* the modalities? When these discrete facets of the sensory distinctions were first explored, they allowed new patterns, insights, and technologies to emerge. In detecting and working with these representational or cinematic distinctions of our inner movies, we can use the finer variables to change experiences. This leads to more precision in introspection, design of strategies, programming in new learnings, developing personal genius, and modeling of expertise.

Primary Levels refer to our first or primary experiences of the outside world via our senses. *Primary States* refer to the states that we experience *about* the outside world.

Meta-Levels refer to the abstract levels of awareness which we internally experience. *Meta-States* refer to our internal states *about* our states. This means that meta-states emanate from the interaction of our thoughts at various levels. As we reflect on our experience we make a meta-move that both transcends and includes the previous state.

Engineering at Different Levels

At the primary level, our immediate perceptual mapping of things induces us into a state. These sights, sounds, and sensations provide us the signals and coding to create our first response mind-body states. Yet just as soon as we experience this, we then experience another thought. We reflexively think and feel about the previous mind-body state. It's as if we can encode a thought "in the back of the mind" and hold that awareness as a frame *about* the thoughts-and-emotions we're experiencing. As this happens, we move up the scale.

When we do, we reflexively turn our thoughts upon our thoughts, our feelings upon our previous feelings, our states upon our states. We create *meta-states,* or states-about-states, such as fear of fear, calmness about anger, joy about learning, love about loving, etc. (Hall, 1995, 1997, 1998). These meta-states are conceptual and semantic states that set the frames in our mind for how we interpret and experience reality.

The Meta-States model makes explicit these internal processes that occur at these higher levels and how they work. We have long known that phenomena at these higher logical levels *drive* and control the lower levels of our primary states.

It begins with a primary state—a state involving *primary emotions* (i.e., fear, anger, joy, lust, relaxation, pleasure, disgust, etc.). A meta-state refers to those states containing thoughts-and-emotions about a primary state. Examples are angering at our fear, guilting about our anger, feeling upset at our disgust, fearing our fear, depressing about our fear, etc.

This model explains the critical importance of the unconscious frames governing our presuppositional lives. They explicitly detail Bateson's insights about meta-levels—that to discern meaning we have to consider not only the words and syntax, but also the *contexts* within which the words and syntax occur. *These contexts are our meta-states.* It's in this way that we create and install our mental and emotional *contexts* and use them to filter experience. It's in this way we create our meta-programs.

This model explains that while we can anchor primary states with sights, sounds, and sensations, we typically need a *meta-mechanism* like language, symbolic symbols, etc. to anchor a meta-state. After all, self-reflexive consciousness operates at a meta-level to the basic modalities level. Mostly it is only when such levels coalesce into the primary level that we are able to use kinesthetic anchors to solidify meta-states. This explains why we typically cannot quickly set an anchor with a touch for such meta-layered states like self-esteem, resilience, un-insultability, etc.

I say *mostly* but that's only if a person doesn't know how to use the meta-stating process to facilitate the coalescing of states and to layer mind-body states and to thereby texture an experience. When a person develops these meta-skills, then meta-stating using kinesthetic anchors becomes not only possible, but a very effective tool.

All of this lets us now distinguish primary and meta-states. Primary states *refer* to the territory "out there." We use primary states as our first line of defense and resource to cope and to master the outside world. I feel afraid *of* a dog, a broken brake line in my car, stepping too close to the edge of a cliff, etc. I feel relaxed when I hear a particular piece of music. We can immediately register these primary feelings in the body.

Meta-states *refer* to high level abstractions like "self," "time," morality (good / bad; right / wrong), relationships, values, beliefs, "emotions," and a hundred thousand other concepts. Here our mind-and-emotion system involves recursive and self-reflexive consciousness. This enables us to *reflect* on our thinking (i.e., meta-think), feel about our feelings (meta-emote), and talk about our talk (meta-communicate). To the concept of "self," I esteem or evaluate it as high or low according to some criteria. Esteeming "self" differs from esteeming the value of a chair in that the chair is "out there," whereas the "self" as a concept of being-ness, dignity, etc. exists in the mind. In so layering thought and emotion *upon* itself, the content of the meta-state structures come to operate as *attractors* in a self-organizing system.

The Structure of Higher Level Excellence
I use the word *meta* here to describe the *higher* level thoughts-feelings that arise when we think about other thoughts. As a Greek term, *meta* refers to something that is "above" and "beyond" something else. When something stands in *a meta*

relationship to something else, it operates at a higher logical level and refers to the lower level.

When we move up the continuum (Figure 3:1), we move into *meta-level phenomena.* "What's that?" you ask. This is the phenomena that we populate our mind with, things that we commonly call beliefs, values, standards, criteria, intentions, presuppositions, negation, understanding, metaphors, narrative, decisions, etc. These are the frames that we set and use to make sense of the world, that we use to create our *matrix of frames.* And since most of the things that matter to us as humans occur at meta-levels, this underscores the extent to which we are *a meta-class of life.* That is, we are a class of life that live for "love," "beauty," "grace," "significance," "contribution," etc.—none of the things that exist at the primary level in the world of physics. We fight about "rudeness," "insult," "failure," "blame," "responsibility"—things that do not exist in the world, but in the world of communication and mind.

When we move to these higher levels, we need *meta-level technologies* to work with, or make changes in, these higher level maps. Actually almost all of the technology for engineering this kind of re-mapping in NLP involve meta-level patterns. That's why the most powerful patterns in NLP are actually *meta-state processes* like the Movie Rewind pattern (also called the phobia cure or the V-K dissociation pattern), the ecology check, the Milton Model distinctions of hypnotic language, core transformation, belief change patterns, reframing patterns, the Meta-Model, Meta-Programs, and of course, Meta-States.

Anchoring At Meta-Levels
In *NLP: Going Meta* (Hall, 2001), I noted that when we set an anchor at a meta-level, we anchor *the method* of how we process the learning context, rather than the learning.

That's an important distinction. Did you get it? Let me quote Robert Dilts to help explain it. From his study of Bateson, Robert Dilts (1983) described anchors working at meta-levels as "context markers." He said that *Learning II* in Bateson's Levels of Learning model involves a change in behavior content. This shows up as *conditioned responses* in response to varying contexts. This makes Learning II a form of behavior rather than content. Bateson's levels of learning start with *No Learning* (no response or habitual response), then *Learning I* (alteration, change of response), then *Learning II* (changing Learning I of how we learn), then *Learning III* (changing Learning II or changing our epistemology).

> "The anchors that stimulate a change in the state of consciousness (the form of processing) in an individual are called *context markers*." (Dilts, 1983, Part III, p. 51)

There it is again. Does that now make more sense? This means that when we work with a meta-level experience, we do not anchor *a state* as much as we anchor *a context*. Let me give an example. Consider the phrase that we use to induce the following state:

> "Think of a time when you felt really tired."
> "Think of a time when you were thrilled and enraptured."

In response we usually access *a feeling state* which that events elicits, and so we can then anchor that mind-body state. Compare that to the following words and what they call forth and anchor.

> "Have you ever stayed up all night writing a paper?"
> "Have you ever been at the birth of a baby and watched that miracle?"

Figure 3:2
Levels of Abstracting and Transformation

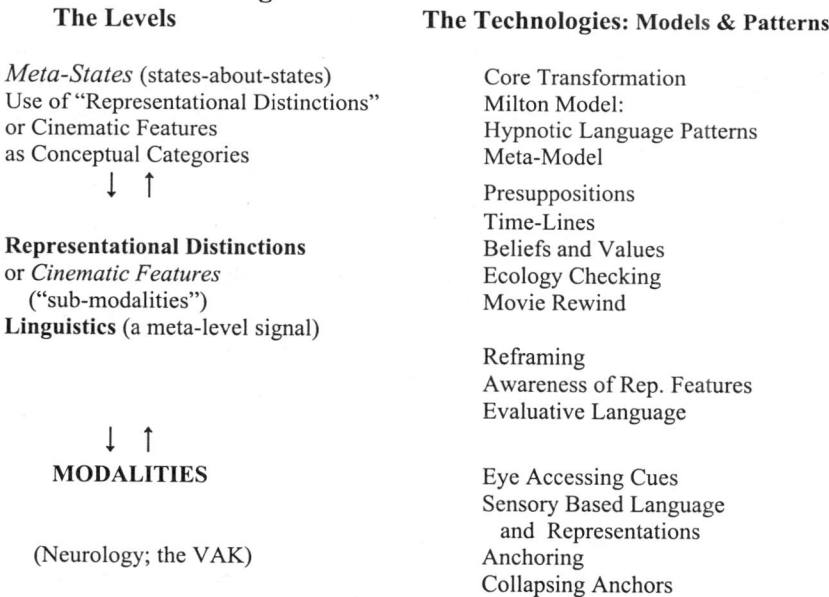

The Levels	The Technologies: Models & Patterns
Meta-States (states-about-states) Use of "Representational Distinctions" or Cinematic Features as Conceptual Categories ↓ ↑	Core Transformation Milton Model: Hypnotic Language Patterns Meta-Model Presuppositions Time-Lines
Representational Distinctions or *Cinematic Features* ("sub-modalities") **Linguistics** (a meta-level signal)	Beliefs and Values Ecology Checking Movie Rewind Reframing Awareness of Rep. Features Evaluative Language
↓ ↑ **MODALITIES** (Neurology; the VAK)	Eye Accessing Cues Sensory Based Language and Representations Anchoring Collapsing Anchors

Robert noted that these words will more likely "indicate the state indirectly *by anchoring a context* in which the desired state would most likely occur" (1983, Part III, p. 53). A mental and emotional *context* differs from a state in that it calls forth and invites *a fuller awareness of an entire set of events and all of the meanings that we give to it*. Whereas when we call forth a state like joy, playfulness, relaxation, anger, fear, etc. and anchor it, we are going mostly and predominantly for the feeling. In this, the content doesn't matter. It's the feeling that matters. And that's what we anchor. At the meta-level, however, the content does matter. The content at the meta-level is the *context*.

Originally Bateson designated these anchors *"context markers."* They identify the frame-of-reference under which we operate. These access the context, and trigger a different kind of processing. In the process we get *meta-anchors.* Would you like another example? Compare the following statements.

      1) What is the color of your bedroom?

      2) What is it like to be in deep meditation?

The first statement invites us to make a visual representation of something "out there," doesn't it? What do you do in response? On the movie in your mind do you not make representations of your bedroom? The words trigger *a representational map.* We see the color of the bedroom and that may (or may not) induce some corresponding "state," perhaps just an observation state.

The second statement anchors us at a meta-level because it invites us to move up a level and create a representation *of* a representation. We now think about "what it is like" (conceptually, emotionally, personally, or semantically) to be in an altered state (an experience within ourselves and not "out there" in the world).. *This anchors a context.* So we may represent relaxing at a beach, practicing meditation, remembering a trance in a workshop, then we rise above that to consider our experience *of* that, "What was that like for me?"

In these examples, you can see how that language itself comprises what Bateson and Dilts called *"context markers,"* and which I have described as *meta-level anchors.* As meta-level anchors, we can include most evaluative terms, terms about classes and categories, complex equivalences, meta-frames about meanings, cause-effect terms, meta-programs that refer to one's meta-processing level, etc. Because such anchors contain meta-levels within them, they involve language and therefore meta-level representations of other representations. These are the terms that send us into the highest matrix of our mind.[1]

Distinctions of Genius

How does all of this apply to states of excellence or genius? Consider the person who has a genius for hearing things musically. What distinguishes this person? He or she can make auditory distinctions as they hear voice productions, distinctions the rest of us miss. Or, consider an artist who sees things that typically escape the rest of us. The mathematical genius has the unique ability to put patterns, processes, and formulas together. The person who has a social genius in handling people senses their emotional states and paces them.

When it comes to *genius*—we generally refer to someone who can do two things.

      1) The person can make *highly refined distinctions* in his or her sensory systems and use such at a higher degree of precision.

2) The person operates from *a set of higher level patterns* which then governs how and why he or she can make these highly refined distinctions.

This gives us an operational definition for *genius*, does it not? We can now speak about the enhanced ability to make highly refined distinctions. The genius distinguishes among, and about, the qualities, features, and properties of mental representation by using appropriate and empowering frames-of-reference (or meta-frames). This description highlights that genius operates simultaneously from a two-fold focus. It has a distinguishing detailed awareness that knows how to specify the key differences as it simultaneously sees the big picture of the overall frame of meaning:

> *1) A specific detailing awareness of genius looks for salient differences* (namely, differences that stand out). Genius operates and arises from the ability to make refined distinctions —to see, hear and feel differences, to sort and separate. This requires a frame-of-reference that governs what and how the genius does that. Genius sorts for differences. The genius sees, hears, feels, and thinks about what others do not see.
>
> *2) A higher embracing frame that sorts for patterns and similarities.* Genius also expresses itself as seeing, hearing, and feeling "the patterns that connect" (Gregory Bateson's phrase). By operating from an understanding of some higher level frame, the genius organizes knowledge according to the pattern. The pattern that formulates schemas of understanding. It detects and expresses leverage points within systems for taking effective action.

In terms of perception, genius involves a balance and integration of several Meta-Programs. This includes such sorting perceptual filters as:

- Specific detailing / General globalizing
- Matching / Mismatching
- Screening / Non-screening (degree of focus)
- Possibility thinking / Necessity thinking

Genius typically operates from utilizing the wisdom that results from a highly developed flexibility of consciousness which emerges when a person can easily move between the perceptual positions. The person of mastery uses the self (1st) and other (2nd) positions, then goes meta to an outsider perspective (3rd). Finally genius tries on the fourth position of the entire system.[2]

When we do this as part of the experience of genius, we access and use various supporting meta-states. This allows us to embed specific skills within higher contexts of motivation, value, belief, understanding, etc. This allows consciousness to intensely focus without interruption, to move in and out of "passionate states," and empowers a person to fully tap their skills and aptitudes. That, by the way, is the theme of the sequel of this book, *Secrets of Personal Mastery* (1999).

The "Sub-modality" Structure of Excellence

What does all of this mean in terms of a highly developed utilization of skills and aptitudes (genius, excellence, expertise) and the qualities and features of our representations?

1) It means that enriching and developing "sub-modalities" alone do not model the essence of genius, but only one component.

> By itself, mere awareness of rich and expansive details in terms of the cinematic distinctions ("sub-modalities") can lead one to getting lost in the details. This can lead one to "miss the forest for the trees." If and when that happens, we have distinctions, but no ordering meta-frame.

2) It means that "sub-modality" awareness actually arises from and is a meta-level state of consciousness.

> The representational distinctions describe *the structure* of an experience, not the content. To even *notice* such features of awareness, we have to "go meta." Yet as we step back from the content, we take a meta-position so that from there we can recognize these distinctions. The ability to compare, alter, transform, and see patterns in various "sub-modalities" emerges when we move to a higher level position.

3) It means that genius inherently involves bringing higher level frames of awareness to bear on the quality level of the representation systems.

> What protects genius from getting "caught up in the details?" The meta-frame of reference. The higher level contexts and contexts-of-contexts keep the genius oriented with a sense of the big picture.

4) It means that genius involves a flexibility of consciousness.

> This mental flexibility enables one to move easily up and down the levels as a given task requires. It facilitates the shifting of awareness, taking on various perceptual positions and frames-of-reference. In doing this, it allows the genius to enrich his or her understandings from many other sources.

5) It means that what empowers and makes salient the cinematic distinctions of our representations comes from the meta-level frames.

> The meta-frames enable the genius perspective which seems so extraordinary and magical to others who lack a particular meta-frame that puts it altogether.

Every genius, whether an Einstein or an Edison, whether a Mozart or a Sheakspeare, operates on the world using the same processes of neuro-linguistic perceptions, thoughts, and concepts as we do. Yet they do so with a difference. The mind of the genius knows what to attend to and how to attend to it in a special way. The meta-level distinctions (including meta-programs and meta-states of the genius) fine tunes his or her eyes, ears, skin, smells, languaging, etc. This gives the highly skilled person, who can perform feats of excellence, the edge. Their high level performances do not emerge magically, without order or form. The excellence operates because of its structure.

Such excellence operates from a *meta-level*. From there, we can see and hear and operate with a powerful focus and clarity on the details and it is these structures and processes that we will be looking at in the forthcoming chapters.

Summary
- There are levels and meta-levels in the mind of genius which endows that higher level of consciousness to see and sort details with more proficiency and skill. To those lacking those meta-level frames, its seems absolutely magical.
- There is a structure of excellence in the meta-levels that we can detect, unpack, and model. Though complex, it is not an inexplicable mystery.
- The Meta-States model adds many new dimensions to NLP, enriching it and providing many new discriminations unavailable before.
- The structure of excellence inherently involves the advanced skill of *meta-detailing* and this operates from a meta-detailing frame of reference. We'll get to that in chapter 17.
- The higher levels of mind and experience operate by the mechanism of reflexivity. This makes the higher levels a system of feed-back and feed-forward loops.
- What we have called "sub-modalities" operate due to the meta-frames that we set. This turns the old "sub-modality" model on its head and alerts us to the fact that they work *symbolically and semantically* —according to the meanings elicited and constructed.

End Notes:
1. See *The Matrix Model* (2003).

2. By the way, these perceptual positions refer to *first or self*—seeing the world from out of one's body, eyes, ears, skin, etc. *Second or other* position refers to the empathy position of seeing things from another's point of view. *Third or meta* position refers to an outside point of view that allows us to see things from a spectator's viewpoint. *Fourth or system* position refers to stepping back to see the whole system of interactions, parts, and components. We can describe every position other than *First/Self* as "dissociated" from the *association* of first position, yet "dissociation" does not mean unfeeling or lacking feeling. It only refers to a different kind and quality of feeling.

Chapter 4

UNMASKING "SUB-MODALITIES"

*"I have never affected an effective 'sub-modality' change
that did not activate a meta-level structure."*
(Bobby G. Bodenhamer)

Having held you in suspense by only hinting and dancing around the idea that we have been deceived by the linguistic fraud of the term "sub-modalities," the time has come to *unmask* the true nature of "sub-modalities"and disclose *the secrets* of "sub-modalities."

In preparation for this, put yourself into a state of playful exploration as you suspend your internal critic. Just *dream and play along* with the ideas, thought experiments, and suggestions here. Doing so will allow you to enter into the process of understanding these *secrets*. Afterwards, you may still not agree. That really doesn't matter. More important is that you get an intelligent grasp on the perspective offered here. Then, with a clear understanding, you can decide whether you buy it or not, find it useful or not, want to go with it or not.

For us, *the very process of thinking and re-thinking* the NLP model is more important than any specific conclusion we draw. After all, regarding the very nature of thought and theorizing, there is always more than one way to map a territory. So thinking and re-thinking a model enables us to move beyond looking for the "one true map," to developing and juxtaposing maps of various degrees of richness, and maps that allow us to accomplish different things.

The Representational Distinctions of Genius
We begin this work from the engineering perspective that *every experience has a structure*. Therefore, mapping the internal structure of an experience enables us to uncover the operational neuro-linguistic (neurological and linguistic)

processes and mechanisms. With these objectives and assumptions firmly in mind, we come to study the structure of *excellence or genius*. Our basic format:

1) First track down the representational steps that comprise the mind-body cognitive strategy.

2) Then sequence the steps to discover its syntax or order.

3) Look for the meta-levels of the higher frames that more fully describes and textures the strategy of genius.

In the first and most comprehensive textbook on modeling with NLP (Dilts, *et al.*, 1980, *NLP: The Study of the Structure of Subjectivity*), the co-developers built a flow-chart model of neuro-linguistic processes. They began with the TOTE model and then added representational steps to flesh out many of the testing operations.

Later, Robert Dilts (1998) collected many other sub-models that NLP contributed to modeling: R.O.L.E., B.A.G.E.L., S.C.O.R.E., and "Neuro-Logical" Levels. In *NLP: Going Meta—Advanced Modeling Using Meta-Levels* I added the Meta-States model to this (Hall, 2001). These later developments included "sub-modalities" in the modeling process whether as *representational steps* in the TOTE or as meta-levels. In modeling today, we pay attention to specific qualities of representations and note how they played into the process.

For example, in a learning strategy, merely seeing a picture of a past memory does not tell us *how* the person actually codes that picture.

—Does *distance* (far or close) effect the learning strategy?

—Does *its clarity* (clear or fuzzy) effect it?

—How about other *qualities* that we can notice in a picture: flat, 2-dimension, 3-dimension, holographic; panoramic or bordered; in color or black-and-white; straight or tilted; etc.?

These *distinctions, qualities, components,* and *variables* of our representational coding make a big difference. No one questions that. These are the *cinematic features* of our internal movies.

- Yet *how* do they make a difference?
- How should we think (or theorize) about this?
- What are these things that we call "sub-modalities?"
- Should we think of them as "things" at all?
- Suppose we run the nominalization test on them. Can you put a *distinction, quality, component,* or *variable* in a wheelbarrow?
- Can we put "close or far" on a desk?
- Can you put clear or fuzzy in your hand?
- Can any *cinematic feature* be touched, handled, or tasted?

Asking these hard questions led us to totally re-think the theoretical basis of "sub-modalities." In this chapter we will offer some refinements about how we think and use "sub-modalities." We will suggest numerous problems with the term "sub-modalities" and highlight the *meta-function* of these representational distinctions. Doing this opens up new space and understandings for new technologies and patterns.

The Focus of The Inquiry

If our proposition is true that *the difference that makes a difference* does not involve "*sub*-modality" coding, then where do we find that difference?

It certainly *seems* that "the difference that makes a difference" lies at the level of "sub-modalities." It *seems* as if "the difference" that really makes a big difference in our experiences, emotions, and responses involves a straightforward shift from one "sub-modality" to another.

When we shift a "sub-modality" back and forth using such distinctions as *Association/Dissociation*, *Color / Black-and-White*, and *Close/ Far* on how we have most thoughts coded, it certainly feels impactful. This process lies at the heart of many NLP technologies such as "Sub-modality Play," "Sub-modality Contrastive Analyses," and "Mapping Over Using 'Sub-Modalities.'" No wonder we have come to so highly appreciate and use them as powerful interventions.

- But what really describes "the difference?"
- And, at what level does this *difference* occur?

The "Sub-Modalities" of Trauma

Let's return to the illustration used earlier. Consider how a person represents and encodes a traumatic experience. Obviously, the cinematic features of our internal representations play a key role in cuing our brains and bodies about how to respond.

If we code the movie of the memory as *associated, close in image and sound, bright, three-dimensional, loud, etc.,* we use a code that enables most people to feel and respond as if the trauma is going on now. That code cues our brain-and-nervous system to enter into the experience of the movie again and to feel distressed, angry, fearful, upset, etc. It cues us to feel and sense that the trauma "is real and present."

On the surface, this seems to prove that "sub-modalities" specify "the difference that makes the difference." Indeed, it *seems* so. And it is this feeling which explains why it has been so easy to jump to that unwarranted conclusion.

While the *cinematic features* of the "sub-modality" distinctions frequently *seem* to provide the switch that governs experience, it does so for a very different reason that the traditional "sub-modality" theory. It does *not* because "sub-modalities" are "the difference that makes a difference." We hinted at this previously regarding the difference between associating and dissociating.

If *associative* processing moves us to think, feel, and act *as if* inside of an experience because we *step into the movie* and *dissociative* or spectating processing moves us to *step out* of the movie so that we think, perceive, feel, and act *about* the experience, then this *"sub-modality"* (and also meta-program) provides an off/on distinction.

First we experience something as if *"in"* the event, then we experience that same thing as if *"out"* of it. In our mind, *we step into it; we step out of it.* We step in and go through the trauma movie again. That makes us feel terrible. We step out of the movie and take another perceptual position, and suddenly we feel more resourceful enough to analyze it as if a spectator.

What hint lies hidden in this "magic?" In this description? Precisely this: we have not only describe association and dissociation as *"sub-modalities,"* but also as *meta-programs.* Consider that!
*   Yet, how could a *"sub*-modality" distinction, something supposedly *below* and *under* the level of the modalities, also be *above* them in a *meta* relation *to* them?
*   How can a *"sub*-modality" be a *meta*-program at the same time?
*   Don't we have two very different models mixed up here?
*   Or could it be that meta-programs are another way of talking about the same thing that "sub-modalities" speak of?

A *Fact* that leads to a *Question:*
     Association and Dissociation are not only *"sub-modalities"* they are also *meta-programs.*

How could a *"sub*-modality" distinction, something supposedly *below* and *under* the level of modalities also be *above* them and sustain *a meta* relationship *to* them? *How?*

The answer?
When we think about, and work with, "sub-modalities," we are not operating at a *sub*-level, but at a *meta-level!*

To think about the *cinematic features* that we discern within the modalities (our mental movies), and operate on them, presupposes that we have conceptually moved to a meta-level. We have *stepped back* from the modalities and have *gone meta* to the representation.

We have to do this in order to elicit the "sub-modalities." After all, thinking about, detecting, and shifting "sub-modalities" works with *structure* and *process*, not *content*. In NLP this is a critical distinction. The structure of information (its form, process, formatting), the *meta-level* structure, governs how we experience it.

This unmasks the first paradoxical secret about "sub-modalities." The *cinematic features* as the qualities and finer distinctions in our modes of awareness (movies) only become available to us when we *rise above* them, when we step back from them, and when we move to a meta-position to think *about* them.

Secret #1: There are no *sub*-levels to "sub-modalities"
The distinctions are Cinematic Features of our inner Movies
We *call* these sensory representation qualities ""'sub-modalities," but using that label does *not* make them a sub or lower class or level. Korzybski described this kind of a thing as linguistic fraud. In a linguistic fraud, the term misleads. It advertises falsely. As radical and unorthodox as this may sound, test this out in your own experience.

A Detection Exercise
1) Think about something—anything.
> What comes to mind? A pleasant experience, your home, a backyard, a memory of a time when you felt creative or confident?

2) Pick out and notice some of *the qualities* or "sub-modalities" of your internal pictures, sounds, or sensations.
- *Where* do you see the experience?
- How close or far?
- What qualities characterize what you see in terms of color or in black-and-white, bordered or panoramic, clear or fuzzy, etc.?
- *Where* do you hear the sounds, noise, music, or voice in the representation?
- What qualities characterize it in terms of volume, tone, tempo, etc.?
- *What* do you feel in terms of sensations?
- *Where* do you feel these?
- What qualities characterize it: pressure, tension, movement, rhythm, etc.?

3) As you now step back, notice *the process of how* you became aware of the *qualities* of your inner movie and its representations.
- Do you go *into* the picture, sound, or sensation more and more?

- Or do you step *out of* the picture, sound, or sensation so that you note *the structure or form* of it?
- Do you not even do this physically by a kinesthetic move-back in your body or head?
- What about others? What do they do when you ask them to notice a "sub-modality?"

Our sensory modes of representation (e.g., visual, auditory, kinesthetic, etc.) provide our basic coding for how we represent information. These modalities make up our inner movies. They also contain certain qualities or properties which we can discern and categorize. In fact, they *cannot* not have various qualities and properties. How could they not have certain *cinematic features* to them?

Test it for yourself. Visualize any picture without some *quality* of distance, clarity, color, etc. Try it... in vain! Yes these properties of pictures, sounds, and sensations may seem to be inside the modalities, yet they are not. How do I know? Because you can *step back* and shift these cinematic features as you *edit* your movies. You can zoom in and out of the image. You can add or subtract sound tracks. You can edit in new sensations and smells. These are things we do *from the outside*, not at some basement level of consciousness.

This means that we mis-diagram and mis-label the VAK *qualities* whenever we attach the inaccurate and unuseful metaphor of *depth* ("sub") to these *cinematic features*. As we have explored this distinction, we have repeatedly asked hundreds if not thousands of people, from novice clients to well-trained NLP trainers, to explain *how* a *"sub-modality"* can be "sub."
- How can a cinematic feature like a picture having movement (a movie) or stillness (a snapshot) be "sub"to the movie?
- How can the color or the black-and-white code of a movie be located "below" the movie?
- How can any quality exist as a smaller part of the whole?
- How can close or far? Fuzzy or clear? A scary sound track or a sound track of classical music?

In response, most people stop ... they pause, and then hesitate (or go into a profound trance!).
- How can the *quality* of a sound like the quality of volume (quiet to loud) be a smaller part of the sound?

Higher and Lower Levels
When Bob first questioned this, he wrote an email to me.
> The *"sub"* part just is not there. When I consider this, my brain goes blank. And I have found that most of the people I do this with also find

that their brain just goes blank. Actually this is kind of funny. I think that if Bandler and Grinder had called them *properties* or *qualities* from the beginning, this facet of the NLP model would not have gotten so confused. It now seems to me that we essentially have to *un*teach that map so we can identify the next secret of "sub-modalities."

We do *not* have "sub" qualities of the modalities in the sense of having a lower, or a more basic, *level*. Quite the opposite. These qualities or cinematic features exist at a *higher* logical level. They are frames over the sensory representations of our movies. Consider what that means.

Now we can re-map these distinctions as simply qualities and properties of the pictures, sounds, and sensations. We can now recognize them as the cinematic features of our mental movies (this was what we did in *MovieMind*, 2003). None of this nullifies the fact that these distinctions exist and are important. It only does away with the theory and the depth metaphor as belonging to a lower level. In the end of this analysis and re-examination, we will show how they actually are a *higher level* or meta-level construction of frames. And that opens up a whole new world of their semantic significance.

We do *not* have "sub" qualities of the modalities
in the sense of having a lower, or a more basic, *level*.

The cinematic features are at a *higher* logical level.
They are frames over the sensory representations of our movies.

To create a *"logical level,"* the higher level arises as an abstraction from and of the lower level. The lower level becomes a member of the class of the higher level. So we put wheels, doors, and steering wheel below the higher abstraction of "car." These are pieces which make up a "car," or members of the class of car. Car is the *class*, they are the members of the class. Similarly, we can classify car, plane, and train as members of the class of "transportation."

Is color, black-and-white, clear, fuzzy, close, far, etc. members of the class of *visual*? No. A picture of Michael, of a mountain, an image of a person skiing, a blue sky, these are members of that class of visual. These terms, color, black-and-white, clear, fuzzy, close, far, etc., are more abstract than "visual." Visual would be a member of the class of close or of the class of far, so would sounds, sensations, smells, etc.

Yes with the term *color*, we have a visual experience presuppose. Yet that does not mean *color* is a member of the class of visual. Specific colors (red, blue, white, green, black, orange, pink, etc.) are members of the class of color.

Similarly, we can move in the opposite direction. We can challenge the so-called *"sub*-modality" by simply asking about the so-called higher "logical level" of the modality.

> How is "visual" an abstraction from "in color?"
> Or, is "visual" a member of the class of "color?"
> How is "visual" a generalization from "close?"
> Or, is "visual" a member of the class of "close?"

This shows the false-to-fact or inaccurate mapping that we have been invited into via the term *"sub*-modality." The cinematic features of our movies do not lie at a lower "logical levels" at all. When we have color, we have an facet, property, and quality that we have brought to a visual representation. Like a movie editor, we start with a film clip, then we add or subtract color from it. Or we change the color adding hues of blue, green, yellow, or whatever.

What does this mean? It means that the prefix *"sub"* quietly suggested the *depth metaphor,* and that in turn led us to view "sub-modalities" as the *molecular structure* of consciousness. Running with this metaphor, the prefix began seducing us into assuming that modalities have smaller elements which are un-decomposable primitives, the building blocks of meaning and thinking. This played off of the periodic table of elements metaphor, a common metaphor in NLP circles, one that I used in several books before I learned better.

Yet none of that is so. The distinctions within the VAK representations (our movies) actually arise from *an interaction* between our experience of the electro-magnetic energies "out there" in the world and our meta-level awareness of the modalities that we construct in our visual, auditory, motor, and associative cortexes.

Today we now know that neither "color" nor "black-and-white" occur "out there." Where do these come from? They *emerge* from the way our rods and cones interact with the electro-magnetic field. *We* construct both "color" and "black-and-white" in our heads. They are concepts—perceptual concepts. We impose them upon our pictures, images, and vision. They are not a "smaller" unit of analysis, but a meta-analysis.

Our awareness of the representational distinctions and cinematic features of anything emerges from the abstractions we construct. *We* are the ones who bring these distinctions to our internal constructing of the world out there. We paint these distinctions onto the canvas of our representational screen due to how our nervous system processing works *and* due to the frames that we bring to them.

What are "sub-modalities?"

"Sub-modalities," as the cinematic features of our movies,
are part and parcel of the meta-frames that we apply to
the representations of our inner movies.

In the end, treating "sub-modalities" as the *smallest building blocks* of subjectivity turns out to be an inadequate way of thinking about these features. Every model allows a person to *do* something or to *go* somewhere. Newton's physics can take a person so far. Aristotle's model of language, thought, and logic takes us so far. But when we get to the edge of those maps, we can go no further. That's when the paradigm blinds us as to what lies beyond. That's when we become paradigm blind.

It is at this point that something new arises—Non-Newtonian or Einstein physics (quantum mechanics) and Non-Aristotelian Neuro-Linguistics (Korzybski's General Semantics, NLP's Meta-Model).

The *depth* metaphor elicited another metaphor, *the periodic chart of elements* and a corresponding theory. It suggested that the cinematic properties which we discern in the sensory representational systems are the "building blocks," a "sub-level" substratum, and the basement of personality. Indeed, that metaphor has allowed us to go far in modeling excellence. It has enabled us to decompose a strategy and identify its elements and facets. But, because it paints an inaccurate and false-to-fact picture, when patterns like *Confusion to Understanding* and *Doubt to Belief* do not work, we are at the edge of the map with no way to navigate except to either give up the pattern or to keep repeating what does not work.

Oh yes, there is a third alternative. We can also revise the theory.
- What if the representational distinctions are *not* at a *sub*-level at all, but at a meta-level?
- What if the cinematic features are constructions of our mind which *we* bring to bear upon our sensory mapping?
- What if we have to *go meta* to detect, apply, and alter these distinctions of our movies?
- What if these facets within the structure of subjective experience exist *above and beyond* our sensory code?
- What if, as in quantum mechanics, we recognize the role that *we* play

in constructing our representational world?   That *we* inevitably influence the system that we observe?

- What if these distinctions and features are our evaluations and abstractions *about* the world?
- What if we recognized these distinctions (i.e., distance, intensity, source, etc.) as nominalizations of concepts?
- What if these distinctions involve a relationship between our movies and higher level understandings and concepts?

The significance? "Sub-modalities" actually arise as map / territory *gestalts*. We start with some lower level abstractions from the territory—the transformations of the energy manifestations "out there" in the form of electro-magnetic energy. Upon inputting this information, we transform it layer upon layer and create our inner world of sensory re-presentations that seems like an inner movie.

There can be no "sub-modalities" as we have traditionally theorized because there is no such thing as "objective" properties in the first place. All "properties" arise and exist in a totally subjective way anyway. Dilts, Bandler and Cameron-Bandler, Grinder and DeLozier (1980) noted and argued for this in their original work. When it comes to "the structure of subjectivity"—it is all subjective anyway.   Yeager (1985) describes the compellingness and inescapability of subjectivity when he wrote, "... subjectivity is unavoidable, which makes it reality." (p. 17).

Secret #2: "The Difference that Makes a Difference" is a Meta-Frame that occurs at Meta-Levels

Gregory Bateson (1972) first introduced the phrase, *"the difference that makes a difference"* in his presentation at the Nineteenth Annual Korzybski Memorial Lecture (January, 1970). What led him to this phrase? He came up with it during his exploration of the classic formulation by Korzybski, "The map is not the territory." In his quest for "mind," and his *Steps To An Ecology Of Mind,* he asked an incredibly important question. He asked, *"What gets onto a map?"*

His answer? *"Difference."* "Differences are the things that get onto a map." (p. 451)

Then he was asked, "What is a difference?" He said it involves "an abstract matter" because with this term we have "entered into the world of communication, organization" (p. 452). In this new world of communication, we leave behind the outside world of forces and impacts and energy exchange. This psychological world of communication, involves "information" or "news of difference."

"... the elementary unit of information—is *a difference which makes a difference,* and is able to make a difference because the neural pathways are themselves provided with energy..." (p. 453)

"The territory never gets in at all. The territory is *Ding an sich* [Thing in itself] and you can't do anything with it. Always the process of representation will filter it out so that the mental world is only maps of maps of maps, ad infinitum. All 'phenomena' are literally 'appearances.'" (pp. 454-455)

From this, Bateson refined his definition of "mind."

"... mind as synonymous with cybernetic system—the relevant total information-processing, trial-and-error completing unit. And we know that within Mind in the widest sense there will be a hierarchy of sub-systems..." (p. 460)

The bottom line is that Bateson viewed "the difference that makes a difference" as *information coding* or "news of difference," which lies in the *qualities and properties* of the representations—in the cinematic features. These qualities and properties of representations lie in the meta-levels that govern or modulate lower levels. These meta-levels consist of *the meanings* that we give our internal representations. They involve the meanings we apply with our words and the meanings we apply to those, etc. Thinking systemically, he viewed "mind" as a system of representation and feed-back and feed-forward mechanisms wherein "the higher levels always modulate the lower levels."

"All communication has this characteristic—it can be *magically modified* by accompanying communication." (p. 230 emphasis added)

How does this apply to "sub-modalities?" Somewhere in the development of theorizing about "sub-modalities," the idea arose that these smaller elements are "the difference that makes a difference." When I first heard this, I accepted it at face value without questioning it and so helped to perpetuate the idea as I repeated it in numerous articles and books. Yet now in re-examining this, it fails as an explanatory map about the structure of subjective experience. "Difference" operates as a meta-level phenomenon.

Bateson's "difference that makes a difference" operates at higher "logical levels" as the meta-frames and semantic meanings that we give to things.

This explains why the patterns and processes for mapping over "sub-modalities" and making "sub-modality shifts" do not always work. It especially explains why meta-level structures (i.e., beliefs, understandings, values, etc.) typically *do not shift* with mere "sub-modality" alterations. It takes something more. You need something higher to get leverage on these structures to create transformation, especially lasting changes.

Revisiting the Coding of Trauma

Let's revisit how we represent a traumatic experience. First note the quality of the cinematic features of your internal movie. These qualities cue your brain and body about how to respond.

Typically, when we code a painful memory using the cinematic features of associated, close in image and sound, bright, three-dimensional, loud, etc., we code it with a structure that as much says or means for most people,

> Recall the experience and fully enter into the movie of that experience again so that you feel distressed, angry, fearful, upset, etc.

Doesn't this prove that the "sub-modality" coding runs the emotional programs? No, it does not. It does not because there's another facet to the structure. *There is the semantic meaning that we give to the code.* What is the basis upon which this code stands? What do these cinematic features "mean" to any given person? Do these "sub-modalities" features have a genetic meaning? Of course not!

And that's the trick, isn't it?

> **Meaning in our human neuro-linguistic processes operates symbolically or semantically.**

That's why nothing means anything inherently. The "closeness" of a picture does not inherently mean "real," "now," "feel it," or "more compelling." If so, just keep at it. Zoom in on the picture even more... and more... and more ... make it a 40 foot by 40 foot screen. Double it. Double it again. Continue doubling it until you can see the dots—see one single tiny dot as 100 feet by 100 feet. Now what does the image mean? At some point the meaning of "closeness" will shift. At some point it will go over a meaning threshold and no longer mean "real" or "compelling."

What is this threshold? It is the threshold of our symbolic system by which we attribute significance and meaning to things.

This explains why we say that *on the surface* it seems that "sub-modalities" mark out "the difference that makes the difference." Yet they do not. We avoid that unwarranted conclusion as we realize that *meanings* (semantics) arise from our frames-of-references. The key lies in the meta-level structure or frame that we put around our representations. If we happened upon the very distinctions that, for most people, stand for and symbolize "trauma," it's those common *meanings* that actually do the damage, not the quality or feature of the picture. Because the picture is "close" does not in itself cause a person to feel traumatized by an image. It is that *closeness* (as a concept and symbol) for a given person (and typically for most of us) have come to *stand for* and *structure* the significance (meaning, neuro-semantics) of "trauma."

How do I know that? Well, try the pattern out on yourself. Think of something that makes you feel horrible, scared, upset, etc. Pick something that elicits feelings of hurt and trauma for you. Now bring the picture closer, and closer, and even more so. Keep doing this until it is "in your face." Then expand your mental screen until you have a picture of the trauma that seems like it is ten meters by ten meters. Now double the size of that picture (20 by 20). Now double that. Again. Again. Keep expanding it up until you have a screen 1000 meters by 1000 meters, and it is in your face. You can now see maybe a few dots in the whole matrix.

How do you feel? Traumatized? I doubt it. Seeing a few dots in a terrible image hardly ever *stands for* or structures the neuro-semantic significance of "trauma."

It is not the *concept* of size or color or dimensions or any representational distinction that *per se* causes, codes, or structures the meaning. We *use* these facets, variables, components of our encoding to stand for and symbolize these higher level meanings. We draft these features into service for our meaning-making. We shanghai them at meta-levels to construct the *structure* of our internal neuro-semantic Virtual Reality map.

So while it seems that the "sub-modalities" flip the switch for our experiences, it only does so because we use them at meta-levels for that purpose. It is not the case that these tiny "building blocks" are the molecules of thought. It is rather that *we use them structurally* to format our frames-of-references in the way we construct meaning. We use "closeness" to *mean* "in our face," "compelling," "undeniable," "full of emotions," etc.

"Sub-modalities" as really Meta-Level Frames
One of the biggest surprises that knocked us off of our feet occurred when we first realized that "There is no *'sub'* in "sub-modalities."

To get to the actual referent of the so-called "sub," we have to go meta. Consider the basic "sub-modality" category of *black-and-white* versus *color*. Do either of these (black-and-white / color) exist "out there" and therefore at a lower level to a picture? Can you have a picture without either? Where is the quality and distinction that we label *"color"* anyway? It is not "out there." Because "color" as an *abstraction* arises from the interaction of the electro-magnetic field impinging upon our rods and cones, it emerges *inside our nervous system* as our evaluation. It arises from the functioning of our nervous system sense receptors and our rods and cones in relation to certain energies. It is therefore *meta to* the event itself.

So with *distance*. How close or far away we "sense" or encode a picture, sound, or sensation depends on *how* we compare, weigh, measure, and judge the event. "Close" does not refer to a "thing." It refers to an evaluative judgment. As a relative term (an unspecified adjective, a comparative deletion) it is part of our abstracting nervous system—part of our neuro-semantic state and experience.

Intermission: The Story of the Discovery

Rest your brain for a few minutes. As you defocus your eyes and rest comfortably, I will tell you some of the story about how we discovered this. Actually, it is not a pretty picture at all. We discovered it by the greatest and most valuable teacher of all, our close friend and constant companion—*failure, inconsistency, ineffectiveness, and getting responses that we did not want.*

It happened this way. We found that the traditional *Belief Change pattern* often did not work. Merely mapping across "sub-modalities" of a doubt to a strong but limiting belief, and from a strong belief to a new idea we wanted to believe, did *not* always work. All too often it did *not* weaken the old belief or create the space in which to introduce a new belief. We actually found that for many people, it *never* worked.

Bob noted this for years as he taught NLP Practitioner Training. Having tried it numerous times, he began to seriously question things. He first began questioning *himself*. "Perhaps I just don't know the right procedure." Later, after we began to publish some things about "sub-modalities," someone else mentioned a similar frustration, "I thought the problem was the client." Bob replied, "I thought the problem was me."

I had a very similar experience with a different "sub-modality" pattern. In using the *Confusion to Understanding Pattern,* I found that merely mapping over the "sub-modality" qualities of *Understanding* to an experience of *Confusion* never worked to make something suddenly clear and understandable. Nor did I find that it worked very often with others. That led me to begin questioning the process.

> So what's wrong? What am I missing here? What would explain this outcome or lack of outcome?

I started inquiring. At NLP trainings and conferences, I began asking about the experiences which others had had with this pattern. At first, people told me that it felt like a "coming out of the closet" kind of experience.

"Will the NLP Mind-Police arrest me, take away my certification if I admit that I never found the pattern all that useful?" Then I heard Charles Faulkner make a presentation in London (Nov. 1998) about his newest work in *Meta-Patterns*. He similarly noted that he didn't believe in "sub-modalities" in the way that they had traditionally been taught. Charles, in fact, utilizing the work of Lakoff and Johnson (1980, 1987) about *embodiment,* presented some processes for externalizing the "sub-modality" patterns. Because we "live inside of these patterns" we also manifest them in our movements, gestures, spatial locating of things, etc.

When I admitted that I never could get it to work and did not find it useful in the lives of many others, confessions began to pour in from all around the world. Literally. Now, I did find *some* people who said that they did find it useful when they did the exercise. So I then asked,

"How often do you use this as a *learning strategy?*
How often in a day, in a week, or a month do you use 'sub-modality' mapping across from confusion to understanding?"

Never. This was true across the board. I *never* found a single person who used the process as their method or strategy for developing understanding. "Strange thing," I thought. "What gives?"

Coincidently, at the London ANLP Conference (Nov. 1998), Joseph O'Connor noted in his workshop on "Values" that trying to change values by changing "sub-modalities" never worked for him. Shifting a value by "Mapping Across 'Sub-modalities'" "works fine as long as you are holding it there. But when you think about something else, there's nothing to prevent it from snapping back." Consciously *holding a new representational distinction* in place with regard to how we think about something needs a higher frame to support it. Joseph noted this when he said, "We have to think about values as a system."

Meta-Level Differences
Actually, the paradox about working with "sub-modalities" involves a very simple explanation.

You have to *go meta* if you want to detect, identify, and then work with "sub-modalities."

Yet you already know *that!* You only have to attend a beginning NLP training to see this in action. Typically, the trainer will elicit an experience (remembered, imagined, or actual) in participants and then debrief by asking about the sights, sounds, and sensations experienced and their "sub-modality" qualities.

For the uninitiated this often seems very mysterious, strange, and inexplicable. A great many people begin questioning themselves. "What's wrong with me? I don't notice my pictures, sounds, tones, snapshot or movie, close or far, focused or panoramic." When NLP newcomers pop in to observe an advanced training in modeling or strategies, they frequently get the impression that everybody has been let in on some incredible secret about running their own brain, except *them!*

Many who come for training will not only *not* recognize such, and may even feel convinced that they do not internally visualize at all. Yet they suffer from no deficiency. They simply live *in content* so much that they simply have not learned how to step aside to notice *the structure* of their thinking. Detecting and working with "sub-modalities" necessitates *a meta-level perception,* the awareness of *structure* rather than content.

"The difference that makes a difference" in our experiences results from the frames-of-references that envelope our lives. Linguistically, we call these "beliefs," "values," and "presuppositions." Conceptually we speak about our assumptions, domains of understandings, categories of knowledge, and our learning history.

Richard Bandler and John Grinder brought this understanding about meta-levels and governing frames-of-reference into NLP with their reframing models. Fritz Perls, Virginia Satir, and Milton Erickson all engaged in changing frames (reframing) to create transformational magic. This also has a pre-NLP history in Gregory Bateson's (1972, 1979) work and his Palo Alto group: John Weakland, Richard Fisch, Don Jackson, and Paul Watzlawick. Their 1974 book, *Change: Patterns of Problem formulation and Problem Solution* predated the first NLP books and explored extensively the importance of reframing.

Bateson argued extensively in many facets of his work (e.g., the double-bind theory, levels of learning, etc.) that *meta-levels govern and modulate lower levels.* This provides a semantic clue about how and why "sub-modality" shifts may work reliably with most people but then fail to work with a given person who operates from a different semantic structure.

Association / Dissociation
Consider again the stepping in and stepping out (poorly called "association/dissociation"). Let's suppose that a person has established a very powerful meta-level frame. Let's suppose the frame operates as an understanding about life, a belief about oneself, "time," and ecology. It operates as a presupposition about how to cope and respond, a value that he appreciates as empowering him. The meta-level frame of reference (or meta-state) goes:

> "Whatever has happened, no matter how unpleasant and distressful, no longer exists and has no power over me."

Now invite this gentleman to recall a memory of a very unpleasant situation. Have him "recall it fully and completely. Step in there and be there seeing what

you saw, hearing what you heard, and feeling what you felt ...."
- Will the induction re-introduce the trauma?
- Will it re-traumatize?
- Will he go back into the state?
- Will it fry his brain and blow out his circuits?

No. It will not. It cannot. With *that* meta-frame, he *cannot* make his pictures so close, vivid, three-dimensional, etc. or his sounds so life-like and vivid, or his sensations to re-traumatize him. *That* meta-frame will protect him from such. "In the back of his mind" (terminology for a meta-frame) he would have, consciously or unconsciously, a presuppositional matrix that would *not* permit it.

Conversely, suppose a person operates from a very different meta-frame. Suppose he has a belief, presupposition, and value that creates lots of pain and distress for himself. Let's verbalize this meta-state frame as:

> "Whatever pain and distress you have experienced in your life will always be with you and will always determine your identity and future."

Now, invite this gentleman to step out and away from a memory of pain, to put it up on the theater of his mind, and to "just observe it from a distance." He will probably find this very difficult and keep defaulting to step back into the memory. *His frame drives that response.* So we ask him to step out from the movie theater where he watches the old movie and to move back to the projection booth—a double step back. Because it violates his frame this will probably be more difficult. Yet even if we get him to do this and he does begin to watch the movie—he may start having traumatic feelings even *way back there* about the movie.

Lots of clients have done that and continue to do that. So what gives? *A meta-frame.* The person has the ability and highly developed skill to feel bad and traumatized *about* the trauma!

Can NLP not do its magic in such cases? Of course! Any proficient practitioner will simply keep interrupting the old program (meta-frame), re-inforcing new frames of distance, calmness, resourcefulness, and comfort and eventually outframes faster than the client. When the gentleman outframes himself with pity, shame, guilt, being a terrible person, hopelessness, etc., as a practitioner we outframe that to jump another "logical level" faster than a speeding train.

> "And as you look at that sad pitiful wreck of a man *for the last time in your life* knowing that change has begun to occur, and will continue to occur even when you do not know it consciously, you can begin to wonder, really wonder, about what learnings you can make from this so

that you never have to repeat it, and can turn around and begin to face a brighter future than you could have even imagined before ... now ..."

When we have a person with those kinds of rigid, limiting, dis-empowering, insulting, and traumatizing meta-frames—working with such a person becomes *a frames war.* Who will set the final frame?

Ultimately human experience results from the frames that we set. These meta-level frames identify where we store our more abstract and conceptual maps of reality and where we set up meanings about self, others, and the universe. Realizing the power of meta-frames, Bob wrote,

> "I have never affected a 'sub-modality' change that produced results that did not activate a meta-level structure. When I first developed the pattern of "Taking a Bitter Root to Jesus" (1993), I thought it operated as it did because of the 'sub-modalities' that it activated. And yes, it does concern 'sub-modalities,' yet it *links* the problem right into a much higher meta-level frame-of-reference and from there it blows the problem out. It does it because of the higher level at which a person represents their image of 'Jesus.' The level at which they put that image inevitably modulates the lower levels. As a result it blows the problems to smithereens."

Secret #3: "Sub-Modality" Shifts work when Meta-Frames are set.
If the realm of *"sub*-modalities" were "the difference that makes a difference" then merely shifting "sub-modalities" should be enough intervention to change most experiences. Yet it is not.

Because the "sub-modality" model began with this assumption, the early developers inevitably drew these conclusions. From the beginning of Bandler and Grinder's discovery of the sensory representational systems, and then later with Bandler's specification of the domain of "sub-modalities," most NLP interventions depend upon "sub-modality" analysis, playing, shifting, and mapping over.

Given the development of the NLP model at that time—this made perfect sense. It did not demonstrate any lack of intelligence in the developers. Having evoked the "building blocks" metaphor of human subjectivity (i.e., the representational systems and their component pieces as "sub-modalities") this provided a world of unexplored territory for them to go rampaging about in. And they did. And out of that wild and chaotic charting of the territory—they came up with many marvelous and "magical" interventions (i.e., the phobia cure, the strategy model, messing up a person's strategy by changing component pieces, reframing, the swish pattern, etc.).

The analysis here does *not* fault the original NLP model in any of this. It was and is a stroke of genius. Rather, we seek to build upon it and offer some finer distinctions as we more thoroughly re-examine the representational model. And we do so fully aware that we have a privilege and opportunity that the original developers did not—we have twenty-five years of hindsight going for us! We have the advantage of more fully developing the Bateson and Korzybski understandings of meta-levels in the Meta-Stats model. With this disclaimer, we now present several reasons why "sub-modality" shifts do not always work —and actually, do not work *at all* alone.

The Inadequacies of Many "Sub-Modality" Shifts
First, "sub-modality" mapping across often does not work because the structure of the problem lies in higher level conceptual states.

In the previous illustration, the gentleman's problem did not arise primarily because of *how* he coded his memories at the level of his movies. His feelings of trauma arose because of the beliefs and maps he had *about* "the past" that he represented. His *meta-level meanings* drove his responses even more so than his specific coding. His meta-state set the frame for his interpreting.

When it comes to *the layering of thoughts* at meta-levels, meta-programs and meta-states govern and control our primary states. They also govern our mental movies and the cinematic features. This means that these cinematic distinctions operate *under the governance* of meta-levels. Simultaneously, due to our nature as a symbolic-class of life, we can transform "sub-modality" distinctions into higher level frames of reference as noted. Doing effective "sub-modality" work necessitates taking into consideration this modulation of the higher over the lower levels. Doing this brings to awareness "sub-modality" distinctions we can utilize at meta-levels. It helps us recognize frames and meta-levels in our thinking, emoting, and processing of ourselves and others.

Second, "sub-modality" chunking down and mapping across can eat up lots of time and trouble without ever pinpointing the governing structure.

We often waste a lot of time and expend a lot of energy in attempting to tear down the structure of an experience by pulling apart every "sub-modality" that goes into the form. Imagine tearing down a building brick by brick and finding that it has an internal metal structure. Thinking about "sub-modalities" using the building block metaphor may pull apart a lot of the structure. Yet in the end, it may simply reveal that there's an over-arching structure within it.

At worst, this process may just take up a lot of unnecessary time and trouble and never touch the real problem. That could leave a person feeling frustrated and hopeless. Breaking down a structure into small chunks without paying attention to its larger structures uses up precious energy that could better be devoted to the meta-levels.

Thinking about the distinctions of sensory representations, on the other hand, enables us to step back and think about *the over-arching structure.* In going meta, it allows us to focus much more on structure and process than content. It can then tune our eyes and ears to see and hear the distinctions that a person may use as a meta-level concept or frame.

>"I don't know what's wrong with me." Bill said. "When I get into a disagreement with someone I feel really defensive and then begin to do things to push the person away. It's like the argument closes in on me and suffocates me or something. I just know that I need to get some distance from it all. I hate this about myself. It's like a weakness. I know that I'm just making things worse when I do that."

Doesn't that tell us just about everything we need to know. When I heard it, I commented,

>"So you need to *think about the person* who disagrees with you as further away in your mind and when you *see him further away because you can easily push your picture of him back*, you can then feel comfortable and listen with more calmness, and maybe compassion, really wanting to understand and help, because it means that you have your space and identity, and you *know that you and your self-esteem are not on the line*, don't you? Have I got that right?"

Bill found himself surprised that "the problem" didn't feel so bad.

>Hmmmm. It seems different now that we're talking about it. When you put it that way, I feel okay.

Of course, I invited him to try really hard in vain to feel as bad about it as he did (another outframing comment). And, repeating the induction several more times, and in different words, I invited him to imagine operating this way in the future.

>Who knows what made the change? Perhaps you just needed a chance to *take a deep breath* about it all, *step back* and gain some perspective, and realize that you can always do that to *feel safe* and resourceful. Then it doesn't have anything to do with being threatened. When you think about it that way, how does it feel to realize that you could use this in the days and months to come?

Here the meta-level distinction of *distance* served to symbolize several meanings for Bill. *Structurally,* when he coded a picture as "close" and "in his face," it stood for a higher level meaning of "intrusion," "invasion," "lack of respect," "assault on his self-esteem," etc. Many people use that so-called "sub-modality" to neuro-semantically represent such things. And many people do not. Instead of "running a pattern" with Bill, I conversationally talked to him setting frames that were semantically meaningful for him.

Third, making changes at the lower level of "sub-modalities," though they may shift a person for awhile, frequently will shift back.

Have you ever run a pattern based on "sub-modality" mapping across and while it worked during the time of the exercise, it did not stick? Have you turned a doubt into a belief, but later found that it had reverted back to a doubt? This is a key problem with "sub-modalities."

Many people have experienced a shift in belief, understanding, decision, etc. when they first run the pattern. But after a little while, they find that things shift and that they themselves are back in the same old mess. The intervention worked temporarily, but did not last. Why not? Why this lack of permanence?

Meta-level frames operate as *attractors in a self-organizing system.* The believing, valuing, understanding, negating, etc. that we do at those levels create a stability at a higher level so that the instability and variability at the lower level can keep reinforcing and validating the higher frame like a self-fulfilling prophecy. For this reason, merely recoding a movie without taking the meta-levels of meanings into account often means that the transformation will not last.

If we do not attend to the higher level meta-states that solidify our virtual realities maps (our Matrix of frames) and give it coherence, the old structure will bounce back. What holds our reality together? What gives coherence to our model of the world? *Our frames—and the frames that envelope those frames.* So we ask, "What frames (beliefs, values, intentions, generalizations, presuppositions, etc.) are holding a given strategy together?"

Adjusting the *cinematic features* of a movie which represents my belief in myself as confident and skilled in persuasion skills will not cohere and hold if I have some higher frames that contradict and conflict with it. Turning your *doubts* about your persuasiveness into *belief* about such by making it in color, three-dimensional, a movie, and with a strong internal voice may work during the duration of the exercise. But will it generalize and stick? Will your matrix of higher frames allow it? That's the critical leverage point for transformation.

Secret #4: "Sub-modality" magic occurs in the activating of a governing meta-frame.
To effectively shift "sub-modalities," we need two things. First we need a clear understanding of the structure of the difficulty.

- How does it work?
- How is it coded?

Second, we need an understanding of the person's symbolic system. We need to discover the "sub-modalities" that the person uses to stand for, and symbolize, the necessary meta-level frame. This introduces the role of our *neuro-semantics*. Why? Because the cinematic coding of a picture, sound, sensation, etc. itself does *not* mean anything.

- What does a *black-and-white* picture mean?
- What does a *color* picture mean?
- What does a *close* picture mean?
- What does it mean *to you* when you see a picture *far away?*
- What about the meaning that you attribute to a *fuzzy, clear, bordered, panoramic* picture?
- What about the meaning of a *close or far, loud or soft, associated or dissociated* sound?

These structural facets or components that make up our movie representations. These variables, features, and facets within our movies *stand for* and *symbolize* higher level concepts. "Closeness" may mean "more real" to one person. Another person, however, may read it as *meaning* "more compelling." Yet another may experience it as meaning "more intense." Yet another may not give it any meaning, "It doesn't mean any of that; it just means the picture is closer."

How we experience any "sub-modality" depends completely on our individual experiences and histories. Via our personal history we learn to attach various meanings to the cinematic features. No wonder merely altering a "sub-modality" does not always work to create change. Merely altering a cinematic feature, apart from taking the higher levels into consideration, fails to recognize our *semantic use* of these representational features.

This explains why we need to understand higher level meta-states, how they modulate the problem, and what distinction or variable of representation we can use to *symbolically stand for* and create that meta-level meaning.

Altering "Sub-modalities" for Assertiveness
When I saw Jenny several years ago, she said that she wanted to become more assertive. She wanted the ability to speak up for herself and to succeed in her career and business.

MH: "Do you have a clear idea of what *speaking up for yourself* would look like, sound like, and feel like?"
    Jenny: "Yes, I do."

"So what stops you?"
    "I don't know."

That's typical. Most meta-frames operate *outside* of conscious awareness. "Go inside, and give yourself permission to speak up forthrightly, assertively, and firmly with all of your female values and traits intact."
    "Oh I don't like that. What if I got rejected? What if someone criticized me for thinking too much of myself? No... I can't ... I just can't do that."

Ah, a meta-frame just popped out in response to *the very idea* of "permission." As we talked, it became obvious to both of us that she had a fully activated and vigorous *taboo program* at work in her mind. Assertiveness was forbidden. "Who set this frame of reference for you? Has anyone ever told you to 'be seen and not heard,' to not assert yourself, to worry about what others think of you, to fear rejection or criticism, anything like that?"
    "Oh yes."
"And do you like that? Does it serve you well?"
    "No, it does not!" she said emphatically.

"Now you're sure that it doesn't serve you well. Maybe it does."
    "No, it doesn't. I'm sure about that."

"So you wouldn't be opposed to *refusing to tolerate* that old frame anymore, would you?"
    "No I wouldn't. In fact, I'd like to refuse to tolerate it."

"You would be willing to emphatically say *'No!'* to that old taboo that has kept you from speaking up? And that has forbidden you to discover your own voice?"
    "Yes."

"Yes? Are you sure of that *Yes*?"
    "Yes I am! I am ready to find my own voice and express it."

Knowing meta-frames you can see the process that intervenes, that identifies the old frame and that loosen it and de-stabilizes it (saying *"No!"* to it), and the next higher frame that validates and affirms that, *"Yes indeed, I want to do that!"*

I went on to identify the *cinematic features* of her *"No!"* and her *"Yes!"* and then updated the particular variables or "sub-modalities" of her internal voice. The structural coding of these representations do not work in a vacuum, but within the larger context of other frames and frames-of-frames. In fact, we can use characteristics as *frames*. For example, with Jenny, I had her *frame her internal voice* with permission, congruence, panoramic, and with the qualities that signified to her strength, confidence, firmness, etc.

Mapping Over "Sub-modalities" For a Loss

Suppose we are working with a woman who has just suffered the loss of someone important to her, whether a spouse, parent, friend, or child. The loss of her emotional investment in that person will inevitably cause her to experience grief, sadness, and a sense of emptiness. Let's suppose that this experience of loss is "clean" in that she does not have any old business attached to it. That is, she has not built any negative frames-of-reference about her concept of losing a loved one.

The *Resolving Grief Pattern* using "sub-modalities" would have us first gather information. We would find out *how* she represents "emptiness" and "loss" and then run a comparative analysis with *how* she represents "fullness" and "connection." With that information, we could then simply invite her to make an exchange. Code the person who has died in the same way that you encode someone who is gone, but with whom you still feel connected and with whom you treasure how they have been a value to you. This mapping over of the "full" code to the content of the person—*applies* these structures to the primary content—and that is a meta-stating process.

This avoids most of the need to explore the person's *meanings or semantics*. We rather directly use the *features, qualities, variables, characteristics,* and *components* of the representations which somehow convey the meaning of "fullness" and "connection." When we bring these structural components to the new content (the primary level) and apply them there—the person *sets a frame* of fullness and connection.

But *if* the person has a higher level meta-frame that prevents this meta-stating, then the symbolic features of the "sub-modalities" will not map over. Or, if they do, they will only map over while we consciously track them over. When we stop, interrupt that process, they will pop right back to the representational distinctions of "emptiness" and "loss." What kind of a meta-frame could prevent that? What about any of the following beliefs, values, understandings, decisions, etc. as a meta-frame?

"Death is a terrible thing that you can never get over."
"When my loved one goes, I'll always be alone until I die."
"I could never meet someone else. That would betray the memory of my dear husband."
"Even if I had another child, I will go to my grave mourning the loss of this child."
"This always happens to me. Whenever I get close to anyone, they

die."

When we shift the "sub-modalities" regarding how we have coded our *values* (a nominalization for the mental-emotional *process* of *valuing*), we have actually moved to a meta-level. There we first observe a person's valuing.

- What thoughts-and-feelings do you bring to this experience that you consider important?
- How do you do this?
- What qualities of the images, sounds, and sensations *stand for* and represent the idea of "important?"

The secret is this: *"Sub-modality" shifts and mapping across work like magic when we use a "sub-modality" that presupposes a meta-frame that effectively and appropriately outframes the old frame and that will govern the new experience.*

This explains what makes them work when they do. The distinction or variable of the representation *stands for* and so *symbolizes* something else at a higher level. For most people, the features of "close," "in color' and "in three dimensions" symbolizes that which is *real* and *present*. "Distance," "black-and-white" and "two dimensional" may stand for and mean "the past" or the not-real.

Summary

- When we unmask "sub-modalities," we find that there is no *substratum*, no lower "logical level"—but just *distinctions, features, qualities,, and variables* of our mental movies.
- In this we have been dramatically mislead to *look down* when we should have *looked up*. The *distinctions* that we can make about our pictures, sounds, and sensations occur at meta-levels.
- Frames-of-references occur at meta-levels. Look there for the magic of reframing, transforming meaning, altering a symbolic system, and the power of your own neuro-semantic reality.
- This means that the cinematic features of our internal movies operate symbolically and semantically. That's why you've got to go meta to do the best mapping and human engineering.
- "The difference that makes a difference" occurs at meta-levels involving higher frames of reference as Bateson noted.
- An empowering frame at a high meta-level can absolutely protect and empower—or sabotage and create havoc in personality. Be careful about the frames that you set.
- "Sub-modality" shifts, mapping across, and contrasts are all guesses in the dark if you don't know about meta-levels, meta-frames, and the symbolic nature of neuro-semantics.

- Meta-level awareness and skill gives your work in engineering and modeling excellence predictability and power.

On to the Applications!

There you have it. In unmasking "sub-modalities" and discovering their *meta* nature, will you ever look at them in the same way? Though they have been masked as the "finer" distinctions that we thought were much smaller pieces like elements of a periodic table of consciousness—we now see that as a masquerade, as a trick costume.

These *cinematic features* of our movie encoding occur in our minds because we take a meta-position and construct them. We have then added them to our internal movies as particular video, audio, and kinesthetic qualities. By doing so, we have *set a frame* both representationally and conceptually.

Now it's time for applications. If you are still hungry for more theoretical understanding about these things—we have 3 more chapters. I originally put them here in the text, but many said, "Too much theory, get on to application. In this book you will find more theoretical chapters at the end:
- Meta-Detailing (17)
- Meta-Levels (18)
- Meta-State Principles (19)

PART II

SIX NEW

NEURO-SEMANTIC MODELS

ABOUT CINEMATIC FEATURES

Since "sub-modalities" are not *sub* at all, but *meta-level* frames, as the cinematic features or frames that we edit into our movies, the refinements that we've identified now enable us to remodel "sub-modalities" and to recognize them as a new meta-domain in NLP.

Doing this gives us four *meta-domains* in NLP. We have 1) the Meta-Model of language, 2) the Meta-Programs of perception, 3) the Meta-States of layers of states and frames, and 4) the Meta-Features of our cinematic distinctions. The first governs language, the second governs perception and filters, the third states and levels, and the fourth the features that quality our mental movies.

To apply this remodeling we have picked out six meta-level phenomena to explore in the following chapters: ground/figure, negation, beliefs, values, understanding, and reframing. These play a significant role in personal mastery and in modeling excellence. The following chapters presents six new patterns for handling meta-level phenomena.

Chapter 5

FOREGROUNDING
AND BACKGROUNDING
RESOURCES

A Meta-Modality Model
For Formatting Mind

"I've never met an image
that didn't stand out from some background."

*"Energy flows where attention goes
—as governed by the intentional frame"*
L. Michael Hall
(*Secrets of Personal Mastery, 1999*)

Suppose you were commissioned to interview a genius for the purpose of modeling his or her strategies?
* What would you explore?
* What would you want to know?
* Where would your questions lead him or her?
* Would you wonder or inquire about what occurs in the *foreground* of the genius' mind?
* Would you explore what lies in the *background*?
* Would you explore how much control and flexibility occurs in the structure of that experience?
* Could such a person's very skill at *foregrounding* certain things and *backgrounding* other things drive the resulting insights and wisdom?
* Could the very *flexibility* in shifting images, sounds, sensations, and words back and forth from foreground to background play a significant role in that person's expertise?
* *How* do they decide what to foreground?
* *What* leads them to decide *when* to foreground it?

All of these facets play a significant role in the cognitive thinking-emoting strategies of a genius, do they not? As you consider times and experiences when you attained high levels of quality performance and those times when you felt stuck, uncreative, unresourceful, what distinguishes the two experiences? What differences occur in terms of what lies in the *foreground* of your awareness and what lies in the *background*?

This meta-distinction is critical. The one thing we know without question is this: if you *foreground* representations, memories, ideas, and feelings of limitation, problems, difficulties, inadequacies, and other things that you evaluate as "negative"—you exponentially increase the probabilities of inducing a state that will definitely prevent you from accessing your own genius.

- What do you *foreground* in your mind?
- What do you put *front and center* that captivates your attention?
- What do you *background* in your mind?
- How do you do the backgrounding?
- How much flexibility do you experience in shifting back and forth?
- How useful and/or productive do you find your foregrounding and backgrounding?
- What would enrich and enhance these functions of mind?
- What thoughts do you have "in the back of your mind" that support your development of personal excellences?

Foregrounding/ Backgrounding as a Meta-Level
Surely you know about the distinction of *foreground and background,* do you not? As NLP grew directly out of the roots of Gestalt psychology and therapy, it should come as no surprise that within the very structure of NLP we have numerous *foreground and background shifts.* Perceptual psychology, cognitive psychology, and gestalt psychology call these "gestalt shifts." This refers to moving to the foreground of our mind the images and internal representations that have been in the background, and to the background what's been in the foreground. And this *gestalt shift* can powerfully and significantly affect responses and emotions.

How much of the gestalt background / foreground distinction do we find in NLP? This "sub-modality" distinction occurs in *all* representational systems. You can find it in *Using Your Brain—For a Change* as "Figure/Ground" (Appendix I, p. 162). Yet it seems that this concept and distinction from Gestalt Psychology has not overtly made much of an impact in many NLP presentations. Isn't that strange? Yet, in every sensory system, foreground and background play a major role. What pictures are in the foreground? What sounds? What sensations? In fact, it cannot *not* play a role. Usually it plays a very significant role in the way we have framed things.

The Gestalt Shift

The classic gestalt example of *the Old Woman/Young Woman picture* powerfully illustrates the foreground/background shift that occurs in perception. Research experiments have even indicated that we can create a cognitive "set" for a person's consciousness which can predispose that person to see one image rather than the other. Then, either by looking long enough or having someone suggest how they can see the other picture—one experiences *the gestalt shift*. Once that occurs, a person can generally shift back and forth at will. And yet even then, even though we fully know and believe that we can see each picture, we cannot see *both* images *simultaneously*. We can only see one or the other. It shifts digitally. Off. On.

How does this work?

Using self-organization theory Robert Dilts (1995) explains it this way:

> "The picture itself is simply a complex combination or 'landscape' of lines and light and dark areas. The women, young or old, are not really on the paper, but rather in our minds. We 'see' a 'young' or 'old' woman because of the basic assumptions and deep structures within our own nervous systems—what Aristotle referred to as 'formal causes.' To move between the 'images' in the 'landscape' we need to first destablize our focus on one attractor and subsequently restablize or 'fixate' our attention around the new attractor." (p. 257)

Something *attracts* us to "see" (perceive) the lines and shades in a certain way. Something *pulls us* toward *foregrounding* the "young woman" or the "old woman." To look at one tiny line as a delicate eye lash, and a thicker line as a necklace, and another line to function as a beautiful jaw allows "the young woman" to emerge from the picture. To see the same lines as the form of a large nose and the thicker line as a tightly pursed lips invites "the old woman" image to emerge.

What we *foreground sets the frame* so that the other pieces *organize* around, under, and in terms of that foreground. By so foregrounding certain elements and using them to construct certain meanings (semantic structures), a *configuration* arises that fits a form, image, and meaning that we bring to the lines and shades.

When a person cannot "see" one emergent image, we sometimes point with our finger and say, "Just look at it this way." "Imagine that this line *is* an eye lash..." "Now do you see it?" Having articulated the details that enable us to configure the gestalt (the overall systemic configuration), we can then begin to intentionally run *the gestalt switch*. We can foreground and background. With practice, we can do this in a split second until it seems that we can almost hold both images simultaneously.

To *highlight* one representation by necessity means that we *downplay* other representations. Frequently, such highlighting will even *hide* other ways of viewing things. Lakoff and Johnson (1980) describe this cognitive mechanism as inherent in "categorization."

> "A categorization is a natural way of identifying a *kind* of object or experience by highlighting certain properties, downplaying others, and hiding still others. Each of the dimensions gives the properties that are highlighted." (p. 163)

They illustrate this at the linguistic level when they assert that "every description will highlight, downplay, and hide."

> "I've invited a sexy blonde to our dinner party.
> I've invited a renowned cellist to our dinner party.
> I've invited a Marxist to our dinner party.
> I've invited a lesbian to our dinner party." (p. 163)

Now *if* each of these descriptions fit for the same person—then each of these descriptions highlights different aspects of that same individual. Each word allows and invites us to *categorize* or frame the woman in a different way. Each may therefore be a "true statement" in what it asserts, and yet simultaneously leave out and hide other things. This depends, in part, upon the author's intention and agenda—which the author wants to make *salient* (standing out prominently and strikingly), and what the author wants to downplay and hide.

This illustrates how we can *foreground* and *background* information (data) at the linguistic level as well as at the sensory based representational level. In this, every single statement that we make foregrounds certain things as it makes those things salient and it backgrounds other things.

Foregrounding Pleasure Exercise

Think about something that you experience as very pleasant and delightful. See, hear, and feel that pleasure fully and completely, and as you do, step into that experience so your very neurology begins to glow with it. Be there fully in that delightfully pleasurable experience and then anchor it with a sight, sound, touch, or word so that you can re-trigger this experience.

Now as you step back from that delightful pleasure, you can begin to notice what you coded visually in the foreground of your internal movie. What do you have in the background? What specifically? If you have "nothing"—what kind of a "nothing" do you have your foreground up against? A white screen or a black one? How big do you have your foreground stretched out upon this background? Are there any sounds? Any sensations?

Specify in the auditory system what sounds, words, music, tones, volumes you have foregrounded and which ones lie in the background. Do the same thing kinesthetically. What sensations do you feel in the foreground? Which ones lie in the background? How about smells and tastes?

As you go through this process, you will undoubtedly begin to notice that to identify the backgrounds in any system, you have to do a *foreground/background shift.* You have to fade out the visual images before you so that you can zoom in more on those in the background, do you not? Or, you have to reduce the volume or tone of the voices or music in the foreground in order to somehow focus in on the sounds and volumes in the background, do you not?

Foregrounding the Background Exercise

If you found it difficult to notice the background in your representations —then you have simply discovered the *power of a context to set a frame.* As long as you see, hear, and feel an experience in whatever configuration of the foreground that you constructed, you will *not* even notice the background. This does not make it go away. It only makes it *un-conscious,* that is, *outside*-of-awareness to you.

Now let's play with this "sub-modality" quality (foreground / background) that *transcends* all of the modalities (what Aristotle called the "common sensibilities") in regard to an experience of pain. Think about something that you dislike, avoid, and find uncomfortable—just a little thing that you would prefer to not have in your world. Recall it fully and completely so that you can feel yourself stepping into it and being there. You will know that you have succeeded in this thought experiment when your neurology and body begins giving you signals of discomfort.

Good. Now stop. Enough of that.

Now as you step back from that unpleasant experience (or *go meta* to observe your experience), go through the process again of identifying what you have foregrounded in the experience visually, auditorially, kinesthetically, and in language. As you check on your foreground—it might try to pull you back into it. If it does, keep stepping back out of it into that meta-position of noticing —just observing, observing calmly and comfortably.

Now *notice* what you had *not* noticed—something in the background. What images lie in the background of your unpleasant picture? How far back do you need to go before you find a delightful resource that brings pleasure to you? How far back in time? In fantasy? Focus in on the background until you experience the gestalt shift ... allowing the background to become the foreground. Do it with the sounds and words that you have in the experience. Then kinesthetically.

As you continue to foreground the background of the representations of this unpleasant experience, how does this affect you? How does it affect the "unpleasant experience?" How does it feel? What kind of a state of mind-and-body have you entered into in doing this?

Exercise Using the Gestalt Shift on Resources
To continue this play with subjectivity, now think about two strong, solid resources which, if you applied them to yourself in the unpleasant experience, would alter the experience completely. You could choose relaxation, presence of mind, sense of feeling centered and whole, a loving attitude, sense of assertiveness, enjoyment, permission to feel more empowered than I have ever before in my life"—anything that energizes you, super-charges your attitude, and invigorates you.

Now look for that resource in your "unpleasant experience" sensory-rich movie. Notice the *you* in that unresourceful time—and notice *the you who has those resources*. They probably exist so far back in the background that you can just barely sense them. Yet, if you allow this process to continue, you will begin even now to recognize those resources in the background... and *call them forth*. You can call them forth to the foreground, can you not? Now. And you can do it with such grace and efficiency.

As you notice *the you-with-those-resources*, you can let the foreground fade in its sights and sounds and sensations only to the extent that you begin to zoom in—closer and closer on *the resourceful you* in the background. And you have your choice—you can do it slowly, gradually, in an ever-increasing fashion, or you can do it suddenly, radically, and with a jolt that all of a sudden, completely and fully lands you there. How's that for an altered state?

Pattern for Detecting and Re-sourcing your Foreground

With your understanding and skill regarding shifting in and out of images, sounds, sensations, smells, tastes, and even *concepts* (words, self-talk, voices from others in your life) from what lies in the foreground and in the background, imagine all of the playful gestalt shifts you can run on yourself and with others? The processes of running a gestalt shifting of background / foregrounds to bring more resources to bear on your experiences goes as follows.

1) Detect the foreground / background structure.

Whatever "thought" comes to mind, *step back from it* for a moment as you make a meta-move of observation to just notice what you find in the foreground. What's up front? What stands out? Next shift your awareness to the background against which it stands. What's there? What is in the far background?

2) Become aware of your foregrounding / backgrounding patterns.

What do you typically foreground? What do you regularly and systematically background? How much *flexibility of consciousness* do you have with regard to these choices? Do they serve you well? Do they enhance your life? What would you like to foreground more frequently? How about a solution-focused orientation? How about courage, love, curiosity?

3) Decide to take charge of your gestalt shifting.

That we foreground some things and background other things simply describes one of the factors about how the brain works. *Taking control* of the way we run our brain so that we learn how to foreground resources, solutions, getting things done, etc., however, describes, how we can use this distinction for running our brains more effectively. So run the ecology check constantly on your backgrounding and foregrounding to make sure that your learned patterns work for you rather than against you.

4) Commit yourself to foregrounding resources.

If you know that you *can* put resourceful thoughts, beliefs, pictures, sounds, music, feelings, etc., then make a meta-level commitment to yourself to do so. In your mind, move up and utter a profoundly powerful *"Yes!"* to that resource. "I will make that idea, feeling, sound, music, etc. *stand out* in my mind!"

If what *stands out as salient* in your mind is crap, non-sense, hurtful old pains, resentments, regrets, etc. —guess what states and meta-states that will evoke in you? Will that do you any good? Are you willing to make an executive decision to foreground the best?

5) *Swish the gestalt shift in.*

> Once you feel strongly compelled to get away from that, then turn around and intentionally *bring mental and emotional resources to the foreground of your mind.* Do it so that your attention shifts to the new referents. *Swish* it there five times as quickly as you can until the shift takes only one second. Every time you think of the background junk —see, hear, and feel it fading out to the background as *the new resourceful You, the empowering ideas and beliefs, etc.* come dancing into the foreground and really stand-out with triumphant music playing and trumpets blowing!

I have intentionally used the term *salient* in this chapter even though it is not a common term. The word refers to something *standing out conspicuously, prominently, and strikingly.* From *salire* (Latin), it has within it the idea of *sallying forth* or jumping out. Has something ever really jumped out, in your mind, in such a way that it becomes totally compelling? That speaks about the power of foregrounding.

Given that we can make both representations and ideas *salient* so that they project outward and upward from its surroundings—what would you like to foreground in your mind? What would you like to fade out and vanish into the background?

Similarly for backgrounds. Sometimes background noise, chatter, self-talk, hypnotic lines, etc. occur just below the threshold of conscious awareness, but still within the scope of influence. Here you might take notice of things in the immediate background that may have an unhealthy influence on your states.

Old woman, beautiful young lady—what do you see? What do you want to see? What kind of a gestalt shift would you like to experience? The gestalt shift actually explains some of the shifting that occurs in many of the NLP patterns such as the Swish pattern, the Movie Rewind (or Phobia Cure) pattern, etc.

Summary

- Stepping aside and going meta to our thoughts can enable us to notice what we have foregrounded in contrast to what we have backgrounded. This gives us the structural format of our representations.

- *Foregrounding* and *backgrounding* pictures, sounds, sensations, and words operates at a meta-level. To run a gestalt switch in your brain, step back from the content of your computations, notice your current foreground and background structure, then decide how to switch it.

- The figure/ground distinction operates as a *meta-modality*, not a "sub-modality." It sets a higher level frame for our neuro-semantic experiences so that we can take charge of the movie's that we play in the theater of our mind.

- As *map-makers* who construct internal movies with foregrounds and backgrounds, we use these patterns as we run our brains.

- Awareness of this structure enables us to choose to put a stop to foregrounding or backgrounding that doesn't increase effectiveness. Knowing *how* the process works, we can now flip the switch and run a *gestalt switch* whenever we like.

- This skill puts into our hands the ability to run mental programs of beliefs, values, understandings, etc. that will function as *attractors* for more empowering configurations.

- *Set the frames* that will organize your internal world to generate the resources that foreground your values and visions.

- Design engineer your own expertise and resourcefulness. This gives you a very powerful process to facilitate the *emergence* of all kinds of exciting configurations which will generate a self-organizing system.

- Since *energy flows where attention goes—as governed by the intentional frame,* develop your own meta-structure for excellence. Set up a background frame from your highest intentions to allow those frames to operate as attractors in your neuro-semantic system.

- Align your attentions with those intentions. Refuse to disorder yourself with *intention deficiency*. Do that and your *attentions* will be all over the place. Instead, align your *foregrounding* attentions to your *background* intentions.

Chapter 6

NEGATING:
THE ART OF MAKING
THINGS GO AWAY

*"Negation only exists in language
and does not exist in experience."*
(Bandler and Grinder, 1981, p. 67)

"Negation is a property of language, not events..."
(Nelson Zink, 1998)

In focusing on identifying the structure of excellence or mastery, we began by unmasking the nature and functioning of the cinematic features that we call "sub-modalities." Doing this has suggested several refinements in the NLP model. The first of these concerned the meta-level of framing that we do in establishing what we foreground and background in the movies that play in our mind.

In *Meta-States* we have discovered that there are a multitude of phenomena that are *meta-level phenomena*. These involve such processes as backgrounding /foregrounding, believing, valuing, expecting, intending, deciding, permitting, giving meaning, imagining, remembering, understanding, etc. In fact we have now identified over two dozen such "levels" of the mind. As we recognize these as meta-level structures rather than sub-level structures, we can now model the forms of these processes.

Negation: Another Meta-Level
We now turn our attention to the unique meta-level phenomenon of *negation.* As we focus on *negation,* I will shift gears from the general approach that I have taken so far. My primary orientation to this point has been to specify the things we need to model or engineer regarding the experience of excellence. Repeatedly I have asked:

> What are the *prerequisites of genius* in terms of cognitive and neurological strategies?

Now we want to explore the things that *we do not want* and, in fact, the things that we *do not need* to access higher levels of excellence. After all, numerous ideas, beliefs, representations, decisions, memories, fantasies, etc. can and do get in our way and sabotage our mastery states. Because of this, we now pose the following questions as important exploration questions in the adventure of modeling and replicating the structure of excellence:

- What *prevents* us from accessing the states of excellence that build up our own mastery?
- What would have to be *eliminated* from our mind and emotions for us to move out more fully and ferociously into life?
- What *gets in the way* and *sabotages* mastery of ourselves, our states, and our skills?
- What memories, ideas, imaginations, etc. stop us from implementing our goals and visions?

All of this speaks about *the concept of negation.* But what is *"not?"* What kind of a representation conveys the idea of "not?" What kind of frames can we set that make some things (memories, imaginations, awarenesses, data) *go away?*

Demolishing Old Things to Engineer New Things
Sometimes before we even engage in the process of eliciting or building up the states of excellence, we have to clear space. Other states, memories, and experiences preempt what we want to build and have to be eliminated. We have to create psychological room for the new.

This suggests an interesting realization, namely, that the structure of excellence and genius inherently involves *absence* as well as presence. Some things need to *not* be there while other things need to be present. Sometimes we have to *get rid of* and *eliminate* the structures that prevent excellence. For example, the positive attributions of genius will not occur where there is laziness, demotivation, despair, overwhelming fear, etc. So even though states of excellence emerge as a gestalt from many numerous things, they can also be sabotaged quickly and easily by just a few toxic ingredients.

It takes much less effort, energy, talent, intelligence, discipline, etc. to *blow up* a building than to engineer and build it in the first place. It takes much less character, love, dedication, rapport, kindness, communication, etc. to *ruin* a relationship, than to build up the trust and invest the care and nurturing that allows another to feel safe, valued, and loved. It's easier to destroy than to create.

It takes a lot less effort, understanding, and work to build up a healthy and vigorous lifestyle that feels energetic and that results in fitness, than to ruin it. To sabotage your personal well-being and health you only need to endanger yourself with exposure to one or a few toxic elements. You can even ruin your health by simply doing *nothing*. Engineering the excellence of energy, health, vitality, fitness, strength, flexibility, and so on involves not only certain healthy attitudes, beliefs, values, and habits, but also *the elimination* of those things that would otherwise undermine it. Procrastinate and do *nothing* and you can ruin many beautiful things.

The structure of excellence not only includes building up resources, skills, knowledge, and practice, it also involves *negating*—making other things go *away or dis*appear. Sometimes we have to *de-construct* old programs, *de-stablize* old habits, *de-commission* old patterns, and *eliminate* those things that prevent us from accessing our resources. In creating empowering meta-states, frequently we first have to slay or tame some dragons. This is the theme of *Dragon Slaying* (2000).

The Human Uniqueness of Negating

In *Turtles all the way Down* John Grinder and Judith DeLozier (1987) identified several phenomena that indicates the uniqueness of human consciousness. They mention self-reflexivity (the ability to think about our thinking), dissociation, syntax, and humor.

> "The three things that distinguish us as a species from other species. One of those is the ability to dissociate ... syntax is another, humor the third." (p. 283)

Upon saying this, someone brought up another phenomenon that they deemed as totally unique to the human species, *negation*. So they asked, "What about negation?" Dr. Grinder quickly responded with his typical dry wit, "I *don't* want to talk about it." After the laughter died down to that humorous meta-level comment about negation, he noted the following in a neuro-linguistic description of negation:

> "... tell me how you know the meaning of this representation:
> **The cat didn't chase the rat.**
> Consuella: I have a slash mark across them.
> ... The previous representation is held constant and the entire proposition is negated by a logical level move one logical level higher than the actual picture —the original representation." (pp. 286-7)
> "Children ... don't compute the negation, 'Don't do that!' The child hears, 'Do that.'" (p. 293)

This raises an important question. What stops a child from computing the negation? The answer is that because *negation exists as a higher level conceptual frame* it takes time before the cognitive development of the higher levels of processing in the brain allow an infant to handle negation. Because negation is a concept, it is a meta-level frame. We do not, and cannot, see, hear, or feel negation. Rather the idea of the absence of something arises from comparing what we expected, knew, or wanted and what does occur.

Making Things Go Away

Sometimes in the adventure of "running your own brain," and accessing resources, whether in therapy, coaching, business, or in everyday life, we turn our focus to *changing* an old limiting idea, belief, or memory. We turn our attention to those things that can get in our way and prevent us from living with power and grace. What interferes with us moving up to the next level? This step toward genius means that before we can fully represent and program in something *new,* we have to *not* think or represent the old ideas.

Perhaps we want to shift our thinking away from defining mistakes and errors as "failure" to just "feedback." So we tell ourselves, "There is *no* failure, only feedback." Here we first aim to make the old concept of "failure" *go away* so that we can then think and represent the current actions, communications, and responses as feedback. The old concept interferes.

Sometimes we seek simply to make some of our representations go away. We aim to access a process whereby we can *negate* the old ideas, concepts, understandings as old programs that we don't need. Yet, how do we accomplish this? How do we make a memory, idea, understanding, awareness *go away?* What powers, processes, and mechanisms facilitate our ability to *eliminate* old programs, to truly get them de-energized and de-activated? To answer this takes us to the unique human "concept" of negation.

The Mystery of the Structure of Negation

Let's begin with the representation question. How do we typically represent *"not"* as an idea? As you think about the following statements, *note* how you represent the *not.*

> "Do not think of a blue car driving down a driveway painted red."
> "The dog is not chasing the cat."
> "I don't want you to feel too comfortable or resourceful too quickly."
> "Your *un*conscious mind does not need to know about this."

Did you do it? If so, how did you do it?
- How do you *negate* a representation and make it so that it does *not* exist in your mind?
- How do you make a memory, idea, concept, word, etc. go away and leave you alone?

When you think about what occurs in so much of therapy and in everyday life itself, a great deal of our talk and effort goes into negating memories, awarenesses, false learnings, limiting beliefs, old programs, dysfunctional habits, etc. So, how do we pull this off? When Bandler and Grinder initiated NLP, they seemed to only know about one kind of negation—command negation. In 1981 they wrote about it:

> *"No single pattern that I know of gets in the way of communicators more often than using negation. Negation only exists in language and does not exist in experience.* For instance, how do you experience the following sentence: 'The dog is not chasing the cat.' ... You have to first represent whatever is negated." (p. 67)

Negation plays a crucial role in the structure of excellence. When we do a contrastive analysis we often find that the expert just *never thinks about* some of the ideas, beliefs, values, understandings, etc. that plague the non-expert. We ask about what the financial genius thinks about the fear of losing money, and typically they will say that they *"never* think about that." The thought just does *not* cross their mind. Robert Kiyosaki (1998), among others, especially noted this in his work on financial intelligence. So we ask, How do they keep such ideas *out* of their mind?

Kinds of Negations

In exploring the structure of negation, we first need to recognize that all negations are not created equal. *There are several kinds of negations.* As we sort out these various kinds of negations, we recognize that some of them make things go away while others actually make the old representations and programs stronger. What kind of negation would work best to create a clean mental slate?

 Do people with different meta-programs (mental and perceptual filters for sorting information and paying attention to things) need to utilize different kinds of negations?   If we have a variety of negations, what determines when and where and with what to use them? Let's begin by enumerating the various kinds of negations:

1) Stated Negations or Command Negations:
> Do not, don't, *un-*, tag questions (don't you?), etc.

2) Metaphorical Negations:
> Imagine sending a representation to blow up in the sun; see an image on a windshield which then gets smashed by a sledgehammer, see something white out, black out, become fuzzy, the sounds of a voice just fade out.

3) Meaning or Frame Negations:
> Reframes, denominalizing terms.

4) Conceptual Negations:
> A void, nothingness, beyond time, beyond words, etc. The concept of

the opposite, reversals.

5) Moral Negations (the naughty negation):

Don't, avoid, Thou shall not ..., shame on you, prohibitions and taboos (you are not allowed, you are prohibited to).

6) Behavioral Negations:

Acting out part of a pattern, but not completing it. Bateson described this as how one dog communicates to another. "I wish to play. I begin to bite, but do so gently and playfully. This signals that I want to play."

7) Indirect Suggestive Negations (Presuppositional Negatives).

Subtly suggestive coding of negation as in *un-* (as in *un*belief*)*, *in-* (as in *in*visible), *less* (as in soul*less*), *dis-* (as in *dis*quiet), etc.

8) Spurious "No."

"I wonder whether you're not being a little unfair."

9) The "No" of stubbornness:

Uttering a strong "No!" or better, "Hell, no!" that indicates that one has "made up his or her mind" and has stubbornly taken a stand. Denial, Refusal.

10) Stated and Command Negations

"Don't think about it not raining."
"Don't covet your neighbor's wife or property."
"Don't think of blue elephants dancing down the street."

In these statements we state a *negation* or use a command negation. We do this using the basic negation words: no, not, don't, *un-*, tag questions (is it not? aren't you? doesn't it?") etc.

How do you represent the *"no"* or the *"not?"* In what representational system? When we use such terms, we generally attempt to negate by some kind of *crossing out action*. We see a big slash (/) across the representation —"Do not walk." Typically, people first see something and then swish it out into the distance until it disappears.

With regard to beliefs, understandings, decisions, and other meta-level phenomena—all humans seem to have a way of *validating or disvalidating, affirming or denying (#9)*. This explains the difference between a thought and a belief. We can represent all kinds of things that we do not believe.
•   What do you *not* believe?
•   Do you know any idea, concept, understanding, etc. that you do *not*

believe?

- How do you know that you do *not* believe it?

Do you believe "Hitler was a good man"? I don't. When I represent those words, I have a meta-voice in my head that dis-avows that idea. "I can stuff my body with all kinds of fatty foods and not gain a pound or clog up my arteries." In other words, I say *No!* to it. What do you do?

Beliefs involve representations which we then either *affirm or deny*. This means that we have affirmative beliefs: "I believe that behind every behavior lies a positive intention." Yet we also have *disavowed beliefs* which we call *disbeliefs* or *doubts*. When I say that I not only really doubt and question the goodness of Hitler, I go further and affirm that I believe he was *not* a good man. This leads me to believe the opposite. "I believe that he was a morally bad person who did much harm and destruction." "I do *not* believe in his goodness; I believe in his badness."

A *doubt* represents a belief *and* a *not*-belief. "I don't know if I believe that ignoring conflict will make things better. Sometimes it might; but sometimes it does not." In *doubting*, we shift back and forth from one belief to another belief. When I doubt, I first believe, then I *dis*believe. "Maybe it is, maybe it is not." "Maybe he can make that shot; but maybe he won't."

An *unsure maybe* represents a state opposite to a belief. "Maybe he is; but then again maybe he is not." This represents the co-existence of both affirmations and denials of the idea. One facet of my thinking says, *Yes,* but then when I look at it in a different way, another facets says, *No.*

The forms of *stated negations* that involve a change *inside* a word itself as in *un*able, *in*visible, etc. involve a stronger form of negation. Lakoff and Johnson (1980) mention this. They contrast, "Harry is not happy" and "Harry is *un*happy."

> "The negative prefix *un-* is closer to the adjective *happy* than is the separate word *not*. The negative has a strong effect ... *Unhappy* means *sad*, while *not happy* is open to the interpretations of being neutral—neither happy nor sad, but in between. This is typical of the difference between negatives and negative affixes. ... The CLOSER the form .. more direct is the experience..." (p. 130)

2) Metaphorical Negations
In negating through the use of a metaphor, we can represent a process that effects a negation by speaking about various metaphors. We utilize something that can "kill," "destroy," "wipe out," etc. the object or focus of our concern. Tad James has popularized the idea of sending a representation of something

(i.e., past memory, hurtful imagination) zooming at the speed of light toward the sun and then watching it blow up as it encounters the extreme temperatures in the sun. We vaporize the idea in the sun. It explodes.

We could just as easily project our representations of some undesired thought, memory, or imagination onto a car windshield as a movie. Then, sitting back in the driver's seat, we could watch that old movie play out as we do when at an outdoor movie theater. We could also hear and feel the jolt—the utter and absolute shock of seeing that windshield shatter into a million pieces as if smashed to smithereens by a sledgehammer. You will find that the Andreas' (1987, 1989) used this metaphor in some of their work in negating.

Since we have seen movie screens white out or black out, we could use that as our referent analogy. As the movie ends, and the reel runs out, all that remains for our glazed eyes is darkness. Or perhaps someone switches on the lights and the screen becomes glistening white. In the visual system, we could also simply see our images and pictures become fuzzy to the point of being indistinguishable. In the auditory channel, we could hear something just *fade out*. We could utilize Richard Bandler's "Bugs Bunny Cure" as he did with the young schizophrenic, Andy. We could see an artist's pen begin to *erase* Bugs' mouth and then tail, and then feet, legs, body, and finally head. Poof. Gone. Nothing. Like the Schwarzenegger movie, *Eraser*.

In this kind of *negating* a representation by the use of a metaphor, we engage in a *meta-level or meta-state process*. Literally, we *bring or carry* (Greek: *pherein*) *over* (Greek: *meta*) some concrete picture or idea and then use that referent to *set the frame* for the item we want to negate. In direct propositional language, we are saying, "Think *nothingness* about this image." "Bring *emptiness, blackness, erasure*, etc. to bear upon this old representation." "What happens if you put this idea *into the void of nothingness?*" In this way, we can use as a metaphor or analogy any process or event that destroys or sends something away. Such referents give us the ability to work metaphorically with ourselves or another to negate.

We can do *housecleaning* and discard the old ideas as used up and no longer of any value. We can *trash* the limiting belief into the *museum* of our personal history. We can click the computer to send it to the recycle bin. Or we could imagine *flushing it down the toilet*. Then there is the *deletion button* on a computer. Click it and old files disappear. They *vanish* from sight.

3) Meaning Negations

How would you negate an idea and a concept like "failure" (as in "I am a failure") so that it goes away? We could meta-model it to reduce the idea to its component elements. As we denominalize the word "failure," we *de-frame* this

word and experience so that it becomes an active process again. That would take it out of the static form and get back some of the movement of the underlying verb. We would then obtain the unspecified verb, "to fail." From there, we could *index* it to discover more specifically how this process works.
> — *When?*
> — *Where?*
> — *How?*
> — *In what way?*
> — *According to what standard?*

Doing this would have the effect of making the linguistic representation *go away.* This describes the power of the Meta-Model for *reducing,* and sometimes *nullifying,* a reality construction. Via meta-modeling we can disperse constructs by breaking down the construction into specifics. This reduces the fluff and creates more specificity, and as it does, reveals the non-sense of the non-referring term. We do this in the Mind-Line patterns of Deframing.

Korzybski (1933) spoke about this kind of process. He did so in his description of the mathematical translation from a static representation (like a snapshot) that the higher cortical processes construct to a dynamic representation (like a movie), and vise versa. Giving the data back to the thalamus part of the brain (given the way it processes information) destroys the former higher order abstraction inasmuch as it translates it back into a more dynamic and emotional representation (*Science and Sanity,* p. 290).

Reframing the meaning of something can also have the effect of negating.
> "When you hear a response that you do not want, it doesn't mean 'failure,' it means *feedback.* It means you have found out something—what does not work. Now you get to do something else. It gives you opportunity for stretching, flexibility, and new learnings. It suggests new refinements for greater skill."

Constructing such new understandings about the events enables us to put new frames around the primary state behaviors. Doing this *re-frames* the old idea which can also have the effect of negating it. The previous unresourceful idea cannot cohere any longer, and so it dissolves.
> "The exaggerated hype that some people have put out about NLP has denigrated the field."
> *Reframe:* "The exaggerated hype now invites the rest of us to take advantage of the opportunity to separate its realistic values and legitimate processes from the unrealistic ones. We have an opportunity to bring a new level of scholarship and clinical proof to the public's attention about the effectiveness of the NLP model."

Anytime we set a higher frame of reference that *forbids* or just *does not allow* the lower representation to continue to exist or cohere—it negates the lower frame.

Bodenhamer (1993) did this when he developed the "Taking a Bitter Root to Jesus" pattern. This pattern involves taking nasty, ugly, bitter, resentful, and hateful representation of some personal hurt and putting it in the same spatial location where one codes and stores spiritual images and ideas. As a minister, he invites Christian believers to think about "Jesus." After they make a bright and positive picture of Jesus who forgives, he asks the person to put the pictures of the bitter experiences in that same place. Doing this *blows out* the resentment and prevents the person from continuing to hold onto it. Resentment can't exist there.

This gives us another way to negate. We can replace an old set of ideas with such new enhancing and powerful ones, that the old ideas can no longer cohere. Resentment cannot co-exist with forgiveness, love, kindness, seeing the sacred, etc. In this instance, *the location* of spiritual images *stood for* and *symbolized* the higher values and concepts of love and forgiveness. When a person tries to see their hateful, bitter, and degrading experience *in that sacred location,* it gets outframed by the sacred ideas. This represents elegant meta-level or meta-state anchoring. In this meta-level process, we leave the sensory-based descriptions the same as we give them a new name, classification, or meaning.

4) Conceptual Negations

We create a very unique set of representations when we represent something like the Void, Nothingness, beyond time, beyond words, etc. With these words, we create a representation (seemingly of a something) yet it is out of, and about, a nothing, a negation. Yet, such *a concept* typically works to negate the content. Bob calls this *the ultimate negation* because the metaphors and concepts involve a person representing *ultimate concepts* around time, space, existence, and beingness.

I find this the most conceptual of all the negation forms. When I think of a statement like "the earth was *without form and void...*" (Genesis 1:2), I hardly know how to conceptualize the idea of such a void. To think about myself before my existence takes me to a high level of abstraction and a very hypnotic state. How do we represent *not-space, not-time, not-self, not-existence not-being*, etc.? How do we represent form*less*ness, meaning*less*ness, *in*visible, etc.?

Here, we may transcend our ability to even language such concepts. We become word*less*. We get to a place "beyond words." Does this mean *non-*words? Of course, we have to also be careful at this point and remind ourselves that merely because we can *conceptualize* something, this in itself does not demand, and much less prove, that it exists.

Korzybski noted that we can create non-referencing words, phrases, and ideas—words that stand for nothing. Actually, no such thing as *not-space, not-time, not-existence*, etc. exists. These only occur *in the mind* of the representer as mental constructions. When we bring a meta-level of *"not"* to bear on anything else, it negates or blows out the lower level. Using Bateson's multiplication of states, we would say, "Nothing times anything equals nothing." So we multiply a something with whatever unit of value it may have for us (1, 2, 3 ....) by a nothing (0). But even 1,000,000 times 0 equals 0.

In this way, when we conceptualize *the opposite* of something, this can have the effect of *negating* it. We communicate a negation when we talk about a man regarding his fear about approaching a member of the opposite sex. He speaks about freezing up with fear when he thinks about making his approach and when he tells himself to *not* feel afraid (command negation). Telling him to *not* think about his fear and nervousness actually adds to the problem. We need to negate in a different way. Instead, we offer statements that will enable him to create representations that evoke ideas and feelings of courage and elegance.

> "Suppose you walked up courageously and in a mater-of-fact way and said something simple, but pleasant like, 'Hi, how are you?' You could then feel the elegance and charm that comes from feeling relaxed and confident. You can also remember *what* to say because you will simply say, 'Hi, my name is...'

Expressing something like this communicates *a negation by implication*. While we have not said so explicitly we have in essence, said, "Do *not* feel scared or freeze up or go into a state of nervousness." We have expressed the *negation* of that by focusing on *what to say* and *how to say it*. To speak freely and openly in a relaxed and confident way negates the fear. It *negates* the nervousness and self-consciousness. This kind and form of negating operates much more indirectly since it directs the brain to *what to think*, rather than to what to *not* think.

To learn how to use it, simply think about what you want to negate. When you have that *idea* in mind, then think of its opposite. The opposite of a "friendly approach" is a "fearful and hesitating approach." The opposite of "learning with ease and comfort and having lots of fun in the process" is "getting all freaked out and serious about feeling inadequate." One negates the other. Talk exclusively about all the problems you have and, by implication, you negate "solution thinking." Zoom in on thinking only about how the past determines you and your future, and you thereby negate feeling free and able to take charge of your destiny.

5) Moral Negations

These negations are *the naughty negations*. A moral negation involves issuing a prohibition or taboo to inhibit and forbid something.

> "Shame on you!" "Don't you dare!" "How dare you?" "Who do you think you are?" "If you do that, it will go to your head." "Only a bad person would say or do that!"

We say such things to *negate* (or attempt to negate) a thought, idea, experience, action, etc. by forbidding it. Think of all the things that you have been conned out of doing because someone *shamed* you, or you shamed yourself. Some things are indeed moral issues, some are not.

> Don't lie. Don't steal. Don't speak up. Don't hit your sister. Don't cheat. Don't use that tone of voice with me. Never embarrass us. You are not allowed to cry or experience any strong emotion in my presence. Get that smirk off your face. Don't confront.

We can code moral negations by using the *modal operators* of impossibility and necessity: "You shouldn't, mustn't, can't..." We can also use the language of prohibition: blame, disqualify, condemn, wrong, bad, etc.

These are also *command negations* and they usually not only do not work, they backfire. In the way they interface, as a meta-level comment about some other thought, feeling, behavior, or state, they generally make things worse. The frame they set about the primary level content tend to make us *more aware* of it—and therefore more likely to think, feel, or act on it. What happens when we chance upon a sign that reads, "Wet Paint — Don't Touch!"?

People who attempt try to run their brain by using these naughty command negations usually find that it only magnifies the content. This explains why a moralistic approach can frequently create more monsters and demons than they eliminate.

6) Behavioral Negations

Bateson (1972) researched and described the kind of negations that some animals use in their communications. Speaking about dogs, Bateson theorized about how young pups communicate, "I want to play," in contrast to, "This is a fight." To do this, they behaviorally have to begin to act out the fight *and not carry it through*.

> "In iconic communication, there is no tense, no simple negation, no modal marker.
> The absence of simple negatives is of special interest because it often forces organisms *into saying the opposite of what they mean in order to get across the proposition that they mean the opposite of what they say*.

Two dogs approach each other and need to exchange the message: 'We are *not* going to fight.' But the only way in which fight can be mentioned in iconic communication is by the showing of fangs. It is then necessary for the dogs to discover that this mention of fight was, in fact, only exploratory. They must, therefore, explore what the showing of fangs means. They therefore engage in a brawl; discover that neither ultimately intends to kill the other; and, after that, they can be friends." (pp. 140-141)

"It appears from ... that play is a phenomenon in which the actions of 'play' are related to, or denote, other actions of 'not play.' We therefore meet in play with an instance of signals standing for other events, and it appears, therefore that the evolution of play may have been an important step in the evolution of communication." (p. 181)

We humans can also engage in *behavioral negations*. In western cultures we do so when we cross our index and middle finger when we speak. Such actions essentially frames the content of the words as signifying, "I'm only kidding. Don't take me serious. I'm not telling you the truth."

A lilt in the voice can also *negate*. Using a teasing or jesting tone of voice, the lilt can set a frame of "not really." Indeed, we can acquisition to ourselves all kinds of behaviors, gestures, and non-verbal expressions to *negate* the content of our words. We can use our hands to slash lines in the air like Zarro with his swords to leave the impression of a sign with a negating slash.

As making a promise while crossing your fingers negates, so shaking your head laterally, side-to-side, as in giving the *"No"* gesture, frowning, or stopping the *"Yes"* vertical gesturing can also negate. In most languages and cultures, shaking the head back and forth linearly from left to right means "No." But not in all cultures. If people "read" such meaning into the pivoting of the head sideways as signifying, standing for, and symbolizing a "No," then we can use that behavior to negate. The same applies for almost any behavior which a person offers, whether within or outside of awareness, when saying "No." Notice the behavior which the person has associated with this state.

These non-verbal processes shows that we can not only *negate* through numerous verbal and linguistic devices, but also with processes that do not rely upon propositional language. We can use tone, tempo, gestures, movements, and other non-linguistic formats to *negate.*

I enjoyed the playfulness and wittiness of the speaker in the following example. It happened one day when I heard some people discussing how two negatives in some languages can make a positive statement. That certainly holds true for Greek. Then one of them said, "But there is no language where two positives create a negation." To that the other gal sarcastically said, "Yeah. Right!"

In this instance her tone of voice served, *at a meta-level,* to negate the content value of the actual words that she used. Normally, "Yeah" and "Right" convey a message of *Yes*. But here, in this syntax and with a sarcastic tonality, they combine to signal the opposite, a *No*.

All of this highlights that we can bring non-verbal facets of our responsiveness into a communication interaction. As we do, we can use such behaviors as *symbols*. When we construct a symbol system like this, we can then reflexively bring it back to the words that we utter. This then uses the non-verbals in a *meta-relationship* to the words. Similarly, we can use words reflexively as we talk about our gesturing. We can say,

>"I am crossing my fingers as I'm promising to be here on time tomorrow. I'm doing that to show what I saw you do the other day."

In this we have put our words in a meta-relationship to the gestures. This simply illustrates that we can make any piece of the communication process *meta* to any other part.

7) Indirect Suggestive Negations (Presuppositional Negations)
In addition to all of the direct *negation words* (no, don't, stop, etc.), there exists in English numerous subtle and suggestive terms that code the meaning of negation. These include such prefixes as

* *un-* as in *un*belief, *un*changed, *un*stable, *un*learning, *un*enlightened, *un*happy, *un*written, *un*intentional, *un*able, *un*like, *un*deliverable.
* *in-* as in *in*visible, *in*distinguishable, *in*flexible, *in*complete.
* *ir-* as in *ir*replaceable.
* *dis-* as in *dis*quiet, *dis*interested, *dis*honest, *dis*count, *dis*trust, *dis*appear.
* *non-* non-trance, non-productive, non-defensive,
* *mis-* *mis*-trust,
* and such post-fixes as *less*— as in soul*less*, fear*less*, hope*less*.
* *With* as in *with*hold (to *not* give).

Further terms and phrases hold the *idea of negation* without expressing it directly. *"Without"* in the previous sentence suggests a negation. Here I have negated "express it directly." I could have written, "Other terms contain the *idea* of negation but does *not* express it directly."

We see the same kind of implication in Either/Or statements.

>"You can't have it both ways; either get in the car and come shopping with us or stay home."
>"Do you want to attend the workshop and improve your skills or would you prefer to remain in your incompetence?"

This structure presupposes that the recipient has *no other* alternative. In so presupposing a binary world, the speaker maps, "This or that."

"You can have this choice, but you can*not* have this other choice at the same time."

"Now I want you to really try hard to stay in the panic and not feel resourceful about handling this problem... Will you just try to do that?"

A common use of *try* implies "will not succeed." "Now really try to succeed." The *try* here actually frames the communication with a presupposition and implication that it will fail. There are other kinds of "tries." There is the *try of attempt*.

"I will try to be more thoughtful."

"I will try to get to the game on Friday evening."

That does not necessarily imply inability. But the *try of not succeeding* does.

"You go ahead this time and go back and look at that panic. See if you can hold it. I want you to try as much as you can in vain." (Richard Bandler, *Magic in Action*, p. 24).

8) Spurious Negations
Sometimes we just throw in a *not* (a negation), and it really doesn't mean anything. It's spurious. Contrast the following sayings,

"I wonder whether you're not being a little unfair."

"I wonder whether or not you're being a little unfair."

"I wonder whether you're being a little unfair."

Each essentially communicates the same message. Now some people will find the *negation* in the first two statements to amplify the effect and so evoke more of a response. For the most part, the *not* is spurious since it does not change the content of the statements. This not does not negate at all!

9) The "No" of stubbornness:
When we utter a strong "No!" or better yet, a *"Hell, No!"* to something that we find unacceptable, toxic, sabotaging, disrespectful, etc., we use the power of stubbornness to draw a line in the sand. This describes a very powerful state. One of the books that Albert Ellis had a wonderful title. I loved the title much more than the book. The title was:

How to Stubbornly Refuse to Make Yourself Miserable about Anything —I mean Anything!

In developmental psychology we experience two stages where we learn to distinguish ourselves from others. At two and during the early teenage years, we individuate from others, first from mother and father and then from family and immediate environment. This individuation is a time when we learn to acknowledge ourselves—our own thoughts, feelings, needs, wants, dreams, visions, values, etc. We're finding our way in the world. We are establishing personal boundaries. And we do so by saying *No.*

The *No* state that we experience in the "terrible twos" or during the troubling adolescence stage is actually the *No* of making up our mind and discovering through individuation of our own preferences. It's an inevitably and important stage in becoming independent and essential for the later stages of becoming inter-dependent in an adult way.[1]

In terms of negation, the *No* of stubbornness is the *no* of having "made up" one's mind, pushing back one's sense of space and values for personal boundaries, and for making dis-valued experiences, ideas, beliefs, models, etc. *go away.* In Meta-States training, we access this state and use it for developing personal power, personal boundaries, and for accessing a strong disconfirming state that we can use in rejecting and refusing old beliefs. (You'll see this again in the next two chapters.)

Different Negations — Different Kinds of Effects

All *negations* do not have the same effect. Some negations actually enable and allow us to *negate,* while others do not. Some negations only stimulate our thinking about negation while simultaneously preventing us actually negating. When this happens, the negation amplifies the mentioned referent.

How paradoxical! *Stated and command negations* amplify the very representation that we want to negate. It has the effect of causing our minds to focus in on the very idea, image, concept, memory, etc.
>   "Don't think about going out for a walk"
>   "It's not possible for you to go into a trance too quickly..."
>   "I don't want you to fly off the deep end when I tell you this..."
>   "It's not that I don't like your outfit, but I don't think it flatters you."
>   "Don't think about this being a problem."
>   "I don't think you're dumb ... so don't worry about that."

Bandler and Grinder (1979) noted this with regard to many people who have weight problems.
>   "They have a hypnotic voice that goes, 'Don't eat that cake in the refrigerator.' 'Don't think about all the candy in the living room.' 'Don't feel hungry.' Most people have no idea that commands like that are actually *a command to do the behavior.*" (p. 65, italics added)

Now suppose all of that occurs in the *background* of one's mind and not in the foreground? So what makes this work in this way? It so functions, because at the meta-level, the *negation* redirects consciousness to focus in on, and zoom into, the primary level representations.

Figure 6:1

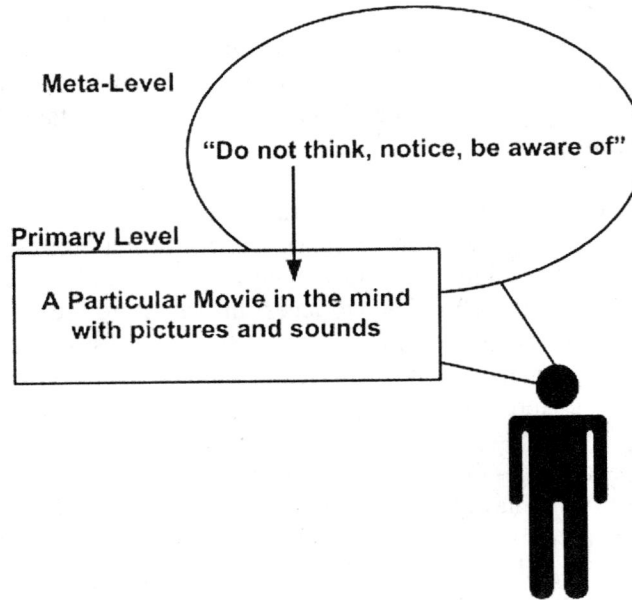

Meta-Level

"Do not think, notice, be aware of"

Primary Level

A Particular Movie in the mind with pictures and sounds

Andreas and Faulkner (1994) offer the following explanation of the process that makes the first kind of negation, command negation.

> "Our brains simply don't know how to put things into negative language. In order to know what *not* to think of, our brains have to first think of it." (p. 33)

This explains why merely *stating* a negation (or worse, *command or ordering* a negation) does not negate a referent but, in fact, amplifies it. Typically, it will *speak about* the concept of negation without facilitating our mind to actually accomplish the negation. Ironically and perhaps surprisingly, it speaks about the idea, while simultaneously preventing the person from carrying it out. As long ago as the first century, the apostle Paul recognized this function of negation. He recognized that it was the very commandment to not covet that brought coveting into awareness and action.

> "What then shall we say? That the law is sin? By no means! Yet, if it had not been for the law, I should not have known sin. I should not have known what it is to covet if the law had not said, 'You shall *not* covet.'" (Romans 7:7)

To negate, we have to set *a different kind of frame.*

- We have to offer a different meaning (reframe).
- We have to distract to other representations.
- We have to offer a process that provides our mental processing instructions for nullifying, destroying, making irrelevant, or making the primary representation go away.
- Or set up a swish so that our brain moves on to replace the first item.

This explains the power of pictorial metaphors for enabling us to actually negate. Pictures of *destruction* (seeing a memory of the past blow up), of *nullification* (seeing a movie shatter, seeing an unresourceful self-image fade out), of *fractionation* (denominalizing a word, breaking a movie down into the VAK representations and then into the cinematic features that frame the movie), of *non-computing* (setting a frame that disallows the primary processing —shaming our shame, procrastinating on our procrastination, hearing something as gibberish.)

Negations and Meta-Programs
Bandler and Grinder (1981) noted this before they had officially specified the domain of Meta-Programs.

> "Negation is particularly effective to use with anyone who has what we call a 'polarity response.' A polarity response simply means an opposite response. If I say to David, 'You are becoming more relaxed' and he tightens up, that's a polarity response. ... People with lots of polarity responses are very responsive; they're just responsive in the reverse direction from what you instruct them to do." (p. 68)

How do you take a *negation*? Well, given the various *kinds* of negations —we have to ask, how do you take this or that kind of negation? Directly stated negations seem to invite resistance, dislike, "feeling controlled," etc. by people who fit the "strong-willed by temperament" meta-program category (see *Figuring Out People*, 1997). When they hear a negation (usually the *stated* kind), they move to a higher level and frame it as "being controlled," "freedom taken away," "put down," etc. It is to this that they refuse to comply. They resist the negation by doing the opposite. By thus *negating* the negation, they now *have to* do the reverse!

The *"Not"* Concept
Ultimately, *"not"* exists in the mind and it exists *only* in the mind. It does not really exist apart from *a processing mind* that can think of opposites, reverses, and absences. We never walk out of our front door and see a *"not"* referent. You, like me, have never stumbled over a hunk of *not* in my front yard.

In the statement, "I see the dog *not* chasing the cat," the speaker compares a map in his or her mind with what is *not* in his or her immediate perception. The speaker seems to have expected or desired to have seen something. But upon checking the actual territory with the mental map, they do *not* find, see, hear, or experience what they expected. "I see the dog *not* chasing the cat" does not describe anything that we would call sensory-based. What *does* the person see? Perhaps, a dog ignoring a cat. Or, a dog playing with a cat. Or just a dog. Or just a cat. Or no dog or cat at all.

Yet sometimes ... we *seem* to think and feel that we do see a *not*. Have you ever seen a not? I bet you have! You walk into a room and do *not* see your friend or lover. You go to the refrigerator and do *not* see the piece of cake that you wanted. "Who ate my piece? I was saving that!" You wait in the baggage area at the airport after de-planing (getting off the plane), and do *not* see your suitcase. "Hey, where's my luggage?" In each of these cases, you had something *in mind* that you wanted, expected, looked for, etc., and then you sought for it in the external world. But you did *not* see or find it.

Suppose that you had regularly, and on many occasions, seen your neighbor's dog chase your precious kitty. Suppose that you then heard some sounds that sounded like a dog and cat mixing it up. Do you hear that? So supposing you arise from your chair to see the mischievous dog from next door, you reach the window and do *not* see "the dog chasing the cat." Your *memory* of previous events, and your *expectation* of yet another instance, may stand out so prominently in your mind (ah, foregrounding) that when you do *not* get confirmation about the event, that very *awareness* of it *not* occurring may suddenly come to occupy the foreground of your awareness. What is *not* happening would become salient and stark.

The same would happen with *not* finding a check in the mail, would it not? Do you know that one? Have you ever seen that *"not?"* Have you ever felt disappointed about something *not* happening? What about feeling strangely uncomfortable when you *notice* that you do not hear an accustomed noise in the house? You suddenly become aware of, and notice a *not*. Seeing, hear, and feeling such *nots* may even seem like a very real, and externally oriented, see-hear-feel experience. But *no*.

There is no *not* "out there." To have a *not*, you have to have a mind.

In fact, we have to prepare ourselves for a *not*. It actually takes a lot of work. We prepare for a *not* by planning, anticipating, wanting, representing, expecting, map-making, etc. We have to use our consciousness, create the representation, and then compare it to actual experience. The awareness of not then arises from the comparison—and so occurs at a meta-level. *It takes a mind to negate.* A dog's mind can even do this as it communicates, "This is *not* 'fight,' this is 'play.'"

This becomes even more complex and layered, however, with human consciousness—a consciousness that never stops abstracting, jumping logical levels, and going meta. With meta-level concepts, which sometimes becomes so much a part of our everyday life, we don't know, or forget, that they *only* exist as "concepts." This includes such seemingly concrete realities (but actually concepts) as "time," "causation," "purpose," "destiny," "dignity," etc. *Not or negation* can also become so much a part of our perceiving that we seem to see it in the world.

The concept of *not* or *negation* arises from, and operates as, a function of language, representation, symbolization, and consciousness. This is why it can come to feel like a real and externally tangible thing. In NLP, we speak of the *nominalization process* as one of the most fundamental processes in language, and even neurological functioning. This refers to how we take processes and turn them into static "things." The term *reification* speaks about our tendency to concretize experience. We take verbs and processes (the most fundamental fact in a dynamic, process, ever-changing world) and we turn them into Nouns (with a capital N). This allows us to handle and control them as if *things.*

Yet in the process of *nominalizing,* we often forget that *we ourselves* created the "frozen world of things," and that it does not really exist. Nominalizing speaks of how we have a natural tendency to take *concepts* that exist at meta-levels and turn them into hallucinated objects which we think we see like rudeness, beauty, failure, or success at the perceptual level.

Nominalizing speaks about how we, as a semantic-class of life (Korzybski), so "naturally" move through the world *projecting* our internal maps on the external world and then failing to remember that we are doing it. We think that *the beauty* exists in the woman that we admire. We think that the *rudeness* exists out there in the way the person acted. We assume that the *elegance* was the performance of the athlete. But no. These nominalizations speak about *our judgments, evaluations, and experiences of the world* which we project onto it. These meta-level phenomena ("values") occur only in the inside world of communication.

The Negation Pattern Exercise
Suppose you do truly want to get rid of some old programs, ideas, beliefs, etc. Suppose you want to do some top-level *negating.* Where do you start? How do you pull it off? Let's say that springtime has come to your mind and you need to do some housecleaning. You feel like you'd like to make some new space for some new ways of being.

In the following negation pattern we offer you one choice for taking charge of your everyday experiences and running your own brain. You can also use the

Movie Rewind pattern (see *MovieMind*, 2003), most Belief Change patterns, or many of the Time-Lining patterns (Re-imprinting, Decision Destroyer), etc. to enhance your results (see *Source Book of Magic*, 2004).

1) Identify something that you would like to negate

What would you like to negate and just make *go away* from your mind, emotions, life?

> It may be a set of memories that have played too intensely in your life and too strong of a role in your life (i.e., a rape, molestation, abandonment, criticism, firing, divorce, etc.). Or you may want to negate an old concept that you once constructed from various experiences (i.e., a belief, idea, understanding, generalization) about some event (i.e., "I will never amount to anything." "I can't learn complex things." "What's the use?").

What would you like to use in practicing "housecleaning?"

2) Fully pull apart the representation and/or idea apart

What do you need to do to fragment the construct into its component pieces?

> Use the cinematic features list (Appendix A) get a full description of the way you have represented and coded it.

Do you see it, hear it, feel it, use words to language it, what?

In what sequence?

> If you begin with a concept or belief, you may first need to tear apart the linguistic encoding using the Meta-Model questions.[2]

3) Outframe the item with a nullifying metaphor

What metaphor could nullify the concept?

> For many things, you will have sufficiently fragmentized the phenomenon by the time you complete step two. If it no longer coheres, you have succeeded in negating it. Congratulations! Pulling human constructions apart is the power of deframing which creates a disintegration. In deframing, we destabilize the old system and remove the old self-organizing *attractors*.

What of the nullifying metaphors that we mentioned works best for you?

> For example, project the movie of your sensory images, sounds, and sensations on a car window. As it begins to play on that screen see and hear a gigantic sledge hammer smashing into it so it splinters it into a zillion pieces of tiny shards.

4) Black it out or White it Out

What happens when you black out or white out the picture entirely?

Which works best for you, making the screen white or black?

What happens when you turn down the sounds until you only hear the "sounds of silence?"

Or would you like to threshold the visual qualities until it blows it out?

5) Run your internal movie backwards
Are you ready to rewind your movie?
> Once you have specified the content thoughts and the memories or scenes you want to negate, go to the end of the movie, step inside, and run it backwards in fast rewind speed.

How much of the meaning and emotion is *negate*d when you do that three times? Five times? Since meaning emerges in part from the sequence of the representations, how many times do you need to rewind to deframe and loosen up the old sequence pattern?

6) Swish it to a more compelling referent
Now you're ready to swish. From the fragments left of the old representation, or from the blank screen, re-train your brain to swish to thoughts-and-feelings that represent *the Resourceful You* for whom the ideas present no problem. How's that?

Does the *Un*conscious Mind Negate?
There's one more NLP Myth that I want to negate or at least blow out. It's the idea that "the unconscious mind cannot process negation." This myth arose from the assumption that there's only one kind of negation, namely command negation. And true enough, the primary operations of the *un*conscious mind does not seem to handle that kind of negation. But what about the other kinds of negation?

Have you ever had a dream in which you could *not* move, you were still and stuck or a dream in which you were moving in slow motion—that is, *not* moving normally or quickly? Has your unconscious mind ever led you to feel *dis*quieted or *dis*turbed, that is, *not* at peace? Have you ever felt, at the unconscious level, fear*less* and full of courage? In a dream, did you ever fear*less*ly fight off enemies or drive dangerously?

Yes, the *un*conscious mind can and does negate. In fact, that's how the NLP and Neuro-Semantic patterns of metaphor and analogy work, we get our unconscious or outside of conscious mind to set frames so that things go away.

An UnConclusion
Try this as an experiment. For a single day, listen to all of the *negations* that you use in thinking, formulating ideas, and speaking. I think it will quickly amaze you at just how often you *negate* things as you move through the world. I think you will quickly feel impressed about the pervasiveness and dominance of negation as a major *conceptual* and *semantic force* in your life. The *negation*

frame plays a major role in our mental computations and reasoning.

"What if he does *not* come through with that proposal?"

"What if we do*n't* get to the chapel on time?"

"If he does*n't* pay me by this Friday, I'll see him in court."

"I do*n't* think I'll ever learn all of this."

"I ca*n't* imagine myself not exercising regularly. I would*n't* even want to think that way."

Summary

- *The structure and strategy of excellence* involves both what we do want and dream about and what we want to avoid and *not* have. Negation plays a critical role in the structure of genius.

- Frequently we find the motivation, drive, and passion to create new things, to excel beyond old limitations, and to generate new innovations because we of a compelling idea in our heads about what we do *not* yet have.

- Genius frequently looks at what has *not* yet been accomplished, invented, or imagined, and asks, "Why *not?*" "How would I?"

- Those who achieve peak performances in various fields often do so by *mismatching*. They sort for what does *not* fit with the norm or the average. They seem to see and imagine and create what others do *not*. What are you *not* noticing yet?

- *Negation*, as a meta-level phenomenon, operates as a meta-state. The sequel volume to this book, *Secrets of Personal Mastery,* utilizes the heart of these negation processes in constructing the genius states. I have incorporated them with the *As If frame* and the Brief Therapy *miracle question* to create a push—pull dynamic that we call *The Miracle Question pattern*. This empowers us to fully utilize the power and magic of *negation* by asking *"not" questions* at meta-levels.

- "Even though it's probably *not* possible, go ahead and just give yourself to the playful and silly imagination of what life would be like if you did *not* have a given psychological limitation. If this or that difficulty, idea, concept, feeling, etc. did *not* get in your way and prevent you from just getting on the highway of life and trucking on down... what would it be like? Now.... as you playfully imagine it?"

- The mind—both the conscious mind and the unconscious mind can and does negate. This is one of the powers of the mind and now that we know the structure of this experience we can use it for our own well-being and empowerment, can we *not*?

Having now specified the power of *negating*, let's switch gears and focus on what we do *represent and believe*.

End Notes:

1. There's an entire chapter in *Games Great Lovers Play* (2004) on the stages of dependence, independence, and inter-dependence.

2. *Communication Magic* (2000) is a book about the Meta-Model —what the model is, how it works, how it grew and evolved in the first twenty-years of NLP.

Chapter 7

IT'S BELIEFS

ALL THE WAY UP

"Behaviors are organized around some very durable things called beliefs.
A belief tends to be much more universal and categorical
than an understanding.
Existing beliefs can even prevent
a person from considering new evidence or a new belief."
(Richard Bandler, 1982)

- What role do beliefs play in the structure of experience?
- What role do beliefs play in the structure of excellence?
- What beliefs organize us for higher levels of mastery?
- Can beliefs make that much difference?
- How do beliefs differ from thoughts?

Suppose I had a bag of enhancing, empowering, and energizing *beliefs* and could grant you any three beliefs that you wanted which would enrich the quality of your life. Would you want them? What *supporting beliefs* you would choose? What beliefs characterize those who achieve excellence and stand out as peak performers in your field?

- Are empowering beliefs a mere coincidence or a causative factor in excellence?
- How do *beliefs* operate in our minds-and-bodies?
- How do belief frames as generalizations enhance or reduce our effectiveness?
- Is it possible to take charge of our believing and belief frames?
- Do "sub-modalities" play a role in the construction of beliefs?
- If "sub-modalities" are meta-level distinctions, how does this influence our ability to change and transform the beliefs that limit us?

Modeling the Beliefs of Genius
Because NLP began as an adventure in discovering the structure of excellence,

the developers sought and identified, many of the key beliefs that distinguish geniuses. Bandler and Grinder did this with Perls, Satir, and Erickson; Robert Dilts did this with numerous other geniuses in *The Strategies of Genius.*

The set of beliefs discovered in the original therapeutic wizards came into their model as *the NLP Presuppositions.* The modelers simply set aside the question of whether these beliefs were "true or false," because they recognized them as liberating, energizing, and empowering influences—powerful operational ideas. As navigational maps, these beliefs enable us to go places and to do things. Because they elicit and organize our inherent powers, they support and reinforce the structure of excellence.

It is because beliefs have the power to "command" the human nervous system that we now turn our attention to exploring *beliefs* as mental-emotional phenomena. Here we will model its structure and dynamic processes. This will enable us to develop and refine the processes and mechanisms for transforming them. Our unmasking and raising of "sub-modalities" now enables us to update the old NLP Belief Change pattern that worked with altering "sub-modalities."

This chapter is the first of three on "beliefs." We'll first explore the structure and then apply to the processes for managing beliefs and levels of beliefs. In the next two chapters, we'll present NLP and Neuro-Semantic processes for transforming beliefs to manage the Matrix of belief frames that govern our lives.

Navigating the Territory via Belief Maps
As you woke up this morning and moved out into the day, you did so by gathering up a host of beliefs to take with you. You put on these beliefs and concepts as you would put on spectacles to view the world.

You have so many beliefs. You have *beliefs* about yourself, your skills, your value and your dignity, etc. You have beliefs about other people— what makes them tick, what they want, how to relate to them, etc. You have beliefs about work, play, recreation, hobbies, volunteer activities, etc. You have beliefs about the world: politics, education, crime, police, the justice system, other countries, wars, journalism, environment, etc. also have beliefs about a thousand different concepts: time, history, the past, the future, causation, personality, emotions, destiny, etc.

In saying that you *"have"* these beliefs, I mean that you *use them as an operation program to navigate territory.* Without doubt, beliefs as mental maps govern our lives, emotions, health, skills, and everyday experiences. These are pervasive maps, frames, ideas, understandings, are they not? Yet calling them "beliefs" does not explain them. Nor does the term provide an operational definition of what we mean when we talk about our beliefs. For that we have to inquire:

- *Where* do beliefs come from?
- *How* do we develop, create, and/or absorb them?
- *How* much validity does a belief have to have to feel valid?
- *What* are the elements that make up a belief?
- How does a belief differ from a thought?
- *How* do we change a belief?
- How can we use beliefs to access our own personal genius?
- What kinds and variety of beliefs are there?

"Beliefs" as Energized Thoughts

As we explore the structure and content of beliefs we realize that beliefs arise from, and exist in the form of, *thoughts*. To believe we have *to think*. Yet believing involves more than just thinking. We can think and not believe. So believing involves a very special *kind* of thinking. But what? To discover this, let's do a thought experiment to explore the composition and nature of beliefs. Begin by simply thinking of something you believe ... and pick something in the following realms:

- Something you believe about politics.
- Something you believe about yourself.
- Something you believe about "time."
- Something you believe about children.
- Something you believe about spirituality.

Now, step back to notice *the form* of how you represent your beliefs and just notice the sensory representational structure of your beliefs.

- What *sights* do you use visually to represent it?
- What *sounds* do you hear?
- What *sensations* or *smells*?
- What *words* did you say, see, or sense that encodes the belief?

In believing we generalize from events to create a *generalization* about something. Beliefs provide us a way to *summarize* experiences and understandings and to code them into some kind of *category*. From this we can now ask critical structural questions:

- How does a belief differ from a thought?
- How do we more from mere thought to "belief?"
- Are there any other critical factors involved in the transformation from thinking to believing?

To explore these questions, let us do some more experimentation. As you quickly read the following list, let your *thoughts* just come and go and notice the snapshots and movies that dart through your mind:

       — The White House   — The Pyramids of Egypt

— Blueberry ice cream	— Ice cream dripping
— Paying your taxes	— Buying a new car
— Making a speech	— Burping
— The red flashing lights of a police car behind you	
— Asking for a raise	— Being rejected
— A crying baby	— Rocking a baby
— Sitting in a hot tub	— Drinking glass of wine
— Making love	— The sounds of such

The "thoughts" of our consciousness zoom about so quickly that to even *notice* our thoughts necessitates that we speed up our noticing so that we can catch our thoughts before they vanish. Another choice would be to slow down the "thoughts" that blast through consciousness and hold on to them longer so that we can recognize them.

How do you differentiate the experience of entertaining a thought that the White House is where the American President lives to believing that? Can you entertain the thought that the White House is actually purple? Can you see that in your mind? Does that mean that you now believe the White House is purple? Can you imagine that it is in Florida? Do you believe that?

Differentiating Thoughts and Beliefs

Undoubtedly you can think about and represent things that you don't believe. Thinking is one thing; believing is another. So what's the difference? We can *think* thoughts without believing. Undoubtedly you just did that, didn't you? Isn't that incredible? We can *think without believing!* Yet if we can, then what's the difference? How does this work? What transforms a thought into a belief?

We can learn and even "know" things (i.e., have lots of knowledge about details and facts) without necessarily believing them. In psychology I can read the works of Freud, Skinner, or any other theorist *and* fully understand their positions while not necessarily believing their ideas. What does this mean? *Mere representation alone does not create a belief.*

If representation doesn't do it, then what creates a belief? How do we give birth to the things we call *beliefs?* To discover the answer, read the following statements with the intention of noticing three things:

    1) How you represent the thought.
    2) *Whether* you believe the thought or not.
    3) How you represent believing or not-believing the thought.

- "I have the skills to take criticism effectively."
- "Adversity doesn't make or break a person, but one's attitudes toward

adversity."
- "There is no failure; only feedback."
- "Acceptance empowers me for adjusting to reality."
- "My thoughts, ideas, and representations are just mental maps."
- "I can easily change beliefs and patterns that don't work."
- "I can find a positive intention behind every behavior."
- "Every person innately has worth, dignity, and sacredness."
- "I am much, much more than any of my functions—more than my thoughts, beliefs, ideas, emotions, speech, behavior."
- "I can significantly contribute to the world."
- "I can effectively manage my states and my meta-states."
- "Making money is easy."

Thoughts take on greater complication and conceptual richness when we reflect on them and create layers of thoughts-and-feelings about our thoughts. In the first statement, "I have the skills to take criticism effectively," we can visualize the subject ("I") by entertain a picture of ourselves on the screen of our mind. But what do we do with the concept, "have the skills..."? What picture, sound, or sensation represents "skills?" How do we code "criticism?" Did you picture a specific person at a specific time saying words that critiqued something and used that memory to stand for "criticism?"

If the entire process of *representation* itself involves this kind of complexity, then how much more complexity will we find in the phenomenon called *believing?* How shall we explain and conceptualize this higher level of thinking?

The answer is this:
> At the primary level of representation, "think" by recording or presenting the ideas using sensory representations or a mental movie. The basic information for the belief occurs on the screen of our mind as images and sounds. We then step back and *think* about those representations. As we jump a "logical level" we embed the movie thoughts with thoughts of *affirmation, validation, and confirmation.* This meta-move sets a confirmation frame and it is this that turns a *mere* thought into a *believed* thought. Our *confirmation thinking* validates our representation and transforms them into a "belief." (Figure 7:1)

In the Meta-States model we distinguish thought and belief in terms of *levels.* Thoughts (even complex ones) occur and operate at the primary level while beliefs (and beliefs-about-beliefs) operate at meta-levels.

When I *think* about the idea of "taking criticism effectively," my consciousness goes "out there" to reference the world of people and the comments they make. I imagine a movie of someone saying something to me that I label "criticism." Then I imagine seeing, hearing, and feeling myself handling it by listening calmly, asking questions to explore in order to understand, using it as information, etc.

Figure 7:1
The Meta-Structure of a Belief

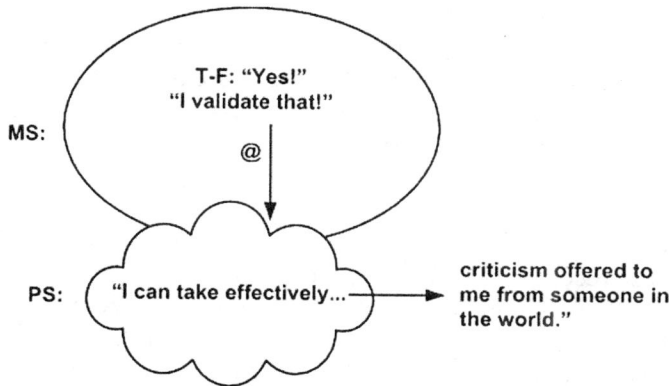

MS:

T-F: "Yes!"
"I validate that!"

@

PS: "I can take effectively..."   criticism offered to me from someone in the world."

[**Note:** In diagrams, "@" symbol stands for "about".]

[Code: T-F stands for Thoughts-and-Feelings. MS: Meta-State, PS: Primary State]

But when I *believe* in the *thought* that "I can take criticism effectively", I move to a higher "logical level." Reflexively, my thoughts reflect on my awareness. I become aware that I agree or disagree with them, that I like or dislike them, or that I think they are true or not. This puts me at a meta-level to my thoughts-and-feelings. My thoughts-and-feelings no longer refer to something "out there" in the world, but to something *inside* my mind—to my idea of my own capacities and skills.

Structurally, a belief first involves *represented thoughts* about something plus validating, affirming, accepting. This explains why merely repeating an empowering belief statement will not have the same effect as *believing* an empowering belief statement. [Although habitual repetition will typically elicit a sense of "confirmation."] How do these psycho-logics work? It probably occurs because we typically equate *"familiarity"* with "confirmation."

This provides insight into the structure of a *dis*belief. To *dis*believe a statement, we essentially apply thoughts of doubt, unsureness, and questions to a primary thought. "I have questions about that idea." Hence, a state of doubt *about* a state of thought.

This follows O'Connor and Seymour (1990) who said that beliefs exist as "the various ideas we think are true, and use as a basis for daily action" (p. 78). "Ideas we *think are true*" describe two levels. At level one are "ideas," at level two is "truth thinking" about those ideas. This defines the meta-level structure of a belief and distinguishes belief from a mere thought. This explains the quality of trust in beliefs. In beliefs, we *trust* or give our allegiance to an idea.

This answers the question that Major (1996) raised about the nature of beliefs in an *NLP World* article, "A Critical Examination of the Place of 'Belief' in NLP." *Beliefs* do not exist as things. Beliefs exist as higher or meta-level constructions of thoughts-and-emotions *about* our representations, a generalization of a generalization.

The Structural Stages of Belief
As we use our mind to become aware of reality as it impacts our nervous system via our sense receptors, we first experience only vague representations of our experience. That is, we *think*. Yet we do not *know*. We have questions and doubts about how to organize our thinking into conceptual constructions of knowledge, how to frame our thinking. Yet as these representations gain more and more clarity, we develop various forms of *knowledge* about things.

Over time, as our knowledge solidifies by repetition, evidence gathering, and experience, our knowing takes the form of *learnings* or *understandings*. We form more and more definite ideas and constructions (our constructed map of reality) which leads us to experience fewer doubts, less questions, and more of a solid sense of reality. At this point we *believe* in the idea. We feel convinced about it and begin to experience the belief as a *conviction*. The next figure portrays this process as the narrowing and focusing of consciousness until we build more and more structured understandings.

Figure 7:2
The Focusing and Narrowing Of Consciousness

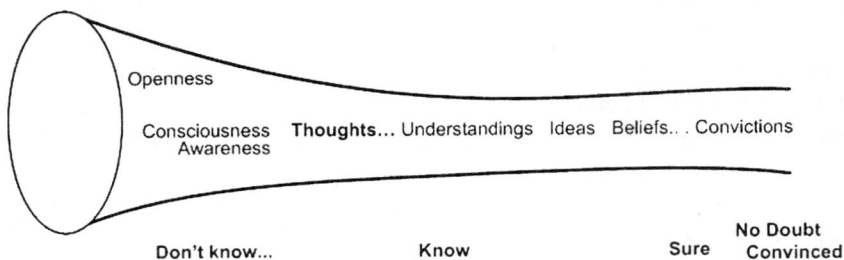

In this way we increasingly wrap our mind around some idea or understanding and move more and more from *thought* to *knowledge* to *belief.* All ideas do not inevitably grow up into beliefs, although they can. Even the mere repetition of any idea (even weird, crazy, non-sense ideas) can, over time, increasingly focus the mind so that the idea seems more acceptable, "real," matter of fact, familiar, and hence believable. This explains one of the contributing factors in how Hitler convinced an entire nation to believe in him and his agenda. If "repetition is the mother of learning," then "repeated learning functions as the mother of beliefs."

Beliefs then emerge from thoughts that we validate and confirm. By moving to a meta-level and using our reasons, experience, and proofs as evidence, we give rise to a gestalt state or experience—a belief.

> *Thoughts are representations in our consciousness ,*
> *beliefs emerge when we validate the representations.*

Quality Controlling our Beliefs

When it comes to thinking and believing our brain has no mechanism for internal quality control. There's no ecology built in that ferrets out stupid, ridiculous, or harmful beliefs. That's because beliefs do not even have to be true in order for us to believe them. They do not have to correspond to anything actual "out there" in the territory. Ask any schizophrenic. For that matter, ask any believer, that is, any human being!

People can, and do, believe all kinds of utterly idiotic things. I certainly have. And I undoubtedly still do. How about you? Even Kant's *a priori* ideas (e.g., time, space, cause, etc.) do not indicate specific innate beliefs, only categories for thinking. The specific content ideas that we believe— can range from the sublime to the utterly ridiculous.

The Meta-Validation Process for Beliefs

Beliefs arise as gestalts. To create such, add some representations, mix in a good bit of confirmation, then let it bake for awhile and eventually you'll get a batch of "beliefs." We already know about the representation part, but what about the validation process? What is that and how does that work?

Because structurally, thoughts need support and validation in order for a "belief" to emerge, we cannot *just "believe"* in something. We believe only when an idea or fact is confirmed and validated. Only when we are able to say to the representations, "*Yes, that's true!*" and have sufficient *reasons* in our way of thinking, can we believe. We have to have a *why* in order to believe. We have to be able to answer the why question: "Why do you believe that?"

Why do you believe any given belief? Because you have something that you consider sufficient "evidence," "proof," "validation," or "confirmation" for believing it. An expert voice, experience, statistics, emotions, something gives you evidence that it's true or valid. For you, it "makes sense," it fits into your model of the world. You have reasons and understandings that support your thoughts. This is confirmation process that then allows you to *believe*.

All of this means that every thought which we believe is embedded inside of some higher frame-of-reference which confirms and validates the thought. It is only when we say, "Yes, that's right." that we create the interaction which then gives rise to beliefs. The thoughts we believe are embedded in higher states of understandings of our "reasons." This creates the psycho-logics of our beliefs and identifies the confirmational structure of a belief.

What do we use to *support* beliefs? We support our beliefs with "proofs." But what *proves* that our idea or fact is real, true, or the way it is? We use experiences, events, testimonies, and such like as "proofs." It's all subjective! There is no such thing as "proof." Proof only means that we feel that we have good evidence for our mental mapping. At a meta-level, we support our thoughts by using some kind of reasoning about our concepts. To flush out the supports that we use for a belief, we only have to ask why:

- Why do you believe that?
- What ideas, understandings, concepts, logic, and reasoning lead you to think that way about this idea?
- Upon what basis do you draw those conclusions and generalizations?

Ask these questions and people will then produce their *evidence*—what for you is sufficient proof for this idea? They will then either provide the data about various experiences, readings, conversations, reflection, etc., or they will describe a *line of reasoning* about those experiences. You may or may not find it convincing or rational. It may or may not fit with your style of reasoning, experiences, beliefs, or psycho-logics. All of us inevitably and inescapably construct our beliefs using cause-effect (C—E) beliefs, meaning equations (the complex equivalence of the Meta-Model) and identity beliefs.[1]

Experiences, events, and arguments play a role in how we develop beliefs. We use the things we've been through as the raw data from which we draw our conclusions. We then draw generalizations and create the meaning attributions. This explains why believing always occurs at a level *meta* to the primary level. People can experience the same event in life, even entertain a similar thought or representation, but then draw different conclusions about that event. They construct different meta-level thoughts (beliefs and belief systems) about the representations.

It is through confirmation that we "hold up" and "support" our meta-level thoughts so they become *beliefs*.. We use confirmation thoughts to set a *frame* on our representation thoughts. In this way, we come to *believe in* the ideas that we do.

Belief Meanings

What anything *means* to us depends on our *beliefs,* not our thoughts. It is by believing that we construct our internal world or Matrix. *Meaning* doesn't exist "out there" in the world. *Meaning* exists only "inside" the mind as we connect and link ideas with experiences in our primary state and in our states-about-that-state.

What does a harsh tonality "mean?" It all depends upon the ideas that you have *connected* to it (associative meaning). It also depends upon the conceptual thoughts-and-feelings you apply to it from a meta-level (contextual or frame meaning). If you connect the experience of "a harsh tonality" with the idea of "insult," "contempt," "disapproving me," etc., *and* then you *feel convinced* that this truly means this, then you *believe* that "a harsh tonality means someone intends to insult, disapprove, etc. you." This becomes your association, your mental frame of mind, and your Matrix.

Did you detect the multi-level structure of a belief in that last statement? The belief state (of feeling convinced) results from the confirmation frame about the tonality statement. Then to move up one more level, suppose you believe in that belief! Belief-about-belief generally locks in place a language constructed map—making it rigid and closed to new information. This describes, of course, the structure of fanaticism.

How Beliefs Grow and Solidify

Beliefs develop. Over time ... and out of our experiences, we *construct* beliefs. We construct beliefs as generalizations about things, generalizations that we confirm with feelings and meanings of validation. In this way we create belief systems that make up our conceptual matrix or model of the world.

At birth, we have no beliefs. We arrive in the world *belief-less*. Beliefs arise as our perceptions, understandings, and learnings grow and solidify. As they do, we experience a focused awareness. In this way, beliefs develop into some very durable internal maps about the territory.
* What helps a belief to grow?
* What processes move us to feel convinced about a thought that *confirms* it as a belief?

Repetition tremendously helps. We can even install non-sense beliefs through repeating an idea enough. Eventually it becomes part of our belief system. No wonder we need to take care regarding what we repeatedly expose our mind to. This includes looping around a fretful thought. The more we loop, the stronger the representation. We might then jump to an unfounded conclusion like, "Since it feels real, it must be real." In this way too much exposure to any thought can lead to a belief. This explains where we get some of our toxic ideas. Looping serves as a form of chronic unconscious meta-stating. Looping intensifies the content of our ideas and beliefs and the repetition leads to a habituation.

Consistency contributes to beliefs growing in strength. Any consistent system of thought supports the development of a belief because it counteracts the influence of contradictory facts and information. So the more we have a coherent systemic thinking about something—the easier it is to believe, and fewer things will be able to operate as a counter-example. It all fits together.

Desirability makes beliefs grow. Many people *only* use desirability for watering their beliefs. If they *want* to win the lottery, they believe that they will. If they *want* to become rich and famous, then they believe that they should and will. If they *want* to believe that things ought to go smoothly for them in life, so they believe. We mostly see this kind of thinking in the mental processing of children prior to the development of "ego strength" for critical thinking in facing reality for what it is. With less of a scientific outlook and less ego-strength to look unpleasant and undesirable experiences in the face without caving in or personalizing, they use *desire* as the basis of believing.

An authority or expert voice cultivate the growth of beliefs in many people. The sense of "proof" or evidence that arises from reliance on authority thinking. "The authorities say ...", "the statistics indicate ...", "the facts lead to the conclusion that ..." "movie stars use X brand." The authoritative voice enables us to texture our ideas with a credibility that makes it easier to assume that they are valid and real.

The Meta-Levels of Beliefs
Given this structural description, we have a lot more thoughts in the form of representations than we have beliefs. We can think lots of things *without* believing them. When we believe—we *trust* our thoughts, *validate* our ideas, and we say "Yes" to those representations as true, right, "the way things are," obvious, valid, confirmed, a reflection of reality, and therefore as something we can cling to without question. We create a belief by adding a meta-level confirmation to a primary level representation.

Getting the Feel of a "Belief"

Emotionally, what does a belief *feel* like? To explore this, recall the earlier mental experiments.

* What did it feel like to have or to experience a belief?
* When we engage in the activity of *believing*, that is, of validating a thought, what emotions do we experience?

The answer depends on the *kind* of belief that we generate, whether a matter-of-fact belief, a strong emotional belief, or a dreadful belief. Most beliefs carry no emotional load. There's no affect because we experience them as feeling "normal." What does *normality* feel like? A matter-of-fact belief will feel *matter-of-fact.* This is the meta-feeling of a belief and this fact makes it difficult to detect our beliefs. To us they just feel as the way things are. We do not experience strong emotions in these beliefs.

Most beliefs involve the simple awareness or "sense" that our thoughts merely reflect or represent reality. There's an *of course-ness* to them.

"Of course, taking criticism positively is hard."

"Of course, taking criticism positively is just a matter of learning the right strategy."

"Of course, you can't change human nature and if you can, it's hard and takes a long time."

"Of course, if you have the right human technology you can make change and even transformation easily and delightfully."

When we enter the matter-of-fact belief state we have a feeling of "reality" because we're thinking and assuming "that's just the way it is." We experience a sense of certainty. The matter-of-fact-ness leads us to feel certain, that is, to feel sure, categorical, definite, and without question. To some extent we have closed our mind on the subject. We "know" that it's this way. In such beliefs, it seems that we are not "believing" at all, only recognizing reality and acknowledging what's real.

The "feelings" of matter-of-fact beliefs reflect our sense and strategy of reality. "This is just the way it is." When someone challenges, disputes, or violates these matter-of-fact the belief beliefs, we are more likely to dismiss them and their comments as non-sense. "Silly thing, he just does not know better!"

A strong belief is different. With a strong and robust belief about something that's important or critical to us we may experience strong or intense emotions of like or dislike. In such beliefs, we do not just take them for granted in a matter-of-fact way, we think and feel passionate about them— excited, motivated, involved, and emotionally invested.

That's why violation of these beliefs lead to a great expenditure of energy in defense, argument, anger, upset, and frustration. Whether it's a belief in a political party or position, a religious concept, human nature, our friends, etc. the more we are emotionally invested in it, the more we will experience the belief as semantically loaded.

The Power of Beliefs

Does it surprise you that the mental constructs of "beliefs" operate so powerfully in our lives, bodies, neurology? Bandler (1982) wrote,

> "Behaviors are organized around some very durable things called beliefs. A belief tends to be much more universal and categorical than an understanding. Existing beliefs can even prevent a person from considering new evidence or a new belief.."

Beliefs send commands to our neurology. This mind-body or neuro-semantic connection explains how our beliefs can make us sick or healthy. Our beliefs inevitably effect our biochemistry, perceptions, digestion, glands, immune system, etc. Because we are neuro-semantic beings, we cannot *not* but act out our beliefs. They are our conceptual center or Matrix from which we live. No wonder we should regularly check the ecology of our beliefs to make sure we have healthy and empowering beliefs, not toxic and limiting ones.

Thoughts differ from beliefs in this area also. While beliefs are *commands* to the nervous system, thoughts are only *signals* to the body. If we are only thinking about wonderful and powerful things, while these may be delightful signals, they will probably have little effect on our body and emotions, they will not be neuro-semantic.

The *self-validating process* of beliefs explains their power and danger. Once installed, a belief functions as part of our perceptual system. Beliefs filter our seeing and perceiving so we eliminate the things that do not fit with our beliefs. Talk about an eliminator and terminator! Beliefs can blind us. Via Meta-States, we say that the meta-level constructions of beliefs function as our canopies of consciousness above and beyond our everyday thinking and perceiving. This endows our beliefs with the power to control, monitor, modulate, and organize our thinking and perceiving. We see the world in terms of our beliefs.

Because beliefs command our neurology and filter our perceptions, they *organize us psycho-logically.* Over time we actualize our beliefs. We *identify* with them. Not only do our beliefs govern our behaviors (if you believe you can't take criticism well—then you won't), but they also motivate us to identify with our belief-behaviors: *"I am* the kind of person who ... (doesn't take criticism well, who does take criticism effectively, etc.)."

Beliefs correspond to our "programs" in NLP and frames in Neuro-Semantics for thinking, feeling, functioning, being, and relating. Whatever you believe is the mental neuro-linguistic *software* that runs your system. Beliefs create our "sense of reality." Every belief we accept and validate seems real, solid, and factual and so governs and manages our reality.

Levels of Beliefs

I entitled this chapter, "It's beliefs all the way up." Why? Because we not only have beliefs, but beliefs about beliefs, belief systems. Robert Dilts' (1990) list of the "Neuro-Logical" Levels describes beliefs on different levels. These levels of beliefs answer to the indexing questions of Korzybski in the Meta-Model: *what, where, how, why, who,* etc. In *Changing Belief Systems with NLP,* Robert succinctly shows how beliefs operate

"... on a different level than behaviors or capacities," and so "they don't change according to the same rules" (p. 8).

Processes of change, transformation, and communication operate in different ways according to the different "logics" of different logical levels. This effects the way we change beliefs. Robert (1990) notes that because beliefs exist at a higher level to the environment.

"A belief isn't about reality. You have a belief in the place of knowledge about reality. Beliefs are about things that nobody can know in reality." (p. 9)

Beliefs are not empirical representations and descriptions of things that occur on the primary level of sights, sounds, sensations, smells, etc. Beliefs function as our higher level maps of conceptual constructions and evaluative conclusions or generalizations. We develop beliefs as *conceptual constructions* about classes, categories, and abstractions: "time," "purpose," "destiny," "self," "mankind," etc. Yet we can't see, hear, feel, taste or touch any of these things. Can you taste "time?" What does "cause" smell like? Picture "purpose." These do not exist on the empirical level where we encounter specifics, but at higher logical levels where we create classes, categories, generalizations, etc.

Beliefs, as generalizations about non-empirical realities, occur at a "logical level" above the see-hear-feel world. There they generate self-fulfilling prophecies. In identifying some toxic beliefs that create personal limitations. Dilts noted the three following areas which represent three really toxic beliefs that we need to address (pages 22-23):

- *Outcomes* — hopelessness,   "It won't work."
- *Ability* — helplessness,   "I can't get over this."
- *Identity* — worthlessness,   "I don't deserve it."

Without explicitly describing meta-levels, Dilts (1990) presupposed them in his explanations of beliefs.

> "*'The clearer I see it the more it makes me feel I probably won't be able to do it.'* This is an example of how beliefs can affect visualization. Ability to visualize is a function of one's capabilities, but what gives the visualization meaning is the belief." (p. 26)

Figure 7:3
Levels of Beliefs
[In diagrams, @ stands here for *about*.]

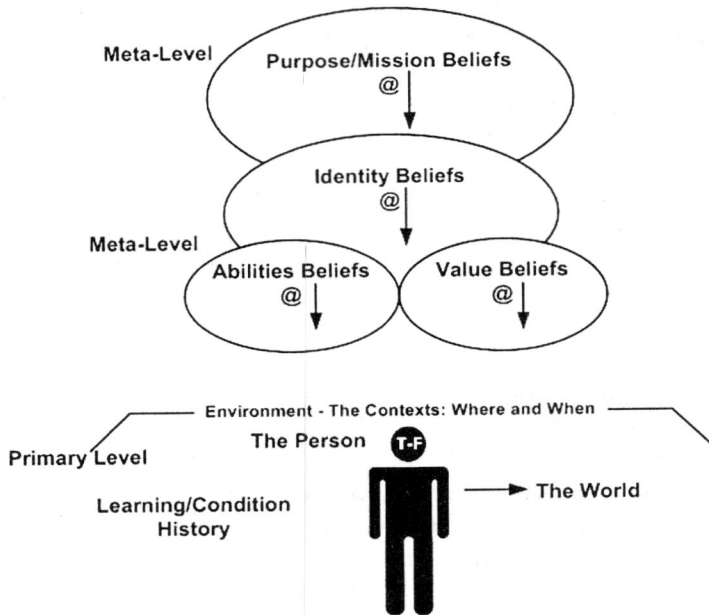

This person has accessed a thought-feeling state involving a cause-effect belief and applied it to himself. He expressed in the cause-effect statement, "the clearer ... the more." This he then applied to his belief and sense of his "ability." His belief refers to a concept about another conceptualization (i.e., ability) and these over-arching constructions drive and organize his primary level experiences.

The *meanings* that we give to concepts (ability, identity, purpose, etc.) are "beliefs." We bring a generalization to *classify* other generalizations. As a meta-state structure, our beliefs function as our classification categories. In the Neuro-Logical Levels model, Dilts has created a short list of beliefs of different levels using the indexing questions.

Figure 7:4
Indexing Questions and the Levels of Beliefs

6. Why? (big)	Spiritual	God/ Universe	Transmission
5. Who?	Mission	Identity	Mission
4. Why? (little)	Motivation Meaning	Beliefs/Values	Permission
3. How?	Process Strategy	Capabilities	Direction
2. What?	Actions/Reactions	Behaviors	Actions
1. Where? When	Opportunities Constraints	Environment	External context

Beliefs differ depending upon the level at which we process the belief. Dilts provides the following example (Figure 7:5, 7:6):

> "The following statements indicate the different levels in someone who is working toward a health goal." (p. 211)

Figure 7:5
Unhealthy Beliefs

5. Identity	"I am a cancer victim."
4. Belief	"It is false hope not to accept the inevitable."
3. Capability	"I am not capable of keeping well."
2. Behavior	"I have a tumor."
1. Environment	"The cancer is attacking me."

Figure 7:6
Healthy Beliefs

5. Identity	"I am a healthy person."
4. Belief	"If I am healthy, I can help others."
3. Capability	"I know how to influence my health."
2. Behavior	"I can act healthy sometimes."
1. Environment	"The medicine healed me."

We can here see the nature of beliefs as meta-frames (i.e., frames about our frames). Robert described beliefs as setting "a frame that determines how everything afterwards gets interpreted" (1990: 133)—a meta-level construct. Beliefs, as thoughts-about-thoughts at higher levels, are not about reality. Beliefs are reflective thinking about concepts—meaning, cause, ability, self, mission, time, etc. Beliefs deal with categories and set-up powerful *attractors* in a self-organizing system.

Beliefs and "Sub-Modalities"
As we move through experiences we construct *meanings* in the form of *beliefs*. We do not create just one belief about any event, person, or idea, but beliefs

about beliefs—belief systems. Our beliefs, as our mapping of reality, make up the meta-levels of our mind, our Matrix of frames. Through the habituation process, our beliefs become more and more outside-of-consciousness so that we just assume them as "the way things are." This makes beliefs *un*conscious.

We work with beliefs when we identify a *frame*-of-reference, when we deframe that construction, or when we reframe it. *"Frames"* and "framing" gives us a powerful metaphor for talking about beliefs. With regard to our perceptual frames—whenever we put a piece of meaning (a neuro-semantic frame) around an event, we create our neuro-semantic world. All of our meta-levels, as meta-state constructions, are beliefs. That's why it is beliefs all the way up. And as beliefs don't exist at the representational level, they much less exist at any imagined *sub*-representational level.

> *No wonder merely mapping "sub-modalities" across from doubt to belief usually do not work to change beliefs.*

Generally, we cannot transform a meta-level structure like a belief using primary level processes. When such mapping across does work, we have activated meta-level processes.

There You Have It
You are now *in* on the secret—the structure of the meta-level phenomenon that we call *believing*. This gives you the key for recognizing limiting beliefs and building empowering ones. You now have a ticket to the domain of excellence.
> "NLP maintains that the critical factor in genius is *how* we use our nervous system and that the mental strategies of a particular genius can be learned by others and applied toward other contents." (Dilts, 1995, p. 370)

In modeling the excellence of peak performers and high achievers, it is critical to clearly distinguish thought and belief. We can now do precisely that. Recognizing *the structure of beliefs* empowers us to detect, identify, and construct the kind of supporting beliefs that will enhance our lives and bequeath to us a rich map from which to operate.

We have just begun our exploration into beliefs. With this meta-model that makes explicit the structural form of beliefs, we can now use these insights to dispense of toxic beliefs, update antiquated beliefs, transform limiting ones, and install empowering beliefs. Interested? Then on to the next chapters.

Summary

- The way we think and believe critically effects the structure of mastery. To access, cultivate, develop, and maintain excellence we have manage our thinking and believing in supportive ways.
- Thinking and believing, as different levels of mapping, set the frames for our subsequent experiencing, feeling, skill development, etc.
- We can now construct higher level thoughts of confirmation about any and every thought we want to turn into a belief. We can now create beliefs as *attractors* to self-organize our skills of excellence. Then our ideas will attract things that correspond to that excellence.
- As we discover the beliefs of highly successful, competent, productive, creative, insightful, and wise people, we can simply track over the encoding to our own representational screen, and then *go meta* to confirm, validate, and solidify those ideas.
- This structure of the magic of believing gives us the ability to choose the commands we want to send to our nervous system. We can also outframe our current beliefs so that we own and *have* them, rather than them *having* us.

End Notes:

1. For more about the use of the Meta-Model in constructing beliefs and the matrix of frames that governs our experiences, see *Communication Magic* (2000) and *Mind-Lines* (2002).

Chapter 8

TRANSFORMING
LIMITING BELIEFS

There's Magic in Rising Up and saying
"Yes" and "No" at Meta-Levels

Knowing that we have to go meta to believe, we now know that it's not enough to just *think and represent* great thoughts. We have to *confirm* them. We have to acknowledge and validate them. We have to say a powerful *"Yes!"* to them. We have to go meta and set *confirmation frames* about the content of our thinking and representing. When we do that, we transform a thought into a belief.

This now puts at our disposal an extremely powerful tool for taking charge of our mind, does it not? Are you ready for that kind of power? It also endows us with the rare and unprecedented opportunity to *believe as we will*. This also expands our actual ability of "running our own brain." We no longer have to wait to believe in something or to feel in the mood to believe. This very moment we can model the thinking and believing of excellence and take on the *thinking* and *believing* of a genius.

Will that immediately transform you into a genius? No. Of course not. Beliefs do not work that way. Why not? Because beliefs occur within belief *systems* and meta-level structures. When we engage and work with meta-levels, we work with *systems*. So, when we set the frames of exciting, empowering, enhancing, and supportive beliefs in our mind, and install them as *attractors* in our own neuro-semantic system ... they initiate new processes: new feedback and feed forward loops are initiated, new commands are sent to our neurology. And with that, *transformation* begins. Magic fills the air when we set self-organizing attractors in motion. Life will become more interesting, more magical, more ferocious, more of an adventure, more fun, and more playful.

If none of that matters to you, skip this chapter. ... Oh, you're still here? Good. So let's move on with *enhancing your meta-levels,* with turning your thoughts into full-fledged beliefs, with layering confirmation, validation and evidence onto your thoughts so that you build a whole system (or Matrix) of neuro-semantic support to enhance your life.

With the structural understanding that you now have about the role, functioning, and nature of beliefs, you have an unprecedented opportunity to do something wonderful. You can identify the beliefs that poison and sabotage you and get rid of that mental garbage. You can also construct new beliefs to empower and enhance you for the strategies of genius. So, as you anticipate this magic:

- What totally empowering belief would you like to get stuck in your head as a frame-of-mind?
- What fascinating and wonder-filled belief would you like to install in your head as a self-organizing *attractor?*

In this chapter we will work with the very processes of actually *transforming beliefs* by using some of the human technology for belief change. As we do, the secrets of "sub-modalities" will challenge the traditional "sub-modality" mapping-across pattern and add the new refinements to the model. This will allow us to use some meta-state processes to build more reliable technology.

A Belief Change Pattern
1) Identify the structure of an old belief you no longer believe.

What is an old belief that you used to believe?
What are some of the old childish beliefs you once believed?
Did you once believe in Santa Claus or the Easter Bunny?
Did you once believe that "chocolate is the most wonderful thing in the whole world?"
How do you represent no-longer-believed belief?
How do you know that you no longer believe it?

2) Identify the form of the belief in its heyday.

How did you think and represent the belief when you fully believed it?
As you go back to a time when you fully believe the old idea and recover it, what insights does that give you about the structure of a strong belief?
What is your "I really believe this!" representation?

3) Experience the evolution of the belief as it changed.

As you now imagine moving up through time—all the way up to the present, how do you represent the old belief changing?
Now from the present, look back and notice *how* the transformation occurred. What shifted your belief?
After you experience the entire process, reorient yourself back into the present to identify the change factors.

Debriefing

As beliefs grow and solidify via the focusing of consciousness, we have fewer questions and doubts in our minds. This moves us to feel increasingly sure. We become convinced. We just "know" that something is "real" or "right."

When we experience *the undoing* of a belief, the reverse happens. We go through the stages in reverse. At first we begin experiencing *questions*. "Well, what about X?" We next experience some confusion, and with the confusion doubt begins to grow. We become a little unsure, and with time, we become even more unsure.

When a thought grows up into a belief, our mind closes more and more around the idea so that it allows less and less openness to other ideas. Conversely, when a belief moves backward to become just a thought, the mind opens up increasingly to other thoughts. It loosens its hold on just one idea. Rather than more focus, consciousness expands and diffuses. It gets broader and wider. We ask more questions. We become more tentative.

When we experience a strong, intense, categorical belief, we have a thought or learning to which we say emphatically, and without a shadow of a doubt, *"Yes!" "Of Course!" "Without question!"* When we undo that belief so that it weakens, we begin to replace it with something more enhancing, we start saying about that thought, *"I wonder..." "What about this other idea...?" "What about these other factors...?"* Then, when we get to the place of disbelief, we definitely, emphatically and categorically say *"No, of course not!" "Ridiculous!" "No way!"* to that thought.

As you do the next exercise, remember that a doubt does not describe the opposite of a belief. When we have an opposite to a belief, we actually have a *dis*belief. We *believe in* the reverse. A doubt operates simultaneously as both an affirmation and a dis-affirmation about the same thought. One minute you say *Yes* to it, the next you say *No* to it. We keep flipping back and forth, "Maybe it is; maybe it is not."

Preparation for Belief Change
1) Identify your representations of doubt.

What do you *doubt?*

How do you represent a doubt? Think about something that you doubt, something about which you really just do not know if you believe or not.

What do you kind of believe, but then there's another part of you that just doesn't know? You have lots of questions about it. As you identify this doubt, now notice how you represent it.

2) *Identify your representation for disbelieving.*

What do you *not* believe in? Think of something that you definitely do *not* believe.

How do you represent it?

How do you *dis*confirm the idea?

How do you say *No* to it? How does this feel?

3) *Identify your representations of not "sure."*

What do you feel unsure about? What is something you just don't know for sure ... you wonder about it ... you have lots of questions about it?

Will you eat salad tomorrow? "Maybe I will, maybe I will not."

Will you do some sit-ups this evening? "I could, but I also could not."

Pick out something small and simple, and get your sensory representations and the cinematic features of your inner movie of it.

4) *Identify your representations for a sudden belief change.*

Have you ever experienced something that absolutely jarred you into a new belief?

Have you ever suddenly discovered a new insight, truth, or fact so that suddenly shifted the way you thought about it completely?

Sometimes, as we move through life, we experience something that totally and absolutely changes our thinking forever. Recall such an event and identify the representations of that *sudden* belief change.

If you do not have such an experience, then just creatively imagine someone like Saul on the Damascus Road. What must that have been like? Imagine him suddenly struck by lightning and experiencing a total conversion from being a Pharisee to becoming a Christian and later an apostle. It does not matter whether you believe the story or not, only that you can create the representations and feel what "a sudden belief change" would feel like.

5) *Identify your representation of your "museum of old beliefs."*

What did you once believe but no longer?

If you think how you now represent this as a mental museum where you store the old beliefs, you can appreciate them as "old" beliefs. How do you represent that museum?

5) *Identify your representation of "openness."*

What are you open to?

Think of a time and place where, mentally-emotionally, you thought and felt in a very open, receptive, curious, and playful way. What is that like?

Debriefing

Representations of doubting give us access to the skills and state of *questioning* (i.e., calling into question, wondering, opening the mind to new and different information, etc.). Here we experience an openness of mind as we become curious, full of wonder, and feeling not-so-sure about something.

This *not-knowing state* offers quite a resource. It generates a broader perspective, less definition, less specifics, much "fusing" together (con-fusion) of thoughts-and-feelings about the subject.

> [By the way, Einstein, Edison, Disney, and others regularly used the state of *not-knowing* to open themselves up to what they did not know —a strategy of genius. Know-it-alls, on the other hand, do not seem capable of learning new things. In workshops, when people complain that they feel confused, I use the traditional mind-line, "Great! You now have the rare and unprecedented opportunity to access your own personal genius as you *feel even more confused*, and let it grow, so that you can *open up new doors of understanding*, and *enjoy* this confusion so that you don't waste it!"]

In your *disbelief* experience, you undoubtedly have a meta-level experience of going above some thought or idea and saying a strong *"No!"* to it. Here, you probably have other thoughts and beliefs that get in the way of saying *"Yes"* to it. Here you will have specific sights, sounds, and sensations that give you clarity of what you do believe in contradistinction to your not-belief.

In your *unsure* experiences, you probably have two (or more) sets of representations vying for attention. As a result, you will internally continue to go back and forth between the representations. "Maybe this... not maybe this... no... " *How* do you oscillate? Do you go back and forth laterally (right to left) or vertically (up and down) or from back to front?

With your *sudden belief change*, your experience of a sudden, shocking, unexpected event, fact, or idea will probably induce a floating feeling of un-reality, a sense of not having a good grasp on reality, a lightness, even a dizziness. In such an experience, your thoughts-emotions will feel as if the very foundation of life and "reality" has crumbled beneath your feet. Sometimes, after a natural disaster like a tornado or flood, or after a man-made disaster (i.e., a bombing, a terrorist act) we see people "in a daze," unsure, dissociated, unable to cope, saying, "I can't believe..."

Your *museum of old beliefs* representations gives you the ability to store away old beliefs that have outlived their usefulness. Here, you can even honor and acknowledge the old beliefs. You do not have to despise or trash the old beliefs. You might feel amused about such old fashioned, non-relevant, and musty beliefs. Or you might appreciate the value they once offered you. Or, you might enjoy knowing that you have outgrown them.

Mapping Over the Transformation

Sometimes, we can simply map over from *belief* to *feeling unsure* and then to *doubt*. In doing this, we take these cognitive-feeling states and apply them to our primary thought. We meta-state the foundational thought. As an experiment, play with this and see if it works sufficiently to deframe and/or transform your limiting belief. Pick out some limiting, sabotaging, and toxic belief that you would like to change.

Now take your representation of the *belief* (typically, a sight or sound— close, in color, associated, bright, clear, etc.) and code it with your codings for *unsure* (two sights and sounds, one to the right, the other to the left, one up and bright, the other down to the right and more of a sensation, etc.). Listen to your internal voice saying *"Yes"* to it, and *"No"* to it, and then *"I just don't know."* Stay in the unsure state and experience until you really loosen up your sense of the belief so that you feel that you just do not know anymore.

Now meta-state over into *doubt*. Use your representations for *doubt* to re-code the old limiting belief. Bring these representational distinctions over to the thought. As you do, let other ideas begin to get in the way of the old belief so that your doubt of the old belief grows stronger.

Do you see what we're actually doing when map "sub-modalities" across from one experience to another? We are making a *meta move*. We are taking those variables of the encoding and using them to *stand for* and *symbolize* the structure (or meaning) of a higher frame. We *symbolize* "doubt" perhaps by a shifting back and forth from two images of two thoughts. Then we bring the representation of two pictures to another thought. Using the structure of *doubt* in this way transforms our experience. Does this work? Yes, sometimes it will. It will work when the particular distinction or "sub-modality" *stands for,* and structurally encodes, a higher level thought about an idea, it creates a powerful influence. Then it will turn the idea into a different experience—into doubt of the idea. Then it will change the belief structure. Before continuing, play around with this on some of the limiting beliefs you want to weaken.

Meta-Stating Toxic and Unbalanced Beliefs

We have been using *the Meta-States model* in transforming old beliefs that do not serve us well or that create sabotage or unbalance. We have utilized the going meta move to bring the *structural coding* of doubt and disbelief to the thought that we want to de-energize and de-commission from running our programs. This understanding of the meta-functions and processes that magically transform a thought into a belief, and then back into a mere thought, gives us the ability to take charge of our higher processing levels.

1) Identify your "belief" representations.

How do you code *the affirmation* of a thought?

What internal representations drive this belief state?

Where in space do you put strong beliefs—down to your right (as "down right" important), up and to your left (as a "high value"), or immediately in front of you (a "forthright" belief)?

Identify all of the critical and driving representational distinctions.

2) Transform your "Yes!"

As you notice your *"Yes!"* and *how* you say *"Yes"* to that belief (tone, volume, tempo, space location, etc.) begin to say that *"Yes"* in a questioning tone of voice.

Use a doubting and unsure voice, weak in volume, small in expression to increase your sense of doubt. Keep increasing the un-sureness until your questioning questions it so much that it feels sure of its doubt.

Experience fully your sureness of this doubt about the belief. "Now I feel sure of my doubt." As you do this, notice where (the location) you store this doubt, or where the *thought* has moved to as it has shifted from a strong belief to a strong *dis*belief.

3) Bring in the new empowering belief that you want to believe.

Represent this new belief fully and clearly as you appreciate how it will make life so much better, command your neurology in an exciting way, and generate a self-fulfilling prophecy that you will love. Again, notice *where* you locate this belief.

4) Say a resounding "Yes!" to this new belief.

Say *"Yes!"* to this new enhancing belief. How does that feel?

Make your internal voice of *"Yes!"* strong and firm, then make it firmer, louder, closer, etc. Use all of the qualities in your auditory system that really make it compelling for you... then double it... until you feel more and sure about the *"Yes!"* How does that feel?

Use all of the kinesthetic variables that further empower the *Yes*: breathing, volume, motor movements, muscle tension, etc.

5) Future pace

As you now imagine, fully and completely, moving out into life tomorrow with *the confidence of "Yes!"* about that enhancing belief, does it serve you well? Does it enhance your life and relationships? What is it like to see, hear, and feel yourself orienting yourself in the world with it ... at work, at home, in all the contexts of importance to you?

Beliefs as Languaged Constructions

Because meta-level phenomena does not deal with "real" things in the actual world, we are dealing with mental constructs of ideas in our mind. This is where we live. We live in the matrix of our frames about things.

Actually in this realm of beliefs, we mostly encode our beliefs using language. In fact, most beliefs are difficult to encode in see-hear-feel terms. That's why we almost always code our beliefs linguistically. Of course, *after* we have done the linguistic work of coding a belief, we can then use a symbol to symbolize the belief: a pair of scales to symbolize our belief about "justice," for example. Yet looking at a pair of scales, or any other icon *alone,* does not and cannot contain all of the rich linguistic concepts and meanings involved in the belief. The nominalizations of cause-effect statements and complex-equivalences enable us to more fully encode the belief. We need language to create beliefs.

Notice the language you use to represent your beliefs. The Meta-Model's linguistic distinctions provide us our primary structures for encoding beliefs in language.

Complex Equivalence Beliefs:
"This external behavior (EB), action, response, event, entity, etc. *equals* or *means* this internal significance (IS)." This gives us the formula: **EB = IS** by which we can describe the structure of the belief.
> "Failing in that business (EB) means I just do not have any business sense (IS)."

Cause-Effect Beliefs:
Here we frame some event as the "cause" of some effect. Often we do so in an ill-formed way.
> "Having a painful childhood explains why I have had, and will have, dysfunctional relationships."
> "The lecturing way he comes across when he gives me a task to do makes me feel like a child."

Mind-Reading Beliefs:
In mind-reading we frame our ideas about certain internal states and intentions of others without checking with them. We second-guess.
> "When she looks at me like that (EB), it means she's upset with me (IS)."

Identification Beliefs:
We structure ideas about our concept of our "self" by identifying this self concept with various ideas, roles, experiences, etc. This creates a complex equivalence between one of our many "selves" and some external event.

"I *am* a depressive." "I *am* a failure." "He can't do anything right; he *is* a loser." "She *is* so emotional because she *is* a woman."

A Linguistic Belief Change Pattern

1) *Write your new belief in effective and compelling language.*

What would be the most succinct and compelling written statement that describes a new enhancing belief that enriches your life?

> "I can trust people and stay alert to signals about who may or may not behave in a trustworthy way."
>
> "I can graciously welcome and appreciate my fallibility, take it into account, and treat myself in a kinder and gentler way when I mess up. I will view mistakes as a sign of my humanity, not my depravity."

2) *Language yourself with the belief statement.*

> What happens when you first take a meta-level position to yourself regarding the subject of the belief (i.e., self, fallibility, relationships, criticism, etc.) and speak the new enhancing belief to yourself?
>
> What happens when you make it more and more convincing and compelling? When you use a compelling voice?
>
> When you future pace it into the months and years to come?

3) *Repeat daily for thirty days increasingly adding more vigor to it.*

> Is the belief important enough to use the neuro-semantic power of repetition to habituate this way of thinking?
>
> Are you willing to do that?
>
> Will you do that? Do I have your word on that?
>
> How will you remember to do this?
>
> What resources do you need to do this?
>
> Will you run your neuro-pathways with this new idea until it becomes a well-worn path? Until it becomes your default Swish pattern?

Changing Beliefs Conversationally

With this understanding regarding the multi-leveled structure of beliefs as confirmation about a representation and your knowledge about how language structures and empowers beliefs, notice the power and elegance of the following. These statements provide a pathway for inviting a change of beliefs conversationally apart from "doing therapy" on others.

Suppose you hear someone say, "I can't believe that..."? "I can't believe that people can change." We have a three-leveled structure:

- *"Can't"*—a state of impossibility thinking-and-feeling.
- *About*—a belief statement regarding some primary state. So "I can't believe that..." translates to, or creates the gestalt of, "I doubt that I have the ability to accept your idea."

- *A primary state or experience.*

Recognizing the structure of this belief, what would be some effective responses to it? We have numerous choices.

- How surprised would you feel if you discovered that this belief, '*People can't change*' suddenly changes so you find yourself *unable* to believe it anymore? What would that feel like to you? Would you like that?

- Yes, I know that you can't believe this, *and* I wonder what it would feel like if you began to, in just a little way, doubt that idea because if you began to have some questions about your inability to entertain such thoughts, you might find yourself at least entertaining the possibility of believing it, can't you, now?

- Let's say that's the sad truth of things. In spite of that, would you ever *like* to *become open* to doubting that this idea is the whole story, or would you like to just let it totally dominate your life and underscore your inabilities? Which would you prefer?

- Do you have even the slightest doubt about that? Do you have even a little doubt about it? A little doubt that you can allow to grow and double ... and become stronger and stronger as the days pass ... so that when you think about this belief five years from now, and turn around and look back to this moment, realizing that your belief has changed?

The Museum and Sacred Temple Metaphor
Belief Change Pattern

We have several belief change patterns in NLP. Apart from the "Sub-modality" Belief Change pattern, we have a pattern designed by Tim Hallbom and Robert Dilts involving spatial anchoring of states. With beliefs that are toxic thought viruses this is a very effective pattern. The pattern involves identifying several different *kinds* of beliefs or meta-states:

- Powerful limiting beliefs that no longer serve us.
- Old antiquated beliefs that have become irrelevant and unuseful. Yet perhaps good to display in the *museum* of the mind.
- Highly desirable new beliefs that are not yet energized or installed.
- Very special *sacred* beliefs that encode our most "core" and ultimate maps.

When we spatially anchor each of these experiences at different locations in a room, we set up *a psycho-geography* . This then makes it easy for us to step in and out of them and use these states to embed other things in.

First invite someone to take the ideas and feelings of a limiting belief and put it in the energy field (or state) of an old belief that has lost all of its juice. This embeds the first belief inside of a larger frame: "old," "un-energized," "no juice or pizzazz left," etc. As such, it takes the punch out of the belief.

Then ask the person to take this another step as he or she puts the *old* belief into *a Museum of Antiquated Beliefs*. This outframes the limiting belief yet another time. This frame says: "Antiquated," and "Good for sight-seeing purposes, not for living." As a result, this frees the person from the limited thinking-and-feeling and creates space for constructing a more desirable belief. Once the new ideas have been formulated, invite the person to step into the place *of the Temple of Sacred Beliefs* and use "of ultimate importance" as a frame.

As a form of kinesthetic meta-stating, this process does not require a full consciousness about either the encoding of the states or of the meta-frames and meanings that we set. This occurs neurologically rather than conceptually. By utilizing the format of old antiquated museum beliefs, we bring the codes and neurological feelings that carry *that meaning* (i.e., old, irrelevant, no longer useful, retired, etc.) and apply it to the old limiting belief. This creates a *felt* de-framing.

Then, take the encoding of *Sacredness,* and its felt kinesthetics, and use these as the new higher frame-of-reference for the new ideas the person wants to install. This *meta-states* the new enhancing ideas using the coding of sacredness or specialness. Because this occurs more kinesthetically using *the feeling and sense of these states* ("museum" and "temple") it utilizes the non-propositional nature of metaphor.

What are we really doing here? We are applying "museum" thoughts-and-feelings *to* the old belief. At a higher logical level this sets the frame that these ideas are now "old," "irrelevant," and part of the enjoyed "archives" of one's life. As a tourist they are nice things to visit when friends come to town, but they are no longer to be used for everyday living. Viewing old thoughts in this way de-commissions them from operating as active beliefs.

This allows us to apply the thoughts-and-feelings of *Very Important, Sacred Importance,* and *Specialness* to our new thoughts. Or, to think of it in a different way, we *embed* the new thoughts into these frames. Seeing anything *in terms of* these ideas cannot but energize and commission them. In this way we set a frame of "importance." It also protects that frame by establishing an even higher frame of "sacredly" important.

Kathy Corsetty and Judith Pearson (1999) in *Healthy Habits,* utilize this belief change pattern. They also have provided the following very powerful conversational layering of meta-states upon meta-states. Here they apply the belief change to moving from self-contempt to self-esteeming.

> "Adopting a new belief can help you *love yourself more fully*. Are you comfortable with that possibility? What do you think will happen if you do *love yourself* wholeheartedly? Do you think the sky will fall in?

Do you envision that you will be struck down by lightning? Do you think you will become insufferably conceited? Acknowledge any irrational fears you have about loving yourself. Be patient with yourself, if you harbor any fears or doubts. Appreciate that you originally (probably at a much younger age) learned to scold, dislike, or discredit yourself in an effort to protect yourself in some way, or to get through a difficult or confusing time, or to adapt to the people around you. Now you can *learn a new way to care for yourself.* Give yourself permission to *let go of old damaging beliefs,* knowing that you can still honor the values and positive intentions that may have formed the underpinnings of those beliefs. Remember that you can also retain all the positive learnings and strengths you have acquired from the past— even those that came from negative, hurtful events." (p. 151)

There You Have It

As a semantic class of life, we inevitably construct and use beliefs as we navigate life. In the process we develop numerous unenhancing beliefs that get in our way. These undermine our accessing of excellence. Yet given the way our minds inevitably seek to validate our thoughts, we find that we can very easily install constructions of non-sense, myths, inaccuracies, and even toxic garbage. Yet toxic beliefs make our minds toxic. Common toxic beliefs sabotaging excellence include:

"You're stuck with your beliefs!" "It's sacrilegious to change your beliefs." "People can't change their basic beliefs." "You better not fool around with these mind games, you may go crazy."

Summary

- The power and pervasiveness of destructive beliefs occurs because that they operate at a level *meta* to specific thoughts. This makes them feel so "real" and "solid" and "unchangeable."

- Once we move to the first level up beyond representational thinking, it's *beliefs all the way up.* We have confirmed thoughts about our thoughts (the first meta-level structure), and then beliefs about that confirmation, "self," the world, thinking, etc. These beliefs-upon-beliefs organize our internal world.

- As beliefs operate at ever higher levels, they become increasingly more *outside of awareness* (or unconscious). As this seduces us to treat them as "real," we *lock in* the lower level beliefs. We assume, "That's just the way it is" and then close the subject in our mind.

- The structure of *beliefs about beliefs* solidifies lower level ideas, thereby making them even more impactful. *Believing in our beliefs* creates *convictions.* It creates a closed loop and cuts us off from feedback creating rigidity. Fanatic know-it-alls absolutely believe in their beliefs.

- If *believing in our beliefs* cuts us off from primary level feedback for updating beliefs, choose to do this only when a *belief* can handle it. Some beliefs can, although most cannot.

- As we keep our *beliefs* flexible and open by *tentative* believing, by *open-mindedly believing*, by recognizing beliefs as just a map in our believing, we are ready to always test them against reality, usefulness, and balance. This makes for sanity.

- We can now aim to change all of our limiting and self-sabotaging beliefs. Whenever we find an old toxic belief that limits our effectiveness in business, personal relationships, or our own personal empowerment, we can change it and replace it with a positive mental map that will take us to more enjoyable places.

Chapter 9

META-YES-ING
EMPOWERING BELIEFS

"An incredible application of meta-stating!
The simplest and briefest Belief Change pattern by far."

A statement is only "believable" to the extent
that we represent it clearly and confirm it
with energy or with matter-of-factness.

- How does it feel now to realize and appreciate the meta-level processes involved in the structure of beliefs and believing?
- What new resources does it give you?
- Are you now ready to use the quickest and most profound pattern for transforming beliefs?

The *Meta-Yes-ing* pattern represents the most dynamic belief change pattern that we have discovered to date in Neuro-Semantics. Interesting enough. it is implied in every pattern for altering beliefs that we have come across.

- Do we sound confident about this new technology for transforming meta-level thoughts?
- Do we exude a conviction that it can change any belief and transform it so that it serves us in accessing our personal genius?
- That we can specify beliefs that accord with the structure of excellence in a given field?

You bet! If you don't feel convinced yet, then take the Neuro-Semantic test. Put the pattern to the test and discover its power for yourself and then you can decide for yourself.

The Discovery of Meta-Yes-ing

I stumbled onto understanding the mental phenomenon of "beliefs" as *a meta-level structure* when I began applying the structural tools of the Meta-States model to beliefs. This arose from thinking about the difference between a "thought" and a "belief" (chapter 7). Upon realizing that a belief involved a primary level idea confirmed and validated with a *"Yes"* at a meta-level, I emailed that description to Bob Bodenhamer to see what he thought about that. He liked it.

Then, true to his *go for it* style, he immediately began practicing it with his clients. In doing so, he quickly discovered the wonders it could work. It especially worked magic on people with whom the traditional NLP Belief Change pattern had not worked. We both felt excited about this and so streamlined the process to create a *Ten-Minute Belief Change pattern*. Bob first applied the *meta-yes-ing* pattern to a particularly stubborn belief that really limited one of his clients. The year was 1997.

Given Bob's attitude of applying and testing things, I can always count on him to *put things to the test*. In the back of his mind, he has a driving question that forever inquires, "What can the theory *do?*" "How can we put it to use in a constructive and life-changing way?" I first discovered this empowering belief in him when he learned about Meta-States. Immediately he began *using it*. And that, of course, deepened and extended his skills and expertise. In applying its power for making desired changes at meta-levels, Bob experimented with using a wide variety of other resources. As he playfully experimented, he began to discover just how so many of the NLP patterns work their magic due to meta-level frames.

Having just written several articles on *Belief Change Patterns Using Meta-States,* I was interested in having Bob use the pattern. In our conversation, Bob asked,

> "If a *belief* differs from a *thought* due to a meta-level structure that *affirms and validates* the thought, then how do we use this understanding to create a more refined and streamlined Belief Change pattern? If 'sub-modality' mapping across does not, in and of itself, necessarily alter a strong limiting belief, what process will?"

He asked these questions rhetorically. And just as rhetorically I said,

> "Well we know that somehow we have to *say 'No!'* to the old limiting belief, we also have to somehow just say *'Yes!'* to the new thought. So why don't we just do that directly and explicitly? Why don't we invite a person to make a move meta to their thoughts and utter these higher level expressions of disconfirmation and confirmation?"

The rest is history. Bob grabbed his next client and tried it out. Nor did he stop there. He ran just about every client and student he could get his hands on through the process. Putting the new Belief Change pattern to the clinical test with real live people, he repeatedly discovered how much it streamlines the process and essentially provides a *ten-minute Belief Change pattern*. Doing so re-confirmed the discovery that "beliefs" operate at a higher "logical level" than thoughts, and that *beliefs* do not always change by merely recoding the "sub-modalities." Rather, beliefs change by the process of inducing or creating a new frame of reference at a higher logical level that disconfirms the old and validates the new.

Jim Polizzi was the very first person to Meta-*Yes* a new belief. As a highly skilled computer programmer, he quickly realized the value of the structure of the process. So it only took a few minutes for Jim to *disconfirm* the old limiting belief that he no longer wanted and to *confirm* a much more enhancing belief to take its place.

In terms of *installation speed*, this one works really fast. When we began, we put it right alongside the "Ten Minute Phobia Cure" in terms of quickness. In our trainings, workshops, and demonstrations since that time, we find that we can run the pattern in just a couple minutes— *and conversationally*. That's its power and elegance.

We now use it regularly in all of our trainings from Accessing Personal Genius (APG) that introduces Meta-States, to Meta-Selling, Mind-Lines, Meta-Coaching, Trainers Training, etc. This includes presentations at several NLP Conferences (London, Toronto, Denmark). This has allowed us to accumulate a great many examples of people making belief changes in a matter of a few minutes—belief changes that last and that make a major difference in peoples' lives.

Because this focuses on *the very structure* of an experience (in this case, *believing*), this pattern fits precisely with the original NLP and General Semantics models. It elegantly shows how *structure governs experience*. Content may more often seduce us and capture our attention, but it's the structural dynamics that determine the experience. So, the more we identify and streamline the structural processes behind or within an experience, the more we'll create effective processes.

Early in 1999, Bob and I presented the Meta-Yes-ing Pattern at the Canadian NLP Conference in Toronto. There we met John Vander Velde, a psychotherapist who lives in the far north country on the tundra where they have no trees. John told us about the Eskimo children there considering eating undigested clams out of slain walrus' stomach and sucking on the eyeballs of slaughtered elks as a real delicacy. Upon describing that in some detail, I just had to comment,

> "If a person can say *Yes!* to *that*, there's no end to the things you can get people to say *Yes* to and create beliefs! If you grow up in a culture that says *Yes!* to sucking the eyeballs of an elk as a real treat —and get

your body and neurology to actually *believe* it, just think of all the other things you could get your body to believe and feel."

Bob later noted, "These children have learned to say *Yes* to something that turns the stomachs of people born in other cultures." He commented that some people even have the ability to say *No!* to the body's natural desire for food, and *Yes!* to being skinny, and can do so to such an extent that they'll over-ride their body's need for food until they die. Talk about the power of Meta-*Yes*-ing and Meta-*No*-ing!

When we first discovered this, we really thought that we had come upon a totally new pattern. Later, however, I discovered some transcripts of Richard Bandler running the *Meta-Yesing* in the early 1980s. Of course, he did not call it that. And knowing him, he would probably deny it. In fact, he did not even know that he was using a meta-level layering of confirmation thoughts back onto a thought. Or, if he realized it, he gave no indication of it then or now. You will find one of those early *Meta-Yes-ing Patterns* by Bandler later in this chapter, and then again in chapter 16.

"Meta-NO-ing" and "Meta-YES-ing"
Jim said that for most of his 39 years, he had struggled with the limiting and toxic belief, "I always alienate and drive away friends." Worse than that, he held another belief, one *meta* to the first belief. "Nothing will ever work to help me overcome this problem." Of course, the second belief *locked in* the first belief frame to protect him from changing. It boxed him in a vicious cycle causing more difficulties.

Jim and his wife tried counseling. They tried weekly sessions of counseling for a year and a half, yet they achieved no significant results. Frustrated, they stopped. About that time, they met a clinician focused on helping people to get results. When Dr. Bob began his consulting work with Jim, he went right after the belief that nothing would work on him. Knowing meta-levels, Bob immediately recognized the importance of dealing with that one first. It rose to the surface as he re-imprinted with some of the childhood roots from which Jim had originally constructed the limiting belief. This enabled Jim to understand where this *idea* came from. From some early intense emotional experiences, he mapped out a meta-understanding that he would always sabotage his relationships with friends.

Then one spring day, Jim told Bob that the old belief about driving away friends "was loosening up." The deframing had started. However, he had experienced some of the old beliefs the previous weekend when he met with some of his peer "computer geeks." After leaving a business meeting, an old internal dialogue nagged at him. "You may have alienated them! You always do this." And that set off some strong negative fearful feelings. So although the limiting belief had been loosened up, and the emotional impact much less, it still ran the programs in his head. Jim was now ready to completely un-install it.

Bob accordingly asked Jim for permission to try out and experiment with the meta-stating process of *Meta-NO-ing* the old limiting belief and *Meta-YES-ing* the new desired belief about his ability to build and maintain relationships. Jim said he was game.

Meta-No-ing and Meta-Yes-ing a Limiting Belief

Jim, when have you ever said *'No!'* to something and *really* meant it?

> "You mean like when I say 'No' to the kids when they do something they shouldn't?"

Yes, I believe that will work.

> "Well just recently I said *no* to my daughter."

How did you do that Jim? *What* did you see, hear, and feel as you expressed that definitive *No*? What tone of voice did you say that in?

> "I experienced saying *'NO!'* high in my chest with a feeling of tightness. How do I do it? Well, like this, ... *'No!'* And I guess it's a pretty firm tone of voice, isn't it?"

Jim, as a meta-stating process, I want you to *bring that 'No!' to bear upon the limiting belief* that says, "You alienate friends." Hear yourself say a strong and firm *"No!"* to that old idea about always alienating friends. Good. Now repeat that meta-level *No!* several more times. How does that feel?

Jim's face flushed as he did this. His head moved forward, and then down firmly as he grunted out a *"No!"* He did so with real firmness in his tonality.

> "This is neat, Bob. It sounds silly that you could bring a *'No!'* that you say to your daughter to bear upon an old limiting belief like this. But, this works, this really works. How neat!"

Then, without any directions from Bob, Jim coached himself to the next state,

> "What do I do when the kids do something good? ... When my little girl does something good, I say, *"Yes, that's right,* you have done good. You have really done well. You can do it!"

He then applied the *"Yes!"* to the desired belief, "I can build friends and relate to them with compassion." He uttered a bold and definitive *Yes* to the idea, "These guys really care about me. I am not alienating them, they really care about me." At this point, Jim started taking notes on a notepad. Then he commented, more to himself than to Bob,

> "I have two powerful resources here. The *No!* I say to the kids, and the *Yes!* I say to the kids."

Bob then decided to test the old limiting belief about him sabotaging relationships through the old belief that he would "come across as arrogant and rude." "Jim, what do you think about the old belief that you have lived with for so long about you always alienating your friends?" Then recalling the experiences of last weekend, he said.

> "These guys really love me. They really love me. They don't believe I am a jerk and arrogant, they really love me."

Interpreting this using the language of the NLP training which Jim had taken, he said,

> "Bob, you just did *an auditory swish* on me with my internal dialogue. Instead of hearing myself say 'I am a jerk' I hear myself saying these guys really love me."

Very insightful! *Meta-NO-ing* an old limiting belief and then *Meta-YES-ing* a new desired belief, essentially gives our brain instructions about where to go—from the old limiting ideas to the new enhancing ones. The auditory swish reflects the meta-state languaging of such.

"This is neat, Jim. You automatically moved from the *Meta-NO-ing* the old belief to *Meta-YES-ing* the new desired belief. I planned to have you do that, but your unconscious mind beat me to the punch and did it automatically." They then checked out some of the previous thoughts-and-feelings that Jim had about his dysfunctional family of origin.

> "I now realize that I may never have had a deep relationship with my family. *And yet* that does not mean that there is something wrong with me. However, I still have a sense of 'aloneness' when I think about it."

"Okay, put that thought aside for just a moment and think of your own family —your son, daughter, and wife." As Jim accessed thoughts of his family, his physiology, breathing, and facial expressions shifted and he seemed to have evoked much more pleasant feelings. Jim thought about his family's nighttime ritual of story telling as the four of them gathered just prior to bedtime. "Now I want you to apply all of these feelings to your thoughts of aloneness that you felt from your family of origin."

Jim immediately brought this *warm and loving family* frame-of-reference and the state that it put him in and applied it to these thoughts. As he did, he became teary eyed, his facial color reddened, his breathing deepened as he generated new neurological connections.

> "It sure is hard to feel alone with a little boy and a little girl on your lap

and your wife sitting beside you. This is *a powerful thing* to apply to aloneness. The aloneness is not congruent with the family I now have. The aloneness is no longer valid. It is not that it is no longer true; it feels more like it no longer matters. My old family does not have the significance it did. I have a sense of connectedness."

The Meta-NO-ing and Meta-YES-ing Pattern
1) Identify a limiting belief and a positive and empowering belief.

Do you have any limiting beliefs that get in your way?

What is one limiting belief that does not serve you at all?

Do you have any beliefs that absolutely sabotage your success, health, or relationships?

What would be a good strong empowering belief that you'd like to believe instead?

What new belief would be more enhancing?

Is it fully ecological? Run a full systems check on the limiting belief. Check for ecology, congruence, health, etc.

- How does this belief limit you?
- How does it get in your way?
- How does it sabotage your success, happiness, resourcefulness, etc.?
- What would you get if you did not have this belief interfering as it does?

Keep meta-modeling the limiting belief in this way to assist the person in deframing it. This will loosen it up and prepare the person for the belief change. Find out how it has not served them well, how it has messed things up, etc. Notice how the person represents the belief, and pace its positive intentions. All of the *ecology* occurs before the belief change process. If we have no innate quality control, we have to check the ecology and make sure we are welcoming in good, robust, and healthy beliefs.

2) Get a good strong representation of saying "No!" to something

What can you think about that you can so *No* to with every fabric in your being?

What enables you to say a definite and unquestionable *"No!"*?

Recall several examples so that you can fully get this resourceful disconfirming state.

- "Would you push a little child in front of an oncoming bus?"
- "Would you do it just for the thrill of it?"

When you elicit a strong *"Hell, no!"* anchor it, invite the person to anchor it by gesture and tone.

Is the person's *"No!"* totally congruent? Does it look, sound, and feel totally congruent?

3) Apply the powerful "No!" to the limiting belief.

Are you ready to refuse, reject, and decommission that old belief?

Then *feel this* (fire anchor for the *No*) and say it to that old limiting belief. Again. Again. Do it until the limiting belief has no room in your life. How's that?

> [If you have any difficulty, re-explore the limiting belief as in the first step.]

What now happens when you apply this *disconfirming "No!"* to the limiting belief?

How congruent are you in saying this powerful *"No!"* to the old belief? Maybe you need this old limiting belief! Yes?

How many more times do you need to say *"No!"* to this limiting belief until you begin to feel that it no longer has any power to run in your mind-body system?

4) Access a powerful "Yes!"

Is there anything that you can say *"Yes!"* to totally, completely, and with every fabric of your being?

Can you think of even one thing that you can utter an incredible *"Yes!"* to?

- Do you want to be healthy, wealthy, and wise?
- Do you love your wife? Your husband?
- Do you adore your children?
- Do you believe in God?
- Do you want to make a significant contribution to the world?
- Do you like sex? Do you enjoy love making?

What gets the strongest and most robust *"Yes!"* from you?

What fully activates your entire mind-body neurology?

How much do you feel this confirmation and validation of *Yes*?

> Anchor with tone, gesture, and voice.

Once you get a good solid *"Yes!"*, reinforce it by asking more about it and amplifying it so that the person experiences a very intense experience of *Yes!* Anchor either with a touch, the way the person says *"Yes!"* and by the person's gesturing of the confirmation. Have them repeat it over and over until they fully access *the confirmation and validating state.* [By the way, be outrageous—do this in public and run it as a Meg Reyan pattern! (From the movie, *Harry meets Sally*)]

5) Apply your Meta-Yes to the desired belief.

What new belief do you want to say *Yes* to?

What is the most succinct and compelling way to express this belief? Have you found the right words for it?

> Keep coaching the person until they are able to express the new belief in a succinct way.

> Keep feeding it back to the person to test its compellingness.
> Get several versions of it to make sure that the person finds
> that the expression truly pulls on him or her.

Do you want to believe this?

Would it enhance your life?

How would it be valuable to you?

How many times do you need to say *Yes!* to it until it feels like you
have welcomed it into your life?

> Keep validating it with a great big *"Yes!"* Do so with intensity
> and congruency.

Would you now want to take this new belief into your future? Into
your tomorrows? Into the weeks and months to come?

Imagine doing that. How does that feel?

Do you like this?

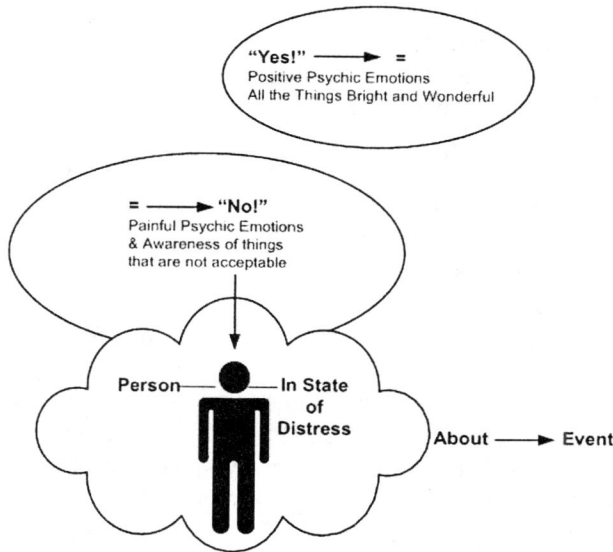

Bandler's Meta-Yesing

As I begin this, I want to issue a disclaimer: Richard Bandler will probably
totally deny what I'm about to write, and deny it like hell. Nevertheless, the
transcript in his work in *Magic in Action* (1984) strikes me as a good example
of *Meta-Yes-ing.* See what you think.

You can see this as you read the section that records his demonstration with
"Susan" regarding *Anticipatory Loss.* Actually I think of this as an excellent
example of his linguistic genius. I say this to his credit. The fact that he did
not have a clue about the structure of what he was doing highlights his
unconscious competence. And when he invented the "sub-modalities" model

to explain things, that actually replicated what happened when he and John Grinder modeled Satir, Perls, and Erickson. At the beginning when he and Grinder modeled the magic and explained what the therapeutic wizards were doing better than they could themselves. Unconscious competence within a system makes it difficult to step outside of it and clearly recognize its structure. This speaks about the need for modelers.

At the end of a Swish Pattern with Susan, Richard had her go back to the old limiting belief she had held about herself. He had previously facilitated a process whereby she created a new way of thinking of herself. She had generated "a picture of you the way you would be if you had made this change" (p. 21).

He then asked her to go back to the old trigger and to let the meta-level representation of her *resourceful self* swish in, the one having made the changes. He asked her to make it a dot in the corner of her trigger picture (the one that had previously triggered her unresourceful sense of loss). Then viewing the composite picture (resource picture hidden inside the trigger picture), he instructed her on how to *run the Swish:*

> "... suddenly the big picture begins to get darker and the other one begins to expand and become brighter until it fills the whole screen. ... you can do it faster than that. There you go. Hurry up. Until you can see yourself the way you would be..." (p. 21)

After instructing her about how to swish her brain, he asked her to do it five more times. "So you go *whoosh.* Do it once. Do it again."

> "What I'd like you to do is go back and do it three times. Only this time I want you to do it real fast. Just whooosh. Don't take any longer than that. That's the amount I want you to take. Do it three times? Okay. Do you like the feeling you get when you see yourself? Confident in the way you would be if you made this change?"

Notice those rhetorical yes questions.

> "Do you *like* the feeling you get?"
> "Do you *feel confident* in the way you would be if you made this change?"

This evoked an affirmation from Susan:

> *"Yes."*

"You like that feeling?"

> [This gets another *Yes* from her to the new confident feeling of her resourceful self.] "Very much."

Eliciting *Meta-Yes-ing* is a great way to *outframe* with a state of validation for any positive change, experience, or emotion. Just ask the person if they like it.

Then question that liking. "So you really like that a lot?" "Nay, you don't. You're just saying that. You don't really want that kind of resourcefulness in your life, do you?"

Do this kind of playful provoking using *rhetorical yes questions* to induce the person into a positive looping that activates lots of repetition. This will drive the validation loop for the new belief or self-image. It's just a pattern. Now, I wonder if you could find a positive use for that?

Summary
- You now know a lot about the structure of excellent beliefs and how to transform the Matrix of an entire belief system.
- Excellence has a structure, one comprised of specific empowering beliefs. The exquisite ability to manage the meta-domain of your beliefs gives you the ability to run your own brain and meta-mind.
- The proof of this pattern lies in testing it in experience. Don't take our word for it, use it with yourself. Give yourself the opportunity to discover the difference that makes a difference between a mere thought and an activated belief.
- Program into your mind and meta-mind all kinds of great ideas that will make your more resourceful. Use your power to confirm, disconfirm, and question ideas.
- Experiment with it conversationally as well. If you are involved in sales, persuasion, education, marketing, personal relationships, or therapy, go ahead and allow yourself to find out just how powerful your *"Yes-ing!"* resource is and what you can use it for.
- Sales people have long known that if they can get seven *Yeses* in a row, that begins to establish a Yes set, which then makes the likelihood of a *no* much less likely. Now we know why, don't we?

Chapter 10

THE STRUCTURE OF UNDERSTANDING

"Understanding is a process that is vital to survival and learning. If you weren't able to make sense out of your experience in some way, you'd be in big trouble. Each of us has about three pounds of gray matter that we use to try to understand the world."
Richard Bandler

- What do you "understand?"
- How do you represent an understanding of something as a movie on the theater of your mind?
- What do you think and/or feel about an understanding that you have?
- Do all of your conceptual understanding of things empower you as a person and enrich your life for high performance?

We know that geniuses, experts, and others who achieve states of excellence, do so through higher levels of *understanding* and *knowledge*. We readily recognize this in the intellectual geniuses: Einstein, Tesla, Aristotle, Freud, etc. Even geniuses in other domains (sports, business, management, finance, therapy, art, etc.) achieve what they do through specialized understandings that set them apart.

In the structure of excellence, we can count on finding higher levels of knowledge and more advanced understandings. Excelling in any given field typically involves comprehensive knowledge of that discipline, new creative models for description and communication, and/or explorations that push the field forward.

If you want to excel in a particular domain, first you will need to attain the necessary base knowledge that allows you to enter the field. This holds true for pilots, architects, dentists, teachers, managers, artists, etc.
- Yet what does "understanding," "knowledge," and "comprehension" mean?

- What do these terms refer to?
- Are they primary level states or meta-states?

In the last three chapters we did not assume that we understood the term "belief." Our curiosity led us to explore *structure:* "How does a thought differ from a belief?" So here too, we will begin with an exploration about what we mean by "understanding." As we here explore, we ask:

- Does "understanding" differ from thought? If so, how?
- How does "knowledge" differ from a belief?
- What is the relationship between "understandings" and "knowledge" from thoughts and beliefs?
- How do we gauge and/or test for knowledge?

The questioning does not end here. Given all of the terms we have for higher level mental phenomena, we can ask similar questions of those terms as well. Once we transcend *thought,* and move into the reality of meta-levels of thoughts, we have a whole range of terms: paradigm, meaning, intention, decision, frame-of-reference, convictions, identity and identification, metaphor, imagination, etc.

By way of contrast, when we lack information and understanding, when comprehension fails and we cannot conceptualize, then we experience states that prevent us from attaining excellence. Ignorance of basic data undermines excellence. So can the inability to use certain intelligences or forms of reasoning. Similarly, lacking a structuring paradigm so that we have too much data begets confusion. In engineering excellence, we have to have enough background knowledge and understanding to talk intelligently about the domain.

These values and benefits of *understanding* as a meta-level state enriches our appreciation about the importance of comprehending the structure of knowledge. Valuing understanding is a good thing and does not in itself lead to dogmatism, arrogance, or closed-mindedness. Knowing something and also knowing that we do not know it all, and never will empowers us to stay open, to take a more modest position about our knowledge. As we frame whatever we know as only partial and time-dated we recognize that all of our knowing is fallible (liable to err).

The Structure of "Knowledge" and Understanding
In the early days of the history of NLP, Richard Bandler developed the *From Confusion to Understanding* pattern. Highlighting the structure of understanding, this pattern seeks to move us from the state of confusion to a state of understanding. In *Using Your Brain For a Change* (1985) Bandler presented the *Confusion To Understanding* pattern as a "sub-modality" pattern. He used it to recode disorganized or confused thinking so that we can organize

what we know.

The basic idea was this: understanding is a state and has a discoverable structure. If we have plenty of data and still do not understand, the problem lies in *how we organize the information.* We "know" lots of things, but we do not have our "knowledge" ordered in a useful and useable form. Rather we feel "confused." Ideas, thoughts, feelings, guidelines, etc. all *"fused"* together (*con-*). Therefore we don't know what to do. We don't "understand." How do we turn disorganized data about which we feel confusion into an structurally organized form that enables us to understand?

The pattern purportedly enables a person to create the state of "understanding" regarding a subject, topic, or concept by directly utilizing the critical "sub-modalities" that make up understanding and mapping them directly over to the content of the confusion. This chases the "fused" thoughts away and gives order to the mind, or "understanding."

But does this work? Can we so shift around these complex *knowing states* just using "sub-modalities?" Well, if you're really good at reframing and can designate that a given "sub-modality" will stand for "meaningful" and "well ordered," and *if it happens to be a sufficient metaphor that fits* with the particular kinds of understandings in a given field, and if the person buys all of this and so constructs his or her inner representations it has a possibility of working.

Of course, that's a lot of *ifs.* Having unmasked the nature of "sub-modalities," it is probably clear that just making a picture bright or close or 3-dimensional may not *stand for,* and symbolically represent, the right kind of frame to turn chaotic data into a well formed understanding. It could. But it is a shot in the dark and not a predictable response.

It was this very pattern that set me on my exploration about "sub-modalities" in the first place. It happened when I began inquiring about the experiences that NLP trainers had with the *Confusion to Understanding* pattern. From that dialogue, I discovered that very few individuals found the pattern helpful. More startling, I found that nobody used it on a regular basis as their strategy for understanding new things. "What gives?"
- *If* this pattern moves one from confusion to understanding, why do those of us who know this pattern not use it more often?
- Why have we not made this pattern our *natural* way to learn and organize our learnings?

Taking my cue from this, I began re-examining the structure and presuppositions of the *Confusion to Understanding* pattern. This led me to entirely rethink the pattern and its dependence upon "sub-modalities." I also began noticing my own strategy moving from confusion states into states of understanding.

Out of this exploration, I discovered that the pattern presupposes several things that just do not hold up under scrutiny. I found out that while *confusion* may occur at a primary level and at meta-levels (i.e., the confusion of levels), *understanding* inevitably always involves meta-levels. We have to go meta to truly "understand" conceptual ideas. We have to *go meta* to organize our sensory representations and how we language or symbolize the knowledge. It is the very move of doing that which *formats* the knowledge in a way that creates a higher level sense of understanding.

The Confusion to Understanding Pattern
Do you know the traditional pattern? You can find it in in *Using Your Brain —For a Change* (1985) and *An Insider's Guide to Sub-Modalities* (1988). This contrastive analysis pattern works by first thinking of something that you *understand* and then of something that you don't understand but which you have enough information to understand. It's something that you feel *confused* about.

Once you identify the two experiences, the focus shifts to eliciting all of the critical and distinguishing "sub-modalities" between the two. We keep asking, *How* do I know that I understand or that I feel confused? The pattern presupposes that the difference will be in the cinematic features of the two representations. When you get that information, you can *map-over* from one experience to the other, from the desired experience (understanding) to the undesired one (confusion). This enables you to recode your "confusion" using the "sub-modalitiy" distinctions which give form to your "understanding" state. And that, of course, assumes that all understandings are the same.

Now undoubtedly, some cinematic features will contribute to a clearer understanding. Generally, a fuzzy and distant picture will not help us with understanding as much as when we construct a clear and close picture. A muffled and blurred internal voice also typically does not facilitate understanding. Yet a clear, coherent, and compelling internal voice might. So, *the better* our representational codings for a particular experience, *the better* our clarity and understanding. Yet, we can also clearly represent data or ideas and still lack understanding. *Clear description* occurs at a different logical level than *clear understanding*. Confusing the levels of description and evaluation falls victim to an error of logical typing.

When "Understanding" Goes Meta
On my first trip to Moscow I stopped at Frankfort Germany to switch planes.

Because that was my first time in Frankfort as well, I felt confused. "Where do I go?" I wondered. "Where am I?" I don't understand where I'm suppose to go to catch the next plane." Catching this internal conversation, I realized that here was a confused state that I wanted to turn into understanding. That led me to wonder:

- How do I represent an airport in general?
- How do I represent a specific airport?
- How do I know where to go when I land at a given airport?
- Which airports do I "know" and "understand" well?
- Which one's do I feel "confused" about?
- How do I tell the difference?

At that time I frequently flew to Salt Lake City and Denver and had a good understanding of those airports. Feeling confused in Frankfort I did a contrastive analysis of the airports. That revealed that I had very similar pictures of the two airports in terms of the cinematic distinctions of closeness, brightness, and clarity. I coded each of them in color, 3-D, and life size. I also represent the sounds about the same—the sounds of people going here and there. I only noticed one difference. I heard the speaker's voice at the Frankfort International airport spoke with a German accent. I had similar kinesthetics for both—the sense of walking, moving, looking about and noticing the smells in an airport.

- How do I *understand* one airport and feel *confused* about another?
- What distinguishes these levels of "understandings?"

I had a mental diagram in my head of the Salt Lake City and Denver airports. I could see on the screen of my mind a picture or diagram of each airport's layout. At a meta-level I knew the overall configuration of the sprawling airport building—and the five terminals at Salt Lake with the connecting gates for flights. This allows me to recognize the *relationships* between "A," "B," "C," "D," and "E" corridors and how they relate to the terminal. What if I now impose that structure onto how I think about Frankfort so that I could then *feel* that *I understand* where I am and where to go? No, that wouldn't work. Frankfort has a different structure. Such mapping would not create useful or accurate understanding.

In every airport that I know and understand, I have an organizing structure in my head, a mental configuration of how the hallways and gates relate to each other. The content of that configuration allows me to know how the various elements and components fit into the whole. This gives me an *understanding* about how it all fits together, the relationship between the gates, the sequences needed to move from one area to another, etc. In other words, the meta-level understanding about the whole illustrates the Batesonian concept of *"the pattern that connects."* Meta-level content forms and orders my understanding. My understanding emerges from a formatting above the specific details that holds the whole together.

What does this mean? It means that *to understand we have to go meta.* We have to go meta because we need a meta-level organizing structure or schema. Then we can understand relationships, ordering, and sequencing. We see this even in Bandler's (1985) original chapter on this subject, *Understanding Confusion:*

> "Confusion presupposes that you have a lot of data, but it's not yet organized in a way that allows you to understand it." (p. 83)
>
> 'It makes sense that if you have a large movie with a narrative sound track, you'll understand something better than if all you have is a small, silent, still picture. You have much more information, *and it's organized in a way that you can comprehend it.*" (p. 86, italics added)
>
> "It's not that something is missing; it's just that *what you have is poorly organized.* You all know *much* more than you think you do. ... Being able to use your mind means being able to access, *organize* and use what you already have." (p. 87)
>
> "For my partner, confusion was a close panorama. So much was happening so close around her that she couldn't take it all in. She had to slow it down, and then physically back up and see it at a distance to understand it." [She had to *go meta* to it] (p. 89)
>
> "My partner is a scientist. When he's confused, he just sees movies of things happening—what he calls 'raw data.' When he starts to understand, he sees *little diagrams superimposed on the movies.*" [A meta-structure about the data.] (p. 89)
>
> "The healthiest thing you can do ... is to become confused, and (while) many people complain about how confusing I am, they don't yet realize that *confusion is the doorway to a new understanding.* **Confusion is an opportunity to rearrange experience and organize it in a different way** than you normally would. That allows you to learn to do something new and to see and hear the world in a new way." (p. 95, bold emphasis added)

Linguistically, the term *understanding* is a nominalization. A verb (to understand, comprehend) has been turned into a noun-like term. It's also a *multiordinal term* (Korzybski) because we can apply it to itself as we are here seeking to understand "understanding." When a word can be used on itself and used at multiple levels, its meaning is general and not specific. As a nominalization we have an unspecified verb hidden inside that needs to be unmasked. The verb here is "to understand." So we ask:

> Understand what?
> Understand when?
> Understand how?

> Understand at what level?
> Understand according to what standards and criteria?
> Understand using what format or structure?

Understanding when we don't Understand

Consider the opposites of understanding: *misunderstanding and not-understanding.* How can we *not* understand and how do we pull off the experience of *mis*understanding?

How can I *mis*understand? I misunderstand when my pictures move too fast or too slow or when I see them as too dim, unfocused, or distorted. If I hear my sound representations as too loud, garbled, fast, etc., or my kinesthetic sensations as too strong, they may then overwhelm me with temperature, pressure, movement, etc. thereby preventing me from understanding. I can also *mis*understand if I organize the details with an untrue structure. If I treat the gates at the Denver airport as if they have the same relationship to each other as do the San Francisco airport. I misunderstand when I use a mathematical formula for a chemical one.

How can I **not** understand? I can lack the necessary information. That would cause me to *not* understand. It takes sufficient information to understand. Yet merely having enough information does not do the trick. With sufficient, or too much information, I might experience con-fusion [the *fusing* "with"] of data. When everything merges, we cannot see the pattern that connects.

We need a higher level pattern. We need an organizing structure or schema to understand, hence the term, to *stand under*. Mere clarity of data, which we create using the most appropriate "sub-modalities," does not create the gestalt of "understanding." This explains why merely having clear and appropriate "sub-modality" codings of an airport will not give understanding of it. For that we need a higher level representation, a configuration (i.e., picture, diagram, even "feel") for how the information fits together and relates to each other. *We have to go meta to understand.*

Going Meta to "Make Sense"

Clarity of representation at the primary level obviously helps significantly with our knowledge of the territory. But to "make sense" of lots of data we typically need higher meta-level representations. This domain of consciousness involves higher or meta-levels symbols (i.e., language, mathematics, etc.). This gives us two levels of "sense." We have primary descriptive *senses* and a meta-sense of language for "making" sense of things.

At meta-levels, we use words that order, structure, format, etc. to understand relationships, sequences, processes, cause-effect interactions, systemic loops, etc. Here also we use *metaphors*. Metaphorical structures play such an inherent role in "thinking" that we typically do not even notice the entirely metaphorical structure of language itself. Lakoff and Johnson (1980) noticed this in such seemingly propositional terms as up/down, in/out, etc. From this, Lakoff has, along with Langacker (1987, 1991) and others, moved beyond the out-dated Transformational/Generative Grammar of Chomsky to the current Cognitive Linguistic models. [*Metaphor* was added as a missing distinction to the Meta-Model in *Communication Magic* 2000.]

The Meta-Move in "Understanding"
To understand, we have to step aside from all of the data before us and make a meta-move so that we can think *about* the data. From that higher perspective we can see the whole including relationships between the parts and the whole. This enables us to think systemically.

Interesting enough, Bandler and MacDonald (1988) knew this and wrote about it in these very terms. The problem was that they did not apply it to the Confusion to Understanding pattern. In describing the Swish Pattern, MacDonald wrote:

> "Being dissociated from the way you want to be also puts you in *a meta position* relative to the change. Not only does seeing yourself having made the change feel good, but you can feel good *about* feeling good [a meta-state]. It is this meta position that makes the image of how you want to behave an impelling one and sets the direction for a whole new set of behaviors that will move you toward its fulfillment.
>
> A critical element in using the swish pattern effectively is *the structure* of the transition to the feelings of the resource state. In the standard model Richard demonstrated, brightness is used to diminish unwanted feelings and to simultaneously intensify wanted feelings. At the same time the associated image is being dimmed (diminishing feelings). The *transitional structure* has to work that way." (p. 63, italics added)

The structure of the Swish pattern itself empowers us to *understand* how to send our brain to a more resourceful referent. The structure itself (resource picture hidden in trigger picture that then explodes to fill the screen of the mind) organizes and formats the details. Merely having lots of information about our unresourceful self and about our resourceful self does not suffice. What does transform involves *understanding* how to move from one position, and that understanding occurs at a meta-level.

The Going Meta to Understand Pattern
•   How can we learn to understand something new?
•   How can we move from list knowledge (knowing lots of facts and details) to a higher level understanding involving a more

comprehensive knowledge about processes, principles, mechanisms, relationships, etc.?

1) Identify the domain of knowledge you want to understand but which you currently feel confused about.

What field of knowledge do you feel confused about?

How much information do you have about that field?

Are you basically conversant with the facts and data of the field?

What do you specifically want to understand?

It really helps to narrow your focus to a specific section or area of a field so that you work with a manageable amount of information. Have you done that? Don't go for an entire field like physics, mathematics, linguistics. Rather, go for a smaller chunk: nominalizations, Kuhn's model for paradigm shifting, Ellis' ABCs model of emotions, how to repair a bicycle, how to remember effectively, algebra #101, marine biology of killer whales, etc.

2) Specify the knowledge and skills you need to understand.

What principles, language, background, experience, etc. will you need to work knowledgeably in this field?

Have you enumerated a list of the variables and elements?

What facts will give you sufficient information to feel confused?

Confusion comes first, then understanding.

3) Explore the organizing principles and metaphors of those who know the field.

Do you know an expert or effective teacher who understands what you don't that you could question and model?

How detailed oriented are you?

How easily can you shift to seeking a global perspective of things? [Confusion is often having too much information and lots of irrelevant data.]

How does the expert do it? How does the expert transform confusion by organizing and structuring his or her knowledge?

Are you ready to move from the *fusion* of data to creating a sorting and separating structure?

Do you have a meta-frame that you can now meta-detail?

What higher level formats hold and categorize this information?

How does an effective person know what to do at what time?

4) Design your own configuration for structuring the knowledge.

Have you tried on various formats and structures?

Which one seems to work best with the domain of data?

What other metaphors can you play with that might reformulate the data of the field to give you more control over it?

What structures, diagrams, and formulas do you know from other fields that you might apply to this domain (i.e., a musical score for emotions)?

Understanding and Domains of Knowledge

What *domains of knowledge* do you know? What knowledge domains have you received training, education, and experience in?

Mechanics	Retail Selling	Cooking
Computers	Insurance	Wines
Teaching	Real Estate	History
Law	Health & Fitness	Geography
Medicine	Baseball	Government
Bicycling	Disney World	Star Trek
Dogs	Cats	Gardening
Psychology	Meta-Programs	Language
Hypnosis	Relationships	Pacing

Most of us have numerous knowledge bases wherein we have some expertise. Just consider some of the things you have studied or experienced, and you will begin to realize that you may have scores and scores of such domains of knowledge of which you can speak intelligently. One domain of knowledge that you uniquely have, and about which you, and you only, can speak authoritatively—your personal history.

• How do you know that you know a given area of knowledge?

• How do you code and store this body of knowledge?

• Where do you store these domains?

NLP authors Lostere and Malatesta (1989) speak to this subject and attempt to squash understandings together.

> *"Collapsing anchors* is an excellent tool for integrating two or more bodies of information or systems of knowledge. When utilizing collapsing anchors for this purpose, the therapist elicits from the client experiences which are representative of each content distinction, establishes an anchor for each and integrates the anchors. ... It is important to address the issue of integrating knowledge versus translating knowledge. We believe that the integration of knowledge vastly improves effectiveness and choices..." (p. 146)

These authors illustrate by using two therapy models, T.A .(Transactional Analysis) and NLP (p. 147). In a demonstration, they asked a person to make an internal representation of each of these *fields*, set an anchor for each and collapsed the anchors. But this doesn't work. After all,

How do I represent an entire domain like NLP?

How do I know and represent such?

How do I organize, structure, and format my knowledge base of NLP?

How *could* I represent such?

With these two *bodies of information* we have two meta-level domains of knowledge, yet we have nothing *above* them that unites or integrates them. Collapsing them could be a useful experiment for generating wild creativity, but not for clarity of understanding. To the meta-level of these knowledge domains, we need to move up to another meta-level to establish that larger frame of reference. It is the higher meta-frame as a metaphor, understanding, concept, etc. that will unify the two.

Domain of Understanding Exercise
1) Pick out some domains of knowledge

> What domain of knowledge do you have?
>
> Pick a domain of knowledge from your learning history that's part of your "library of references" which you use as resource information.

2) Identify your way of representing this information.

> What is your mental movie like?
>
> What do you mainly use—pictures, sounds, somatic body feelings, words, conceptual categories, diagrams, etc.?
>
> If you have a listing menu, how do you represent it?

3) Specifically identify the meta-levels within your knowledge base.

> If you picked baseball, for example, you probably begin (at a primary level) with a diamond, the four bases, perhaps a movie of a game in action, players, etc.
>
> What about the "rules" of the game?
>
> How do you represent that conceptual realm?
>
> What about specific teams, players, dates, etc.?
>
> If you picked something more conceptual, like NLP, what do you start with at the primary level?
>
> Do you think about *neurology* by imagining a human body and nervous system?
>
> Do you think about *linguistics* by hearing words?
>
> What structures format the different sub-models in NLP?
>
> If you picked computers, do you begin with seeing a computer or feeling a keyboard?
>
> Or do you see the internal mother board?
>
> How do you represent hardware, software, programming, applications, etc.?

4) Specify the pattern or model that connects.

> What is the pattern that connects these things which allows you to know, and to know that you know you know?
>
> What meta-level distinctions allow you to effectively use your knowledge?

Momentarily give yourself permission to let the pattern that connects fade out and notice what happens to your knowledge domain. Now reclaim that pattern. How was that?

Obviously, representing and anchoring *a domain of knowledge* represents a meta-level experience itself. It differs radically from representing and anchoring a fear object, a pleasure, or any other primary level experience. Why? Because language is a meta-representation, a metaphor, a representation of experience. It is a powerful organizational tool that creates clarity and understanding. That's why to create understanding we mostly look to higher level language.

This is where the Meta-Model comes in as a great tool. And even though it was based on Transformational Grammar that Chomsky disowned and disproved in 1976 (the year after the publication of *The Structure of Magic*), today *Cognitive Linguistics* by Langacter, Lakoff, and others continue the search for structure. In fact, I like this model better because of its use of representational space ("mental space," Fauconnier) onto which we project our understandings. Categories and classes of information provide a knowledge base for constructing internal pictures, sounds, sensations, etc.

Lakoff and Johnson (1980), and Lakoff (1987) highlight the central value of *prototypical categories* from Rosch as the natural way we "make sense" of things.
> — Think of a prototypical dog.
> — Think of a prototypical chair.
> — Think of a prototypical house.

As you do, you do a transderivational search to your domain of knowledge, do you not? You go in and then *up* to that meta-level where you store your categories, classes, and knowledge base which, in turn, governs and organizes your experience.

Stepping into Another's Understanding
The structure of *understanding* typically involves frames-of-references and meta-levels. As we discover the various kinds of structures we use to format different kinds of information, we can then use a variety of formats for expanding, experimenting, and playing around with new and different ways to understand things. This insight also gives us the ability to begin to elicit understanding structures and metaphors that others use. Doing this provides a streamlined way to engage in accelerated learning.

If my current *way of understanding* (i.e., structuring and formatting details) does not seem to lead to clarity or high level skill, wouldn't it be a sign of wisdom to inquire of an expert regarding how he or she thinks and understands the field? We could then take on his or her way of understanding. What does that say about how to very deeply pace someone's model of the world? Trying on another's *understanding structures* give us other ways to learn and to "understand"—to *stand under* them, supportively, as we listen and enter into their structured reality.

In modeling the strategies of genius, Dilts (1994, 1995) not only described the domains of knowledge that informed Freud, Leonardo de Vinci, Nikola Tesla, Aristotle, Sir Arthur Conan Doyle's Sherlock Holmes, Disney, Wolfgang Mozart, and Einstein, but also the meta-levels involved in such knowing. Using "Neuro-Logical Levels" he explored what they knew and understood about many things at various levels. Using the Meta-States model, we would also want to inquire, "And what do you know about that knowledge?"

Dr. Martin Roberts (1998, 1999) brought up this subject of *background knowledge* in his articles on modeling in *Rapport.* In thinking about modeling an expert pilot, what do you need to know? What do you have to know? After you get his strategy for piloting the plane, even his supporting beliefs and values, how it affects his identity, and any other facets that may touch upon his sense of spirituality, would you not desperately want to know *what he knows about the field of aeronautics?* Would that not be important? Without some insight into that background knowledge—that meta-level frame-of-reference, I would not want to attempt to replicate the pilot's skills.

And what about the non-propositional and non-verbal background knowledge of a pilot's development and training of his or her vestibular system (inner ear balance)? This is the system that controls our sense of orientation, direction, balance, etc., and it plays no small role in the skill and knowledge of flying a plane.

The Multi-Ordinal Nature of Mental Phenomena
All thoughts are not equal because they do not occur at the same level. With our thinking and understanding occurring at different levels we invent labels of different terms. Each term offers a little different view of these facets of meaning and understanding. Each of these mental phenomena is a different facet to the same diamond of experience and so sheds a little different light on things. We can think, believe, value, know, understand, intend, decide, value, identify, etc. These mental or conceptual powers enable us to build thoughts at many different levels. Failing to notice the levels is to confuse the levels which creates confusion and category errors.

All of these terms are also *multi-ordinal* which adds to the complexity since they can and do refer to themselves, and to each other. With so many terms which lack specifically, we have to specify *the level of abstraction* at which they occur in order to determine their meaning.

Because we can *think* about our *thinking*, this is a multi-ordinal term. As we think and understand at multiple levels, with each meta-jump we create multiple kinds and qualities of understandings. In Meta-States we have applied this (the levels of abstraction) to the process of thinking and to the products of that process to more specifically identify the vast array of conceptual terms and to operationalize these terms. These terms also identify the many kinds of "logical levels" of meta-phenomenon that we can and do create.

We do this, as we use the Meta-Model, to de-nominalize our terms and make them more precise and accurate. This lets us speak more precisely about all of the mental phenomena that we experience at meta-levels. In Figure 10, start at the bottom of the chart and move upward.

Level One: Sensory-based "thoughts" / "understandings"—the Movie.
>   The language of thought consists of our sensory representational systems that enables us to experience an inner movie in our mind. We encode and construct our internal sense of reality by mapping the territory in terms of sights, sounds, sensations, smells, tastes, etc. that we put into the movie. Here "thoughts" occur as senses, awareness, intuition, knowing, and feeling.

Level Two: "Thoughts" / "Understandings" as Words in the Movie.
>   When we move up a level, we encode level one "thoughts" using *words*. If we have a snapshot or movie of a strawberry, we can now use the word "strawberry" to stand for and refer to all of the sights, sounds, sensations, smells, and tastes that comprise that referent. This meta-representational system operates as a secondary experience, thoughts of our first thoughts. "Thoughts" here take the form of ideas, knowing, understanding, representations, etc.

Level Three: "Words" about Words— Abstract Terms.
>   Move up yet another level and we can put a term like *strawberry* into numerous higher level abstract categories: fruit, food, plant, nourishment, organic life, red objects, cultivated plants, things that weigh less than a pound, squashable items, etc. The *abstract category* that we use, invent, or discover gives us additional ways to think about the item. As such, we map our previous map and generalize, delete, distort, conceptualize, etc. "Thoughts" here show up as beliefs, meanings, understandings, knowledge, concepts, conceptualizations, abstractions, values, decisions, etc.
>   *Beliefs* arise when we validate a previous thought confirming that it is

valid, true, accurate, or real.

Values are beliefs about importance and significance.

Decisions involve choosing one thing above another, saying no to one thing, yes to another, "cutting off" alternatives.

Understanding involves creating a framed or structured format that enables us to relate the variables and elements of something.

Ideas involve inwardly "seeing" a concept.

Maps refers to constructing, formatting, and framing one thing in terms of another.

Meaning involves "holding" something "in mind" so that we link one thing with another.

Level Four: Abstractions about Abstractions.

With our self-reflexivity, abstracting never stops. It's an unending process and so it leads to ever increasing levels of abstraction and complexity and builds up our matrix of frames about a thousand things.

Convictions are beliefs about our beliefs.

Domains of Understanding are areas of knowledge.

Paradigms are complex models that govern a field.

Belief systems refer to the embedded belief frames about other beliefs.

Frames of reference refers to our referent event that we use as a benchmark for understanding something.

Identifications refer to our identity beliefs.

Figure 10:1
The Meta or "Logical Levels" in our Matrix

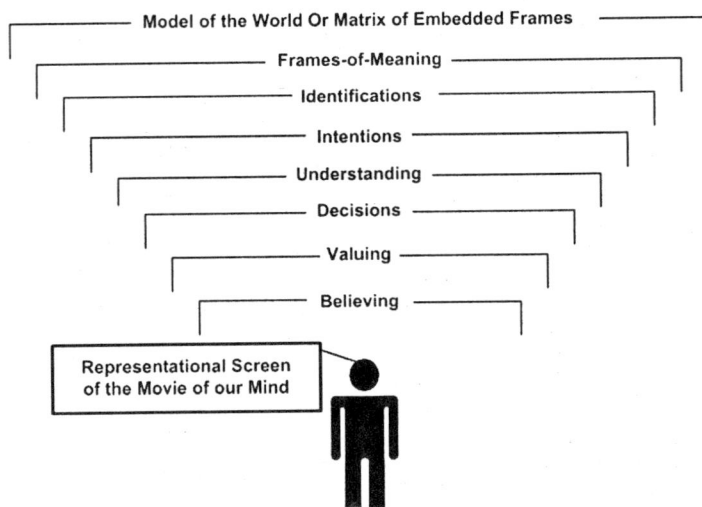

Model of the World Or Matrix of Embedded Frames
Frames-of-Meaning
Identifications
Intentions
Understanding
Decisions
Valuing
Believing

Representational Screen of the Movie of our Mind

Summary

- To cognitively and conceptually "understand," we have to *go meta*. We move above the details to organize them within a higher structure. This enables us to then meta-detail.

- It takes a lot of data to become confused. Once confused, we have to go meta. Gathering more and more information without knowing how to organize it keeps us at a clinician level, rather than an executive level.

- This ability to take charge of the *organizing process* that governs "understanding" is the essence of genius. Because now you have an enriched ability to organize and reorganize information using various categories and patterns so that you can incorporate your valuing, believing, identifying, deciding, etc. in such a way that your mapping truly serves you well.

- Modeling the structure of experience necessitates that we develop expertise at both the representational level *and* the meta-levels of frames. When we combine both and sequence them in effective patterns (e.g., the Movie Rewind pattern, the Swish Pattern), we develop higher level *understanding* about how to run our own brains.

- Even when we structure our thoughts with the distinctive cinematic features of our representations ("sub-modalities"), we do so at a meta-level of awareness. This separates those who can operate at higher levels from those who get caught up in the details and don't know what to make of things.

- Genius in every field moves above details and constructs a synthesizing perspective or a higher paradigm to unite and structure things. The larger picture enables one to see the details afresh. A holistic meta-detailing perspective nourishes a new way of thinking about details. It elicits metaphors, models, theorizing structure, etc.

Chapter 11

THE STRUCTURE OF
VALUES AND VALUING

- How do we *value* and *give importance* to something?
- What ideas and experiences do you consider *important?*
- How much importance do you give to such values as achievement, power, love, affection, spirituality, honor, sex, family, success, health, or fitness?
- What do you value as highly significant and meaningful in your work, hobbies, relationships, etc.?
- What do you value about love (or curiosity, learning, achievement, or any other value)?

These questions direct our attention to an extremely important and determinative process in our experiences—*the meta-level of valuing* and giving importance. From this *valuing process* comes the nominalized term that plays such a pervasive role in our lives, *"values."*

At first glance, a "value" sounds like *a thing.* It is not a "thing." *"Values"* do not even exist in the world "out there," they exist only in human minds and hearts in the world of communication. They emerge from how we mentally and emotionally give worth and significance to something. *Valuing* arises from how we attribute importance, meaning, worth, significance, importance, etc. to things. This makes valuing (and hence, "values"), a *meta-function.* [In this chapter, I put "values" in quotes to highlight the care we need to give to this term.]

The Importance of Importance
An experience is a set of actions, reactions, events, words, feelings, thoughts, responses, etc.—the raw data of the experience. Yet we inevitably and inescapably e*valu*ate experiences. What does this entail? In the process of

*evalu*ating we find, give, or create value. In evaluating, we discern that something is valuable and important or without value and unimportant. In this way, the structure of our experiences inherently contains our valuing and dis-valuing, hence "values." Our "values" are critical due to the role they play in meta-programs, emotions, motivation, congruence, success, mastery, self-control, etc.

Meta-Programs: We talk a lot about these internal evaluative phenomena ("values") because these are the processes that *drive, control, govern, and regulate* our lives. We could even say that we live in order to fulfill our "values." Ultimately we move toward and away from those experiences, events, ideas, and people that we value or dis-value. And because every driving meta-program which governs our perception involves values we literally see the world in terms of what we value and dis-value. These meta-level phenomena start out as meta-states and then they coalesce so that they become incorporated in our neurology and in that way, they "get in our eyes."

Emotions: Nor does the role of these values end there. Our *emotions* (another nominalization which speaks about the *somatizing of our thoughts)* function according to how we *value* and *dis-value.* When our experience in the world of things, events, and people confirms and fulfills what we *value as important* —we experience "positive" feelings.

At the subjective level, we experience these "good" emotions as the positive feelings of joy, satisfaction, completeness, safety, dignity, love, appreciation, compassion, excitement, desire, etc. In this, the good feelings provide us a *reflection* and cue about the fulfillment of our values. Such emoting registers the relative sway or weight between two things—between our model of the world and our experience of the world. Like a scale tipping one way or the other depending on the relative match or mismatch between our model of the world is either confirmed or dis-confirmed. As this happens what we experience as our emotions is the *tilting* toward either fulfillment and accomplishment of our values or the lack of such

Conversely, when our experience in the world of things, events, and people disconfirms, fails to fulfill, and even violates what we value as important—we experience "negative" emotions. It's at that point that we feel upset, angry, afraid, disgusted, frustrated, stressed, discounted, unfulfilled, threatened, etc. These emotions indicate that the *tilt* has shifted in the reverse way and indicates that our experience of the world does not match up to our expectations and model of the world.[1] Later we'll see the critical value in motivation, personality, being congruent, and other facets important to developing expertise.

Valuing in the Structure of Excellence

In the structure of excellence is the ability to distinguish different levels of "values" as we discriminate between *what* we value and *how* we value. In excellence we not only understand higher principles and processes that we value, we also structure our understandings of those valuable meanings. Doing this creates the states and empowering beliefs that positively motivate and drive our passion for excellence and keeps us focused.

We value this as important because it structures our focusing powers. Excellence emerges from the power of focus that allows us to be of one mind in our engagements. The laser beam focuses on a synthesizing vision (the meta-frame of importance) to maintain our value frames and solidify our focus. This can be dangerous. If our focus is unbalanced we could undermine the strategy of excellence and become unbalanced and unecological. We avoid this by developing a crystal clear and balanced focus regarding what we deem significant.

With this in mind, we now focus on *the valuing process* itself. In this chapter we will specify a process for detecting, creating, constructing, orienting, and prioritizing our valuing so that it healthily contributes to go for excellence and develop a healthy personal genius state.

Where do "Values" fit into NLP?

Where do we put "values" in the NLP model? Given that we understand that the nominalization ("values") comes from the verb which points to the process of *valuing*—where do we put "values" in the NLP model?

- Are "values" simply internal representations at the primary level?
- Are "values" a higher "logical level" to the movies that we play in our inner theater?
- How do "values" relate to beliefs? If I *believe* in my *values*, does that put beliefs above *values?* If I *value* my *beliefs,* does that put *values* above beliefs?
- Are "values" constructs of "sub-modalities?"
- How do *values* relate to meta-programs? Do we use our *values* as part of our perceptual filters for sorting information? If so, how do *values* differ from meta-programs?
- What relationship do *values* have to meta-states? Does our thoughts-and-feelings of *valuing* operate as a state of consciousness above other states? If so, how do values differ from meta-states?

Positive and Negative Emotions and "Values"

When we experience *positive* and *negative* emotions, we actually experience somatic (or body) signals about our valuing. *Good feelings* emerge when we feel that our values are being fulfilled; *bad feelings* emerge when we feel that our values are being violated. Good feelings are the signs and expressions of the somatic and personal energy to *keep doing whatever we have done that brings about the fulfillment of our valuing.* As "go" or "keep on going" signals, this explains why we experience most positive emotions as gentle, less energetic, and easier to "live" in. Only in a few positive emotions (i.e., ecstasy, total surprise, etc.) do we experience them as very strong and intense.

Bad feelings have a different function and feel. They generate an *emergency kind of energy and response.* Negative emotions grab our attention, jarringly knock us on the side of the head, and alert us to an immediate and unacceptable danger. They alert us with bells and alarms and lights, *"Something has gone wrong!"* "What we value and hold as meaningful is in immediate danger!" This explains why the *"Stop! Look! Listen! Do something!"* message of our negative emotions can create so much intense somatic energy. They provide a tremendous *power surge* within—good energy for the immediate moment and for the short-run, but not the kind of energy to "live" in.

Positive emotions operate more like the acceleration pedal in a car. They give a *"Yes" signal* for continuing and sustaining our present direction. Negative emotions operate more like the *"No!" signal* of the brakes. With them all the dashboard lights light up and sound off alerting us to the fact that *something is wrong.*

Positive and negative, go and stop, pleasure and pain—we need all of these energies and signal systems to operate productively, maximally, and healthily. We need them and even though they serve different purposes. To that end we have to sequence them properly.

To drive down the highway of life without any brakes or warning system invites disaster. It's not a smart way to go. We need negative emotions to alert us to dangers that threaten what we value. Yet to drive through life by riding the brakes, and only looking for warnings, invites a cynical attitude, burnout, a missing of the journey, and tremendous wear and tear on the engine.

Neurologically, our nervous system innately moves us *toward* what we value and *away from* what we do not value (or *dis*-value). Our feelings of *attraction* and *aversion* reflects the things (ideas, experiences, people, etc.) that we have decided to value. This sets up the *value propulsion system* that our emotions reflect.[2]

Backtracking Emoting to their Source in our Valuing
Where do these *"Go For It"* and *"Stop, Look, and Listen"* signal systems of our positive and negative emotions come from?

They come from our *thoughts*. We construct them over time via our thinking, reasoning, representing, and evaluating as we map the territory. This explains how and why positive and negative emotions may become misaligned, distorted, and irrational. *Emotions* only reflect the *e-valuational* thinking that we do as we move through the world valuing and dis-valuing. They're only as good as the *quality* of our thinking and perceiving.

To the extent that we have *valued* something in a distorted way, or in a way that undermines our well-being, health, or productiveness, our emotions (or more accurately our *emoting*) will not operate as a useful *rewarding and warning system*. Emotions do *not* have an inherent rightness or wrongness. Nor do they give us accurate or useful information about what exists "out there" in the world. That's why we should *not* use them as information gathering tools. They are not designed for that. The quality of our emoting depends upon the *thinking* that generates our valuing and dis-valuing in the first place. They rather reflect a contrastive comparison between our model of the world (our evaluative judgments) and the world that we experience in our body in interaction with people and things. Emotions are designed as signals of the interface between the "values" in our Matrix of frames and the experiential world we live in.

As adults, we often have "values" driving and governing our lives which reflect childish or adolescent thinking rather than up-to-date adult "values." Such valuing will inevitably set up an internal model of the world and corresponding expectations that will have difficulty finding a match in the experiential world.

"I must be first." "If you're not right, it means you're stupid." "Any driver who pulls in front of me quickly is asking for a fight."

In this, our *valuing* reflects another kind of *meaning-making* or believing. In valuing, we think, represent, and conceptualize something (a person, place, thing, idea, etc.) as having worth and value, as holding importance and significance, or of having no value to us. The thinking involved in *valuing* does not differ from any other kind of thinking. It is preeminently neuro-semantic in nature and so we experience our "values" as emotions and intuitive knowledge.

Recognizing and Appreciating "Values"
We learn our "values" by constructing them over time from how we think about various experiences, people, events, concepts, etc. By valuing them as contributing to our experiences of pain or pleasure, we learn *what* and *how* to value. When we ask, "What do you value?" we are essentially asking,

"What do you believe brings pleasure to you, increases your effectiveness, adds worth and significance to your life, etc.?"

Later we nominalize this mapping by succinctly summarizing such thinking, believing, and values as "values" and "value systems." As nominalizations, these terms are deceptive because they invite us to think of them as static. Yet within these statical terms is the valuing process of what we think will contribute to our well-being, safety, excitement, and pleasure. We, conversely, *dis-value* what we believe will bring us pain, illness, hurt, danger, threat, etc.

This provides an understanding about the nature and role of *valuing* (evaluating) in human personality. What we value, or do not value, inevitably connects to the learnings that we have made. It involves the pain and pleasure that we experience and associate with various events, experiences, people, ideas, etc.

Show me someone who does not *value* reading, studying, and learning, and I'll show you someone who may very likely have had experiences with "learning" that caused them pain (boredom, embarrassment, inadequacy). A nun may have struck the back of their hand with a ruler time and time again. Or some kids may have laughed at them for not getting it. "Billy's a dummy! Billy's a dummy!" Either physical or psychic pain can lead us to conclude and feel that "Learning brings pain." No wonder they do not value it! What worth or importance could the experience of "learning" hold if it resulted in insult, put-down, shame, embarrassment, etc.?

"Values" are not given, we *learn* them. We learn to value. We take our experiences and use them to map value, worth, and importance. We learn to believe in the value of certain things. When someone is teased and hurt, laughed at for not getting something, in *that* situation the person might easily conclude that "trying to learn" only brings insult. The larger problem lies in over-generalizing, in treating *that* experience as representative of all learning experiences.

Our valuing and values explain and summarize our *learning history* about pain and pleasure. Do you value or dis-value authority figures? It all depends, doesn't it? What kind and quality of experiences have you had with someone who fell into that conceptual category? Did it result in pleasure (protection, dignity, excitement, admiration) or in pain (insult, punishment, distress)?

To know the *values* of someone puts us deeply in touch with that person's matrix or model of the world. It informs us about what makes him or her tick, what the person moves toward and what the person will move away from. To *not* know what a person truly and deeply values means that we do not know that person very well. This prevents empathy, understanding, rapport, connection, and persuasion. Andreas and Faulkner (1994) noted this.

"Persuasion is the ability to offer compelling values to *others*." (p. 162)

But how can we offer something of *compelling value* to another if we do not know what they value?

Motivation (activating lots of emoting) grows out of, and demonstrates, our "values." We *move* toward what we value as producing pleasure, significance, and meaning, and we move away from what produces pain and violates our "values." The degree, quality, and nature of our motivation emerges from our values. Value little—build few *motives* (reasons or values) for *moving,* and you will have little or shallow *motivational energy.*

This shows how our *valuing* and *values* powerfully relate to our personal congruence. When we live and act in a way that fits with our valuing, we come across as congruent. It gives us the sense of self-integrity, wholeness, integration.

Building Propulsion Systems Using "Values"

When we simultaneously move toward highly valued appreciated "values" while moving away from those things that we strongly *dis-value* and reject— we experience *a propulsion system.* Putting these pushing and pulling energies together into a system enables us to develop an accelerated motivation process. This allows us to positively use the power of both the "positive" and "negative" emotions. Yet we must do this with intelligence and care. If we don't, we can structure such energies and forces in a way that they turn against us.[2]

Merely having had a hell of an experience in the past, whether from abuse, neglect, physical trauma, war, rape, divorce, bankruptcy, betrayal, etc. does not, *in itself,* create any damage, pathology, or discord. In fact, strong negative emotions should occur during such. They help fight against hurtful things. They provide us the energy to take effective action. What creates damage in human personality arises from our mapping, from how we map those events. We experience pathology only when we construct toxic maps about the event that says we are worthless, nothing will ever work out, we are powerless and impotent.

To re-arrange things neuro-semantically, we need to welcome and accept the pain, hurt, and distress of our negative emotions (i.e., fear, grief, anger, stress, disgust, confusion, etc.). Once we do that, we can let it create a powerful push in us away from anything and everything that violates our "values," that harms our life, and that does not enable us to fulfill our nature as valuable, loving, and contributing beings. [In the following figures, the equal sign (=) stands for the things that we move away from and the arrow —> stands for what we move toward .]

Figure 11:1

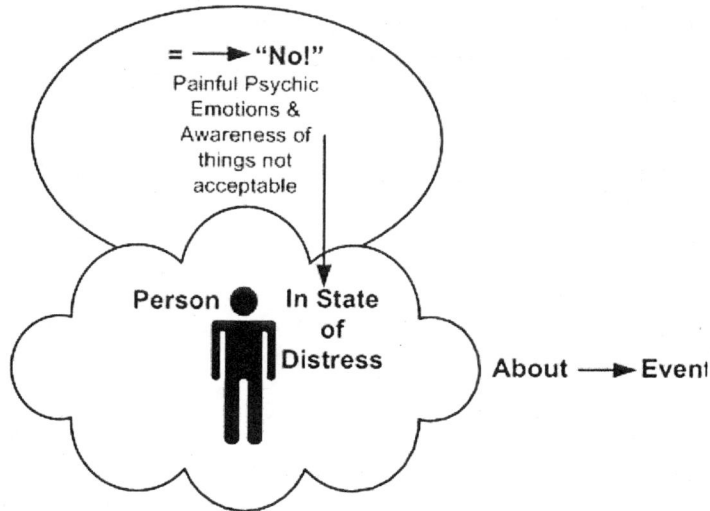

Merely *accepting* the negative emotions, as powerful and accepting important messages about what *not to accept,* does not suffice. We need to build an even higher frame of reference. We need to go meta one more level and identify what we do value, the things to which we say a strong and positive *"Yes!"* The *psychic push* of the negatives provide us a wonderful kick in the butt. But we need more. Once we get that kick-start to our rear end, we also need a pull, a magnetic pull to something higher, better, and grander.

Figure 11:2

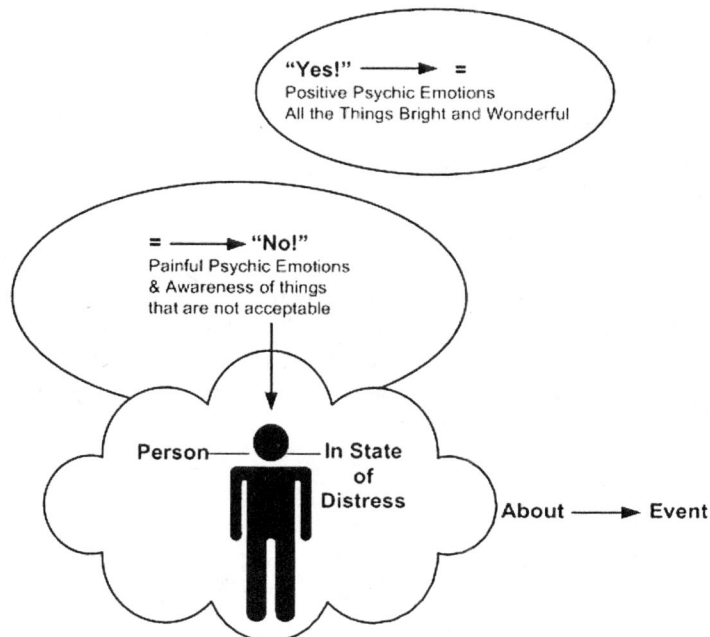

Valuing— The way we Structure "Values"

"Values" identify and determine our standards or criteria by which we make judgments, decisions, and e-*valu*ations. Typically, "values" show up in language as nominalizations. Common nominalizations that name and code the value states include:

being right	happiness	fun	enjoyment	success
relaxation	learning	sex	useful	beauty
accomplishment	power	health	excellence	saving time
pleasing others	money	love	the past	security
discovery	exploration	family	praise	neatness
spirituality	humor	truth	learning	autonomy
dignity	perseverance	playful	self-reliance	wisdom
solving problems	creativity	order	freedom	courage
contributing	mastery	caring	simplicity	synergy

So we make another meta-move and access the positive emotions that result when we value, see worth, declare compelling goals, etc. This enables us to have a great big *"Yes!"* pulling us into a bigger and brighter future that becomes more and more real to us with each step we take into our future.

Valuing— The way we Structure "Values"

"Values" identify and determine our standards or criteria by which we make judgments, decisions, and e-*valu*ations. Typically, "values" show up in language as nominalizations. Common nominalizations that name and code the value states include:

Make a list of your "values." What do you value? As you make this list, you will find that *context* asserting its importance. So identify several contexts: home, work, hobby, church, friends, relaxation time, children, career, etc.

As you do this, notice the front and back sides of your "values." The person who highly values fun and enjoyment may give such so much importance that he may find it very difficult to ever getting around to accomplishing much. The work, discipline, struggle, etc. may really put him off. Conversely, the person who highly values success, achievement, the struggle of accomplishment may find it difficult, if not impossible, to kick back, relax, and enjoy the benefits of his success.

Valuing in the Structure of Strategies

Since a *strategy* refers to the step-by-step process that creates an experience, it operates like a recipe as it details specific steps. It specifies a procedure for running our brain and neurology to produce an given experience. As an injunctive structure of experience, strategies allow us to work systematically, sequentially, and methodologically with mind-body-emotion responses. We use them to do all kinds of things, from spelling to managing, from parenting to partnering, from writing to skiing, from discovering something new to marketing something old, from keeping fit and healthy to restoring health and activating wellness responses.

- Since we create our realities and response patterns via our strategies, how does our *valuing* relate to the structure of our experiences?
- How do our "values" relate to the strategies of excellence?

Generally, the presence of a systematic way for running our own brain and neurology to produce a given state or skill indicates that we *value* that process (at least we once considered it important). We do it in order to accomplish something of significance for ourselves. What does this mean? *Valuing empowers our strategies.* We activate our mental processes of representing, believing, understanding, deciding, etc. to achieve something of value for us.

So where do we locate values in the NLP model? We locate them in *the positive intention* behind or above every behavior, belief, and strategy. As a higher frame to the experience, they function in the intentional system of our beliefs about importance which then *drives* our behaviors. As *beliefs about pain and pleasure,* our valuing sets our higher frames and energizes our emotions to move us toward pleasure and away from pain. No wonder we find specific "values" in the structure of every experience and in the structure of every specific excellence. No wonder we will want to meta-state ourselves with high level "values." By embedding our strategy inside of such, then we have "a motivated reason" for getting off our rear ends and getting at it.

An early understanding about strategies in NLP said that "the last step in a strategy was the kinesthetic," and that "strategies work by creating a V/K synesthesia." Yet these statements do not do justice to the NLP model, let alone the Neuro-Semantic model. After all, the **K** (*kinesthetic feelings*) only refers to *body sensations*, not "emotions." An emotion refers to meta-level phenomena, hence the designation K^{meta} to indicate an "emotion" and differentiate it from a "feeling" (sensation).

- What puts in the final K^{meta} in our strategies?
- What finally kicks the program into gear with a genuine and intense K^{meta}?

The answer is— *a meta-level frame of valuing.* We have to go meta and evaluate:

> "This is important!" "This makes a difference!" "I really, really like this and want this very much!" "I have to do this!" "This counts!"

Figure 11:3
Meta-Level Frame of Valuing

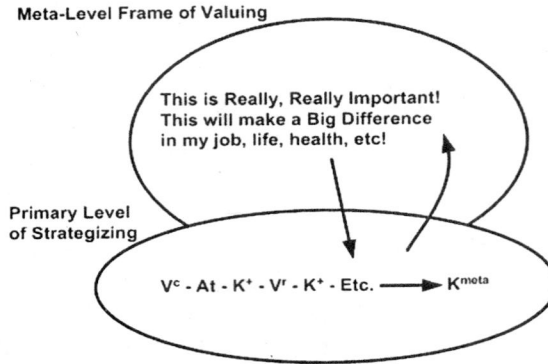

We have to set a *valuing* frame over the set of representations of our computations about how to do it, our beliefs that it's real and true, our decisions that we ought to do it, etc. This means that instead of thinking about the structure of a strategy as simply a V/K synesthesia, think about it as a **MS—>K^{meta}**. Bob expressed it this way,

> "The **K^{meta}** at the end of the motivation strategy will represent *a 'value'* to a person. I have checked many instances of this and, at the end of the motivation strategy you will find a 'value'—often an unconscious 'value.' I learned from Tad James to first elicit conscious 'values.' 'What's important to you in this context?' From there we have the person access a time when he or she felt highly motivated and associate into it. Tad would then have them roll it back a little and get *the feeling* that pushes or motivates them. That feeling usually represents an unconscious 'value.'"

The Meta-Level Nature of "Values"

As I have de-nominalized the static term "values," I have been highlighting *the process of valuing.* This reflects a meta-level experience. How does this work? What does that refer to? How do we actually value? How does the process of valuing relate to meta-levels?

This description provides a behavioral and operational definition of what it means "to value" something. We *language* or frame it as important, significant, meaningful, emotional, etc. in words, pictures, sounds, etc.

- We *value* when we *apply thoughts-and-feelings* of importance, worth, significance, or meaning to something.
- We value *by framing* an idea, event, person, concept, etc. with beliefs about its importance.

Mere representation at the primary level of experience does not lead to valuing, or to a "value." As noted about the meta-level structure of beliefs, we can represent things that we do not value. Can you "think" (i.e., represent) of something that you do not value? Certainly! Even full vividness of representation does not create a "value." Take anything you dis-value and turn up all your sensory representations so that you make your movie of it in-color, close, 3-D, and with close and compelling sounds. Do you now *value* it? I doubt it. Do you not have a higher frame that discounts it from having importance to you?

You can go through a list of dis-valued states and "values" and represent them so that you fully understand them, even believe that they are real and actual, and still *not* value them, can you not? Represent an old worn out soda can. Represent various dis-valued states (i.e. boredom, stupidity, dishonesty, over-seriousness, hurting people, disharmony, sloppiness, entitlement, ugliness, injustice, feeling stuck, disorder, etc.).

Representation, without *the meta-level confirmation of valuing* that attributes significance, results only in having a representation. It does not create a "value." You have an emotion-less and unmotivated representation. We see, hear, feel, smell, and/or taste it. We can even say words about it, but it doesn't matter. We won't care. We won't value it.

Yet when we do *value* something, we make vivid representations and then frame it as significant, worthwhile, and important. And because the represented idea matters, we represent it again *and again and again.* Doing this causes it to habituate. Our mind goes out to that referent (event, person, concept) frequently so we develop a predisposition for it. The tendency *predisposes* us to it keep repeating the process. We then give it *meanings* of importance (whether positive or negative, important to esteem or important to avoid). This gives us important *toward* values and important *away from* values.

At a meta-level, when we keep applying the same thought or internal representation to frame something, that frame holds meaning for us. It may simply represent the value of "familiarity." But usually, it holds meanings that increases our well-being, pleasure, purpose, etc.

This explains the structure of *valuing* as a meta-state experience. To value, we meta-state a primary level representation (or a meta-level idea) with *thoughts-and feelings of importance and meaning.* This sets a value frame. This creates the *"value."* We engage in this process as a never-ending process. We can value a "value." I can value my loved one (i.e., love and appreciate that person). Then I can value my loving and appreciating. Then I can value my identity as a loving and appreciating person.

To *value* means that we *believe* (i.e., confirm or say "Yes!" to) the value or importance of something. I believe in the importance of loving, of living life with vigor and purpose, I believe in enjoying the process of taking on a challenge. A *"value"* therefore simply represents one kind of belief—a belief in the value of something. We can also *believe* in our "values." Do you *believe* in the importance of having, knowing, and articulating your values? Valuing (at whatever level) involves the believing in the importance of something. Believing in that value moves you to the next highest level and solidifies the valuing.

We have no "values" in our mind as *entities.* If we over-use the nominalization of "values," and think of this mental-emotional process in a rigid and thing-like way, we populate our mind with pseudo-ideas. The truth is that the structure of "values" lies in *how we use our mind-body-emotion consciousness to value.* Because value operates as a multi-ordinal term, it has no specific meaning until we specify the level at which we use it. This is why we can easily confuse low level "values" with high level "values" and forget that we construct "values" within "values."

Consider, for example, the *value* that we nominalize with the term "love." At the primary level we take the thoughts-and-feelings involved in this *valuing* of *loving* and extend them out beyond ourselves and "love" a child, a mate, a dog, ice cream, etc. At the first meta-level, we might "love" our love to then experience "infatuation." We might "love" our learning to create the gestalt of motivated learning. If we move to yet another meta-level we could "love" our "hatred" of other people. At each level, we see the nature of a multi-ordinal term. It means something different at each level.

The Quality of Our Valuing
- When you value, how do you value?
- What quality, richness, and style do you bring to this process of attributing significance?

• How much *intensity* do you endow your internal representations with?

Suppose we measured the amount of energy that you invested in your valuing. We could then range the energy level from low to high: from worthless, trivial, frivolous, to compulsive, serious, supreme. This structural analysis speaks about the relative *importance* of numerous items that we value. After all, we do not value all of our values alike or with the same degree of importance. *Valuing relates to emoting.* How we value results in our felt sense of its degree of importance in something. How important do we consider this or that item? Generally, the more vivid, close, colorful, etc. we make our representations —the stronger the emotional pull we feel.

Implied "Values" and Valuing in our Frames
Structurally, every frame-of-reference we create operates as a "value" because we treat that frame as significant and meaningful. This explains *how* we get "values" installed in ourselves which we may no longer even consciously value.

For example, as a child we might have really *valued* being the fastest, best, smartest, etc. We valued competing and beating others. If that valued became really really high, it may continue to operate at the highest meta-level— to our detriment and chagrin. If it does, it may undermine our ability to get along with others, play as a team member, and align ourselves with others.

Value-Frames Elicitation Pattern
Use the following pattern to help you identify your values: the things you highly value, the things you do not value, and the things you value moving away from.

1) Eliciting Valuing, "Values," and Value-Frames
Eliciting great importance representations:
> What is of something of great importance to you?
> What is something that you very much deem as important, of lasting importance, and of durable importance?
> What is something you really go toward and really want?
> How do you represent this in see-hear-feel terms?
> What else is there? As you represent this, notice if you have any *other* thoughts "in the back of your mind" about these thoughts. What are they?

Eliciting trivial representations:
> What is something that you consider trivial and *un*important?
> What is something neutral that you respond with a ho-hum kind of attitude? (e.g., a plastic cup, a pencil, a discarded sheet of paper).
> How do you know that you think of this as *un*important?
> What quality of cinematic features and distinctions of it?

What voices, pictures, thoughts, or feelings do you have *in the back of your mind* about this?

Elicit something important to avoid:
What is something that's important for you to *avoid*?
> (i.e., driving fast and reckless, reacting with defensiveness, putting your hand in fire, driving without insurance, etc.).

How do you represent this?
What meta-level ideas do you have about it?

Eliciting a compulsive "value:"
What is something that you feel driven toward compulsively?
To what do you say things like, "I have to have..." "I must have this..."?
What do you have to have? Something over which you feel you have *no choice*?
What "sub-modalities" or cinematic features drive this so that it stands or leaps out? (e.g., halo, brighter, glowing, close).

Elicit former values and un-values:
What is something which you once deemed *un*important, something that didn't matter, but which now does matter?
What is something that you now have to have and that you drool over?

2) Run a contrastive analysis.
How do you distinguish between the things that are *important* and those that are *trivial?*
What are the "sub-modality" distinctions?
> When I do this, I find that I have coded my desirable wants in such cinematic features as: in-color, a 3-D movie that's close, that's immediately in front of me or to my right. By contrast, I have my trivial items coded as a dim black-and-white move or still snapshot off to my left side.

3) Identify the meta-level structures for important/ unimportant.
How do you cue yourself or say to yourself, "Important!" And "Not important."?
After you represent an item as valued or not, what enables you to know which category to put it in?
> When I do this, I have the words "Important," or "Yes, that's true!" "I value that!" coded in a matter-of-fact tonality which grows to an enthusiastic affirmation in a moderate volume. Conversely, I have coded "unimportant" using numerous verbal expressions. "No!" "Unimportant," "Not important,"

"I don't care about that." The tonality in these begin with a matter of fact tone, then grow to a more emphatic and stern tone as it increases for some things, and more of a nonchalant tonality for others.

The Structuring of Value Frames

Bob elicited his *valuing* around the subject of relationship faithfulness. He thought about how he values being faithful to his wife, Linda. First he made a representation of her. This evoked in him positive associated feelings. Where did these emotions come from? We have to back up. When Bob did that, he noticed that they immediately came from "the back of his mind" (i.e., a meta-level) and arose as thoughts and awarenesses of enjoyment about that. This was his "yes" to the "value."

When he thought about the idea of "cheating on my wife," his mind went to the place (or frame) where he had *"No"* stored. This led to experience a very strong unpleasant feeling which caused him to "bounce out." What frames did he have that *"No!"* embedded in? I asked him. "Why did you say 'No' to that?" This elicited many of the higher frames of his understandings, beliefs, reasons, and decisions. These were the levels which supported his *"No!"*

I elicited my *valuing* about staying fit and healthy. When I thought about this as a "value," I put it in my *space* to the right ... as if in my immediate "future" (immediate as in *"today"*). I coded it as a movie of my future self moving and taking physical actions that will bring that value into existence. I have the picture in color, close, 3-D, panoramic, with appropriate sound track .. and "in the back of my mind" I have a resounding "Yes" echoing. When I asked the why question of myself, "Why do you say 'Yes' to that?" it elicited all of my higher frames of understandings about fitness, beliefs about health, and decisions regarding why I want it.

We do not just say 'Yes" and "No" to things, to ideas, to people, etc. We express our affirmations and denials *because* of higher frames. We have our reasons, our understandings, our beliefs!

When I shift to the opposite thought, when I think about "getting out of shape, fat, and unhealthy" I picture it over to my left as if away from me in my "past" (even though that has never characterized me). I see a black-and-white picture, small, dim, flat, and I hear a resounding "No" in my mind dis-avowing it.

If I shift all of the representational distinctions in my "getting out of shape" picture and code it with the "staying fit and healthy" features (in color, close, bright, 3-D, etc.), my "No!" voice gets louder and I have a sense of taking my left arm and wanting to shove it back out of the way and further to the left as if "to make it go away." My meta-level awareness refuses to let it stay so coded.

Encoding Inside and Outside

Because *structure* governs experience, as we detect and identify how we code our valuing and "values" this clues us into understanding their nature, structure, and operation. It also enables us to work with values more efficiently.

- How do you represent *value or importance?*
- How do you signal your brain to know the difference between important and not-important?
- What did you discover in terms of your inner movie of see-hear-feel representations, their qualities, as well as meta-level affirmations and negation?

In identifying how you encode "values," notice your use of various orientation metaphors. Charles Faulkner has utilized the work of Lakoff and Johnson (1980) regarding such metaphors. This has led him to rework the "sub-modalities" model similar to our work here.

The embodied metaphor of orientation that has to do with *high and low* in space leads us to look for such terms as linguistic markers and actual spatial locations in our sense of space. Many people encode their *higher* "values" as "up" in actual space. They will look up, to their right or left, and locate them at that place in their personal space. A similar thing occurs with the intensity metaphor of *high and low* in terms of sound volume and pitch. Many people will encode *higher* "values" by using more volume and a higher pitch.

Others will code *real and unreal* using big versus small in size, a picture having color or black-and-white, located close or far; or being clear or fuzzy in focus. Such individuals may give something more of a sense of "reality" by making their pictures and sounds closer, more forefront to them, and as if "closely held" to them. We may similarly encode values using other "submodality" distinctions such as light versus heavy; tight versus loose; firm versus loose, etc.

Externalizing "Sub-Modalities" and Meta-Levels

Shortly after the field of NLP began, Bandler, Dilts, Woodsmall, James, and others began to notice that most people use various *symbolic internal metaphors* for encoding the meta-level concept of "time." Most (or at least many) people think of this concept of "time" *in terms of* (hence, metaphorically) a line. Others picture or feel it as a circle or spiral, or a boomerang, or a number of other configurations.

The early NLP developers also noticed something else about this. When we mentally map out "time," we typically project our internal maps into actual physical space outside of ourselves. We not only keep our ideas of "time" and the metaphors that we use for the encoding in our head, we externalize it. This means that we *spatially locate* our "sense" of "time" by *emboding* our ideas and metaphors in an external way.

The modelers noticed that most people have "a sense" of *where in space* they put "the past," "the present," and "the future." What a marvel! We begin with a high level *concept* like "time." This conceptual understanding involves representations of previous events and happenings, current circumstances, and imagined future activities. Then we metaphorically think about this concept using an orientational and spatial figure like a line or circle. Then, with that *frame*, we map out a configuration in our heads ... and then we *act it out in our bodies*. This shows up in our pointing, gesturing, and feeling of "time" as out there.

Incredible. Who would have ever predicted that our internal 3-D holographic maps in our heads could actually be seen, heard, and felt on the outside? Yet this is precisely what the modelers stumbled upon and began mapping. In NLP, this has lead to all kinds of wonderfully *magical* processes for "Time-Line Therapy" (James and Woodsmall, 1988) and "Time-Lining" (Bodenhamer and Hall, 1997). The classic elicitation for a person's internal Time-Line goes as follows:

> "Think about something simple you did last week like brushing your teeth. Now think of doing that one year ago, two years ago, five, ten. Now think about brushing your teeth this morning. Think about doing it tomorrow, next week, next year, two years from now, ten years from now. Typically, most people put their representations for these things in different places in space. So, now, if you imagine these representations along a line, point to where you experience your 'past.' Point to your 'future.' To 'today.'"

Via this elicitation, we can externalize a time-line which then gives us the ability to work more explicitly with the way we or someone else mentally maps out the idea of time. Where has this led? In NLP, this has enabled us to use time-lines in therapeutic ways to get over old hurts and painful memories of "the past," to sort out the "time" zones, to work with desired outcomes in building more empowering and compelling "futures," to utilize kinesthetic time-lines for building more resourceful responses, to conceptualize other kinds of "time," etc. (See *Time-Lining*, 1997).

> W have a propensity to project or externalize our internal 3-D holographic model of the world and our internal movies into actual space.
>
> If we look, we can see ourselves and others projecting the internal matrix world on the outside if we open our eyes to look for it.

Externalizing Other Meta-Level Maps

- If we can take a meta-level concept like "time," encode it using metaphorical referents like a line, circle, boomerang, etc., and then *externalizing* it, what else can we use this very process with?
- What other conceptual states can we do this with?
- What if we expanded this process to other "logical levels?"
- What if we externalize beliefs, values, affirmations and negations, understanding, etc.?

Ah, the possibilities!

Richard Bandler explored this idea for more than a decade in the DHE trainings (Design Human Engineering). Yet there was a certain weakness embedded in DHE. What was the flaw? The central weakness in DHE is the assumption that the "sub-modalities" are the sub-elements of experience, the building blocks out of which we can design new experiences. That's the flaw. No wonder DHE processes was found inadequate and lacking. No wonder DHE produced no results in over ten years. As we have unmasked "sub-modalities" and revealed the meta-level secrets about the qualities of our cinematic representations, we now know that "the difference that makes the difference" occur not at the so-called "sub-modality" level. The difference occurs at meta-levels—at the level of our *frames*.

Regarding "values" and the valuing process, we encode, store, and project these concepts of importance, significance, and meaning in *3-dimensional space*. Like "time," we can also learn to see people projecting "values" if we know what to look for and how to look for such.

How? Begin with the realization that we humans innately develop a sense of "personal space" as we grow up and develop. In different cultures and sub-cultural groups, this "space" or sense of "territory" differs in size, shape, etc.

Yet we all experience it. This sense of space, in turn, governs how close or how far we stand to each other, the degree that someone may "get in someone's face," or intrude into their personal space, how comfortable or uncomfortable we experience some people, where "rudeness," "insult," and "defensiveness" begins and ends, etc.

If you want to see (and feel) just how "real" our projected maps are, just step into someone's "space" and activate their meta-level frame of reference for "too close," "intrusion," or "insult." That should serve as a good demonstration and a convincer!

As we begin with this construct and think about *the externalization of our valuing* in terms of a 3-D spatial area, begin by simply noticing *where* in the actual space around a person and within which a person functions that he or she "puts things." Do the same for yourself:

> As you think about something very, very important to you ... notice *where* you put that. Now think about something worthless and trivial... and notice. What metaphors do you, or another person, use in these orientations. Do you use up-down, close-far, in-out, bright-dim, loud-quiet, etc.? How do you know that you *highly* value something? What voice, picture, or metaphor do you experience about the value? How do you experience yourself making this meta-move? Do you feel yourself *taking a step back?* Do you *float up?* Do you gesture in any particular way? Where does your first meta-level begin? How high off the ground? How does another person signal or gesture with regard to this?

"Values" and Meta-Levels
The structuring of *important* and *unimportant* begins with cinematic distinctions in our representations. After that, we use meta-level structures to set frames of reference as our or internal context. By these we categorize one concept versus the other. We do this because, after all, "importance" and "value" and "meaning" do not occur at the primary sensory-based level of existence, but at meta-levels.

What happens when, if you represent something as closer, brighter, and more to the right? Typically this increases the vividness of the representation and therefore the intensity of the feelings. Does this automatically cause the brain-body system to respond to it with the meaning of "important?" No, not necessarily.

Mere representation alone, no matter how "juiced" up, will not make the shift and hold it. Sometimes, it may invite us to adopt a certain way of thinking and feeling, unless some meta-level shifts occur it will not maintain the perceptive as our "value." Therefore at a level higher than the representation, you use some meta-frame to distinguish these categories, "Important" from "Unimportant." How do you do this? Perhaps you use one or more of the "sub-modality" continua. If you do, you may thus code "less important" as further away, dimmer, and more to the left.

The Meta-Governor

The meta-modality nature of "sub-modalities" means that our movies with their cinematic features and frames actually govern our states and experiences. How we encode our movies with various cinematic features and the metaphors we play with determine the structure of our experience and the subsequent emotions and actions that result.

If we use the metaphor *"Up is more, Down is less"* as a frame-of-reference for gauging the idea of "more/less," this will modulate our "sub-modalities." So with other metaphors that we could use:
>   "Heavy is more, Light is less"
>   "Light is more, heavy is less"
>   "Up is more, down is less"
>   "Down is more, up is less" [the more you go down, the more you enter into hypnosis]
>   "Closer is more, further away is less"
>   "Further away is more, closer is less"

To illustrate the last one, consider what a seminar participant asserted in Andreas' (1987) work:
>   "My least important criterion was close in front of me and the most important one was far away! I'd respond to what was close even though it was trivial, and I didn't respond to what was actually important to me off in the distance! When I realized this [a meta-state] then, I said to myself, 'That's nuts' and switched the whole thing around. And that really changed his state. " (p. 83)

It's *the metaphor* that we apply to our thinking about the intensity of an experience ("more or less") which governs and determines *how* the "sub-modalities" will work.

Metaphors, as meta-level structures, is to thinking about one thing *in terms of* another thing. Lakoff and Johnson (1980) have written extensively on the existence of the "orientation metaphors" hidden in our everyday language (in/out, up/down, front/back, etc.). While we do not generally think of such as "metaphors," this does not reduce their power. We generally use more *concrete* and highly defined facets of our experience (facets that grow out of our embodiment and the physics of our nervous system) to explain the less well defined.

Frame Governs "Sub-Modalities"

Realizing that frames govern our cinematic features explains the variations in how different people use "sub-modalities" and why shifting these variables and features of the representations has different effects on experiences. It boils down to the fact that we have and use different meta-levels framing in our understandings and representational formats. So we have to ask, "What does 'close,' 'bright,' 'loud,' etc. *mean* to you?"

Generally, people from the same culture will use similar meta-frames in their *meaning attributions*. In the West, when we make a picture or sound closer, louder, brighter, etc. it *increases* an experience, making it feel more compelling and important.

Similarly, most right-handed people in Western cultures code their "time-line" from left to right or back to front. The more they move an internal representation into the "present" and "future"—the more real and compelling it becomes to them, therefore the more valuable and important. The more they move an internal representation to the left and into their "past" the less compelling, real, and so more unimportant it becomes.

This is why we have to keep checking on any given person's frames. Doing so allows us to discover their meta-structures. Understanding their frames gives us significant clues about *the meanings* of their "sub-modalities" just as understanding how their cinematic features work clues us to their meta-frames.

At the conceptual level, if someone believes that *"the past as all important and determining"*—how will this effect *where* they put their past, how *close* or far it stands from them, the *direction* of their time-line, etc.? To change this—we can address it at the meta-level with a belief change pattern or at the primary level by editing the movie.

Whenever we put an internal representation up in a certain spot, the representation will typically *activate* the meta-level meaning, *"No, not important."* Conversely, when we put it in another spot, it will activate another meta-level meaning, *"Yes, important!"* We can activate meta-levels via "sub-modality" and conversely, we can activate "sub-modality" or cinematic editorial shifts via meta-levels.

This is why if a "sub-modality" shift works, it works because it activates a meta-level structure. For primary states, we need to map across these distinctions, but for meta-states we need to *map across* the meta-level structure or frame. From where do we make "sub-modality" shifts? From a meta-level. We go meta, step back from the *structure* of our experience and from "sub-modality" formatting, run the contrastive analysis and shift the representational distinctions.

Summary

- Valuing ultimately involves a meta-level of believing *in the importance* of something, believing that it will enhance your pleasures or that it will help you to avoid pains.
- Mapping across "sub-modalities" from similar experiences sometimes works marvels in transforming personality and human reality. This almost always involves primary states, not meta-states. Shifting primary states from hateful and disliked to liked and friendly, from boredom to fascination, from serious to ludicrous, from unmotivated to motivated, etc. recodes at the primary level to do its magic.
- Mapping across "sub-modalities" typically does not work with meta-level phenomena: confusion to understanding, doubt to belief, indecisiveness to decisiveness.
- To transform meta-level phenomena, we have to use meta-level processes (language, higher symbolic systems) to set higher frames.
- Working with the meta-level phenomenon of "values" we use our knowledge of the cinematic features of our representations and meta-levels. Then we can make "values" and valuing more or less important.
- Discover the features in your representations that carry a meta-level meaning of "more important," "more significant," etc. Then you can use them to set conceptual frame of reference.
- Discover these features in the way others talk and gesture and use their personal space, and you can increase your ability to pace their model of the world and influence them in considering what you have to say.
- What do you need to value that will add to excellence in your field?

End Notes:

1. For a fuller description of the Neuro-Semantic description of an "emotion," see *Meta-States Magic* (2002) or *The Secrets of Personal Mastery* (2000).

2. A "propulsion system" refers to a synthesis of the push—pull dynamics. For more about this, see *Propulsion Systems*: Accelerated Motivation (2003), the Axes of Change in *Coaching Conversations* (2004) and *Meta-Coaching* (2004), and *The Spirit of NLP* (1996/ 2000).

Chapter 12

THE STRUCTURE OF MEANING AND REFRAMING

Transforming Meaning Frames

"Magic is hidden in the language we speak.
The webs that you can tie and untie are at your command
if only you pay attention to what you already have
(language) and the structure of the incantations for growth."
Bandler and Grinder (1975)

"The explanatory world of *substance* can invoke no differences and no ideas but only forces and impacts. And, per contra, the world of *form* and communication involves no things, forces, or impacts but only differences and ideas. (A difference which makes a difference *is* an idea. It is a 'bit,' a unit of information.)
Gregory Bateson (*Steps,* pp. 271-272)

"Words and magic were in the beginning one and the same thing, and even today words retain much of their magical power. ... By words one of us can give another the greatest happiness or bring about utter despair; by words the teacher imparts his knowledge to his student; by words the orator sweeps his audience with him and determines its judgments and decisions. Words call forth emotions and are universally the means by which we influence our fellow creature. Therefore let us not despise the use of words in psychotherapy."
Sigmund Freud (1935, pp. 21-22)

In living the human experience—we constantly dance between two very different dimensions. In this ongoing dance, we have to keep adjusting for the different rules, principles, and logic that govern each arena. We do this because a different logic governs two things. The things that operate in *the external world* of physics differ from the logic that governs *the internal world* of communication. In the external world, phenomena are tangible, empirical, measurable, linear, and rational way. The subjective reality of the inner world is a very different dimension. This is the strange world of *psycho-logics* that govern thoughts, feelings, perceptions, values, beliefs, memories and all of the systemic features of our Matrix.

Making this *distinction* between the "world of physics" and the "world of communication" (Gregory Bateson) differentiates the men and women of excellence and those who still live in a primitive Aristotelian world. Similarly, NLP began with Bandler and Grinder saying that the ability to distinguish descriptive sensory-based information from evaluative data distinguishes the incompetent communicator from the professional.

Korzybski went further. He said that the inability to distinguish these levels of abstraction, means a *confusion* of levels and leads to *unsanity*. So the excellence of both sanity and science depends upon recognizing and distinguishing meta-levels.

From Frames of Reference to Frames of Meaning

Meaning always involves a frame. Without a frame, nothing "means" anything. A bell is simply as a bell and signifies nothing. But when a person *associates* a bell with "time to start," "food," "train leaving," "exercise now," or any other significance, we say that the bell *means* something. Such *associative meaning* is the first level of meaning which even the simplest of minds and most primitive organisms experience. Pavlov studied this level of meaning and articulated it in his laws and principles of conditioned and unconditioned associations.

For a thing (person, place, object, event, process, etc.) to take on *meaning* to a responsive mind, repetition of an association creates a *frame-of-reference*.

For example, if I grow up in a place where every parental communication focuses on what I'm *not doing right*, on criticizing, on pointing out mistakes, I could soon link and anchor together "the talk of my parents" (external event) with "being criticized" (internal state or significance). If I continued to generalize this, then all experiences falling within the category of "people in authority wanting to talk to me" might become connected with "criticism, put down, being wrong." Continual repetition of this could install this as my basic *frame-of-reference* for anything in this category. Then I reference my previous experiences and my generalizations (along with the beliefs, values, decisions, understandings, etc.) that make up this conceptual category. The *reference* explains how and what a thing *means* to a given organism. In this way, we create primary and meta-level meanings.

"Frames" As Meta-Level Structures

At the primary level of our everyday experience, we have *associative meaning*. What something "means" depends entirely on what we have associated to a

stimulus.
- Does a pointing index finger *mean* "insult," a condescending attitude, a scolding?
- Where does your mind go when you see that stimulus?
- What ideas does it evoke within you? What feelings?
- What references from your history?

Over time we all develop associations. These grow out of our past experiences as well as our vicarious and imagined experiences. In this way, it lies in the nature of mammals to link things together. Today we call such linkages and relationships Pavlovian conditioning.

In concept and in language, the Stimulus-Response (S-R) connections that we develop in our nervous system show up in our mental mapping. What we map such relationships they appear linguistically as the Meta-Model distinctions known as Cause-Effect, Complex Equivalence, and Identity statements. This begins what we recognize in NLP as the structure of meaning.[1]

Yet our meaning-making and associative powers do not end with linking. Above the primary level of associative meanings, by layering associations one upon another, we build up another kind of meaning. We construct *context* meaning or *frame* meaning. All kinds of various *contexts* significantly influence the semantics or meaning of an event:
- The physical context: where one says something.
- The conceptual contexts: the mental ideas spoken about.
- The interpersonal context: with whom we speak.
- The intentional context: the reasons or purposes for speaking.

The frame (as the mental paradigm or conceptual category) within which we put an idea, belief, or awareness textures, qualifies or generates *meaning*. This distinguishes *content* reframing from *context* reframing. Every *meaning* or neuro-semantic significance involves some frame of reference. This applies as equally to even the simplest Pavlovian linkages. When a researcher or dog owner *triggers* a dog to *associate* the sound of a whistle to the experience of eating food and that activates the unconditioned salivation response, the dog eventually *relates* and *connects* the whistle to the *eating* frame of reference.

Yet the whistle *is* not the food. The sound of the whistle as vibrations in the air *is* not the same thing as the smell and taste of food in the dog's mouth that activates the salivary glands. Yet through neurological linkage —the dog's nervous system and brain *anchors* the external stimuli to his or her internal experience of salivating... the dog treats and responds to the whistle *as if* it **is** the food. This confuses *levels*.
"In primary process, map and territory are equated; in second process,

they can be discriminated. In play, they are both equated and discriminated." (Bateson, 1972, *Steps,* p. 185)

Bateson described this as confusion of logical types; Korzybski described as *identification*. What is the backside of confusing items that belong to two different worlds, two different dimensions of existence, and two different logical levels to identifying items as if they refer to the "same" thing when they do not?

Figure 12:1

Stage I:

External Stimuli	Internal Response
In world of physics	In world of neurological abstracting

1) Experiencing the smells
   and tastes of dog food   —>   Salivation

Stage II:

Experiencing food—>salivating   **and**   Hearing the sound of a whistle

Stage III:

Hearing the Sound of a Whistle   —>   "mind" and neurology *represents* the Eating Food Experience, thereby activating the salivation response

Stage IV:
Meta-Level:
Frame-of-Reference for whistle

"It *is*, means, leads to, causes eating food"

Primary Level:

Dog   —>   Hearing Whistle

Treating, relating to, responding, and feeling *as if* "the whistle" or the auditory sounds *is* "the internal neurological response of salivating" (the responses of the nervous system kinesthetically so that it activates the olfactory and gustatory senses, the autonomic nervous system's glands, and motor programs, etc.)

confuses different things and *identifies* them as "the same thing." Yet this maps out a model of the world that is false-to-fact. As it does, this creates an unsanity that if unchecked can lead to a breakdown in discerning what's real.

Korzybski noted that *on the macro-level* and in the world of unaided nature of animals, we can get by with such confusions and identifications for the most part. Using them creates no damage or adjustment problems. As long as the sound of an owner's walk indicated "feeding time," "playing time," or whatever, then for the dog to treat those "sounds" as being the same as food, play, etc., that map will assist the dog in thinking and responding.

But when we use our nervous systems similar to animals (i.e., confusing logical levels and creating identifications), we reduce our response patterns and style to a primitivism that is basically unsane and set ourselves up for *semantic reactions*. A semantic reaction refers to an unthinking reaction. Rather than thinkingly responding, we react and project our meanings onto it. As an evaluation process for making meaning, this can powerfully misdirect us and can create all kinds of false-to-fact conclusions. The "stressed tonality" of a person's voice does not necessarily *mean* anger, hatred, insult, put-down, worthlessness, etc. Nor does it have to trigger or cause us to experience such.

As a neuro-linguistic and neuro-semantic class of life, we use *symbols* to stand for and represent other things and we can rise above our mapping to reflect on our symbols. As we step aside from a stimulus and our symbols of it, we can recognize the gap between stimulus and response. What is this gap? It's consciousness. The gap is where we think, map, and create meaning. We can now evaluate, at a higher level, whether our response to the stimulus serves us well or not. We do not *have to* confuse the external stimuli with some conditioned or pre-programmed response. We can design and create the responses we want which will enhance our lives and put us in charge of how we adapt to the world.

It is this higher level quality of *mindfulness* (thought about thought, awareness about awareness) that empowers us to consciously construct the associations, linkages, anchors, and semantic responses that we want.

Constructing Meaning—an Inside Job

Meaning does not, and cannot, exist "out there" in the world on its own. We cannot measure it with a yardstick. We cannot weigh it on a scale. We cannot stumble over it in our background. People do not drop pieces or chunks of it as they walk down the street. They do not flick it out of their car window as they drive by. *Meaning* does not exist in that dimension. So what is meaning?

Meaning refers to what *we* do on the inside (via our nervous system and mind) as we create associations, linkages, anchors, contexts, contexts-of-contexts, "ideas,"concepts, etc. Meaning is *neuro-semantic* in nature. Meaning emerges an inside job—something that we do in our heads and in our entire embodied neurology.

We inevitably and inescapably make meaning. We have to. Our body and nervous system operates by abstracting from the world. It encounters various energy manifestations (the electromagnetic field, vibrations, etc.) and responds to such as sense receptors (eyes, ears, skin, mouth, tongue, inner ear) transform that energy into a neurological product. Light energies impact our rods and cones and via the interaction, sets off neurological impulses and then chemical transfer of neuro-transmitters to the visual cortex so that we then *have the experience of "seeing"* something.

In this *"seeing"* we *construct* what and how we see. We construct color, form, shape, etc. We do not see the hole in the back of our eye that lets in light. Our brains fill in that hole. Nor do we see things at the microscopic level or any aspect of the light energies outside of a very narrow band. We do not see ultraviolet light, x-rays, etc. We do not even see many things at the macroscopic level.

If we look at an electric fan as it turns, we "see" a disk. We could even take a picture of it and the photograph will show a disk. But there is no disk. As we turn the fan off and continue to watch it, we will come to "see" four fan blades. When those blades move faster than our eyes can compute the information, the blades disappear and we construct a disk. They move faster than we can see. Our eyes in interaction with the energy manifestations do what all neurological sense receptors do—they abstract (summarize, delete, generalize) as best they can to create a neurological-mental product for our consciousness, in this case, a non-existent disk.

Does this mean that this *emergent neurological-sense sensation* (the disk) really did exist for a time? No. It means that via the nervous systems of our mind-body-emotion system, *we created a map* about the world—a neurological map (what we "saw") and a linguistic map (what we call it, "disk"). Yet, our "map is not the territory" only a product of our embodiment.

What does the electric fan and its spinning blades mean? It means *nothing!* In and of itself, it has *no meaning*.
- What meaning do *you* give to it?
- What do you *associate* with it?
    — Useful technological for keeping cool.
    — A dangerous piece of equipment that could hurt you.
    — An indication of human ingenuity and inventiveness.

— Modern capitalistic greed.
— A present for a friend.

It all depends, does it not? *Meaning,* as an inside job, depends entirely on your learning history and the higher level abstractions that you apply to it. *Meaning* exists at a higher logical level than the events in the world beyond our nervous system.

In the human adventure of discovering and making meaning—we do so, always at meta-levels. You have to *go meta* to identify, work with, construct, reframe, deframe, and outframe meaning. Our neuro-semantic lives arise from, emerge from, and receive their impetuous from our higher level frames-of-references or meta-states from where we encode our beliefs and mental paradigms. This makes up our Matrix. There we construct beliefs about value, importance, and significance ("values"). There we invent beliefs about self and identity, purpose and mission, teleology and ontology ("identity," "mission," etc.). There we construct beliefs about knowledge, understanding, reason, etc. (epistemology). These meta-level phenomena do not exist "out there," they emerge from our cybernetic system of consciousness.

Reframing Content and Context
Reframing requires that we *step aside from* our meaning constructions (both associative meaning and contextual meaning) and evaluate them. Once we do that, we can then alter them, if we so choose. When we do, we make a *meta-move* and if we consciously recognize the map/territory distinction, we can do so with grace, power, and elegance. This prevents us from confusing levels or identifying our mental ideas (meanings) with reality.

What does "watching TV" mean? What does it mean *to you?* What do you have associated or linked to that experience? Which of the following do you have associated to it? Relaxation, entertainment, a social event, a way to isolate yourself, what to do when you feel bored, a status symbol. You may have multiple meanings connected to it—depending on the various states you experience over time, who you are with, what's happening in your life, where you are, etc.

When televisions first appeared in American homes in the 1950s, having and watching TV functioned as a status symbol for a great many people. It meant "being up-to-date and modern." Fewer people experience those meanings today —unless, of course, they keep buying the latest equipment in digital, cable, internet technology and take pride in having the largest and most expensive sets.

Beliefs "are" not real. They are the mental constructs we create as we map out our model of the world. We use beliefs to explain to ourselves our understanding about what "causes" (leads to, triggers, activates) what—cause-effect relationships. We develop understandings about what *equates to* and *is* "the same" as something—complex equivalence or meaning equations. We develop opinions about what others think-and-feel and intend (the mind-reading structure). We articulate various "identities"—what we have *identified* with (e.g., ideas, definitions, experiences, etc.).

This explains why we change beliefs at meta-levels. As a higher level and layered phenomena of human cognition they are not highly amendable to "sub-modality" shifts. The only exception is when we use a cinematic feature in a way so that it *represents*, or stands for, some higher level concept. If, "a black and white picture" represents the meta-level concept of "not real," and "a picture in color" represents the meta-level concept of "real," then we could apply this "sub-modality" feature to our representations so that it sets the frame of "real" and thereby reclassify a set of internal representations into a "belief" (a validated, affirmed thought).

We can use any of the *cinematic features* of our sensory-based representations to perform meta-level transformation if, and only if, we create an association between the "sub-modality" and a higher level concept.

For most people, an *associated* picture, sound, or sensation means "feel this," "represent this as real, now, and compelling." Conversely, for most people a *dissociated* picture, sound, or sensations usually means "don't feel this directly," "represent this as not real, no longer real, not now, and not compelling." This explains how this "sub-modality" distinction (associated/dissociated) is also a meta-program. (see Appendix A.)

Unmasking this secret shows us how we can use "sub-modalities" for meta-level transformations. It offers a pathway for analysis and exploration about why a given "sub-modality" distinction can have different results with different people. Because the cinematic feature that we edit into the movie will mean different things to different people, we have to consider *the symbolic significance* or meta-frame that the person connects to it.

A person who *associates* a loud and tonally stressed ("harsh") tone with anger or insult can use it to feel bad, to go into a defensive state and mode, or to insult themselves for the rest of the day. A person who has learned a different meaning ("he must be feeling upset or stressed") to it may use the same stimulus to feel compassion or pity. The stimulus of the "sub-modality" in and of itself *means nothing.*

Outframing All Maps
Would you like to *loosen up* your maps, meta-states, beliefs, paradigms, and

other meta-level phenomena so that you operate in the world with more flexibility, more "consciousness of abstracting," and more choice and adaptability in using your meaning-making powers? The following pattern provides you an opportunity to do just that. When you do that, you will be able to *observe* your observations and to *evaluate* your evaluations. Do it to empower yourself in truly managing your meta-mind.

We have designed these exercises for developing a more flexible *mindfulness* about our maps, ourselves, and our Matrix. It helps us to facilitate a greater neuro-linguistic relaxation (Korzybski). In *neuro-linguistic relaxation* we move through the process world of continual change more playfully, less seriously, more flexibly, and with more of a sense of adventure. This gives us a calm alertness as we apply the scientific mindset of experimentation to the way we move through life.

When we make meaning we move up and down the scale of abstraction. When we move up, we create meaning, when we move down we either deframe meanings or we install meanings. We make lateral moves to create a metaphorical meaning. This uses the Meta-Model, the Milton model, the Meta-States model, and the Metaphor model respectively. We adapted the following from John Overdurf.

Exercising Mindfulness of your Maps and Meanings
1) Take an observer position to your maps.
> Realizing that "the map is not the territory," and that whatever you think is just a map, how do you represent this?
> In observing your maps, how do you know that they emerged via your perceiving and representing?
> What is it like for you to realize that even this awareness is a mapping?
> How do you feel as you experience yourself as a symbolic class of life?
> Take a moment to fully notice how you feel to realize that you operate in the world by your frames of meaning.
> What do you feel about this whole neuro-linguistic process and the recognition that no map *is real* in any external sense?

2) Repeatedly go meta until you go up and away "beyond words."
> Continue this process of awareness as you continue to make one meta-move after another and do so until you move to a level beyond all of your languaged mappings and into what we may call "the void," the inexpressible, and the metaphoric.
> What is this like?
> As you do this, keep reminding yourself that whatever you think, conceptualize, format, believe, etc. is only a map.
>> "It's not real. I created it. I constructed it in my nervous system

and brain. It offers me one way to map things, but not the only
way."

3) Return from the meta-heights to the ground level.

What is it like when you move so high that you're in the ozone of your
consciousness?

Once you have "zoned out" all the way up beyond words to experience
a *transcendental sense* of your unexpressible reflexivity, come back all
the way back down the levels.

As you return to the ground level before you represented anything, to
the unspeakable level, what is it like when you bring with you all of the
meta-awarenesses and feelings?

Take a moment to let it all settle ... this transcendental sense of yourself
as a meaning-maker and a map-maker.

4) Future pace this map mindfulness.

Imagine moving into the world with this meta awareness in the days
and weeks to come. What does it do as you engage in conversations?
What does it do for your own awareness of your self-talk?

If you moved into tomorrow and next week and the rest of your life
with the full realization and ownership of your powers as a map-maker
... free and empowered to construct the kind of mappings that will serve
you well, do you like that?

How well does it work to enhance your life and empower you as a
person?

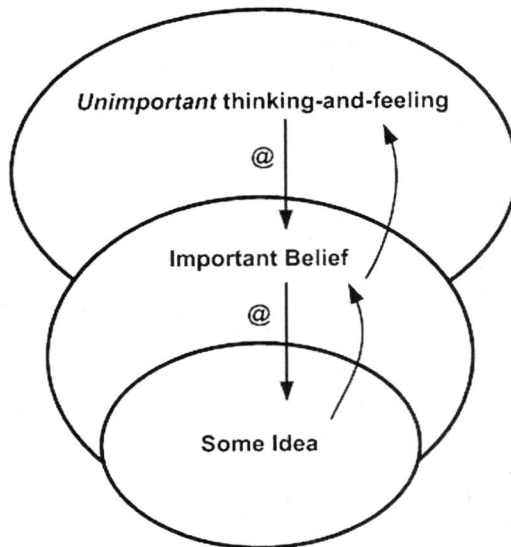

Summary

- Have you decided to take charge of your own meaning-making powers and set out to attribute the most enhancing meanings to the events of life? Making that executive decision changes everything.
- The *step back skill* of going meta to ourselves gives us the ability to detect frames. And that frame awareness gives us the ability to deframe toxic meanings that get in the way of developing excellence.
- It is when we go meta to our meanings that we can then apply other evaluations, ideas, and frames to our meanings and the events of the world. This describes the structure of making meaning.
- In *going meta* we are able to transform meaning. Setting a new frame enables us to perform the *magic* of meaning making is because the magic is hidden in the words we speak. Use this skill to magically transform life, perception, behavior, skill, emotion, and experience itself.
- *Genius* emerges from exercising this ultimate power of the mind in processing information, working with ideas, handling understandings and beliefs, etc. Without the ability to reframe, deframe, and outframe—we are limited in developing mastery.

End Notes:
1. For an extensive description of the structure of meaning, see *Mind-Lines: Lines for Changing Minds* (2002).

GOING META
FOR NEW APPLICATIONS

Part I:
- Presentations of the details about the cinematic features (the so-called "sub-modalities") and how they work semantically. A description of how we can use them in modeling the structure of experience and of the excellence of any mastery.

Part II:
- Six new patterns for working with and handling meta-level or Matrix phenomena. When "sub-modalities" *go meta* we are able to work with the higher processes of our Matrix recognizing the semantic frames that govern them.
  - —Foreground / Backgrounding
  - —Negating
  - —Believing
  - —Understanding
  - —Valuing
  - —Making meaning and Reframing

- We are now ready to use all of this for *pure application*. In re-modeling the "sub-modality" model, we can now reformat various NLP patterns for running our own brain with a view of building more enhancing experiences of excellence:
  - —Changing Personal History.
  - —Inserting Resources in the Middle of our Ideas
  - —Reading and Externalizing "Sub-modalities."

- Afterwards, we will put it all together by presenting and analyzing the magic of a master modeler at work.

RECAPITULATION

We began by unmasking "sub-modalities" to reveal that they are not *sub* at all but *meta*, that they are the *cinematic features* which we edit into our movies. We discovered that we have to *go meta* to both detect these features of our coding, to alter them, and to rise up to discover the frames they are embedded in. In this we discovered that these meta-level features are actually semantic structures or frames. These discoveries enable us to re-model the NLP model making it more robust and powerful.

Recognizing cinematic features or "sub-modalities" as the fourth meta-domain means there is a relationship between them and the other meta-domains—Meta-Model, Meta-Programs, and Meta-States. This gives us four meta-domains —four avenues into the same thing.

This is exciting because it gives us entrance into the very heart of NLP—into *modeling the structure of excellence.* We can now inquire about the original genius of Bandler and Grinder in how they modeled some of the excellence in Satir, Perls, and Erickson. What drove that genius?

Each person who demonstrates excellence makes distinctions that others do not. They see, hear, and feel things that escape the awareness of others. What enables them to do this? What meta-level *frames*-of-references (i.e., beliefs, values, understandings, decisions, intentions, etc.) provide them a *structure* for making distinctions?

The original three "therapeutic wizards," each had his or her own theories, hypothesis, and understandings (Family Systems Therapy, Gestalt Therapy, and Ericksonian Hypnosis). These models about human functioning gave them a *meta-understanding* about what to sort for, notice, and address. Then the two modelers, using the theories, hypothesis, and understandings of Transformational Grammar, General Semantics, computer science, mathematics, cybernetics, etc. stepped back to build a *meta-model* about the frames and meta-frames of the wizards. This bequeathed a meta-legency to NLP. Not surprising, the majority of NLP patterns involves meta-levels.

On the surface, these patterns often seem to only involve "sub-modalities." Yet they actually operate by recognizing how we are using the various features of our representations symbolically and semantically. We use the cinematic features to invoke and set higher level frames. This is how they work so magically. To now use these technological advances in runing our own brains, we have to learn to skillfully make meta-moves in the way we handle the neuro-semantic symbols.

And now, on to some of the technologies that build excellence in our lives.

Chapter 13

CHANGING
PERSONAL HISTORY

"It's never too late to have a happy childhood."
Richard Bandler

Bad things happen and they happen to good people, even sincere, honest, and hard-working people. When they do—then what?
- How do we respond?
- How do we feel? How do we think?
- What maps and meta-maps do we create from out of such experiences?

We experience *bad things* as not only unfortunate, undesirable, and challenging to our thinking, feeling, energy, responding, etc., but we generally treat such experiences as *bad* and *horrible*. Sometimes we go further and treat them as totally determinative of who we are (identity) and what the future has in store for us (our sense of fate). We interpret them as meaning:
- We are deficient, flawed, and no good (Personalizing).
- It affects everything about us and life (Pervasive).
- And it will affect everything forever (Permanent).

Seligman (1975, 1990) described those three *"p"s* as the structure of "learned helplessness." These are dependable features for a recipe of depression. Feeling "bad" describes our *felt interpretative* response to stimuli, not the innate character of *what* happens. The actual empirical events that occur at the primary level (not reaching goals, dreams not coming true, achievements unrealized, bills to pay, jobs dismissed from, conflicts with people, ill-health and accidents) describes the events that we have to cope with.

Yet above and beyond such unpleasant realities occurs something worse. We create meta-frames that load the event with too much meaning. This happens when we take an event and process it as a *bad* thing, when we keep representing it to ourselves, day in and day out, hour after hour, and use it as our primary *frame*-of-reference. In this way we do even greater damage to ourselves. *Using* unpleasant, painful, and traumatic events of the past as a perceptual filter, belief system, frame, orientation in the world, and attitude creates a "dragon state" that will come back to devour us. It never makes things better. It programs us for limitation, distress, pain, inner torture, unresourcefulness, etc.

This does not contribute to personal excellence. It does not create the foundation for developing genius states. To the contrary, it undermines human expertise and creativity, resourcefulness and happiness, hope and proactivity.

To so misuse our experiences of negative things and to *mis-evaluate* events is not a healthy way to manage our mind. Yet a great many people have gotten caught up in doing this very thing. They go through some hurtful, ugly, and distressful experience. Then they *represent* it so powerfully, vividly, and graphically so that it takes over the screen of their mind. As the trauma movie fills their mind, they empower it with fear and dread so that it becomes their primary reference experience. They use it as their frame to judge, interpret, understand, and process everything else. Then, as they keep replaying the movie again and again, they use that garbage to build even more toxic beliefs, perceptions, decisions, and understandings. Ugggh! That's no way to run a brain!

Nor does anybody have to do that. We can represent the "bad things" that we have been through as things we *have been through—past* things that we have moved on from and that we will continue to move on from. We can replace it with much more positive and empowering referents. We can set new frames that reflect healthier and more enhancing beliefs, values, decisions, and understandings. Doing this describes the structure of excellence and the foundations for developing new masteries. We can choose how we want to think about and respond to unpleasant experiences. We can stay focused in the here-and-now with a bright eye on a compelling future.

The Magic of Going Meta
Is it really any surprise that the majority of NLP interventions and models depend upon the process of making a meta-move or *going meta*? It shouldn't. After all, NLP is a meta-discipline.
- What then explains the power or magic of *going meta*?
- Why do we have to get a client, customer, or ourselves to make a meta-move to a higher "logical level?"
- Why do we have to go there to create the magic of change that transforms mind, emotions, and life?

First, the majority of the things that trouble us occur at meta-levels, not primary levels. Most human problems, challenges, and distresses do not occur at the sensory-based level of mere description. Most occur at the levels where we *evaluate* and attribute higher level *meanings*. It is this that creates our conceptual states and neuro-semantic frames, the beliefs, understandings, decisions, and values that makes up our operational model of the world or Matrix.

Second, *change takes a lot more time and trouble when we attempt it from within a system.* If we stay inside a system of thinking, emoting, and responding, change takes a lot of work and typically a long time. It is only when we step out of the system that we can see the system for what it is and work with the system itself. At a higher level, we can make systemic changes that work more pervasively and that last longer. It is in this way that magic occurs when we go meta.

This also explains why merely altering the distinctions of representations in higher level phenomena (like beliefs) usually do *not* work. "Sub-modality" alterations of that kind only infrequently alter the meta-level frame that creates the inner *context* of the experience. Unless we specifically apply the cinematic, representational distinction which *stands for* and *symbolizes* some appropriate meaning, the experience will not change. The matrix structure will not be affected.

Because "sub-modality" patterns only directly affect how we *encode* our mental movies they do not necessarily transform the meanings or higher level frames that govern the experience. Sometimes the patterns work, but only infrequently and only sporadically. Sometimes the force of personality of a highly confident change-agent will facilitate a change. Yet if a highly skilled person like (Richard Bandler) sometimes get changes using a so-called "sub-modality" pattern, in actuality he or she is meta-stating. Chapter 17 shows Bandler's "sub-modality" patterns working *because of his meta-stating* and thereby enabling clients to apply meta-resources to their problems.

What we need to change is the meta-level structure (or frame) and its meanings. And since most problems and all beliefs operate at levels *higher* than the primary level of experience, they only infrequently yield to mere editing of the movie.

Bob began using "sub-modality" shifts on beliefs early in his NLP career as a trainer and in his work with clients. Eventually, however, he stopped because he felt he could not obtain consistently predictable results. Later he discovered the reason. What did he discovered? He discovered that *cinematic editing* ("sub-modality" shifting) *does not always alter meta-level structures.*

Understanding meta-levels and the nature of self-reflexive consciousness originated with the insightful works of Korzybski and his neuro-linguistics and neuro-semantics models. Korzybski noted that we seldom have problems with "first-order abstractions." At the sensory level—we map from the world using our basic neurological mapping mechanisms. We map over the sights, sounds, sensations, smells, and tastes that we to construct our internal "sense" of the same—our internal VAK movie.

When we move into second-order abstractions, third-order abstractions, etc., we use *the meta-representational system* of language, mathematics, music, poetry, visual diagrams, etc. Now we make *maps of our maps,* abstractions of our abstractions, and conceptual generalizations of our concepts. This moves us up the scale of abstraction into the land of nominalizations and generalizations. Yet we often create concepts that do not serve us well. We create toxic beliefs, morbid conclusions, and false-to-fact understandings.

Conceptual States

Abstractions that are especially problematic include concepts about time, space, causation (cause-effect), self, past, future, purpose, destiny, nature of the world, of people, relationships, materialism, spirit, ability, responsibility, being told, authority, etc.—and this is just the beginning! Our self-reflexive consciousness generates concepts about concepts. In the end, we can fill our mind with maps full of cognitive distortions, inadequacies, and irrationalities. If we then *believe* in our concepts or think that we are forever stuck with certain ideas, our belief in our beliefs make them seem unchangeable, that they are our "fate."

Once I worked with a young man who felt that he just could not get rid of a certain limiting belief. He was talented, smart, and had a passion for an area that could easily become a pathway to financial independence for him. He had done his homework about wealth building and developing business sense, but there was still—in the back of his mind—a old dialogue.

> I'm just fooling myself. Others can "think and grow rich," but not me. It's never worked. You're just fooling yourself. As a minority male in this culture, it will just never happen. You're just hoping for the impossible. Even running this belief change pattern won't work in the long run.

What do you think of all of that self-talk? Do you like it?
> Of course not. But I'm afraid it's true.

You're *"afraid* that it is true." That's also in the back of your mind as one of your frames of reference about all of this? And you have historical *evidence* to back it up?
> Yes, I do. I've tried and tried to defeat this one and just can't.

And what do you think about that? What's further in the back of your mind about that frame?

> Well, I'm doomed to live a minimum existence and to barely get by.
> This is my fate.

And you believe that?

> Well ... Yeah.

Do you want to? You probably really want to believe this and not break free from its control over you!

> No. I don't want it!

So you're at a decision point, aren't you? What will you choose to be the highest frame in your mind? Will you set up the frame that you have the right, privilege, and even responsibility to succeed or will you bow down to this limiting belief?

When we map things by *believing in our beliefs* we give our power away, we give our frames the ability to perpetuate traumas. We then develop the ability to feel really bad, traumatized, and tortured decades after a traumatic event. This structure of pathology empowers us to continually traumatize ourselves by how we remember a past experience. However, we do not have to engage in this kind of neuro-linguistic unsanity. We do not have to create morbid second and third order abstractions. We can map things out in much more enhancing ways.

What can we do about a set of unenhancing maps about past events that we didn't like then or now? *We can change them, we can change our history.* We can alter and transform the way we code our memories and our meanings. For this purpose, the Change History pattern works marvelous magic. The following reflects some reformulating of the *Change History pattern* to incorporate and show how it operates as a meta-level pattern to remap toxic meta-level structures.

"Past" and "Future" as Conceptual Meta-States

Specific images, sights, sounds, sensations *alone* do not encode the "time" dimension and matrix. The concept of "time" is an intangible idea—a semantic category which we cannot see, hear, feel, smell or taste. In fact, we can even say that *there is no such thing as time.* "Time" isn't a thing of the world; it's a thing of the world of communication.[1]

We have to move to a higher level to conceptualize the idea of "time," the idea that some *events* have occurred, some are now occurring, and some may one day occur. When we move down from the meta-level of "time" at the primary level there are only *events.* At that level, there are things happening. It's only when we step back and hold *events* in mind and compare them that we have "time." And after we have time, we have a sense of history, destiny, purpose, etc.

Of course, the problem with a sense of *personal history* is not that we have been though some hurtful or ugly experience, no matter what kind of a hell we might have experienced. The problem lies in *what we think* about that experience —what frames we embed that movie within, what matrix we build from it.

- What meanings have we given to it?
- How have we interpreted it?
- What significance have we endowed it with?
- What does it mean about our identity?
- What does it mean about our future?
- What does it mean about our skills and abilities?

To change our personal history, we could *blank out* the events that we find painful, unacceptable, inhuman, etc. Or we could *negate* such and just make them go away. Or we could *re-edit* the internal movies so that we develop a different response to them—humor, compassion, anger, disgust, relief, calmness, etc. Or, we could *set new frames* so that those experiences mean something different to us.

Check out your personal history: your memories, what you recall, how you encode those events, what you say to yourself about them, etc.

- Does it serve you well?
- Does it enhance your life?
- Does it empower you to move through the world more resourcefully?
- Does it make your life a party?
- Does it enable you to develop mastery in areas of your talents and passions?

Mere representation, and even "accurate" representation, that keeps putting us back into state and traumatizing us will make things worse. It is a concept or belief that "We have to accurately represent and keep representing whatever actually happened." And as a belief, it is an especially toxic one. Why keep an old video if it was B-rated the first time?

Going Meta to Change "History" Pattern

We can now meta-state our personal history containing memories and meanings to transform them so that they contribute to our development and create a forward movement for our growth and development. If the way you have been running your brain about the "past" has not empowered you, then use the following pattern to coach your brain to operate in a new and more productive way. Do it repeatedly and it will habituate to become a meta-pattern for your mind.

1) Identify an incident you'd like to change in your personal history.

What event or incident do you believe has a continuing *un*desirable influence on your life today?

Do you have any old incidents that involved a hurtful or ugly act imposed upon you by another person?

Did you ever experience a long series of unenhancing interactions with someone that sours you today?

Have you ever had experiences of derision or failure in some area of life (sports, academics, relationships, having fun, music, etc.) that keeps you from engaging in that area today?

What problematic or distressful event have you drawn some conclusions that still affects you?

What event occurred, which *if* it had not, you would think, feel, talk, act, and relate in a different way today?

What B-rated movie still plays in your mind from time to time?

2) Identify one or more powerful resources.

What resource of thought, emotion, or skill would have made all the difference in the world if you had it available at the time of the event?

Menu list: confidence, competence, self-esteem, etc.

What *resourceful* understanding about yourself, others, the world, how something works, etc. would have made a positive difference?

For example, "Dad just didn't pass his Parenting 101 class." "If a person acts in ugly or hurtful ways—the responsibility for that belongs to him or her."

Fully recall the resource, amplify it if you need to, and anchor the resource so that you have ready access to it. Strengthen it through appropriate amplification processes. Use a key cinematic feature or a driving meta-program. Really *juice it up* so that you experience it in full measure ... and enjoy that resource as you wonder just where you could apply it.

3) Meta-state your past experience with the new resource.

What do you feel when you take that resource back to the earlier incident and relive it with that resource?

How does your experience change when you take the resource back and relive the memory with it? In what ways specifically?

Repeat this process with the resource, or even other resources, so that with each re-run through the incident—you find that the event keeps changing and transforming into something more and more useful. How many times do you need to do this?

What happens each time you take a meta-position to your "memory" and *apply the resource to the memory*?

How else would you like to *outframe* your old frames with new empowering thoughts-and-feelings?

4) "Grow up" with the resource to create a new memory.

When the memory change is completed, what is it like when you now imagine growing up with that resource?

What other new memories do you create?

As you imagine moving up through your personal history along your time-line with that changed experience, enjoy inventing a history of resourcefulness that you can keep with you.

5) Future pace the resource.

What situation may occur in your future that you might need to fully feel and use this resource?

As you imagine that future event, imagine moving into that situation having *changed your past* and having *grown up with that resource*, notice all of the ways in which you respond so differently from what you otherwise might have done. Do you like that?

Are there any other resources to add to this?

This pattern enables us to outframe many of the old contexts and contexts-of-contexts as we bring thoughts-and-feelings of developing ("growing up") with a resource. We keep embedding our experience in the resource. And, if we do this in a trance-like state of relaxed comfort and inward focus, we will activate all parts of our brain and nervous system to *real-ize* it in terms of neuro-semantic processes.

Changing Suzanne's Personal History

Susan recalled a painful experience from her childhood when Bob invited her to do so during a Master Practitioner training. He asked about the representational distinctions of the old experience and invited her to make an image of herself and to step back from it so she could see it, "See that younger Susan, so that you can see it clearly—from a distance."

As Susan did, she saw an image of her younger self and saw the images as if out in front of her. "Where do you see the image at?"

Susan: "The image is right here ... out in front of me, down low, and about six feet away. There's also some color in it."

Bob: "Susan, I want you to focus on that image ... Good. Just be with that. Now, you of course realize that the event that happened to that younger Susan, happened many years ago. And that it is no longer happening. It once happened. But it is no longer real in that way. That event happened way in your past, and the people in your life at that time have changed ... they have changed dramatically, and so have *you*... You have changed to become much more resourceful, haven't you?"

At this point, Susan had moved through Steps 1 and 2 as Bob invited her to apply several resources to the old representations. Together they applied *a sense of distance, a sense of change,* and *a sense of "no longer real"* to her old memories.

Bob: "As you look at that picture now, I want you to begin to bring to bear on it some of your current resources ... resources that enable you to feel confident and courageous and which allow you to know fully your own value and dignity and as you do this, just begin to notice how it changes that no-longer-real memory from your past ... How does it change it?"
Susan: "It is disappearing."

"That's right, Susan, and that image can totally disappear as your resourcefulness increases, can it not?" It did. The image disappeared. As it did, Susan was struck with the realization that her map really is not the territory, but only a map of it. She also realized that she was no longer ten years old.

Bob: "So as you enjoy this experience of the old disappearing, you can begin to imagine yourself moving up through time, growing up as it were with that resource ... and as you imagine this, and feel this fully, you can anticipate arriving at today with this resource that has grown up those memories so that when you imagine your future—and other experiences, you can imagine being the you with all these resources and history... now."

In this instance she applied the *"The map is not the territory"* realization to the old movies playing in her mind. Interesting enough, while Susan "knew" that; she had never really *felt* it until this experience. Now she truly knew in her body that her map of the old memory was not the territory. The original territory from which she developed her map was over thirty years old. It occurred to her younger self—to a little girl of ten years of age.

Changing *History* Changes *Now*
Another client we met had been diagnosed as suffering from "manic depressive disorder." Due to this diagnosis, she received disability payments and at first she thought this was great. But after living four years under this diagnosis, she became tired of the label and felt anxious about not working and contributing. To make her life better, she took a part time job.

Yet this act of strength and courage evoked several fears. First she feared that she could not keep her new part-time job. Then she feared she would regress back to being a non-achiever. She also feared that she was defective and inadequate. The list went on and on. When enough was enough, she called Bob and asked that he "do some of his NLP magic." When she showed up, her presenting problem was a seemingly simple thing, "I'm afraid that I can't keep this job."

Bob inquired, "*How* do you know you feel afraid about this?" He asked because he wanted to know what references and meta-frames that she used for thinking and feeling this way. He sought to identify the higher belief and understanding frames which enabled her to justify and explain the fear to herself.

As it turned out, she had an old memory of a bad work experience. This "history" meant a lot to her. Bob explored it in terms of *what* she represented and *how* she encoded it, what it meant to her, and how she was using it to create her current experience of fear. Out of that exploration, he discovered that she had an image of herself as if watching a movie. On her mental screen she saw the former experience and her younger self losing a job. She then created her current fears by creating a panoramic image of this right in front of her face seeing herself getting fired. Then when she brought this up closer—it began feeling exceedingly real and compelling. And of course, coded like that, no wonder it scared her!

Knowing that the *Change Personal History pattern* could take care of this short measure, Bob used it with her. Afterwards, her image totally disappeared. Actually, it vanished. What explains this disappearing of a memory? It disappeared simply because the memory was *no longer meaningful to her or real* to her. In his case study notes, Bob wrote:
> "Prior to the therapy, she had essentially meta-stated herself into an almost panic by using the memory as her frame-of-reference for how to think about the current job. But now, utilizing the same neurological processes that she used to negatively meta-state herself, she meta-stated herself with new resources and applied them to that memory. When she did that, her image disappeared."

The 10 Minute Change Personal History Pattern
1) Set a frame that sorts out the past, present, and future.
> Hear a strong and compelling voice in your head for the following three time frames. When you have a good representation, anchor it.
> *Past:* "That's the past. It only describes experiences I have been through and nothing more. It means nothing about me at all. It rather describes the heavens and hells that I have journeyed through."
> *Present:* "Today is ... the day I have to live, to love, to discover, to grow, to experience, to plan, to take the first step or the hundredth step of an adventure. I will make the most of it."
> *Future:* "Tomorrow only exists as an idea and hope in my mind—and I will spend some time in preparing and anticipating it as I create a bright and compelling future to move toward while also taking full

advantage of the present moment...'

2) *Float up to your meta-level time-line.*

Where is your past when you float above your time-line?

Where is your present and future?

Are these positions sorted out so that your memories and imaginations serve you well?

Where do you have these located spatially? What voice tone and tempo? What visual qualities?

3) *Set a new time orientation.*

What resourceful ideas, beliefs, understandings, decisions, etc. would enable you to live more fully in the present, using the past for learning and wisdom, and the future for motivation and exploration?

Identify the frames that give you more space, energy, and focus in the present. How many do you have?

How often do you have to apply these frames until you feel alive and that you have fully come into the present with a compelling future?

Are you now empowered to move forward into your future and to enjoy the process?

4) *Super-charge your attitude for an energetic state to face the future.*

As the resource state gets stronger and stronger, let it feel more and more energetic as you apply it to *this moment* so you can come into full sensory awareness as you look around. How aware are you of your surroundings? Of your sense of your goals, values, and desired outcomes?

Let this simmer for a few minutes as you experience this hyper-synesthesia of past wisdom and future dreams in the moment and imagine using this as your basic life orientation from this day forward. Do you like that?

When it comes to brains, *brains follow directions literally.* If we tell our brain to represent a past horror, it does so. If we tell it to fully re-experience insult, humiliation, distress, or abuse, it will. If we do it repeatedly, under some delusion that if we keep going through it, we will get over it, we will only re-enforce the representations and toxic generalizations that we drew from it.

This means that we must be very, very careful about the *instructions* we sent our brain. It contains no quality control mechanism—no ecology check. If we want to have quality management in our mind—we have to make a meta-move and establish that frame.

Summary

- If we keep representing trauma and playing trauma movies in our mind we will eventually set *trauma and pain* as our frame-of-reference. Then numerous higher states and frames will keep us spiraling in that cycle.

- We can take charge of running our own brain by deciding to give our brain specifically enhancing instructions.

- The structure of excellence for any expertise or mastery involves the willingness and ability to take charge of our own sense of "time." This means learning from mistakes and putting ""bad things" behind us. Only then can we have enough freedom, safety, excitement, and passion to move full force ahead into a bright future.

- Our "past" is only a construct that we created. To use our memory movies as a resource, recode past events as learnings about what to avoid *and* what to go for with wisdom and power.

- It's never to late to have a happy childhood—so go have one now!

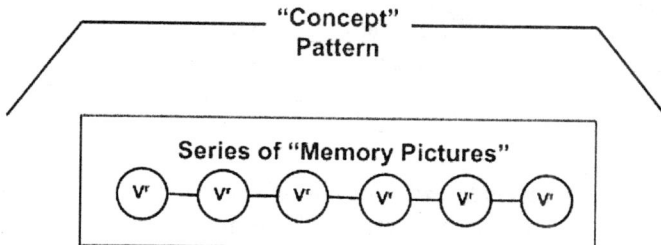

```
            _____ "Concept" _____
           /               Pattern              \
          /                                       \
         /    ┌─────────────────────────────────┐  \
        /     │      Series of "Memory Pictures" │   \
              │  (Vʳ)─(Vʳ)─(Vʳ)─(Vʳ)─(Vʳ)─(Vʳ)  │
              └─────────────────────────────────┘
```

Chapter 14

INSERTING
RESOURCEFUL IDEAS

Inside the Void of a Pause

There's a funny thing about the way we *think*. We actually *think by making movies inside our heads*—we make movies full of sights and sounds, and we also make movies that also are full of smells, tastes, and sensations. It's the wildest movie theater in the world!

As a species, we are inveterate *movie-makers*. We think by recalling and re-presenting inside of our minds various scenarios. The result is that it seems like we are seeing, hearing, feeling, smelling, and tasting things again. *Think* about the Big Ben, the Pyramids of Egypt, the Grand Canyon, the Twin Towers, Napoleon, Caesar of ancient Rome and so on and what happens? A *movie* happens.

Of course, none of this is *literal*. We know from modern brain research and the neuro-sciences that we do not actually have movies or pictures, or sounds or sensations or tastes or smells occurring *inside* our brains. It only *seems* like we have movies playing there inside the theater of our mind. It only *seems* like we experience a world of sensory experiences there.

Yet our bodies certainly respond as if we do have movies playing there. Ultimately all we have in our brain is the exchange of neuro-transmitters, the exchange of ions and positive and negative charges in neurological activity, the activation of cell assemblages, and other bio-electro-chemical processes. No movie theater, no screen in the mind. No movies.

What actually occurs in our brain? How do we *sense* things there that seem like a representation of the outside world? It is still too early to say. There are yet mysteries to unravel before we can explain or replicate this magic. What we can say is that somehow we use the external senses as a way of mapping or representing things. Somehow we have the sense that we are seeing, hearing, smelling, tasting, and feeling again and that reproduction of our sense modalities operates like a facsimile of the outside world.

Philosophically this way of understanding and "knowing" what we know (epistemology) is known as *phenomenology*. It only *seems like* what we have seen and heard. We are actually only dealing with our representations of the phenomena we experienced.

Regardless of what we call it, we think by re-presenting to ourselves what we have seen, heard, smelled, felt, and tasted on the outside. NLP describes this in terms of sensory representational systems—the VAK movie. We map things by making movies in our mind.

Renewing the Mind By Inserting New Pictures
Knowing about these component distinctions of our thoughts gives us many leverage points for renewing our mind, changing our mind, running our own brain, and taking charge of our mental-and-emotional states. Thinking about our internal movies as the way we represent information and encode understandings gives us a powerful metaphor to play with. And that's what the following is all about.

Notice what happens when you *stop* your internal films of whatever internal movie you are playing ... notice the effect it has on your body and emotions when you turn them into mere *snapshots* of the thoughts. Does not the process of *stopping* the movies have the effect of solidifying your pictures? When you freeze-frame your movies and turn them into snapshots, they typically become more static ... more solid, and more real. What happens then? Do you not then respond to them as being more real, static, and unchangeable?

Symbolically, representing *movement* conveys actions, progress, change, instability, emotion, and so on. Conversely, representing something as a snapshot can easily come to stand for "stable," "permanent," and "real."

Now as you continue to play with your brain ... as you remember and realize that these constructions are just that—*mental constructions*, internal mappings, then *visualize the space between* one image on the screen of your mind and the next image as individual snapshots—whether you have 32 images per second or 64 images, or however many. If you now just **stop the movie** and all of the moving pictures, allow yourself to become aware of *the space **between*** the images. You can do that, can you not?

So what happens if you now send your brain to those spaces, and then *into* them? Do you not end up in ... *a void* of sorts, a kind of nothingness of potentiality? Play with this and see where your brain goes. Because inside of that *pause* ... inside of that pregnant pause in-between the pictures of your movie, in the place where you *stop* ... in your mind, with the knowledge of the previous picture ... and awareness of the upcoming picture, then *in that void* we have a place in which we could insert a whole new images that could totally transform everything, if we choose to do that. And I wonder just what would you like to stick in there? And what would someone else like to stick in there?

In that *void of the pause* ... we could actually embed all kinds of things. Then later, when we could rewind the picture a bit and then let it go forward as pictures normally do so that all of a sudden *a whole new image,* and even an entirely new world could magically pop into existence. Something new that had not been there before could not emerge. How about that for a different kind of a way to swish the brain to new referents?

From this thought experiment, Bob and I put together and tested the following *Insert Pattern.* Bob used it with many people in his trainings and consulting. In the following case studies Bob demonstrates how to apply and install entirely new ideas inside of ideas.

Meta-Stating Your Movies With an >*Insert*>

The inserting process involves a meta-function because you have to *step back* and out of your internal movie, stop it, and then from a higher level, apply some resource (that you code as a part of the movie) to the original movie.

To illustrate visually how this language pattern works in stopping a movie (i.e., a strategy interrupt), Bob had some of the participants in one of his courses experiment with it. They ran an internal mental movie, and then *stopped* it abruptly. They did this just to see what would happen. For some, this minimized the negative feelings connected to the internal memory.

When he asked one participant to stop the movie, all of the frames that occurred before the place of the stop simply collapsed. However, she could still re-run the unpleasant movie and feel bad. Bob then coached her on running some additional meta-stating processes to completely blow out the traumatic movie.

After making sure that his participants knew how to abruptly stop a movie, he asked them to *insert a spiritual resource* such as their representations of God, Jesus, a Wise Mentor, being centered, feeling loving, etc. He asked them to insert them at the point of the stop, and to then finish the movie. As preparation, they had to first identify and fully access their representations of this spiritual resource. When they did, he asked them to re-run the total movie with the new insert in it. As a result, the *Resource >Insert > pattern* made a lot of difference for every one of them. It provided specific instructions for putting off their old mind, and putting on a new mind.

Recovering Insights from Korzybski

True to his engineering background, Korzybski compared the *structure* of primary states full of emotions and energy (first-order abstractions) and meta-states (second-order abstractions). As he did, one of the metaphors that he used was that of the analogy of *watching a movie.* In watching a film, we can focus on experiencing its drama and movement or we can focus on stopping the movie in order to gain understanding of its structure, form, and *nature.* Content and structure. Lower experience and higher experience.

When our internal pictures operate as a dynamic and ever-shifting *movie,*
> "... our 'emotions' are aroused, we 'live through' the drama; but the details ... are blurred. ... The picture was 'moving,' all was changing, shifting, dynamic, similar to the world *and* our feelings on the unspeakable levels. The impressions were vague, shifting, non-lasting, and what was left of it was mostly coloured by the individual mood..."
> "But if we *stop* the moving film ... and analyse the static and extensional series of small pictures on the reel, we find that the drama which so stirred our 'emotions' in its moving aspect becomes a series of slightly different static pictures, each difference between the given jerk or grimace being a *measurable* entity..."
> "The *moving* picture represents the usually brief processes going on in the lower nerve centres, 'close to life', but unreliable and evading scrutiny. The *arrested* static film which lasts indefinitely, giving *measurable* differences ... allows analysis and gives a good analogy of the working of higher nerve centres, disclosing that all life occurrences have many aspects ... The moving picture gives us the process; each static film of the reel gives us stages of the process in chosen intervals." (*Science and Sanity,* p. 292)

Commenting on the nature of our internal abstractions, Korzybski separated and sorted out two kinds. He noted how they correspond to two levels of brain processing. The ever-shifting nature of the lower levels (thalamic processing) and the more static nature of the higher levels (cortical processing) corresponds to our primary level states and meta-states.
> "The thalamic regions ... are a vestibule through which all impulses from the receptors have to pass in order to reach the cortex" (p. 290)

Here the *dynamic* and shifting nature of data creates in our experience as the highly affective nature of "thoughts," namely *emotions and somatic responses.*

> "The cortex receives its materials as elaborated by the thalamus. The abstractions of the cortex are abstractions from abstractions and so

> ought to be called abstractions of higher order. ... The receptors are in direct contact with the outside world and convey their excitation and nerve currents to the lower nerve centers..." (p. 290)

The *thalamic* thinking at the lower level needs to be "re-educated" by the "development of poise, balance, and a proportional increase of critical judgement and so 'intelligence'" from the higher levels. These higher level abstractions "have *lost* their *shifting* character" and "are further removed from the outside world." (p. 291).

Korzybski noted that the lower level of brain processing, the thalamic processes, corresponds to the quickness, fluxations, and movement of data. This leads to more emotionality, reactivity, and inability to control "thoughts." He said that when we send this thalamic material up to the higher levels of brain processing, so that we abstract one or more levels from it, we can slow down our images and control them more. This makes our pictures more solid and real.

Korzybski's engineering attitude led him to write about the process of translating static data to dynamic data and vice versa. In this way we develop choice and control over running our own brain. The *Inserting Resources* pattern taps into the power and usefulness of both dynamic and static images. We begin with the dynamic flow of "thoughts." We then stop the internal movie, insert a new resourceful awareness or feeling, and then put it back into a dynamic form which will then react with new and different and more resourceful emotions.

Inserting a Moment of Spiritual Peace
Several years ago Alethia's father shot himself and so ended his life. At the time of the shooting, Alethia was in the house and saw her father's body immediately after the event. This memory of the traumatic event gave her problems for years.

In the NLP course, she ran the movie and stopped it midway through the horror to insert her resource (at image of Jesus). Upon doing that she ran the movie again and at the insert point suddenly became aware that her spiritual resource had been there all the time. This enabled her to finished the movie. She next ran the entire movie consciously and enjoyed seeing *this new image pop into* it at the point where that resource assisted her. Alethia reported that by becoming consciously aware of this presence, it allowed her to see her deceased father being ushered into heaven. Later she reported that this procedure removed "much of the negative emotions that had been associated with the memory."

Getting a Divine View of the Situation
David decided to use the *Insert Pattern* on an incident that happened during his

teenage years and which had continued to bother him into adulthood. It concerned an especially vivid movie in his mind about a confrontation between himself and his parents.

He began by running the movie of his parents "discussing" his bad deed. About midway through the movie, he stopped it, *inserted his new resource,* and then let the movie play out to the end. This procedure immediately lowered his negative emotions about it. He then went back and ran the movie from the beginning to the end to put it all together as one piece. As he did, he saw himself, his father, and his awareness of a divine presence in the context of the old confrontation over his misdeed.

This astonished him.

> "Wow!" David said. "The content has stayed the same, but I see God as meta to us. The anxiety I have always felt is gone. This works great! It's like I have a sense of my spiritual values right in there when I really need to have that awareness."

Hell Embedded in the Glow of a Protective Guardian Angel

Calion chose a really bad scene with which to test this procedure. Though now divorced, Calion endured a horrific marriage with a terribly abusive man. Her husband had wanted her to go with him somewhere, and when she refused he followed her into the house and physically assaulted her, severely beating her in the face and bruising her eyes.

When Clarion described the movie before inserting the resource, she was fully associated in the memory. Tears flowed down her face and she grimaced as if in pain. In questioning her, she described the scene as "click," "click," and "click" indicating that she focused in on each frame as she slowed the movie down. As she described this, I (BB) thought about Michael's words about how slowing down representations tends to make things more solid. When we slow down our painful movies and run them frame by frame, we intensify the feelings because we are able to focus on the hurtful content encapsulated in each frame. Calion was seeing each frame distinctly and clearly and this caused her to re-experience all of the hurt and pain.

After placing *her resource* into the old movie, and re-running it as one new edited piece, she said,

> "I saw a new presence, maybe an angel, come in the room with me and like an angel he stood with outstretched arms, protecting me from my husband. He can't get to me anymore!"

In spite of the fact that her abusive former husband had been in prison for years, she had continued to live with the fearful anxiety of seeing him return and doing his worse. Now, however, the *Insert pattern* enabled her to set up a new frame of reference for her mind and emotions—the meta-protection of a guardian angel. This allowed her to recall that scene with laughter. What a change from how she first recalled the memory!

An Insert That Annihilated a Movie

In all the previous examples, I (BB) have used anonymous names from students. Now for the final and best test for this procedure—my wife, Linda. I asked her if she would like to try out a new procedure that we had been playing with. She said she would play, so I invited her to run an internal movie of some negative event at work. When she thought of one, I asked her to begin the movie and to let it play out, in her mind, until she got to about half way through it, and to *stop it* there.

Then I suggested that she could *insert a resource,* like her image of Jesus, at the very point where she stopped the movie, and to then finish the movie with an awareness of that spiritual resource in it. But she said that she could not even run it anymore.

"Bob," she said, "it won't run with Jesus in it."

I asked her to insert her resourceful image at the beginning of the memory, and to let it run all the way through with the resource in it.

"I can't run it! It just will not run that way!"

A day later, I checked with her, and then again two days later to see what had happened to her thinking and feeling regarding that event. She said,

"It was an old hurt that occurred when Barbara was teaching me about Human Resources. Hmmm. No! That event doesn't mean anything to me anymore."

If You Insert Calmness, Don't Outframe with a Sword!

I worked with Sharon over the period of a few weeks. We had two meetings, plus a more recent one with both her and her daughter, Carla. As a single parent, Sharon raised her daughter since she was six years old. When I briefly met the daughter it was obvious that she carried a lot of intense anger and that her mother had lost all control with her. Soon, my worst fears came true.

When I next saw Sharon, her daughter Carla had run away from home. Sharon eventually located her at the home of a girlfriend who also came from a broken home. Sharon didn't want Carla to spend one more night because her friend was in the custody of the Department of Social Services and had a history of rebelliousness.

When Sharon first notified the police of Carla's disappearance, they could do little because children over sixteen are considered adults in North Carolina. Yet over-determined to take her daughter home, Sharon tricked her out of the friend's house. A fight then ensued between mother and daughter. Just at the point when Sharon lost her temper and struck Carla, the police arrived and so Sharon was arrested. Carla had to go live with her grandmother in another state.

In describing the trauma of these events, I asked Sharon to run a movie of the confrontation and subsequent arrest. We discovered that she had dissociated from the event. I asked her to run the movie and *stop it* abruptly right before the fight. She did. I then invited her to re-run the movie and *insert a spiritual* resource into the movie just before the fight, and to then complete it. I finally asked her to run the movie from beginning to end with this resource in it.

Afterwards, Sharon described how she would have behaved much differently had she *realized and felt the presence of this resource* during the event. She then said something most fascinating. On her way over to get her daughter, she had prayed and thought about "suiting up" for a spiritual battle. "I put on the breastplate of righteousness and grabbed ahold of the sword of the Spirit." Sharon said this raising her arm up, symbolizing the sword in her right hand.

"You went as a soldier and so you ended up fighting, didn't you?"
     "Yes, I sure did." she said.

This reflects the power of the *metaphors* that we apply to our thoughts and emotions as Lakoff and Johnson (1980) mentioned in *Metaphors We Live By*. As Sharon *framed herself using the War Metaphor* that contained ideas of being a soldier, she went forth in a fight mode, and nearly got herself locked up. How much better of an outcome would Sharon received had she gone to her daughter with a resource image conveying more gentleness, love, and compassion?

Using The *>Insert>* Pattern
Since we construct all of our internal movies, *we have the power to change them at will.* We can also refine them, tune them up, add all kinds of resources to them— and we can do so in multiply ways. This describes the genius of NLP and Neuro-Semantics. The *>Insert Resources> pattern* takes the metaphor of our internal movies and maps it out so that we can alternate from dynamic to static representations. We do this to activate and utilize both our affective and somatic nature as well as our higher level meta-states of understanding, belief, values, etc. In doing this, we maintain and balance all facets of our mind-and-neurology nature.

Summary

- The cinematic features of our sensory representations or internal movie provides a symbolic or metaphorical way for us to encode information.
- Many people use "closeness" in sight and sound to designate "more compelling" and "more real." We typically use "brightness" to designate "encouraging, hopeful, and positive." This describes how we use these distinctions so they take on a meta-function for symbolizing *meanings* and embedding experiences inside such meanings.
- This also explains how and why "sub-modalities" work. When we discover *what* it symbolizes to a given person and *use* that encoding as a code for something else—we can map over a limiting state to the distinctions that use the key the meta-frames to set new, different, and more resourceful frames.
- Since it's all constructed—the idea of *inserting* new resourceful ideas, feelings, memories, etc. in the very middle of our mental processing, offers us some new meta-patterns for running our brain.

Chapter 15

EXTERNALIZING
AND READING
"SUB-MODALITIES"
ON THE OUTSIDE

"All sub-modality shifts are demonstrated in external behavior."
Richard Bandler
Using Your Brain—For A Change (p. 151)

Using NLP we know we can see and detect the cues that a person is using various sensory codes (visual, auditory, and kinesthetic) in running their mental movies. Eye accessing cues especially give clue to this. Is it also possible to *see* the cinematic features of the pictures, sounds, and feelings in our internal movie?

- Can we engage someone in a conversation and *see* "sub-modalities" on the outside?
- If we could, what do they look like externally?
- What do we pay attention to?
- How do we discern "sub-modalities" in gestures and "body language?"
- How do we *externally* act out, gesture, move, breathe, etc. that indicates a "sub-modality" distinction in an internal movie?

As a book about "sub-modalities," the questions in the bullet points here focus on whether the cinematic features of our movies can or do show up in our physiology and neurology. The surprising point of this chapter is that *Yes*, we do demonstrate and project "sub-modalities" on the outside and can learn to read them.

We manifest the qualities of our inner movies because those properties and cinematic features of our thinking and internal experiencing occur within our mind-body-emotion system. To some degree they are expressive in our neurology. We also manifest them, at least a little bit, because we physically operate in the world in our movements and gestures using the *holographic maps* we have in our heads. In other words, we don't merely create flat 2-dimensional maps or snapshots, we create full holographic maps or 3-D movies, and we then move through life *inside of them*. The movie that repeatedly plays fit our Matrix.

Similar to how we use *eye accessing cues, breathing patterns, gesturing patterns,* and even *body types* in NLP to detect the visual, auditory, and kinesthetic systems, it's really no surprise that we can learn to detect and calibrate to the behavioral cues of "sub-modalities." Supposing this is so, this raises numerous questions:

- *How* do we learn to read "sub-modalities" on the outside?
- What processes can assist us in developing this skill?
- How can we learn to recognize various cinematic features externally in a person's behavior?
- What do we need to do to fine-tune our senses to detect "sub-modalities?"
- Why would we want to do this? How is this of any value?

"Sub-modalities" as Frames and Within Frames
In unmasking "sub-modalities" and finding that they are an editorial meta-level of our movies, we discover that the structure of experience is not at a *sub* level, but at the conceptual level. There is no *sub* or *lower* level to our movies. The idea of a lower level arose from the misdirection of a false-to-fact term.

The distinctions we make about the sensory features in our movies occur at a higher level and reflect our conceptual framing. As we set frames, the concepts recruit the cinematic distinctions to encode our representations for the corresponding effect. In this way, we abstract the concepts of distance, location, volume, brightness, etc. Then we set "close" or "far" as our frame of reference, "bright" or "dim," etc.

This means that merely representing the brute facts of images, sounds, and words do not *per se* create the quality of our subjective experiences. Rather, the *quality* of our life, behaviors, skills, emotions, experiences, etc. arise from the qualities and meanings we encode via our editorial frames. As we make *a meta-move* to frame what we see, hear or sense with various qualities and features we cue our brain-neurology system about how to feel in response to a stimuli.

Consider the goal of staying fit and trim as an example. Represent that idea. As you do, create and hold a picture of that goal in your mind.
- Does that representation *in and of itself* cause you to implement it?
- What does, or would, *activate* your nervous system to actually move

you to exercise?
- How do you need to code the representations of "the fit and trim you" so that it gets you off your rear end?
- Can sufficient neurological energy emerge from the *qualities* that we encode an internal movie in?
- What cinematic features would we need to use?
- Would it happen for you if you saw your fit and trim self movie with lots of vivid colors, rather than a snapshot?
- Or, would it happen if you code with crystal clarity the images and see them close and large?
- Perhaps you need to see the movie up close and personal, from an associated position while you hear the words, *"Just do it!"*

If so, then these qualities and codings are the cinematic features that tell your brain-body system what to feel and how to respond. Using your critical cinematic features ("sub-modalities") they will set the frame that switch on an experience of motivation. Yet, even cranking up *all* of your "sub-modalities" so that the movie looks vivid, bright, close, 3-D, with surround-a-sound, etc. may still not get your neurological juices going sufficiently. Suppose you have all of that embedded in conceptual frames like: "Why go through all the sweat and bother?" "That would take too much effort, too much time." "I don't like to exercise." The frames would nullify the movie. And that's why frames govern.

Reading "Sub-modalities" and Frames
We have repeatedly suggested the possibility of learning to see "sub-modalities" and frames on the outside as we do VAK representations. Eye accessing cues, linguistic markers, breathing patterns, etc. have traditionally made up the domain of NLP as pathways for recognizing a person's representational systems.

Are there additional pathways that can put us on the road to seeing other mapping structures on the outside? In *The Spirit of NLP* (Hall, 1996/ 2000) on mastering NLP, we addressed this subject about learning to recognize "sub-modalities" on the outside. In *Figuring Out People* (1997) we applied the same to seeing and hearing meta-programs on the outside.

Eliciting our Movie Cinematic Feature
Use the following exercise to tune yourself in recognizing the qualities, features, and characteristics of your movie representations. As you do, give yourself a chance to slowly and intentionally (but maybe not consciously) sort out the *driver* or critical "sub-modalities" in yourself and others. Simply discover the range of variation that occurs in the cinematic features. As you play with this process with others, you can further train your senses to become more intuitive

about these distinctions.

The Elicitation Pattern

1) Access and anchor an uptime state.

What best invites you to step into an intense state of sensory awareness? How much do you feel in "uptime?"

What do you need to do to amplify this state?

What are you seeing right now in your *external* environment? What are you hearing? Smelling? Sensing?

How much more fully can you come into *the now* of this moment?

Do you have permission to to "lose your mind and come to your senses" (Perls)?

2) Elicit a strong positive experience.

Have you ever thoroughly and completely *enjoyed* something? What have you enjoyed so much that you got lost in it?

Are you willing to use this as a *content* for the purposes of this exploration?

What is it like right now, on the inside, when you *see* what you saw, *hear* what you heard, *feel* what you felt, and *smell* what you smelled in that enjoyable experience?

What do you need to do to amplify that experience?

3) Experiment with detecting the following cinematic features.

As you hold that experience in mind and just enjoy it, access the analog distinctions using the following features as we here do with *location*:

Where is it located? How far away from you? If you were to point to it, where would you point? What if it was closer? Farther away?

Is there a sound track? What is it? Where is the sound coming from? How far?

What sensations are there? Where are they located? What if they were in your legs? Back? Etc.

Take one cinematic feature at a time, inquire in a similar way so the person can become aware about that distinction. Slowly vary each distinction to get a sense of what such shifts do for the person's inner subjective experience.

Visual	**Auditory**	**Kinesthetic**
Location	Location	Location
Distance	Distance	Intensity
Movement	Volume	Duration
Brightness	Pitch	Movement
Contrast	Tone	Rhythm
Focus	Rhythm	

For example, brighten the image to the point where the feeling or experience begins to change. This typically indicates that you have pushed the experience to some sort of threshold. Stop when you get to this stage. Back off slightly and vary the "sub-modality" feature in the other direction (from brightness to dimness). Again, stop and back off slightly.

When you have finished experimenting and playing around with the range of a distinction, ask the person to restore it to the way it was originally.

4) *Invite a meta-awareness of the experience.*

As you notice your positive state and how these shifts of the "sub-modality" distinctions effect you and the range of variation you experience, which cinematic features really *drive* things for you and which just provide *some* alterations?"

So what was that like?

Would you comment on your experiences as we played with the "sub-modalities" to help me more accurately calibrate to you?

What changes made the biggest differences for you?

> Expect some changes that are big on the inside to be very subtle on the outside.

What variables seemed the most useful in changing the intensity of the experience?

What are the person's driving or critical "sub-modalities?"

How much more do you need to calibrate and experiment from your own state of sensory acuity until you have a sense of reading the person's "sub-modalities?"

5) *Combine "sub-modality" drivers.*

Do you now know three of the main driver distinctions?

If so, combine them and run them at the same time and notice the cumulative effect. What happens?

Are you now beginning to develop insight with regard to *how* your own "sub-modality" distinctions effect your own subjective experiences?

As you work with someone in this process, you will begin to tune your eyes and ears for recognizing this kind of mapping in the external expressions of others. With practice, this will train your intuitions to give you a natural sense about this.

Excuse Me, But Your "Sub-Modalities" are Showing

Fifteen years ago, Bandler (1985) suggested this area of research:

> "All sub-modality shifts are demonstrated in external behavior. For instance, when someone brightens a picture, the head rotates back and up, but when a picture comes closer, the head moves straight back. If

you observe people when you ask them to make sub-modality changes, you can calibrate to the behavioral shifts that we call 'sub-modality accessing cues.' Then you can use those shifts to determine what someone is doing inside, even when he's not aware of it. I always use this calibration as a check to be sure the client is doing what I ask him to." (p. 151)

What do you *believe* about the idea that we can learn to read "sub-modalities" on the outside in external expressions? To what extent do you think you can fine tune your calibration skills that you could tell when a person entertains an internal image in color versus black-and-white? Or, a fuzzy picture versus a clear one? Or have an image which they code as close versus far away? Or a sound that they hear inside in a panoramic way versus one located in a single location?

During my original training with Richard Bandler, Eric Robbie focused on this feat of calibration as an advanced kind of Master Practitioner "mind-reading." Taking his cue from the NLP eye accessing cues, he sought to find ways to read "sub-modalities" on the outside. He wrote about such in *The Journal of NLP International* under the title, "Sub-Modality Eye Accessing Cues," (1987, Vol. I, No. 1).

To a great extent this skill depends on the ability to access, cleanly and intensely, a strong uptime state. This assists with calibration to the internal experiences of others. If you are not fully and completely present with all of your sensory awareness, you will simply miss most of the cues in another's experience. Amplify this even further by accessing a "fast time" trance state. Sense yourself going twice as fast as the speed of things in the world.

Begin by calibrating to people's *internal dialogues.* Learning to calibrate to this facet of internal experience means training yourself to watch for *the analogs of the language* representations. Watch for movements in the jaw and lower mouth while a person uses words to "think."
* Does the person sub-vocalize?
* Can you see the person "talking to him or herself?"
* What kind of a rhythm does he or she generate with the internal dialogue that may show up as muscle movements in their jaw and/or mouth?

With some people, the eyes will sometimes move down and to the left. With others, eyes will make quick lateral moves. What do you notice? What about detecting a person experiencing two dialogues going on simultaneously? Practice this by finding a partner and asking him or her to mentally *debate a decision* back and forth without talking aloud. Now just sit back (or forward!)

and notice.

- What do you see? Hear? Sense?
- Do you see the person's head moving back and forth?
- Do you discern any pattern to the internal experience of debating a decision?
- Does the person seem to have representations or voices stored in different places to which he or she goes back to, from time to time?

Typically a person in internal debate between two lines of thought will code the two internal voices by *sorting them out spatially* in different locations. This seems to occur more often than not.

While in the internal debate, invite your partner to drop the jaw. As he or she does, notice how this affects things. Ask the person how it affects his or her experience, body, feelings, etc. Typically this alteration of the kinesthetics of the jaw and mouth will cut off the internal talk completely. With some people, it will just reduce the amount or speed of the internal dialogue. What do you notice in yourself? In your partner? By changing the kinesthetics of the mouth and jaw, we can often *interrupt* those kinesthetic—auditory synesthesia patterns, and/or powerfully affect the internal experience. This also suggests that we use our jaw and mouth as part of our internal dialoguing over conflicting choices.

This means that we have a way to encode our learnings, understandings, memories, etc. regarding our language representational system. It gives us a tracking system for recalling and retrieving these higher level thoughts. Use these processes as a way to organize and train yourself to recognize the presence of words.

Most of us have grown up in a culture and neuro-linguistic environment that highly values language as the medium of choice for thinking. Most educational systems highly reward the language dimension for learning, intelligence development, problem solving, etc. And rightly so. Yet some people overly trust this meta-representational system. They over-value words. A person can live too much in the language system and so become too much removed from the primary level of sensory experience. Korzybski described this as an *intensional orientation* rather than an *extensional orientation.*

An over-reliance on words can have harmful effects. As it removes us from the sensory-based level, words can get in our way from experiencing things directly. Fritz Perls argued that sometimes we just need to get "the words out of our eyes." To that end, he said, *"Lose your mind and come to your senses."*

Reading "Sub-modality" Features Externally

Take some time to use the following exercise to play around with "sub-modalities" in order to tune your *intuitions* about them and their external expressions. This exercise will enable you to calibrate to others' internal experiences with more accuracy.

1) Access an experience in a group.

With three people, take turns playing the role of experiencer, coach, and meta-observer. The coach will begin by inviting the experiencer to access a strong positive or negative memory experience.

2) Calibrate from an intense uptime state.

Experiencer: Will you access a referent experience of a joyful time?

Coach and meta-person: Access a strong uptime state to fully turn on all sense receptors to calibrate the experiencer. Watch and calibrate the person's breathing, posture, eye movements, skin tone, etc., while listening to the person's story.

What "sub-modalities" does the person express? What are implied and presupposed?

If you need to, ask the experiencer questions about the "sub-modalities" of the experience until you feel satisfied that you have begun to calibrate them. Do this once or twice.

3) Repeat the process in silence without words.

Once you have "set your calibrations" to the experiencer, invite the person to access another strong experience but *without* speaking about it. Let the person tell the story and just quietly experience it.

After a few minutes, the coach and meta-observer can begin *wildly guessing* about the "sub-modalities" of the experience. Make a written list of your guesses and see how many each person guessed correctly. When you do this, *go as quickly as possible*. The speed will help. Don't think about it, just quickly make guesses. Simply look, calibrate, gauge, and guess. This will help you to avoid thinking about it. Just do it quickly. This very process will assist you to turn off your internal dialogue so it will not get in your way. This will help you move into the "unspeakable level." Use the following list at first, later you can add to it.

Color   — Black / White
Bright — Dim
Focus   — Defocused
Near   — Far
Moving — Still
Big   — Small
Border — Panoramic

Flat — 3D

Once you develop some expertise with these, then begin to play around with other distinctions: tilting, shimmering, spinning, moving in unusual ways, translucent pictures in front. Experiment to see what you happens.

Debriefing the Finer Calibration

How did you do? How much did that put you into a place of feeling that you were calibrating much more—noticing, detecting, and reading "sub-modality" cues on the outside? How much more calibrated did you become? Do you have any awareness about signs or signals of various distinctions?

Can you tell the difference when a person processes a big internal picture versus a very small tiny one? Try that by having someone engage themselves with each of these distinctions. What difference can you see on the outside that may function as an analogue marker? Does the person lean back and look more upward when processing a really big picture? Do not most people lean forward and closer when they think about some small particular detail of a picture? This same pattern will occur when a person thinks about a picture as close or far away.

What would you guess relates to the "sub-modalities" of a trance state? Take a moment to see if you can identify them. Then, when you have a list of them, use this list of language by presupposition to assist someone going into that state. Do this by giving the language to the person which includes the very cinematic features that will lead them into that state.

Practicing the Skill

1) Access and anchor a state of ecstasy.

> Have you ever experienced an exquisite experience where you felt just ecstatic? When and where? What was that like?

2) Identify the cinematic features of ecstasy.

> What are the cinematic features that code your referent experience for ecstasy?
> What are the "sub-modalities" that *drive* it?
> How many of them are you able calibrate?

3) Pick a new desired activity.

> What can you not do, but that you would like to do?
> I want you to now close your eyes and see a picture of yourself doing this desired activity. That's right. Just enjoy it.

4) *Access and apply the feature.*

As you are now stepping even more fully into that state, let it amplify, that's right. And what is it like now when you apply your ecstasy "sub-modalities" (including tastes, sounds, and smells) to this movie? What happens? How does that feel? Do you like it?

5) *"White out" the picture.*

How easily can you now brighten the picture until it whites out?
When the picture becomes completely white, nod and I want you to *feel this* (immediately fire the ecstasy state anchor).
And *the more* you feel the feelings of ecstacy, *the more* the picture of doing what you would like to do will come back."

Use all of the cinematic features and analogs that match and increase the ecstasy state.

Now I want you to white-out and let the picture return three times and very quickly.

6) *Break state and test.*

What time is it?
That reminds me, what did you eat for breakfast last Thursday?

As you do this, keep calibrating to seeing and hearing the "sub-modalities" on the outside. Keep using analogs that match and amplify the internal state so that you can keep learning to match the internal "sub-modalities."

Externalizing Internal Maps and Movies into External Space

The previous processes and patterns operate by increasing sensory awareness, calibration skills, and training intuitions regarding the states of others. Yet there is another way to approach this subject. We begin with the assumption that we *externalize* our internal maps and movies. Starting from that concept, we can now ask someone to exaggerate the externalizations and watch, listen, and feel what happens.

This approach comes from the same presuppositions which enabled Bandler to discover and articulate the model of externalized "time-lines." Consider how we externalize our concept of "time" and to then sort it out using the metaphor of a line, path, or circle. In *Time-Lining: Patterns for Adventuring in "Time"* (1997) we noted that at a level above and beyond the actual passing of *events* (primary time), we have numerous *concepts* of "time." Past, present, and future "time" are our first level "time" zones. We have atemporal "time," eternity, Western "time" and Eastern "time." We have personal and cultural "time," psychological fast and slow "time," mathematical, religious, and mythical "time."

All of these meta-level abstractions about various kinds and dimensions of "time" arise because we do stop when we recognize and represent an event, we rise above that and notice the passing of events. We take the next step to sort out events. We sort out the events that have happened, events now happening, and events that we anticipate will happen. As we then *compare* events, we create a code to tell the difference. We use a line, path, circle, semi-circle, spiral, or boomerang as a metaphor. The metaphor enables us to put previous events in a certain place in our mental world, to encode and punctuate how much "today" or "the present" takes up, and the location for storing events yet to come.

All of this takes place in our mind like a holographic 3-dimensional representation. That's pretty incredible. Yet even more incredible is the fact that we *project it outward* into the actual space around us.

In time-line eliciting and processing, most right-brained persons put their *past* to their left or behind them, the *present* immediately in front of them or around them (close to their sense of personal space) and their *future* to their right or straight out in front of them. We can detect these conceptual *spatial encodings* of past, present, and future if we simply watch *where* the person looks and gestures when talking about these time concepts.

Woodsmall and James (1988) described many of these facets. Later Andreas and Andreas (1987, 1989) offered other refinements using "sub-modality" distinctions about time. In these works, the processes are based upon the *externalization* of our internal processes and codes. Detection depends upon looking *where in space* a person puts things.

We hinted at this earlier in the section, *Debriefing the Finer Calibration.* There, the external behavior of *moving in* or closer as if looking for more details, and *moving out* as if trying to get a larger perceptive illustrates *the behavioral externalization of internal representational distinctions.*

If we look at other subjective experiences, will we find similar patterns? If we use this *externalizing of our holographic maps* as a formative principle, what other ideas, concepts, and representations will we find externalized?

Charles Faulkner uses the work of Lakoff and Johnson (1980) and the Cognitive Linguistics principle of *embodiment* to suggest a similar thing. Given the kind of bodies we have and the kind of relationships we have to gravity and to the world in general, we develop orientational metaphors that we use to encode our understandings. Orientation metaphors include such simple terms as up/down, in/out, before/behind, near/far, right/left, continuities/discontinuity, under /around/ over/ through, etc. Embodiment metaphors include: containers, objects, paths, forces, cycles, links, etc. These govern the most primary physical components of our world: space, energy, movement, etc.

Faulkner (1998) in a tone that seemed a bit rebellious, asked his workshop audience at the ANLP Conference in London:

> Why bother with reading "sub-modalities" on the outside? Just ask yourself, "What would a person literally **do** in an actual experience?" If something was bright and far away would he not squint his eyes? This is no big secret. You don't need to have to wait for this until you get to the Master Practitioner level. You don't need to promise to *not* do this without certification, or to tell people the secrets!

Bandler moved in this direction with his DHE work claiming that we can see and detect all kinds of things in the actual location of a person's space. For years he has said that we can see in actual space a person's beliefs, values, meta-programs, decisions, motivation, etc. You will find in *Appendix A* the beginning of this exploration and the need for unique and personal calibration for each given individual. Just as we find people's time-lines in different places and with different configurations, so we will find idiosyncratic differences in where and how any given person *externalizes* his or her *internal holographic mapping*.

To assist in this detection, pay special and literal attention to a person's linguistic markers about embodied reality. These will provide lots of clues as to the person's *internal landscapes*.

> "These are my *highest* values."
> "Well, I hold that as *downright* important."
> "I would have gone for it, but it was *bigger* than both of us."
> "Now just *step into* the goal..."
> "I feel *beside* myself today; something's just not right."
> "It seems that we're always *in sync* with each other."
> "When I engage in that, I feel I'm *dancing with* my destiny."

Question: Where do these things come from? How do we end up with the constructed landscapes or mindscapes that govern our thinking and feeling?
Answer: For the most part, we use our actual external experiences, our embodied experiences, to construct our internal coding systems. These exist almost entirely implicitly, and almost never explicitly. Now, all we have to do is to externalize what we introjected.

Once we have done that, we can also begin to examine and evaluate the kind of landscapes with which we have used to populated our world. Do they serve us well? Do they assist us in *moving forward* as we desire? Or do they create various kinds of *traps and pits* for us so that we get *stuck* and cannot *proceed forward?*

"Sub-modality" Transformations "On the Outside"

As we do various kinds of things with *kinesthetic* time-lines, using actual external space for anchoring, re-imprinting, moving into the future, we can also do other "sub-modality" interventions on the outside. This gives us the freedom from the hypnotic induction, "Close your eyes and go inside, and now picture."

Faulkner says that we literally *in-form* our world as we create patterns and impose structures. We construct our world and then we live inside that matrix. This leads to new explorations:

> How have I structured the distinctions in my world?
> What patterns have I constructed and now live within?
> Do they serve to enhance my life?"

If it is all mapping, then we can re-scale our maps. We can re-configure our landscapes. We can pull down *walls and barriers*. We can build *bridges* and *propulsion forces*. We can do all kinds of wild and wonderful and magical things. If we grant that all of this *externalizing* internal maps and detecting them on the outside is true, so what? What can we do with this information? How can it empower us in our communications?

The value is that we can perform elegant magic with our words and non-verbal communications. We can learn how to spatially anchor concepts. For example, we could gesture to indicate that old negative memories and thoughts can *move over* into a person's "past" and out of the way. We can gesture and mime that the person can open up new "future" space as the person moves out more courageously. We can move to stand immediately in front of someone's pictures and then begin to tear them up with wild gestures. We can invite someone to *step back* to get a broader and more expansive vision of something. And the magic goes on.

Summary

- The cinematic distinctions or "sub-modalities" that give more detail and specificity to our internal coding are meta-frames. We *go meta* to detect them and we *go meta* to play with them, alter them, transform them, and use them to empower our life.
- Though seeming invisible and outside-of-consciousness, these components are not beyond the ken and scope of our awareness. We can learn to recognize and detect them "on the outside."
- We can develop greater sensory awareness and skill in learning to calibrate to these cinematic features in our mental movies. We can learn to see, hear, and feel them as we talk and interact with people. And when we do, we increase our power in using neuro-linguistic magic.
- Knowing about the *externalization* of internal mapping enables us to be more precise and elegant in our words and non-verbal communications. We can anchor things *spatially* in and around another's semantic space.

Chapter 16

META-STATING
IN ACTION

The Magic of Richard Bandler

- Though Bandler calls them *"sub*-modalities," what if they are actually meta-states and meta-frames?
- What if the magic was meta-stating all along?
- What if Bandler has been meta-stating and just didn't know it?

When "sub-modalities" *go meta* and we *unmask* their meta-levels, we discover several new refinements for the NLP model. We once thought it was about some lower level structure when it was about the *meta* or editorial level of the framing of our mental movies.

As I first came upon these secrets of "sub-modalities," I immediately relied upon the experiential clinical testing of the processes by Dr. Bodenhamer. Together we created numerous *meta-distinction patterns w*hich, in turn, led us to reformat several of the classic NLP patterns. Formerly, these would have been classified as *"sub-*modality" patterns. Today this has changed. We now perceive them as meta-level operations which perform their magic by applying various distinctions or qualities to some experience.

In another sense, this theoretical re-modeling of these processes and structures does not change the fact that people have been able to make numerous *meta-level transformations* using *"sub-*modality" shifts. To illustrate, I want to replay some of the "cutting edge" *"sub-*modality" patterns that Richard began introducing in the mid-1980s.

I have pieced together the following from some old videos from *NLP Comprehensive* when Richard Bandler first revealed some of his "new" discoveries in 1987. The tapes were recorded as "the best of Bandler" in the context of the then new "sub-modality" distinctions. At least Richard presented them as *"sub-*modality" patterns.

As far as I'm concerned, the linguistic genius of Richard Bandler that one can see and hear in those presentations occur *in spite of his theoretical understanding.* He thought and conceptualized what he was doing as "sub-modalities." He thought it had nothing in the world to do with meta frames, states, or processes. For so he said. In spite of that, as you will shortly see, his language patterns present straight-out *meta-stating.*

Of course, he did not know that he was meta-stating. The *theory* he operated from and presented involved "sub-modality" shifting and mapping across. And so it seemed—in 1987.

Today, with the hindsight of *the Meta-States model,* we see many of the processes that he performed as just straight across the board *meta-stating.* If you have access to any of those video-tapes, check it out for yourself. You will find that he even used some of the language that we now identify as *meta-stating.* For me, this demonstrates Richard's genius. In this chapter, I have extracted some of that genius and highlighted how it reveals meta-stating using "sub-modalities." Feel free to notice the rich interplay of both meta-modeling and hypnotic language, reframing, anchoring, and setting meta-frames with metaphors.

Meta-Stating "Problems" and Seriousness With Humor

"Now, *with this in mind* (i.e., curiosity, fun, playfulness, etc.) when you think about that old thing (an internal critical voice full of seriousness, etc.)—what do you feel?"

In this expression, Bandler brings several states, whether curiosity, fun, and playfulness, etc., to bear upon the state of feeling serious and criticized. This sets the primary state in a context of silly and ludicrous.

The same occurs in the video about Andy, diagnosed as schizophrenic with whom Richard worked. Bandler in that video did some *sly meta-stating* as he snuck in various frames to set upon Andy's schizophrenic thinking and feeling. When Andy tells Richard in a very serious tone of voice about "what a powerful person Mary is" (referring to his hallucinated Mary of *Little House on the Prairie*), Richard asks him to push her out into the background as a dot, and then take the artist's eraser from a Bugs Bunny cartoon and erase her mouth. Andy laughs at this.

Of course, when you get a schizophrenic to *laugh* at playing around with his internal images of some "powerful figure" that makes him angry and gets him to rage and do stupid things, you have induced a new element into his mental world and reorganized his psycho-logics. Somehow, you have set a very different frame of reference about that internal world. This illustrates much of the power and pizzazz of Richard Bandler (as indicated in *The Spirit of NLP).* Part of Richard's genius lies in how he constantly applies *the most ridiculous images* to primary states. This inevitably has the effect of interrupting and altering things.

Later when Richard confirmed with Andy that Andy did see these images "in his mind" rather than "out there," he noted that Andy made them.

> "And if you made them—then they are yours. It's only a question of who's in control, isn't it, Andy? And you don't like to be controlled, do you?"
>
>> "No."
>
> "So you may think that Mary is powerful, but *you* made her that powerful and you can make her less powerful by pushing her away, can't you, now!"

Here Bandler got Andy to say a *meta No* to the state of "being controlled," and then he drove home the *ownership* of internal pictures, and the power of that ownership. That's meta-stating pure and simple.

Meta-Stating Schizophrenia

When he first began with Andy, he found that Andy judged things and experienced strong emotions far too quickly, as if in a reactive way.

> "Take a break, you need some peace and quiet up there. ... It's your brain. ... Take a deep breath, you don't have to do anything else. Just slow down ... Just admire her as a beautiful woman. ... Look at that lamp, and go, 'Lamp.'"

Here Richard identified the state of internal rushing and racing and recommended instead the primary state of calm relaxation. He also provided some new lines, "Just admire her as a beautiful woman." Next he presented a so-called *"sub-*modality" shift.

> "Change the voice and hear it like this, 'Ah, a beautiful woman,' [in a smooth and nice tonality] all you have to do is just enjoy her." [This outframes the experience with *pleasant tonality* and *just enjoying.*] Isn't that easier? ... This is called 'being mellow.'"

This confirms the power of a meta-level to re-classify something, to give it a new meaning. As it does, it sets a frame (or meta-state).

Setting Frames of Provocation and Exaggeration

In another instance of Richard Bandler *meta-stating,* he inquired of a man who went through all kind of gyrations to avoid meeting the very women he felt attracted to. In so *meta-stating,* he utilized Frank Farrelly's style of Provocative Therapy. Accordingly, he began by asking in an incredulous tone of voice,

"Don't you feel foolish doing all of that?"

"Well, yeah."

"Are you *sick and tired* of that foolishness?" [*Sick and tired* is here put in a meta-position to foolishness.]

"Yeah."

"No, you're not! You need to live this way! With this fear you have no other way to live. You *have to* live this way!" [Here he brings "No Choice," "must," to bear upon the behavior.]

Doubting Belief and Getting Outrageous About Meeting Girls

With a young man who said he always felt nervous and anxious about meeting girls, Richard elicited enough information about *how* the fellow was able to fill his body with fear to just the idea of meeting a girl. It turned out he scared himself with scary words and tones about rejection and abandonment. To this description and process, Richard mercilessly exaggerated it.

"So you think she will look at you and run out the door screaming? That kind of thing?"

"Yeah."

"And you believe this?" [Applying doubt and questioning to the experience. He say *Yes* to the exaggerated idea, so Richard asked a question that *doubted* it in a doubting tonality. This brought doubt to his belief.]

"She'll think I'm boring and a nerd. ... like I get nervous... She'll think I'm bad." [The young man here attempts to re-assert and reclaim the belief.]

Bandler then presents a wild counter-example, speaking the following in a bold, brash, and mischievous kind of tone.

"Well, that's not my way. I have some internal dialogue that goes, 'I'm going to give you a chance to get to know me!'" [This outframes the young man's entire mapping about meeting girls and his belief with a counter-example full of brash outrageousness! It offers an entirely new frame of reference.]

Outframing Anger With Various Qualities

In reference to a man who had "an angry voice" inside of his head which made him feel bad, Richard conversationally meta-stated by saying, "Well, you could make that voice sly and curious ... or you could make it soft and gentle. When you listen to it in these kinds of voices, and then in the old angry voice, which one do you want?"

Bandler here meta-stated the gentleman by offering him a menu list of new qualities he could pick from: sly and curious, soft and gentle, etc. To even answer the last question, he would have to apply each of these states to his anger state, and then decide which of these he wanted.

This presupposed a higher meta-level of *choice* about resourceful frames.

As I watched these classic NLP interventions, it became clear that the central meta-states that Richard Bandler used at that time and which he continues to use in working therapeutically with people actually involves a short menu list of his favorite resource states. These involve those states that uniquely define the very spirit of NLP—humor, curiosity, provocation, ludicrousness by exaggeration, you're-not-broken, but work perfectly well, you have a positive intention behind this crappy behavior, etc.

This suggests that part and parcel of *the spirit of NLP*, and the genius of Richard Bandler, lies in the kind of states that we apply to ourselves and to others. In other words, there is something much, much more important than the particular mind-body-emotion state you experience at any given time, even anger, fear, disgust, frustration, or any other negative and unpleasant state. What is more important? Your second state, the *state* that you experience about the first state, the higher frame.

When we *meta*-state, we put one state in a meta-relationship to another so that the second state becomes the frame or class or category for the first. The first state becomes a member of the class of the second. This shows up in language so that the meta-state becomes the modifying term or phrase. As such, this gives us such states as *bitter* anger, *resentful* anger, *distressful* anger, *hateful* anger, *enraged* anger, *suppressed* anger, *feared* anger, *repressed* anger, *cold malicious* anger. And how different are those complex states from *respectful* anger, *calm* anger, *thoughtful* anger, *loving* anger, *gentle* anger, etc. Can you tell the difference between these choices? Which ones are you wanting to choose for your life and relationships? How well installed are they?

The same applies to every other *negative* emotional state. Beyond the brute fact that we experience thoughts-and-emotions of stress, grief, pain, tension, upsetness, etc., we have to consider *the qualities* that govern or outframe the primary level experience.
- What *kind* of frustration do you experience?
- What is the *quality* of your grief, sadness, sense of loss?
- What are the *properties* of your fear, apprehension, worry?
- What is the *kind* and *quality* of your stress, tension, distress?

This domain of focusing on the kind of qualities, characteristic, and features that we apply to our states—we have moved into a meta-level, a meta-level that has been traditionally subsumed under the category of "sub-modalities." Strange.

And yet perhaps not so strange. After all, to mentally discern *qualities,* features, and characteristics requires a higher consciousness. We have to go meta. We have to concern ourselves with higher level concepts like location, distance, volume, tonality, etc. These do not refer to things "out there" in the world. You have never stumbled over a "location." Perhaps a specific rock, but not the *abstract* concept of "location." Location is not an actual thing or externally real, it is a conceptual–semantic of the mind. It results when a *mind* discerns, classifies, and categorizes things and sorts out a conceptual world. Such words are not sensory-based terms, but evaluative terms.

With another gentleman who experienced "flash-pan anger" that would just "flame up" in anger, Richard first got his strategy for how he did that. "Okay, so how do you do that?" To answer the content details of the question, the man has to move to a meta-level of awareness about the process and also own that it is his anger, and that he creates it. And with that, the frame had been set. In his case, he created anger by seeing a big panoramic picture of things that could go wrong. If he then brought it closer and closer, he would feel more and more anger. This would then activate some internal dialogue about being mistreated.

To highlight the stupidity of getting into a rage even before something insulting or unfair has happened, which the man also understood, Richard exaggerated this without mercy.

> You must be fun to live with! You get angry *before* something happens just by thinking that it *might* happen!? Are you married?

This brought down the room in laughter. He then told the man to take his big picture of the thing that makes him angry and to put a little picture *inside* it that says, 'Isn't this ridiculous?!' Richard then had him *swish* this "Ludicrous Picture" *in* his mind so that it entirely covered the other picture.

> "In fact, in that new picture that comes sliding in I want you to see something that causes you to drool it's so pleasant ... it can even be X-rated. Yes. Like that. And when that *pops up*, how do you feel?"
> "Better."

A Quick Belief Change Shift

In what follows, you will find a belief change shift that Bandler used as a therapeutic process. This illustrates that, in spite of teaching and believing that the process works by "sub-modalities," it actually is a *meta*-state process. Here you will see him working with the meta-level phenomena of beliefs supposedly using a *"sub*-modality" mapping across the coding from *doubt* to *belief,* from *weak belief* to *strong belief.* Yet unknown to him, he actually performed a different process, as we can now discern in his languaging.

"Think of something that you believe which you think of as really important. And you really believe this is important. Just to try something [notice the meta-

levels in the words *just* and *try*], pick something *totally* important."
    "Yeah."

"When you do this with someone, notice where their eyes go. Then pick the belief that they have trouble with, and spatially anchor it to the place where their eyes indicated that they put their *unimportant beliefs*. Then say, 'So this is really important?' in a questioning and skeptical tone. And they'll go, 'Well, no...' Then say, 'Ah, ha— it wasn't a real issue, was it?'"

Do you now see the trick? Richard found and used the *quality* of location, which the person used in his encoding to sort and separate the higher level ideas of "important" versus "unimportant." He found this *encoding of the information* in the externalized "sub-modality" of location (e.g., where the person spatially put his beliefs) which symbolically stands for the concepts of "important" or "unimportant." He then applied that to the current belief. This essentially created the meta-level structure as illustrated in figure 16:1.

Figure 16:1
The Meta-Level Structure
of States and Frames

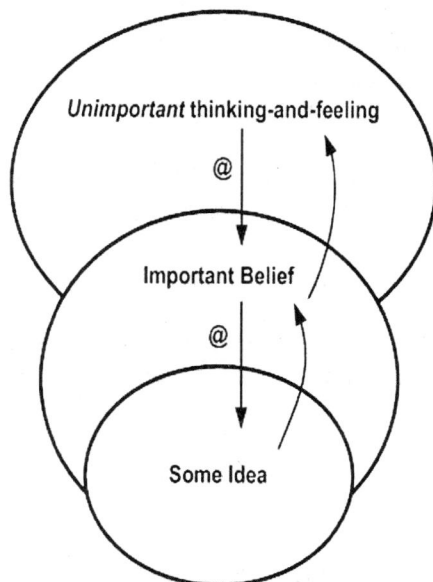

Outframing a limiting and undesired belief with *"Un-importance"* reduces its power and believability. So does challenging it quizzically and skeptically (bringing these characteristics to bear on the belief as well). It layers more *doubt* about the *belief*. Then with the new line, "Ah, ha! So it wasn't a real issue!" this outframes it yet one more time, now bringing *not-real* and applies to it at yet another level. That's elegant and wonderful, don't you think?

Richard then said,

> You have to build up a belief in your client that it's silly to live that way, and that they would rather be involved in lustful ecstasy. When you set off with a client, part of your job is to trick them out of their stupidity. So say to them, "Isn't that idea ludicrous? If it was a *real* belief, you'd still feel it was important, you'd still believe it, but you don't, do you? ... now."

More layering. Now *silliness* about the seriousness of the unreal belief. Then a *swish* to lustful ecstasy. By moving their eyes to the place where they symbolically encode "unimportant" and asking them to *try to feel it as important* adds a convincer piece into the Mind-Lining here. It enables the person to say *No!* to the old limiting belief, which then speeds up the belief change.

To do this kind of *meta-stating*—bringing various mental characteristics, evaluative features, and thinking components (previously labeled as ""sub-modalities") to bear upon a thought, Richard uses rhetorical questions, and especially *the Rhetorical Yes*. This moves one above the everyday primary state to a higher level and facilitates thinking about setting a higher frame as a life attitude or an orientation about how to move through the world.

"Wouldn't you rather do something that felt better and more lustful for your life? Wouldn't you rather enjoy flirting or aim to make lots and lots of money?"

> How do you answer such questions?

Do you not respond with your own *rhetorical yes*? "Well, of course!" Well, rhetorically **yes-ing** elicits our self-reflexive consciousness as it gets us *thinking* about our states and how we want to live. It facilitates us to set a new frame.

This kind of belief change occurs by making the old belief ludicrous, "bozo ridiculous," stupid, or unfamiliar.

Outframing Discouragement

In one video, a man offered a problem. He said, "I feel discouraged." To this, Richard used the classic NLP Meta-Model response,

"How do you discourage yourself?"

> "I'm just aware of my feelings."

"Yes, that's the end. We have to back up to the beginning. That's how we play this game." [And of course, this sets a frame about the *conversation* as a playful,

experimental, and non-serious kind of thing.]
        "I don't know how to back up."

How would you respond to that excuse? As the client, he now presents himself as *stuck*. Now what? To this, Richard used a line that he used repeatedly throughout the videos and that you will hear him often say. It's a line that outframes by setting a frame that creates a sense of empowerment, ownership, and response-ability. He said,

> Well, it's *your* brain! Tell it to back up. Let it make the picture bigger ... and closer ... faster... That's right.

The man then commented,
        "This seems to be only as fast as I can go."
Oops, stuck again.

> So as they speed up, what happens? ... You know, you'd be surprised ... people aren't used to doing this deliberately ...

Beginning with the presuppositional term "as..." the focus shifts to "What happens?" Then before giving too much time to think about it, he meta-stated him with ideas of *surprise* and *deliberateness* as he delivered the Mind-Line that explains it all(!), "People aren't used to doing this deliberately."
        "Slowing the picture down really makes me feel worse."

What an orientation this guy had to getting stuck and complaining about it!

> Well, of course, this is about making the pictures go faster ... so go ahead ... make them go faster. Then oscillate them, so that you slow them down and then speed up a little faster, just keep doing it and see what happens ...

Meta-Stating Stuttering

One man complained about having stuttered all his life until he learned to take more control of it through learning some breathing exercises. Richard inquired about whether he had an internal critic that offered judgments and criticisms about his talking—which, of course, the man had. Humorously and teasingly Bandler then said,

> Well that won't make you smooth and suave! [Laughter.] So start it up ... now change its tone. Make it sweeter, more and more soothing. Keep doing this, now slow down the rate ... and notice what happens.
>   "It has a lot less energy, it takes the punch out of it."

Next, Bandler joked about people having to go to T.A. (Transactional Analysis) to get an Internal Critical Parent.

> Before they went, they didn't have an internal critic, so that they had to go and pay money to get one." [Laughter.]

As the group began laughing at his exaggerated story, he followed it up, saying,
> Yeah, I know this stuff is funny, but it's just that we never stop and think about these things. How do you make your pictures go faster?

The man said that the voice "wants to go back to the critical tonality."

How do you know that "it wants to?"
> It says, "I've been here protecting you."

"If it spoke to you in a nicer tonality, would you be willing to listen to it?"
> "Yes."

"Well, we're going to be sneaky now. Start the loop and slide it into a pleasant tonality, then let it loop back to the beginning. Do this five times. I figure, if you're going to rag on yourself, you might as well use a pleasant tonality. Now rag on yourself with that tonality! Then you can *decide* whether to listen to that voice or not. Sometimes we ought to listen to our inner voices."

In this maneuver, he first invited the man to bring thoughts-and-feelings of *pleasantness* to bear upon the *critical voice*. This created the meta-state sense of a *pleasant* critique and it presupposed *a sense of power of choice* about whether to listen to (or not) the particular content.

Take this Philosophy With You
Another young man struggled with pessimism. He had an internal voice of pessimism. When he was out at a public restaurant with some friends, he saw a beautiful woman and said to himself, "God, she is so beautiful."

Richard asked him, "Well, did you go over and talk to her?"
> "Oh no, she would never go out with me."

Richard then responded, "You're right; I'll go."

That brashness got young man laughing ... to which Richard told him to turn his internal voice into one that teases. "Can you *take this philosophy* of life and just lighten up, and let the voice just tease you?"
> As he tried that on, he noted that "It went away."

Teasing him some more, Richard said, "Well, run the voice again; we'll catch it." Then, talking in the tone of the pessimistic voice as if in response to the humor. "Have a sense of humor? My ass. I'm out of here!"

In this exchange, the language of meta-stating shows up in terms of *taking this philosophy with you*. Because when you think about a state, a thought, an idea, an emotion, or some other facet of one of your experiences, and then take some philosophical attitude about that, then you have framed the subjective experience with that higher level abstraction. Then the quality and properties of that philosophy will qualify the state, such as, *humorous and light-hearted pessimism.* Richard reinforced this later when he shifted and *pessimistically put down humor.*

Outlandish Assertiveness

One woman wanted to speak up for herself more and to feel good about herself in speaking up. So Richard invited her to say something nice about herself. Say something like, "I have a sweet disposition." She struggled to do that. So he prompted her, "You can even lie. This is just for fun." She said, "I have a lot of curiosity."

"Do you feel comfortable saying that?" he asked.
    "Yeah."

Having established that base, he then suggested, "Okay, now say something more risque ..." and then, in a teasingly seductive tone that drew out the last word in a slow and deliberate way, he said, "something *dangerous.*" [Outframing now with these qualities.]

As she processed this, he suggested more cinematic *"sub*-modality" shifts and alterations using a sexual tonality. "Hear that voice inside your head in the tonality that says, 'Don't do it. It will be *dangerous.*"

As she seemed hesitating or unsure, he offered more prompting. "Pull out into the fast lane. Pull the fun meter to the red line, see the sparks fly on the guard rail!" [Laughter.] "If you can do it here, all the rest of the world is downhill. .... Now think of something even more risque ... just to see how comfortable you can feel."

On the surface, this seems like *"sub*-modality" alterations in how one merely represents something. Yet knowing now that we can make any thought, awareness, or distinction *meta to* another, this demonstrates outframing thoughts-and-feelings of self-affirmation with *taking the risk to think way beyond the borders* of the usual self-definitions.

Thinking *"In Terms Of"*

Finally, a nice and very non-obtrusive way to meta-state some distinction or quality that you might otherwise think of as a *"sub*-modality" use the phrase, "in terms of."

> *"In terms of* distance (the conceptual frame], just look at that memory which has given you so much pain at a greater and greater distance, in fact, one that just keeps moving further and further away from you."

"Well, *in terms of* just enjoying life and having a good time, how would that effect your thinking about that disagreeable guy?"

"Now *in terms of* getting the best buy for your money and working with a trustworthy company, I think that when you buy this one, you've really maximized your choices, don't you?"

Summary

- If you have altered a *"sub*-modality," or mapped one over to another, and transformation occurred, then you accessed and utilized *a meta-level* frame-of-reference, meaning structure, or meta-state.

- We have discovered this in the magical language patterns of Richard Bandler. It's his genius. He gets changes, as do others who have mastered *neuro-linguistics,* in spite of the old "sub-modality" theory.

- Metamorphosis occurs due to the power of higher levels. Meta-level principles always govern and describe the interface relations when we construct state-upon-state structures.

- To replicate Bandler's genius so that you can achieve dependably transformations, thoroughly learn about how "sub-modalities" work *at meta-levels* to establish new frames. This will give you a predictable explanatory model.

- Many who tried and "failed" with *"sub*-modality" shifts and patterns have drawn false conclusions either that "NLP doesn't work" or that they are incompetent. The third alternative is that we have followed a misleading term ("sub-modality") and operated from an inadequate theory.

- Rethinking the matter using meta-levels has enabled us to construct a more useful theory and explanatory model. Now we can focus simply on the *cinematic distinctions, features, elements, qualities, and components* and think about how they work symbolically to semantically access higher implied frames.

- This corrects the misdirection that the term "*sub*-modalities" initiated. It gives us a more accurate understanding of the actual mechanisms that create change and transformation.

- We have to *go meta* to detect and work with the features of our movies. "Sub-modalities," refer to meta-level concepts, frames, constructions, and formats, which we apply to our states and representations.

- This re-modeling does *not* do away with "sub-modalities," it *refines* the model to make it more powerful. It highlights the pervasive power of meta-level phenomena and principles.

PART III

META-THEORY

FOR

NEURO-SEMANTIC FRAMES

When "Sub-modalities" are Unmasked

They Go Meta

Chapter 17

META-DETAILING

A Holistic Synergy of Going Meta and Detailing Specifics

When "sub-modalities" go meta we strip away the old misunderstandings from the so-called "*sub*-modalities" and recognize the *meta* nature of *the cinematic distinctions* in our movies. This leads to lots of new refinements on many NLP patterns, giving us a new appreciation for the higher or meta structures of beliefs, understandings, values, negations, backgrounding and foregrounding, etc.

Is our task now completed? Almost, but not quite. We have yet to present one of the most exciting consequences of these refinements. We call it *meta-detailing*. Meta-detailing plays a key distinction in experiencing the genius state and in the process of moving toward mastery or excellence.

When I first wrote this chapter I discovered many examples and practical applications of the meta-detailing skill. Then over the ensuing years, I continued to find them again and again while modeling the excellence in several fields. In modeling "selling," I have found it in selling excellence (*Games Great Sales People Play*). In modeling wealth building, I found it in translating one's passion into a viable contribution, in creating a ten-year plan for becoming financially independent, budging, handling money, working with others, etc. (*Games for Wealth Building*). I also found that meta-detailing plays a key role in business leadership and management (*Games Business Experts Play*).

In this chapter I refer extensively to Robert Dilts' work in *Strategies of Genius*. I do so to present some of the incredibly insightful things he has written about the relationship of "sub-modalities" and states of genius.

A Distinction of Genius
What *distinguishes* a human being so that he or she can operate at a high level of expertise, excellence, quality, or intensity (i.e., "genius") from those who do

not?   Grinder and DeLozier (1987) have enumerated the following characteristics in their work on *The Prerequisites of Genius*:

> Commitment, intensity, focus, clean state shifting, using meta-levels to shift from state to state, and let the "demon" (or genius) state loose "within a controller's cage to *kick!*" (their language).

A genius makes finer distinctions in one or more of the sensory systems than the rest of us. This may occur visually (artists, visionaries), auditorially (musicians, speakers, statesman), kinesthetically (athletes, craftsman, technicians), using the olfactory system (chefs), in the gustatory system(chefs, wine tasters), or in the vestibular system (athletes, astronauts). It may also occur in the linguistic system or in the meta-linguistic system (conceptually; philosophers, scientists, etc.). Generally we think of these finer distinctions of sound, sight, sensations, smell, etc. as identifying the domain of *"sub-modalities."* But, the quality of genius or high level expertise, cannot emerge from mere awareness of representational qualities. It emerges and develops and grows and expands *by the frames and meta-frames* that it discovers and adapts about the representational features. We describe this quality here as meta-detailing.

Some years ago, I went to a concert with a girlfriend who loved a pianist of a particular group. As the music started, I noticed that the sounds began to have an enormous emotional impact on her. I became curious.

> "What are you experiencing?" I asked.

She said something to the effect about the beauty and grace of the music. Pretty global.

> "What are you hearing specifically that gives you this experience of beauty and grace? I'd like to hear it that way!"

She spoke about the tempo and melodies, and the tonal overlays of patterns and things like that.

> "I'm not hearing any of that. Teach me how to hear it as you do."
> "You don't *just feel it* in your body soothing you?"

I did not. Nor did she want to stop her experiencing *at that moment* to make her strategy explicit. But later, back at home, with some CDs, she attempted to train my ability to notice the auditory qualities and features and distinctions that stood out so saliently to her. And as she did, she also gave me many of her higher level frames of reference that governed her thinking, hearing, perceiving, and experiencing of the patterns in the sounds.

Afterwards I reflected about this and realized that *all of the sounds* were present to my ears. I heard them. But I did not hear them *in the same way*—using similar *patterns* (meta-level structures) in my head as she did. And without those higher level patterns—I did not know *how* to use the experience to cause the representational distinctions (or "sub-modalities") to stand out in the foreground of my consciousness. But now I do. Now I know *the structure* of her genius that sorted for the crucial distinctions.

Dilts on the Meta-Levels of "Sub-modalities"

When you read the following quotations you will see that it is both natural and inevitable that I utilize the writings of Robert Dilts on this subject. Given his extensive research and writing on the subject of finding the structure and critical factors in genius *and* the fact that he has penned some amazingly insightful things about "sub-modalities" you might think we collaborated in working to unmask the *meta* levels of "sub-modalities."

The following references from *Strategies of Genius* reveal Robert's insights that recognize "sub-modalities" as involving meta-level abstractions. In the first quotation about Sherlock Holmes, Robert expresses this key secret of "sub-modalities." In the second set of quotations from the genius of Aristotle, Dilts (1994) describes "sub-modalities" as *"common sensibles"* that occur at a higher level. The genius of Sir Arthur Doyle's "Sherlock Holmes"—

> "Unlike the average person, when Holmes is observing he pays more attention to *the more formal qualities* of what he is observing than to the content of his observations ... While "sub-modalities" could be considered 'details' in a way, they are actually *not* just a smaller piece of an experience *but rather a more abstract and formal feature* of the object under observation. By extracting key features and using them as his basis for a memory search, Holmes is open to a wider variety of associations than someone who simply sees 'mud.'" (p. 119, *italics* added)

The genius of Aristotle:

> "As Aristotle put it, *'[I]t is not the stone which is present in the soul but its form.'* In other words, the 'form' is more important than the 'content'—our perceptual model of the world is more important than the objective reality of the world. And ***these 'sub-modality' qualities are the fundamental 'formal cause'*** of our mental models of the world." (p. 49, ***the bold italics*** added)

> "Sub-modalities are the particular perceptual qualities that may be registered by each of the five primary sensory modalities." (p. 48)

> "According to Aristotle the process of inductively identifying universals from particular sense-perceptions took place through the 'common sense' —the place in the 'psyche' where all of the senses met. One of the functions of the 'common sense' was to register something which repeated in a number of experiences—a pattern. *Patterns or 'universals'* were perceived in terms of a set of content-free qualities

that Aristotle called *the 'common sensibles,'* which were the discriminations that were shared by all the senses.

> *"'Common sensibles' are movement, rest, number, figure, magnitude, unity; these are not peculiar to any one sense but are common to all."*

"For example, 'intensity' is something you can register in any sense. You can have intensity of color, sound, taste, smell or touch. The same with 'number'; you can see three things, hear three things, feel three things, etc. Location and movement are also perceptible via all the senses. You can see, hear, feel or smell something from a particular location or moving in a particular direction. These qualities are not a function of only one sense. They are something that can be shared by all the senses and facilitate the transfer of information between the senses. According to Aristotle, common sensibles allowed us to do our *higher level mental processing."* (pp. 54-55, *italics* added)

If the "common sensibilities" are "higher level mental processing" that involve concepts, patterns, and higher abstractions, then "sub-modalities" are not *sub* are all, but *meta.* Robert, in these quotations all but seems to argue for the meta-level structure of "sub-modalities" as we have in this book. He has argued that the very *features* of our pictures, sounds, and sensations operate at a higher level and so involve higher abstractions or frames.

Meta-Detailing as the Essence of Genius

The theme in this chapter relates to the *meta*-nature of "sub-modalities" is this:

> The heart and essence of genius and genius states is the ability to sort for, pay attention to, and recognize critical details *from a meta-position.*

The trained or natural genius has somehow learned to recognize and operate from some meta-pattern or principle that, in turn, allows him or her to see, hear, and sense the richness of details. What does this term mean?

> *Meta-details* and *meta-detailing* summarize a gestalt of two kinds of thinking that are synergized at the same time— precision processing from the perspective of a larger perspective.

Meta-details refer to the crucial and essential details that we can discern and differentiate by using various meta-level distinctions or frames. This means that the genius state and the excellence that emerges from it occurs when we establish a meta-level frame-of-reference which, in turn, allows us to configure the critical and essential details in some skill or performance.

Meta-Detailing Creativity

Robert Dilts (1994) noticed this very thing in the Genius of Walt Disney.

> "In summary, Disney's major representational system as a Dreamer was

his vision. But it was not necessarily directly only toward specific pictures of things. He used the quality of movement as a 'common sensible' to overlap other senses onto imagery and to see underlying forms and patterns. As he maintained in response to a question about the future:
'What I see way off is too nebulous to describe. But it looks big and glittering. 'That's what I like about this business, the certainty that there is always something bigger and more exciting just around the bend; and the uncertainty of everything else.'" (p. 169)
"'In animation it's what to draw, not just the ability to draw. It isn't just drawing the darn thing, it's thinking about it and giving it personality. I was into technique before I should have been. I needed more life." (p. 170)

Disney here talks about *the details* of the art work involving and manifesting such qualities as animation, color, contrast, movement, etc. Yet these details are driven by a higher frame of reference. He viewed the details as important, but only as the served that higher frame.
"[Making our characters ...] It must, above all, have that elusive quality called charm. It must be unsophisticated, universal in its appeal and a lot of other things you can't nail down in words but can only feel intuitively." (p. 174)

Disney's *Creativity Strategy* involved the flexibility and discreetness of three particular states or roles—Dreamer, Realist, and Tester (or Critic). From that strategy, Dilts invented an NLP process for accessing and installing these states so that we could use them in a way supportive of creativity. In doing so, he sequenced them in a way that specifically utilized *the meta-details principle* and a meta-stating process.

It begins with *the dreamer* as your first position—in a vision that catches the whole story. In doing this, you *begin meta* and establish the meta-patterns and principles that will govern the details. Disney said,
"The story man must see clearly in his own mind how every piece of business in a story will be put."

From this frame as a meta-principle, we shift to *the realist*. From second position, we associate fully and completely into the experience. In Disney's words, "He should feel every expression, every reaction." Finally, we shift back up to a meta-position to let *the spoiler* arise. Now, from third position we have the distance to take yet another look at the whole thing. "He should get far enough away from his story to take a second look at it."

Dilts noted this very structure and process in the Disney strategy.

"Whole story: 'To see whether there is any dead phase.'
Individual characters: 'To see whether the personalities are going to be interesting and appealing to the audience.'
Specific behaviors of characters: 'He should also try to see the things that his characters are doing are of an interesting nature.'" (pp. 184-185)

Meta-Detailing Music Excellence

In modeling the musical genius of Mozart, Dilts related the same strategy of the genius using a meta-level pattern to perceive critical details that similarly operated in other geniuses. Beethoven,

"I begin to elaborate the work in its breadth, its narrowness, its height and depth [the specific details], and since I am aware of what I want to do, the underlying idea never deserts me [the meta-level principle or frame]. It rises, it grows, I hear and see the image in front of me from every angle, as if it had been cast, like a sculpture, and only the labour of writing it down remains..." (p. 240)

Composer Paul Hindemith similarly writes,

"A genuine creator ... will.... have the gift of seeing —illuminated in the mind's eye, as if by a flash of lightening — a complete musical form ... he will have the energy, persistence and skill to bring this envisioned form into existence, so that even after months of work, not one of its details will be lost or fail to fit in to his photographic picture."

Similarly, Pulitzer prize winning symphony composer Michael Colgrass writes:

"Because as you detach yourself, you are getting a gestalt view of what's going on here ... " (p. 241)

In summary, the gestalt of *a big picture—governing the details* (meta-detailing) provides us with the structure of excellence or genius. It gives a larger picture about how to run our brains. As it does, it synthesizes and unites in the two polar ends of the General/Specific meta-program. We no longer need concern ourselves about "being *either* global *or* detailed." We need *both,* and we need both sequenced so that we can focus in on details from the perspective of some meta-frame. This empowers us to sort out the trivial details and zoom in on the incredibly relevant details in just the right way.

"You might also choose to just dream about the first step of something instead of the whole thing. But I suggest you keep a broad view. Usually the problem that we have in pursuing an idea isn't because we don't think about it precisely enough, it is because we don't have a broad enough vision." (Dilts, p. 198)

Theorizing about Meta-Detailing Frames

Dilts (1994) also describes *how* meta-detailing works. He describes the following in the context of relating it to self-organization theory. This theory, about the process of order formation in complex dynamic systems, describes how the details come together, organize, and emerge by the meta-level form, structure, and attractor (pp. 245-248). Order arises from *attractors*. In visual perception, the "attractors" function as the focal point in the phenomenon, around which the rest of our perceptions become organized.

In human neuro-linguistic and neuro-semantic states, *ideas* operate as the attractors. Our perceptions, behaviors, and neurology organize around our meta-frames—belief frames, value frames, meta-program frames, understanding frames, etc. These organize our entire neuro-linguistic state giving us genius *eyes, ears, and skin* for the particular area of expertise. The second part of this book describes this as when we examined how various meta-level phenomena (foregrounding, negating, believing, valuing, understanding, and framing) work to give us such eyes, ears, and skin.

Meta-Detailing—the Pervasive Pattern in Excellence

In his conclusion regarding some of the larger patterns characteristic of geniuses across the board, Dilts enumerated "ten main elements that seem to be common to all of the geniuses covered thus far in this study." These included the following:

1) Have a well developed ability to visualize.
2) Have developed numerous links between the senses.
3) Use multiple perspectives.
4) Highly developed ability for switching between perceptual positions.
5) Ability to move back and forth between different chunk sizes and levels of thinking.
6) Maintain a feedback loop between the abstract and the concrete.
7) Balance of cognitive functions: Dreamer, Realist and Critic.
8) Ask basic questions.
9) Use metaphors and analogies.
10) Have a mission beyond individual identity.

Among these central elements of genius, numbers four and five summarize what we mean by *meta-details* and *meta-detailing*. These terms refer to this highly developed ability of a person to move back and forth between different chunk sizes or levels of thinking, between the gestalt of the complete picture and to zoom down into tiny pieces without getting caught up in the details. It refers to the ability to maintain a feedback loop between these little concrete facets and the larger and more abstract categories.

Meta-Detailing Alfred Einstein

In Volume II of *Strategies of Genius,* Robert provided abundant information about the genius of Einstein and specifically the cognitive strategies that governed his thinking. He modeled the process as involving a kind of "higher level 'big picture' i.e., *'visual survey'*" that governed a *"feeling of direction"* process. In between this, Einstein had a *"combinatory play"* and *"logical concepts."* Einstein describe this himself in these words:

> "Two directions are involved: getting a whole consistent picture [the meta-frame], and seeing what the structure of the whole requires for the parts." [the details seen and accessed by the larger structure] (p. 51)

Robert then diagrammed this *meta-detailing* of Einstein with a meta-level frame —the "thinking" of the "visual survey" or "big picture" of the "connection between those elements and relevant logical concepts" which created a "feeling of direction." (V^i—>K^i). Under this comes the feedback loop of the "combinatory play" back and forth from concept level to sensory based level. Again, quoting Einstein about his own processes:

> "When a certain picture turns up in many such series, then— precisely through such return—it becomes an ordering element for such series, in that it connects series which themselves are unconnected. Such an element becomes an instrument, a concept." (p. 52)

Thinking in terms of a concept became for Einstein the "ordering element" which enabled him to notice the details that counted. The concept as a meta-frame operated as the attractor and then self-organized the entire system. Dilts illustrated this with a diagram of a meta-level or meta-state structure that he entitled, "A 'Concept' is an 'Ordering Element' that Connects a Series of Experiences" (p. 53).

Figure 17:1

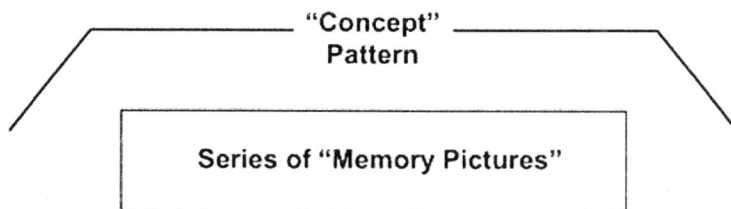

Meta-Detailing In Freud, de Vinci, and Tesla

In Volume III of the series, Robert noted the following regarding the strategies of genius.

"Freud not only came up with a completely unique and startling perspective on the statute [Michelangelos' Statute of Moses], but also on Michelangelo, Moses, and the Bible itself! This characterizes one of the fundamental qualities of genius —finding a detail which does not fit the accepted paradigm ... which consequently leads to a reformulation..." (p. 83)

"For Freud, it is the details which seem contrary to the context or typical cultural assumptions often become key elements. The strength of Freud's strategy, and of his genius, was to be able to find what was significant in the clusters of details that most people overlook." (p. 92)

About Leonardo, he certainly had incredible powers to see details:

"Leonardo's own powers of observation must have been remarkable. The drawings in his famous Codex on the Flight of Birds revealed details that no one else was able to discern until the invention of high speed photography." (p. 304)

What created his genius? His higher level skill that enabled him to "know how to see." This was the ability to connect visual observations to cognitive and behavioral processes. Regarding Leonard's statement, "This constitutes the science of painting, which is in the mind of the theorist who conceives it..." Robert wrote,

"Leonardo talks about the 'science of painting' which he relates to the discrimination of what are called 'sub-modalities' in NLP. ... According to Leonardo, the perception and discernment of the interrelations between these qualities takes place in the 'mind of the theorist' and form the basis for the 'execution' of the painting." (p. 305)

"... it is only the individual who had both the subtle powers of perception *and* the ability to pictorialize those perceptions who is in a position to achieve true knowledge." (p. 305)

In Leonardo's case, the meta-frame from which he did his meta-detailing was *proportion*. He loved "harmony and proportion and viewed it as *virtu spirituale* ("spiritual property") (p. 335).

"Leonardo claimed that there were 'ten attributes of sight, namely darkness, brightness, substance and color, form and place, remoteness and nearness, movement and rest ...' One of Leonardo's greatest skills was in being able to see the attributes of things and not just the things themselves." (p. 343)

So There You Have It

In the beginning of NLP, Bandler and Grinder looked out over the troubled waters of the human models of consciousness and mind. They saw chaos and confusion about the very components of mind. Then, as they modeled the three therapeutic wizards, they said, "Let there be Representational Systems and let these Representational Systems make up of *VAK modalities.*" And so it came to pass. And Gregory Bateson saw that it was good, and he wrote a Preface to say so.

Then on a later morning, they said, "And now let us call the *qualities* of the representational systems "*sub*-modalities" so that humans everywhere can play with their internal pictures, sounds, and sensations with more precision. This will let us expand our study of the structure of subjectivity as we model excellence." And so that came to pass. Robert Dilts said it was good and wrote it down in a book, *NLP Volume I.*

This discovery created an Edenic garden for workshops, trainings, and NLP Centers. It provided new technologies and interventions to help all creatures here below to move out of stuck states. It also created a more extensive language for talking about, and modeling, human excellence.

Then one day a voice was heard in that garden. This voice was heard asking some tantalizing questions about the whole *sub*-thing about "sub-modalities."
> "How can these distinctions be *sub*- when you have to *step back* and *get a larger perspective* so that you even see what you're doing?"
> "How can these be *smaller pieces* of the pie when they involve *meaning* and higher level frames-of-reference?"
> "Why do we refer to these pieces as the *structure* of the content, yet act as if they are the details of a sub-microscopic level? What gives?"

And there was a deafening silence in the Garden. Had someone eaten of the Tree of Knowledge and needed to be punished by being kicked out of the Garden? No word came from on high to answer the challenging questions. What does this mean? Does this mean we must figure it out for ourselves?

Summary
- In the process of unmasking "sub-modalities" we have discovered meta-level symbolic frames-of-reference lurking behind the mislabeled term. And with that we have stumbled upon an absolutely marvelous neuro-linguistic tool: *meta-detailing*.
- Geniuses do not just have "big ideas" and see "the big picture." Nor do they just "focus in on the details that everybody else is missing." They experience a higher level synthesis—they *see, hear, feel, or language the details* that others miss *from the perspective of a higher frame.* Meta-Detailing governs the structure of their excellence.
- It now seems obvious, does it not, that we have to *go meta* to detect and recognize the structural elements of a representation? We also have to use the meta-function to play, shift, alter, and "map across." We have to *go meta* to recognize them as *setting frames of references* for our thinking.
- Recognizing this enables us to see how the meta-function creates our meta-programs and meta-states. This means that meta-level *framing governs* and *organizes* the thinking-emoting system as a self-organizing attractor.

Chapter 18

HIGHER LEVEL MAGIC

The "Magic" of the Higher Frames

"The whole is always in a meta-relationship with its parts.
... in matters of control,
the smaller context can never determine the larger."
(Bateson, 1972, p. 267)

"The living man is bound within a set of epistemological
and ontological premises which—
regardless of ultimate truth or falsity—
become partially self-validating for him."
(Bateson, 1972, p. 314)

"All communication has this characteristic—
it can be magically modified by accompanying communication."
(Bateson, 1972, p. 230)

In Neuro-Semantics we take it as axiomatic that the highest and best *magic* occurs at meta-levels. When we *go meta*, we move up into a realm of mind, into the Matrix of our frames, where we can do all kinds of wonderful things. Going meta describes the *transcendence factor* which drive our states. Going meta gives us a broader and more extensive view, as it allows us to step aside and just witness things. Going there invites us into the larger system or god-view of things.

In systems theory, *going meta* describes the very factor that enables us to not only *transcend* a system but also to *transform* a system. As we move out of the lower level structures, frames, and content—we step aside from our agendas, limitations, hang-ups, and self-fulfilling prophecies and this gives us the ability to take a second, third, fourth, etc. look at ourselves. Herein lies wisdom.

Herein also lies the mastery or excellence that the genius state facilitates.

Einstein described it succinctly, "The kind of thinking which creates the problem cannot solve the problem." The kind of thinking (i.e., reasoning, framing, assuming, etc.) that creates problems cannot solve those problems. When we are *thinking inside the box* we cannot get an outside view to even recognize the box or discern how the box as a frame that influences our perceiving. When locked inside that way of thinking, we can't see the limitations of our seeing which actually create or contribute to the problem. When inside a bottle, it's difficult to read the label. To solve such difficulties, we have to rise to a higher level.

What do we call this move to a meta-level?

> This is the *meta-function* which enables us to discover a higher kind of *magic*—the magic that Bateson spoke about which emerges in "the world of communication."

I first discovered the *meta-functions and moves* when I came across the writings of Gregory Bateson. In his studies of schizophrenia, meta-communication, art, play, evolution, form, learning, "self," alcoholism, epistemology, cybernetics, etc., he utilized the model of *logical types* (from Bertrand Russell and Alfred Whitehead) to theorize about the structure of these experiences. After discovering Meta-States, this led me to understand many of the processes that seem *magical*.

What is the relation of this to "sub-modalities" and genius states?

> The higher frames which govern experience and set up self-organizing processes translates the energy of those higher meta-states into the lower states, texturing and in-forming them. That way our skill in detecting and working with higher frames empowers us to set the kind of frames that will work their magic on the lower levels—on emotions, behaviors, and skills. This gives us the power of meta-detailing. As we construct the higher frames, meanings, beliefs, values, etc. for specific expertise, we program into ourselves the eyes, ears, and heart for collecting and utilizing such details. Our meta-level frame operates as *an attractor* in a self-organizing system empowering us to move down to *the details* that support and enhance the frame. This actualizes the genius states creating a primary state focus of flow.

Bateson's Two Worlds

To understand Bateson, we have to understand his two worlds. In a wonderfully provocative piece entitled, *"The Group Dynamics of Schizophrenia,"* Bateson extensively described two worlds. He separated two facets of reality in a similar way in which many other thinkers have distinguished them. Bateson not only separated map and territory, he demonstrated in numerous ways how *confusion* of these two domains causes unending troubles and stupidity. Frequently he alluded to the work of Korzybski nearly half a century earlier as the basis for this distinction. The engineering perspective of Korzybski (who first enunciated the map/territory distinction) pinpoints *confusion* of the two as the central force for unsanity. This is also the heart of Aristotelian reasoning, thinking, logic, and language.

What are these two worlds? Bateson distinguished them as *"the world of physics and forces"* and *"the world of communication"* or mind. These worlds radically differ from each other. The first describes the territory, the second, the map.

In *the "world of physics"* Bateson spoke about how it innately involves the kind of cause-effect processes that Newtonian dynamics characterizes. In this world of things "out there," actions or things become energized by the transference of energy from other actions and things. This operates in a pretty direct and straight-forward way. When this event occurs, it transfers energy to another. We can use the principles and understandings of the physics of impact and gravity to model how billiard balls move on a pool table. You hit the ball with your cue stick and the ball moves in accordance with the energy transfer of that force. We can measure such events. We can predict the amount of movement, direction, etc. Certainly other contributing factors enter into the picture. Yet overall, the processes of energy transfer (especially at the macroscopic level) operate according to a set of "logics" that even a child can understand and use.

Not so with *the world of "mind."* When we move to the world "inside" the human nervous system, things are a bit messy and can even seem a bit crazy. It becomes more like an Alice in Wonderland world. Now *magical relationships* seem to govern. What are the entirely different set of "dynamics" and "logics" that occur here?

Consider the "magic" involved in this world of communication when we kick a dog. What will happen? What can we predict in terms of energy transfer? *The movement of the dog,* in response to our kick, will *only partially* partake of a "Newtonian trajectory," says Bateson. To predict the trajectory of the dog, the intensity of the dog's response, etc. not only do we need to consider the amount of force applied, but also the dog's own metabolism, internal energy system, his learning history, and his relational nature with the kicker.

Given all of these other contributing factors, when we try to compute things logically, the "logic" isn't always so "logical." "Magic" is afoot. And that's why it is much more difficult to work out the laws and principles about what will happen in that world of mapping.

From Mind to "Magic"

Bateson (1972) even noted that while we may use the word *dynamic* when referring to processes *within* psychological nature, we must remember that we use it in a different sense from the way physicists use the word in their domain (p. 229). Upon making this distinction between these two realms, Bateson (1972) then noted how this relates to what we can only call *magic*.

> "This, I think, is what people mean by magic. The realm of phenomena in which we are interested [psychological, mental, communicational, etc.] is always characterized by the fact that 'ideas' may influence events." (p. 229)

Ideas may influence events.   This lies at the heart and source of both the structure of magic and the secrets of magic. In introducing the word *magic* into the realm of communication, Bateson may have unknowingly provided the original inspiration for the seminal book in NLP, namely, Bandler and Grinder's (1975) *The Structure of Magic.* In this regard, Bateson also used other phrases, "the realm of magic," "the magical realm of communication" (p. 231).

What did Bateson precisely mean by the use of this term *magic*? What did it mean in the Batesonian context?

> "It might well be sufficiently confusing to be told, that according to the conventions of communication in use at the moment, *anything can stand for anything else.* But this realm of magic is not that simple." (p. 230, *italics* added)

Bateson used the word magic in the realm of communication or mind to refer to the cognitive-neurological understanding about how *ideas can influence events.* It seems magical because in the realm of symbolization, we humans as a symbolic-class of life use and manipulate symbols to map and navigate our way through life, where a wide range of things can *stand for* many other things.

The flexibility that allows many things to stand for many other things explains a lot about human "psycho-logics." It explains why our experiences, understandings, meanings, and emotions can be so fluid, complex, plastic, unpredictable, and even wild. It explains why people can come up with, invent, construct, and believe all kinds of incredible things. It explains the extremes from human pathology and psychosis to human excellence and genius. The arena of mind, inside the human neurology and brain, transcends the laws of physics, and is *not logical* according to the standards of Aristotelian logic. It operates by a different set of principles, those *neuro-semantic* in nature.

This is the kind of *psycho-logic* that rules when we scratched our head with regard to another's response and wonder, "What planet did she or he grow up on?" Or, "Where in the world did that come from?"

In a dimension where so many things can stand for other things and where *ideas* may influence events, we have to shift our expectations from Aristotelian and Newtonian logic to a non-linear and systemic logic which is governed by *the semantics of frames*. If we do not, we will be disappointed. Our internal thinking, reasoning, and logic do not operate in the same way that things out there in the macroscopic world operate. The structuring that we experience "on the inside," via our neurological and linguistic abstracting, operates by a systemic process involving *neurology, linguistics* (including words, language, associations, emotional connections, frames, movie representations, editorial cinematic features, and metaphors), and *semantics* (meaning, intentionality, significance). We construct our Matrix from our experiences.

To a larger extent than we typically imagine, *we invent our reality.* Schizophrenics do it wildly and with little, if any, connection to the territory. The rest of us at least attempt to make maps that correspond to the territory in a useful way. Because we all begin with basically the same kind of nervous system, brain, genetic structuring, sense receptors (i.e., eyes, ears, skin, etc.), we construct maps that are similar—a shared reality. Still, we invent our particular construction of reality.

These theoretical ponderings of Bateson (1972, 1979) and Watzlawick [*Change: Principles of Problem Formation and Problem Resolution,* (1974), *The Language of Change (1978),* and *The Invented Reality* (1984)] articulate the theoretical foundations of NLP and Neuro-Semantics.

This establishes the world of communication with its "dynamics" which we experience as "magical" and gives us the meta-structure of genius. Bateson (1972) wrote:

> "All communication has this characteristic—*it can be magically modified by accompanying communication.*" (p. 230, *italics* added)

How can we *magically modify* one communication message or representation? We do so by using other communication messages and putting one into a meta-relationship to another. That is, one message stands in an *about*-relationship to another; one message is *about* another message. As evidence, Bateson illustrated this by using the example of speaking with one's fingers crossed behind one's back. The meaning of the symbolic representation of crossed-fingers qualifies and modifies the previous message (as a lower-level message) about the speaker's words.

The structure of humor provides another example. How does the humor of a joke emerge? The "punch line" arises at a different logical level from the primary level syntax of the joke set-up. We hear it on one level —at the level of content, the details of whatever is being described. Yet at another and higher level, it suggests or implies another thing. The joke sets up our predisposition to expect one line of thought, one anticipation. Then suddenly it shifts logical levels and in doing so, it jars our consciousness. We were not *minding* that thought. The jar shifted us to another level or frame. This produced the experience we call "humor."

This illustrates the determinative role of meta-communication signals. Higher level messages can get us to play out things in our minds and give rise to new configurations. In this way, meta-messages modify and qualify lower-level message in ways that seem utterly "magical."

Of course, being a scientist, Bateson did not leave his ponderings about the world of communication and mind in the magical format. He turned to mathematical symbols to convey this understanding of the relationship between messages. In this way he showed how the meta-messages can operate in several relationships as symbolized by the mathematical signs:

+	plus or addition
-	minus or subtraction
X	multiplication, or times and
÷	division

By such relationships, we can radically alter and modify the original state. Bateson asserted that this means that "the world of communication is a Berkeleyan world" (p. 250). In the world of communication, no true "things" exist—only *messages* (representations with many variables and qualities). Actual things and events cannot enter into this world. "I" as a material object (p. 251) cannot enter it, but "I" as a message, as part of the syntax of my experience, can.

External objects can only enter into "the communication world" by representation or mapping them (correctly or distortedly) into the communication system. Because this makes up and drives that world, our mapping can take on "magical" functions, so to speak. This provides the basis for the "word magic" and the languaging "wizardry" that we can do with ourselves and others.

The Meta-Magic of Conceptual Mathematizing

I find it absolutely fascinating how messages and messages-about-messages can structurally relate to each other in ways that we can analyze mathematically. Do you? What do you think of Bateson's comment that communication signals can operate as pluses (+), minuses (÷), multiplication (X), or division (÷) processes?

When I first read about the mathematic relationships in communication, I did not see the relevance. Later, the Meta-States model gave new significance to

Bateson's comments. Today this provides a provocative area of research similar to that suggested by Korzybski (1933) with regard to the relationship of second-order, third-order, etc. level of abstractions to each other (pp. 440-441).

Bateson described how messages interact with each other in a mathematical way in the following quotation.

> "All messages and parts of messages are like phrases or segments of equations which a mathematician puts in brackets. Outside the brackets there may always be a qualifier or multiplier which will alter the whole tenor of the phrase." (p. 232)

Figure 18:1
Interface of Message Upon Message

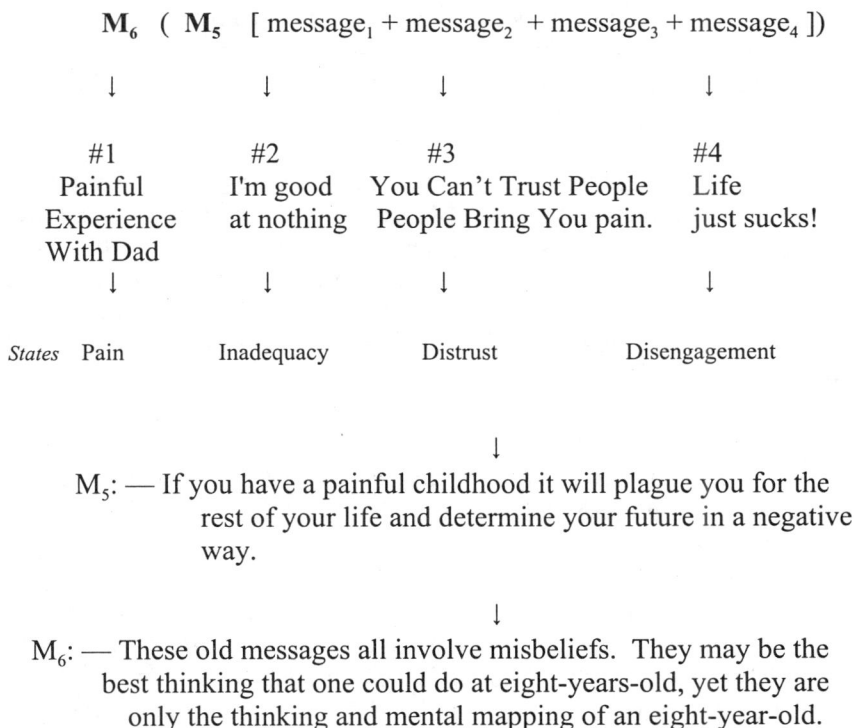

$$M_6 \; (\; M_5 \; [\; message_1 + message_2 + message_3 + message_4 \;])$$

     ↓   ↓   ↓   ↓

#1	#2	#3	#4
Painful Experience With Dad	I'm good at nothing	You Can't Trust People People Bring You pain.	Life just sucks!

     ↓   ↓   ↓   ↓

States   Pain   Inadequacy   Distrust   Disengagement

↓

M_5: — If you have a painful childhood it will plague you for the rest of your life and determine your future in a negative way.

↓

M_6: — These old messages all involve misbeliefs. They may be the best thinking that one could do at eight-years-old, yet they are only the thinking and mental mapping of an eight-year-old.

Diagraming this, we begin at the primary level. There we horizontally (or linearly) experience messages 1 through 4 in terms of *addition,* of one pain added to another pain. Painful message after painful message (each comprising a primary state of pain, distress, and negative emotions) simply *increases* and *adds* onto the message's content. From the original experience of trauma each *additively* increases the person's mental-emotional pain. Each textures the primary state with more distress, trauma, distorted beliefs, limiting decisions, etc.

As a meta-message, *message 5* functions very differently. This message-*about*-the-other-messages stands at a level *above* the other messages. It *classifies* them. It is not a message about another painful thing on the same level as the other experience. It operates as a concept, category, and classification. It operates as a conceptual message of distress about the other messages. As such, it communicates and represents a different level of painful message. In this case, it does not merely *add* to the individual's personal misery, it *multiplies* that misery. It does so because it multiplies the primary messages/states together (1—4). So while message 5 also represents a painful message, structurally its syntax generates a different kind of pain. It does not represent a mapping of a primary experience. It rather maps *the meaning* of the other messages as within its category. Therefore as the frame about the other messages, it amplifies the boy's distress and trauma. It does so by establishing the higher level *neuro-semantic frame* for the other messages.

Finally in the diagram and illustration, we see another meta-message. Actually, in this case a *meta* meta-message. Message 6 also *multiplies* the other messages, yet in doing so it does not increase the trauma, but *negates* the sense of trauma. Structurally, its message about all of the messages at lower levels *reverses the sign* from − (minus) to + (plus). This negation message multiplies a minus (−) to the lower level messages and thereby effects a transformational reversal.

Bateson (1972) offered this explanation:

> "What exists today are only messages about the past which we call memories, and these messages can always be framed and modulated from moment to moment." (p. 233)

A meta-message modifies the lower level messages. Meta-messages operate like the procedural parts of a fax message. Such procedural messages indices for the recipient meta-information about the source, sender, intended recipient, date, time, etc. All of these messages in the text communicate about the text, and in that way modifies the text. They set a frame for the text and create a contextual meaning for it. An unlabeled fax offers a message, but one that the recipient might find confusing and ambiguous. It raises questions, "Who is this from?" "What is this about?" Etc.

Figure 18:2
The Mathematizing of Meta-Levels

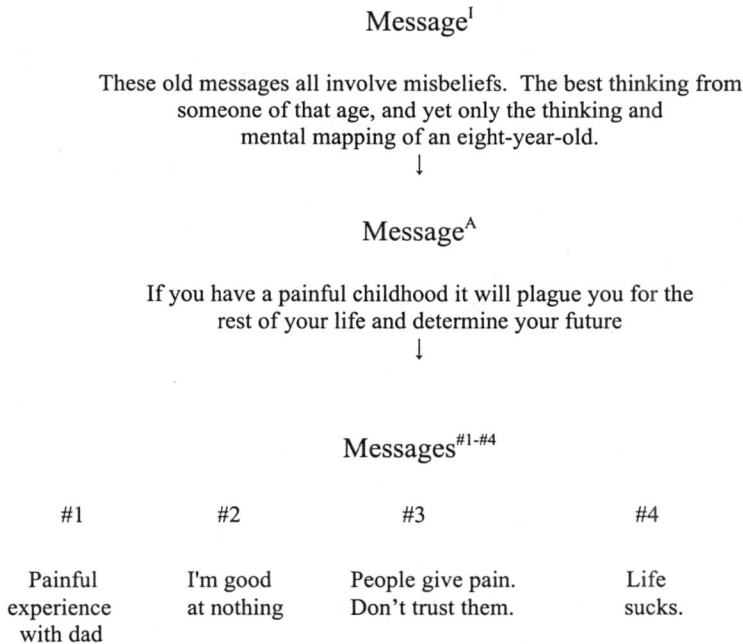

Message^I

These old messages all involve misbeliefs. The best thinking from
someone of that age, and yet only the thinking and
mental mapping of an eight-year-old.
↓

Message^A

If you have a painful childhood it will plague you for the
rest of your life and determine your future
↓

Messages$^{\#1-\#4}$

#1	#2	#3	#4
Painful experience with dad	I'm good at nothing	People give pain. Don't trust them.	Life sucks.

Meta-Stating up the Levels

Mind-body states inherently involve two things 1) the internal representations of the movies of our mind which induces and 2) the corresponding physiology in our bodies. Therefore the thoughts-and-feelings of the primary messages (e.g., messages #1—#4) function at the level of primary states. *Above* these primary states, the higher-level meta-message creates another state. It reflects a state *meta* to the primary states, and the message that qualifies it stands at a meta-level to it. Figure 18:2 shows this set of relationships.

Bateson (1972) noted that psychotherapy itself involves a context of multi-level communications (p. 224). It involves multi-levels of meanings that involves such multiple levels as:

    1) Immediate, direct languaging that the therapist does with his or her clients.

    2) The more indirect languaging which the therapist's particular theory provides as the psychological paradigm from which the therapist comes.

    3) The languaging that the context of a particular problem, role, expectation, etc. provides (for example, the languaging involved in the

"script" of restaurant behavior, visiting the school principal, going dancing, applying for a job, engaging in conflict resolution with a mate, etc.).

4) The languaging that one's larger culture provides.

The diagrams show this complexity of levels within contexts and contexts-of-contexts and shows how we move from embedded frames to the overall Matrix.

Figure 18:3

The Embeddedness of Communications Within Higher Levels of Messages

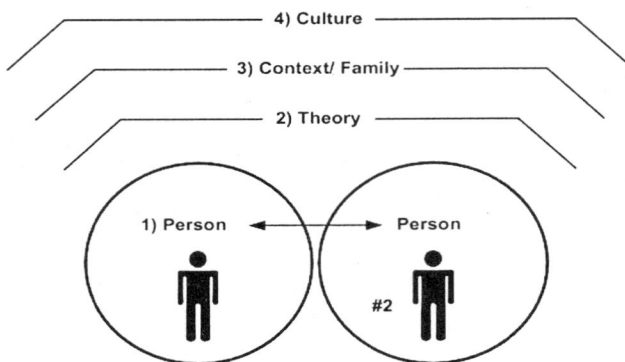

Using Meta-Levels to Transform "Sub-Modalities"

If psychotherapy involves multiple *meta*-levels of messages that set the frame and apply healthier, more sane, more reality oriented, and map-updating ideas to our old ideas, how does this relate to the cinematic features of our representations? Consider *how* we encode some of the ideas that torture us and which sickens us and makes us candidates for therapy.

• The "past" is close, compelling, "real," and unavoidable (i.e., in my face), etc.
• I can't get over, or away from, my "past."
• I "am" my experiences—or thoughts, emotions, actions.
• People are determined by what happens to them, not the thoughts they map about such.
• Once a victim, always a victim.
• When you get violated, something very deep gets broken inside that can never be fixed.
• You condone a perpetrator if you forgive him or her.
• Keep your anger and nurse it; that will keep you strong.

We encode and represent the first idea by making our internal pictures and sounds very close so that we have no sense of distance. When we *push the pictures back* and get some "space" from them so that we no longer see them as "in our face." This enables us to feel them as less compelling and less "real."

Doing this essentially sets a new frame-of-reference. If in-color, three-dimensional, and loud functions as our symbolic coding for "real" and for "compelling," then making the internal movie black-and-white, a flat two-dimensional slide, and soft in volume will probably serve as the coding for "not real" or "unreal."

Doing this leads us to reference those pictures and that movie less and less. With less referencing, and less swishing our brain to those ideas, they bother us less. They influence us less often and with less emotional energy. As we make a meta-move to think about *how* we have organized and *structured* our thoughts (that is, detection of these representational variables), we can then do something about them. We can then begin to "run our own brain." When we note that having our pictures too close does not serve us well, we can decide at that meta-level to push them back. From this, we will experience a sense of emotional release. Setting this new frame will transform our mind, emotions, and behaviors. This is the power and the magic of meta-moves.

Now consider the second *idea*. Here we undoubtedly have encoded our thoughts about a *concept* like "the past" (already a meta-level phenomenon) using the modality features of close or near. In encoding our time-line this way, we have easy access to the "past" referents which inevitably then *empowers* them as our reference system. We may create another meta-level structure (i.e. a cause-effect structure). *"If* these thoughts are close to me—*then* they determine my feelings, actions, identity, etc."

We again perform *transformational magic* by moving to a meta-level and simply notice our time-line and its configuration and questioning whether it serves us. If it doesn't, we clear out a space for a new decision. We set a new and more empowering cause-effect frame: *"As* I see those events disappearing further and further into my past, I feel less and less impact and influence by them."

The third toxic *idea* ("I am my experiences") indicates someone operating from the meta-level of *identity*. The linguistic distinction of complex equivalence indicates that someone has taken an experience and equated it to some concept.

So we ask, *"How* do you know that you *are* your experiences, emotions, or behavior; how do you represent this?" This probes the structure of the madness. In response, some people will describe images, sounds, and sensations. Others will just use words—vague and non-referencing. In the cinematic features of our movies, what see-hear-feel term does the person use to stand for and symbolize the meaning of identification with some experience?

We often discover that the person suffers from a seventh grade image of self identified with an experience (i.e.,"You don't count. Nobody likes you."). So shifting to a meta-level, we then run an ecology check to examine it.

Does this serve you well?
Does it enhance your life?
Would you like a better way to identify yourself?

There You Have It

How curious has the meta-levels of mind made you in regard to thinking, feeling, and communicating? Is it not fascinating that we not only deal with messages, but layers of embedded *messages-about-messages*? As we learn to take these messages at different "logical levels" into account, it enables us to notice how one level of messages can magically affect other levels of messages. This structural knowledge of the form of experience serves as the basis for becoming a Neuro-Semantic magician.

It provides a way to more systematically deal with the complexity of messages. This explains much of the magic of the Meta-States model, and how we can use it generatively to design engineer new empowering configurations. This explanation seeds the ground for learning to create larger-level generative change. Now we can do all kinds of near-magical things: negate old messages that used to generate intensive pain, divide old childhood pains in half, and then half again, multiply representational equations with new resources, subtract hurtful and irrational beliefs that serve no useful function.

If NLP began these explorations into the structure of experience by showing how words work so magically at the representational-neurological level, then the Meta-States model continues it by bringing "logical levels," self-reflexive awareness, and the syntax of meta-levels into play. We now know how "sub-modalities" work which informs us how to model and replicate the structure of excellence.

Summary

- What seems like "magic" in human experience is actually *messages* operating at the meta-levels of our mind and experience. These higher frames run the show in our mind-body-emotion system and texture our everyday states of mind-and-emotion.
- Attempting change in ourselves, others, and in organizations without awareness of the governing frames of reference is like using a bicycle to fly. It will not work. It will also leave us feeling frustrated and disappointed.
- Skillfully facilitating change and transformation comes when we use meta-level processes and principles. This cues us into how our Matrix works and how to perform magical transformation from higher levels of awareness.

Chapter 19

GOING META
FOR STRUCTURAL
THINKING AND FRAMING

NLP arose originally as a *meta-discipline* about the language patterns which Bandler and Grinder found in Gestalt Therapy, Family Systems, and Ericksonian hypnosis. It did *not* create a new psychology, it rather organized itself as a *meta-domain* about various models of human functioning.

About the same time, in another discipline of human study, the field of *Meta-Cognition* came into being. Theoretically and epistemelogically, NLP fits into the field of Cognitive-Behavioral Psychology. Various textbooks on psychology and communication have located NLP as a sub-field of Cognitive Psychology.

One of the most determinative distinctions at the heart of NLP and Neuro-Semantics is the difference between *content and context.* Differentiating these two dimensions separates NLP from merely being a psychology and moves it into the field of *Meta-Cognition.*

This distinction also lies at the heart of modeling. To make a distinction between the *content* of something at the primary level and the *process, structure,* and *context* at the meta-level enables us to move beyond details. Developing this awareness is crucial for working at meta-levels and exploring this domain is critical in getting to the heart of the structure of excellence.

- How well do you move from exclusively thinking in terms of content where it is so easy to get lost in the details to thinking in terms of process?
- To what extent can you now move back and forth from *content* thinking

to *context* thinking without losing track*?*
- How easy or difficult do you find it to move from thinking about content to thinking about structure and process?
- What helps you move easily between content and structural thinking?
- What have you found best facilitates this shift in others?

Engineering Excellence from a Structural Perspective

This focus accords perfectly with the emphasis in the original writings of Alfred Korzybski who went so far as to state that the only content of "knowledge" is *structure*.

> "A map *is not* the territory it represents, but, if correct, it has a *similar structure* to the territory, which accounts for its usefulness. ... If we reflect upon our languages, we find that at best they must be considered *only as maps*. A word *is not* the object it represents; and languages exhibit also this peculiar self-reflexiveness, that we can analyze languages by linguistic means. ... Antiquated map-language, by necessity, must lead us to semantic disasters, as it imposes and reflects its unnatural structure... As words are *not* the objects which they represent, structure, and *structure alone*, becomes the only link which connects our verbal processes with the empirical data. Words are *not* the things we are speaking about ... If words are *not* things, or maps are *not* the actual territory, then, obviously, the only possible link between objective world and the linguistic world is found in structure, and *structure alone*. The only usefulness of a map or a language depends on the *similarity of structure* between the empirical world and the map-languages. That languages all have some structure ...we unconsciously read into the world the structure of the language we use ..." (pp. 58-60)

If "the map is *not* the territory," then to use language as a map of reality highlights the importance of the correspondence, relation, and structure. Words and what is externally real occurs on different "logical levels." This distinguishes the inward or neuro-linguistic "reality" of words from their referents on the outside. To add to this complexity, there is the fact that the territory keeps changing. The maps we create of the territory have to deal with a territory that is a "moving target." Why? Because no event ever stays "the same in all regards" over time. In a process universe where every "thing" and every event keeps changing, how do we language this? Typically our language fails to reflect this. Indexing and time-dating provide two devices for communicating this ongoing dynamic change. "Identity" as absolute sameness does not exist in the world.

> "Anything with which we deal on the objective levels represents a process, different all the 'time,' no matter how slow or fast the process might be; therefore, a principle or premise that 'everything is identical

with itself' is invariably *false to facts."* (Korzybski, 1994, p.194)

In a proverbial form Korzybski (1933) wrote: *"Whatever we say a thing 'is' — it 'is' not."* (p. 35). Our words, descriptions, and models can never fully say what anything *is.* With everything in flux and everything continuing to change, we have to not only think structurally, but structurally in a *dynamic way.*

> "Once we abstract, we eliminate 'allness,' the semantic foundation for identification [create stable but rigid maps]. Once we abstract, we abstract in different orders, and so we *order* [levels], abolishing fanciful infinities. Once we differentiate, differential becomes the denial of identity. Once we discriminate between objective and verbal levels, we learn 'silence' on the un-speakable objective levels, and so introduce a most beneficial neurological 'delay'—engage the cortex to perform its natural function. Once we discriminate between the objective and verbal levels, *structure becomes the only link between the two worlds.* This results in search for similarity of structure and relations ..." (p. 404, italics added)

By this mindful "consciousness of abstracting" Korzybski referred to an "awareness that in our process of abstracting we have *left out* characteristics" (p. 416). We become aware of how we delete in making our mental maps. Lacking this consciousness, we *identify*—we *confuse* words with objects and feelings. Doing this means we fail to make a proper evaluation, and that, in turn, effects our adjustment to reality.

Structural Awareness

To notice, detect, identify, and then work with *the structural or process nature* of our thoughts, representations, and coding necessitates that we go meta. It is in making this conceptual meta-move that we step up to a place (conceptually) where we can *think structurally.* We can then discern *the form* of our representations and frames, the form of our sensory systems, our words, higher abstract terms, and our perceptions. These areas correspond to the territory discerned by the meta-domains: the Meta-Model, Meta-Programs, Meta-States, and Cinematic Features (or the Meta-Modalities).

To think structurally about "sub-modalities" we first have to make a meta-move in order to detect them. Once we go meta we can then recognize them and alter these editorial features of our movies and recognize their semantic significance for formatting our states and experiences.

All of this means that to develop expertise or mastery we have to go meta to develop higher forms of thinking. Only by going meta can we then engage in *structural thinking.* Conversely, it is when we get lost in content or get caught up in details that we arrest our development.

Structural thinking means a meta-awareness for noticing form, pattern, and process. Thinking structurally about "sub-modalities" takes us to the *cinematic features and distinctions* in our mental coding that cue our brain-body system about how to feel and to respond. It takes us to using "sub-modalities" to format our framing *symbolically or semantically*. We use cinematic features (i.e., distance, intensity, volume, tone, etc.) to *stand for* higher level concepts and meanings. In this, the distinction *sets a frame* on the content of our thinking. The frame is our reference point or system determining *how* we view, evaluate, interpret, and judge the experience. Structurally it classifies our experience telling us what the content *is* to us.

For example, if I structurally use black-and-white to *stand for* and *symbolize* concepts of "old," "the past," "not-now" then this "sub-modality" / cinematic features is my code for these meanings. Conversely, if color stands for and symbolizes "now," "new," and "currently real," then this representational coding or cinematic editorial feature set these classification frames. "Sub-modalities," in and of themselves, do not mean anything. They only mean something through *standing for* and *signifying* higher level conceptual or abstract ideas. Only then are they semantically active.

If I use the feature of "distance" ("close" or "far") to encode the concepts of connection and disconnection, these may stand for and symbolize "close" in dimensions of time, in feeling, and in reality. Here I would set a frame using location as a metaphor for structuring these concepts.

Structurally, we think about these concepts using what we have labeled "sub-modalities." In doing so, we have applied a *distinction* or element of a sensory modality to a thought, feeling, idea, or representation. This sets a frame of reference by simultaneously constructing a symbolic system.

Meta-Misunderstandings
By mis-conceptualizing ""sub-modalities," and by utilizing an inadequate metaphor (i.e., going *down* to a *deeper* level), we have inadvertently created several distortions and misunderstandings. I will mention two of these here briefly.

1) Misunderstanding the Emotions of the Meta-Positions
When we step back to notice the form, structure, and process of our thinking, emoting, and responding conceptually, we step into a meta-position. Doing this enables us to *step out* of the emotion of the primary state and to simultaneously *step into* another point of view with all of the thoughts-and-feelings of that new perception. Think about a time when *you* criticized someone, recall it as if there—seeing, hearing, and feeling the experience as you did then. Now step back from that memory and view it from the perspective of the person you

criticized. Imagine what *you* looked like from the perspective of the listener to the criticism. How do you now think about *that you?* How do you feel?

Traditionally, we have described this second perspective using the term *"dissociation."* Yet using and labeling this way of perceiving by the nominalization *dissociation* makes it sounds as if it is a "thing" and as if we will experience "no emotion." Yet this is not so! Our emotions may shift in nature and quality, but we will still be embodied and have emotions. We have stepped out of the thoughts and emotions of one state and have stepped into another mental and emotional state.

The very *idea* of having "no emotion" illustrates the extent to which we have fallen victim to the dualism of "mind" and "body" and are still not holistically mapping "mind-body" as a system. This *elementalism* dichotomizes the world and creates a false-to-fact mapping. Actually we can never have one without the other—"mind" apart body. Where, after all, does the "mind" occur? We can have no "emotion" apart from "mind." After all, the *body* itself functions as an information gathering, sorting, and coding device. To more effectively map this facet of our experience we use the holistic phrase: *mind-body-emotion.* This describes a holistic, interactive system not separated into independent elements.

There is no actually dissociation from our bodies. "Dissociation" only refers to a conceptual feeling (i.e., feeling numb, weird, not feeling what we usually feel). In the processes that we label as *dissociation,* and the "dissociative disordering of personality," we actually speak about people thinking, emoting, and responding in strange ways that are outside of the norm (i.e., weird, strange, "floating," etc.). Usually, we experience an emotional flatness or neutrality when we dissociate. We may experience thoughts-and-therefore-feelings of being "weird, strange, not-me, outside of my body," etc.

Such meta-level awarenesses and descriptions indicate our search for words as we describe these odd and strange sensations and ideations. The person experiencing such is still inside his or her body and is still using the central and autonomic nervous systems to breath, talk, move, etc. This shows the power of the Meta-Model for helping us to avoid reifying our descriptions as if they were entities. The nominalization "dissociative Personality Disorder" *is not* a thing, but a process.[1]

In this, we differ from a side comment by Robert Dilts in an article where he made a distinction between dissociation and dis-association (*Anchor Point,* September, 1998). We see no such distinction. Robert noted that whenever we take another perceptual position or point of view, we *dissociate* from our previous perception (and all of the thoughts-and-feelings that it generates) and adopt or *associate into* another. The person who suffers from the psychiatric disorder of dissociation has simply *disordered* his or her thinking, feeling, and responding in such a way as to become *stuck* in one position. The person now has various frames-of-references (meta-states) that prevent and forbid them from stepping back into first or self position.

2) Meta-Level Emotions

What can we expect to *feel* when we move to experiencing at meta-levels? Many things. *Going meta* does not put us out beyond the realm of humanity. In fact, it enables us to step into higher states of awareness that exemplify the best of the human condition. Going meta and stepping into higher level states takes us into such wondrous meta-states as proactivity, forgiveness, self-esteem, self-appreciation, magnanimity, etc. Conversely, we can go meta and step into some *hells:* self-hatred, self-contempt, self-condemnation, resentment against the past, a collector of injustices, etc.

The *emotions* that we experience at meta-levels involve our kinesthetics just as much as do the emotions of our primary states. Yet at meta-levels, they take on new complexities. Concepts merge and mix with our body sensations to create all kinds of new mixtures and configurations. Here we experience the awesome and the dreadful gestalt states: from courage, self-esteeming, seeing and seizing opportunities, to living for revenge and retaliation, seeing dark and pessimistic futures, etc.

The Meta-State model identifies sixteen kinds of interfaces that occur in the interface of one state with another state (Appendix B). These interfaces provide a basic template for understanding how the emotions of states at meta-levels can generate new and very different configurations.

Meta-Principles

As NLP training begins by setting forth foundational presuppositions, so in Neuro-Semantics we have a set of assumptive frames or meta-principles. These presuppositions describe the mechanisms or processes that govern how meta-states work and how to use the Meta-States model effectively. These govern the cinematic features of our movies since the "sub-modalities" actually set and elicit implied frames that work as meta-states.

1) *Meta-levels govern. Higher "logical levels" always and inevitably drive, modulate, organize, and control lower levels.*
Gregory Bateson (1972) formulated the dynamic of this first and foremost of the meta-level principles. Meta-levels are the frames-of-reference for the activity (thinking, feeling, responding) that occurs at the levels lower to the frame. The meta-level operates as an "attractor" in a self-organizing system. This is what we mean by a "logical level." Whenever we set a frame of

reference at a higher "logical level" that frame will govern all lower levels. The interface between higher and lower levels generates a whole list of effects from intensifying the lower states, defusing them, negating them, multiplying them, creating trance, creating paradox, etc.

2) Someone (or something) will always set the frame of reference.
The question is, *"Who* set the frame?" Sometimes the frame occurs by "osmosis"—we simply breathe and live in it as the cultural, linguistic, familial, professional, etc. frame. Marshal McLuhen was the one who said that while he didn't know who first discovered water, he knew it was not the fish. Meta-levels typically operate outside-of-consciousness. This *un*conscious nature of meta-levels gives them more power. Because they operate at a level *above* conscious awareness we assume them and take them for granted. You can count on many, if not most, of your meta-states becoming unconscious frames—your "way of being in the world," your attitude.

3) Whoever sets the frame will govern the experience.
Since higher frames govern, and since somebody also sets it (no need to allow Lost Performatives here), the person who sets the frame exercises control over subsequent experiences. The resulting thoughts, ideas, concepts, beliefs, emotions, behaviors, language, problems, solutions, and experiences derive their existence from the governing frame.

4) The whole determines the parts and from the parts, the whole emerges.
This describes the systemic nature of the mind-body-emotion system and speaks about the *gestalt* nature of our neuro-linguistic processes. The system that emerges from the meta-levels that govern the lower levels brings about an overall gestalt (or configuration of interactive parts) which define the character of the whole. This highlights the fact that we have to look for emergent meanings and properties when it comes to a system of interactive parts. We can analyze and break down *courage* into its component parts: fear, vision, desire to achieve an important outcome, etc. Yet the gestalt that arises is greater than the sum of the parts.

5) Outframing involves setting up a higher frame-of-reference that will exercise greater control and influence.
In detecting and identifying a frame we are able to step aside from a frame (and from the thinking and feeling which creates that frame) and to set a whole new frame. This transforms everything. It performs meta-level "magic" as it installs a new self-organizing attractor at the top of the semantic system. Our highest frames operate as the self-organizing attractors in our neuro-semantic system.

6) Experience differs radically and significantly at each level.
Korzybski's levels of abstraction template models how the nervous system

abstracts at different levels. Each order or level as "second-order abstractions," "third-order abstractions," etc. describes a different experience. When we can use a word at different levels, we have a *multi-ordinal term*—the term only has a general significance. To determine its specific meaning we have to specify the level at which we are using the term. *Love* at the primary level differs from *loving love* (which we may experience as infatuation), and *love of loving love* at the third level (perhaps, romanticism) is even yet different.

7) Reflexivity endows our consciousness with systemic processes and characteristics.
Reflexivity is the process that governs and drives our levels of abstraction and meta-level experiences. Reflexivity is consciousness *reflecting back* onto itself or its products (i.e., thoughts, emotions, beliefs, values, decisions, specific concepts, etc.). As we reflect back, we set up feed-back and feed-forward processes and create a circular system. We commonly speak about "getting into a loop" or "going around in circles." In systems language, we experience and create both vicious cycles and virtuous cycles. If we become fearful of an upcoming test, and then worry about our fear of that test, and then become afraid of our worry, and then fear our worry-of-our-fear, etc., we have a *vicious* closed-loop circuit. Recursive thinking solidifies higher frames and sets up our conceptual atmosphere or canopy of consciousness. To think about the meta-levels of our higher states and the gestalt state that then arise, we have to shift from linear thinking to thinking in circles and loops.

8) Meta-level disorientation and conflict can create living hells.
Generally speaking (exceptions do exist), whenever we bring *negative* thoughts-and-feelings (states) against ourselves or any facet of ourselves, we put ourselves at odds with ourselves. This creates "dragon" states. And when our self-relationships (relation to ourselves) become disturbed, we begin to loop around in vicious downward self-reinforcing cycles. Then self-disturbance in a closed loop (i.e., self-condemning, self-contempting, self-repressing, self-hating, etc.) creates a disturbance for all of our relationships with others. Unchecked, this creates neurosis, psychosis, personality disorders, character disorders, etc.

9) Paradox governs many meta-level solutions for health, integration, balance, and empowerment.
The only way to rid ourselves of unwanted thoughts, emotions, behaviors, habits, etc. involves, *paradoxically,* welcoming, accepting, appreciating, and celebrating that very thought, emotion, behavior, etc. By welcoming it into consciousness we can take counsel of it, reality check it, learn from it, etc. To *not* reckon with it leads to unuseful suppression, repression, self-rejection, etc. This creates many of the counter-intuitive solutions in Neuro-Semantics.

10) Setting a frame necessitates neuro-linguistic energy and repetition.
How do we actually *set* a frame or establish a meta-level state? Merely "thinking" or even "feeling" will not do it. Thinking, knowing, and feeling does not necessarily establish a higher level frame-of-reference. To do so, we need to use drama, energy, repetition, etc.

11) Altering higher level frames alters identity and destiny.
Frequently, we can't change what we *do* (so that it lasts in a pervasive and generative way) without also changing *who we are.* Does our higher frame of self-definition support the change? Our behavior typically operates like a printout of our operating programs.

12) Symbols derive their meaning from references.
What anything "means" depends on both what we have linked it to (associative meaning) and the context in which we apply it (contextual or frame meaning). After inquiring about what something means, we have to specify what it points to or references. Since meaning operates in these ways, we enter the Matrix of our frames to search out the layers of embedded contextual meanings within yet higher frames.

13) We construct our meanings and our meaning-of-meanings.
There can be no meaning apart from a human mind that connects and associates and constructs layers of frames. In and of themselves, nothing means anything. Meaning arises from the interaction of a human mind embracing and appraising some event in the world. *People are the meaning-makers*—we are the ones who attribute, construct, and appraise meaning.

14) Higher frames typically make us paradigm blind.
The self-organizing nature of ideas, beliefs, and meanings set us up to become trapped in our own world of thoughts—paradigm blind to evidence, information, and data that contradict our thoughts and feelings. When we experience internal conflict or *dissonance* between antagonistic thoughts, our cognitive dissonance motivates us to reduce the contradictions.

15) Meta-levels never stay "meta" in a heady way" for long, they are forever coalescing into the primary state.
While we "conceptually" move up to higher levels and layer our mind with additional thoughts, these levels or layers of frames do not stay conceptual for long. Repetition, emotion, decision, and habituation bring them back down into our flesh, our muscles, and our eyes. This explains how meta-states become meta-programs and how the "sub-modality" frames code and recode our representations and semantically commission our emotions.

16) We experience a critical difference in how we sequence the syntax of our meta-levels.

The structuring of our higher levels arise from how we order and sequence the layering of our thoughts-and-emotions as we meta-state ourselves. In this way the syntax of our frames determines the quality of our states.

The structural work isn't complete when we identify meta-frames. We still have to construct the right kind of supporting frames, the necessary number of them, successfully install in the right context. Otherwise we could "get lost in the clouds of abstraction." We could have absolutely brilliant ideas that we don't translate into practical forms.

Summary
- The key for modeling experience and working effectively with human functioning lies in distinguishing *content* and *structure* and developing the ability to *think structurally.* This is the legacy that Korzybski has left NLP and Neuro-Semantics.
- It is the ability to *go meta* that empowers us in becoming highly skilled and proficient in the *Neuro-Linguistic* and *Neuro-Semantic* models.
- Because the structure of excellence emerges from how we layer our mind and emotions with higher frames-of-references, it's critical that we know and learn the principles of the meta-levels.
- The lack of this understanding has led to several mis-understandings about the meta-levels, about the nature and working of "emotions" at higher levels and the meaning of "dissociation."
- In the end, when we take the prerequisites of genius and meta-state ourselves with those qualities that we set the frames that enable us to move toward mastery and excellence. This meta-stating then initiates a self-organizing process in our mind, emotions, bodies, and behaviors.
- Since higher frames inevitably govern, we will want to set quality meta-frames or meta-states which will support the excellence we desire.

End Notes:
1. *The Structure of Personality: Ordering and Disordering of Personality using NLP and Neuro-Semantics* (2000).

SUMMARY:
Sub-Modalities Going Meta

- What is the bottom line?
- What have we discovered from *"sub-modalities" going meta*?
- What have we discovered about the meta-frames of the so-called "sub-modalities?"
- What difference does knowing about the meta-nature of the cinematic features make?

In unmasking the meta-levels in "sub-modalities" in this work we have discovered that a mis-labeling has created a lot of confusion and misdirection. Re-labeling them *cinematic features*, in turn, has opened up a new meta-domain of cinematic and editorial features of our mental movies. The unmasking process has led to discovering a whole new meta-domain. We could call it *meta-modalities* (rather that "sub-modalities") yet that seems equally awkward, and even a bit esoteric. In the end we're simply talking about the features that every movie editor works with. So, what happens *when "sub-modalities" go meta?*

We find the cinematic meta-domain. This then gives us *four* rather than three avenues (or meta-domains) for describing human experience and for modeling the structure of excellence. This opens up many new refinements and revisions of NLP patterns. It opens up new understandings of how the fluid meta-levels operate. It opens up the neuro-semantic nature of these cinematic features—that they operate by standing for various concepts and higher level meanings.

When "sub-modalities" go meta we have more tools for modeling the structure of excellence or expertise. We can now more fully enjoy and succeed at detecting, unpackaging, modeling, and replicating *excellence..*

Where do we go from here? Originally I intended to publish a second volume of this work as *The Structure of Genius* as an application and next step. I wanted to write about the patterns we use in "Accessing Personal Genius" which is our introduction training to Meta-States. But a shift of focus occurred and so we published that work under the title, *The Secrets of Personal Mastery* (2000). Today that work makes explicit the meta-stating process for setting frames as self-organizing attractors in mind and neurology to create personal mastery. In that book we identify the *prerequisites of genius* in the levels of the mind-body-emotion system and use such for developing personal mastery.

Would you like a simple, easy-to-read version of this work? Then *Movie-Mind: Directing the Cinemas of the Mind* (2002) is the book. In that book you will find the basics of NLP and Neuro-Semantics without the jargon. There we run with the movie metaphor and speak about using cinematic features for taking charge of our minds.

Finally, there is the website for Neuro-Semantics. There you can find egroups and thousands of pages of free materials.

www.**neurosemantics**.com

ISNS — International Society of Neuro-Semantics®
P.O. Box 8
Clifton, CO. 81520—0008 USA
(970) 523-7877

From Representational Codings
To Meta-Level Meanings

What does a *"sub*-modality" as a representational distinction or cinematic feature refer to?

- What does it mean when you encode a visual image "close?"
- What does it mean when you picture it as "far away?"
- What does it mean when you see it in three-dimensions versus two-dimensions?
- What meanings arise or are evoked when you encode a voice with a serious tone versus a more humorous one?

Because we learn to use the features of our mental representations symbolically and as metaphors, they come to *stand for* higher level frames of meaning. This creates our neuro-semantics. We may cue our brain and nervous system to respond to something as "real" versus "just fantasy" by using a color, close, 3-D, and panoramic movie. We may learn to encode the concept of fantasy similarly except we see our pictures "on a screen" with a pink border. In this way, we encode our representations using various *distinctions* ("sub-modalities") or *cinematic features* so that they take on, and elicit, higher level *meanings*.

"Sub-Modalities" **Cinematic Features of our Movies**	*Meta-Programs* **Evaluative States Or Processes**	*Meta-States* **Higher Conceptual Frames**
See-Hear-Feel Movie Representational Systems Sensory-based descriptions the form and structure of thought	Conceptual and Thinking Patterns about Representations, Higher Meanings about thought	Semantic States Higher Level Evaluations

Visual
__ Brightness
__ Focus/ Defocused
__ Color/ Black-&-White   <u>**Real, Current**</u>
__ Size   <u>**Old, Past**</u>
__ Distance: close or far   **Chunk Size: General/ Specific**

                                                           <u>**Impactful**</u>
__ Contrast   **Global / Detail**   <u>**Compelling**</u>
__ Movement   Options/ Procedures
__ Direction   Sensor / Intuitor   Uptime—Downtime
__ Foreground/ Background Judger/ Perceiver   Controlling / Perceiving
__ Location   Self- Referencing
                                  Other-Referencing/ External Ref
__ Associated/Dissociated   Assoc./ Dissociated
__ Changing/ Steady
__ Framed/ Panoramic
__ 2D (Flat), 3D (holographic)   <u>**Real/ Unreal**</u>
__ Speed: fast, slow,   Match- Mismatch /
      Normal   Same— Difference

Auditory

__ Pitch   Toward / Away From Values   **Motivation**

__ Continuous or Interrupted **Associated/ Dissociated**   **Assoc./ Dissociated**

Goal Sort: Optimizing/ Perfectionism/
__   Skepticism

__ Tempo: fast/ slow   Value buying: cost, Time, convenience

__ Volume: loud/ soft   Time Tenses: Past/ Present / Future   **"Time"**

__ Rhythm   In Time / Through Time

__ Duration   Affiliation: Independent/ Dependent/ Team/

__ Cadence   Manager

__ Foreground/ Background   Extrovert/ Introvert / Amivert

__ Distance

__ Location   Convincer/ Believability —VAK or Words   **Proof**

__ Clarity

Kinesthetic

__ Pressure   MO: Impossibility— Possibility

                      MO: Necessity — Desire

__ Location & Extent

__ Shape

__ Texture

__ Temperature

__ Movement

__ Rhythm

__ Duration

__ Foreground/ Background

__ **Associated/ Dissociated —>**   **Thinker/ Feeler**

__ Intensity

__ Frequency

__ Weight

Appendix B

META-STATING EFFECTS

What happens when we meta-state? What happens when we create a state-upon-state structure, when we layer states and frames upon each other? What kind of interfacing effects result? What kind of responses, consequences can we create by using various meta-stating patterns? The following are among the key results that arise when we jump a "logical level" and set one state upon another.

1) Painfully intense states are reduced. Some meta-stating will reduce the intensity and power of the primary state: calm about anger; doubt about doubt.

2) Intensify states. Some meta-states will amplify and turn up the primary state: worry about worry; calm about calm; loving learning; anxious about anxiety (hyper-anxiety); love love; passionate about learning; appreciate appreciation.

3) Exaggerate and distort states. This increases the intensity factor. Generally, when we apply negative state to another state, we *turn our psychic energies against ourselves*. Anger about anger; love hatred of; fear about fear; hesitating to hesitate (talk non-fluently) creates stuttering; sadness about sadness (depression); mistrust of mistrust.

4) Negate states. In doubt about my doubt, I usually feel more sure; resist your resistance; in procrastinating my procrastination, I take action and put off the putting off. Mistrust of mistrust, ashamed of shame; hate your hatred.

5) Interrupt states. It jars and shifts the first state, it totally interrupts it. It can arrest the psycho-logic: humorous about seriousness; anxious about calmness; calmness about anxiety; intentionally panicking.

6) Create confusion. By getting various thoughts-feelings to collide and "fuse" "with" each other in ways that we do not comprehend. Ludiculous seriousness.

7) Create paradox. Paradox isn't real—you can't see it, hear it, touch, smell or taste it. Paradox doesn't exist "out there" in the world, but inside the mind-body-emotion system as a map/territory confusion. It is a category error. It arises when we confuse levels. The classic paradox is the "Be spontaneous now!" paradox. So with: try really hard to Relax; "Never say never." "Never and always are two words one should always remember never to use." "I'm absolutely certain that nothing is absolutely certain." The Title of book: *"This Book Needs No Title."* (Raymond M. Small, 1980)

8) Create dissociation. The word *meta* does not mean or equate to "dissociation." Yet when we *go meta* and step back from one state we can sometimes step out of our comfort zone and reality zone so much that we feel weird, strange, outside our usual self, floating, numb, spaced out, etc. We "dissociate." And if we dissociate dramatically enough, amnesia may result. Actually any time we switch states too rapidly and without a grounding anchor for reference we can produce amnesia and other trance phenomena. When we meta-state ourselves with distance from pain, observing old trauma, etc. we can create what we call "dissociation."

9) Create the beginning of a new process. By setting one state upon another, we can sometimes *initiate* the first step of a new experience, we can create a new emergent experience as in courage to have courage; playful uncertainty; learning how to learn; gentle anger; willing to become willing.

10) Grab and focus attention and swish the mind: this can provoke more thoughtfulness as it leads in a different direction. It can arrest attention, overload consciousness, stimulate new thinking, and question axioms, beliefs, reasoning, memory, etc. (hence deframe). Calm about anger; appreciative about anger; lovingly gentle about anger; resistance of resistance.

11) Induce trance and trance phenomena. Most people experience third-order abstracting and above as "trancy." It invites one to "go inside" so much that the "inward focus" of trance develops as one engages, consciously and unconsciously, in an internal search for meaning. We especially experience meta-stating that shifts logical types *and* sets up double-binds as initiating trance. Example: Rebel against thinking about just how comfortable you can feel if you don't close your eyes before you're ready to relax deeper than you ever have before, now. I wonder if you're going to fail to succeed at not going into trance at exactly your own speed or whether you won't.

12) Create gestalt states. States-about-states frequently generates gestalt experiences so that something new emerges from the process that we cannot explain, as a summation of the parts, it partakes of a systemic and non-additivity quality. Suppress excitement creates anxiety; worrying about what any given activity or meaning means leads to existential concern.

13) Creates humor. The jolt and jar of state-upon-state often results in the gestalt of humor (Plato: that which we experience as "out of place in time and space without danger"). It tickles our fancy, delights our consciousness, surprises, amazes, shocks, etc.

14) Qualify experiences. Higher level states *qualify* all lower level experiences by setting the frame for them as in joyful learning, an accomplished liar, a devious negotiation, a boring learning, a charming lie, ruthless compassion. In this we *texture* the quality of our states.

15) Solidifying frames and levels. When we *believe* in a primary state, *value* it, *take pride* in our learning, believe in the importance of feeling fully our depression, etc., we make the lower state more permanent, solid, and lasting. This works as an installation pattern.

16) Loosening frames. Conversely, we can not only use higher states to solidify a level, but also to loosen a frame and level. Thus, doubting in the importance of learning, questioning our confidence, being playful about our serious beliefs, etc.

Appendix C

PRE-NLP "SUB-MODALITIES"

In 1977, Caryl Marsh wrote a chapter in *Altered States of Consciousness* and presented a framework for describing subjective states of consciousness. At the time, Marsh served as Consultant to the Drug Abuse Council, and was completing a Ph.D. in Social Psychology. The following predates the formation of *"sub-modalities"* in NLP.

> "For most of us, the images, thoughts, and feelings of consciousness are difficult to describe. They are complex, continually changing. Skillful artists —poets, film makers, painters, photographers, novelists, musicians—often capture and communicate vividly the unique contents of their awareness. Despite the unique *contents* of each person's awareness, there are underlying similarities, a discernible common *framework*. This *framework* enables us to characterize the contents of our awareness at any particular moment and to distinguish among different states of awareness." (*Italics added*)

Marsh begins by describing structure as a frame—as *frames* that order, structure, format, and characterize context. *Content* looks different in a global frame (zoom out, larger picture, larger view of the surrounding area) than a detail frame (zooming in, more tunnel vision effect).

Focus
Marsh uses "focus" of External/ Internal Focus similar to how we describe the meta-program of Self and Other Referencing, and Uptime and Downtime. He uses a continuum metaphor, decreases of Internal/External focus... along an analogue.

> "By *focus* I mean the direction of one's attention, outward to *external* objects and conditions or *inward* to one's own thoughts, feelings, images, awareness of oneself. Focus of attention can be thought of as a continuum. One end is deep within us, as in meditation when we totally block out all external stimuli. The other end is complete absorption in something outside ourselves, as when we are engrossed in reading a book, listening to someone, solving a puzzle, watching a film, or playing a game."

Next he describes the flexibility of focus, the meta-program of Screening and Non-Screening, an intense focus state of flow ("genius").

> "Focus of attention is like a spotlight that we move about. It has also been compared to a tuning system. We constantly *tune in or out* whole segments of stimuli much as we switch channels on a television set and then adjust the images and sound. Often, we are unaware of the extent to which we are shifting the focus of our attention from outside to inside and back out again or from one set of stimuli to another. Hence, we tend to be unaware of how and to what extent we control consciousness by refocusing and what the full potential of this capacity might be."

Structure
Here Marsh describes the cinematic feature of Foreground / Background which contains many meta-levels including many domains of knowledge that govern the matrix of our understanding. He also includes the Global meta-program.

"By *structure*, I mean foreground, background, and overview or aeriel view. In the *foreground* of awareness are the sense impressions, thoughts, feelings, memories, plans, wishes, strivings that capture our attention at any particular moment. In the *background* are the more general, persistent awareness of time, place, social reality, and personal identity. We know roughly what time it is, the date, how long we have been awake, how soon we will be going to sleep. We know where we are, in what place, what city or area, what country. We have our culture's frame of reference for assessing reality. In the background of our awareness, there is also a sense of the steady, silent workings of the body."

Next he speaks about *reflexivity* as that which allows us to develop meta-cognitive states and all of the meta-levels of awareness.

"By *overview or aerial view*, I mean one's awareness of oneself being aware. You can observe yourself observing your own consciousness. Philosophers call this the reflective mode."

He then speaks about the fluidity of our meta-levels of awareness, the fluidity that can quickly shift awareness, that creates new and different gestalts.

"An important characteristic of this structure is that the relationships of foreground and background can change at any time, more swiftly than we can talk about them. The sensation of a sudden pain in your body will immediately move to the foreground of your awareness. Any unfamiliar change in the background of awareness tends to draw attention to itself and thereby shift the pattens of your awareness so that what was background becomes foreground. What was foreground may shift to background or fade away entirely. In some states of consciousness there may be only foreground. Background awareness may vanish, as in dreams or intensive activities that have no sense of time or place."

Attributes

"By *attributes*, I mean *the qualities* that describe the perceptions, images, thoughts, feelings, and memories of awareness. Any of the qualities may be present in varying degrees or may be completely absent. Some qualities, combined with structure and focus, distinguish one state of consciousness from another. Sample attributes are:

clear / blurred	— **Visual**
whole/ fragmented	— **Visual/ Auditory**
jumbled	— **Meta-judgment**
familiar/ unfamiliar	— **Meta:** judgment compared against knowledge background
meaningful/ meaningless	— **Meta:** evaluation of degree that something "makes sense"
colorful / colorless	— **Visual**
real / imagined	— **Memory/ Imagination; recalled/ Constructed**
like / dislike	— **Meta:** Emotion Attraction/ Disattraction
expanded / contracted	— **VAK — Extended/ Tight**
purposeful / purposeless	— **Meta**

Attributes of One's Roles

In this category, Marsh puts what we call first and second perceptual position and the "sub-modality" distinction (also a meta-program) associated in a movie or outside of it as a spectator. He speaks about the sense of Owning or Disowning our movies.

> "Within one's own images during a daydream or sleep dream, one sees oneself anywhere along the continuum from active and involved to passive spectator to helpless victim in regard to the events taking place in the images."
> "One also perceives one's role in relation to the degree of control one has over initiating the images. For example, in studies of the hypnagogic imagery that some people experience as they are falling asleep, subjects report that the images just seem to produce themselves automatically like a series of lantern slides. ... Sleep dreams are often seen as foreign to the dreamer, who finds it difficult to accept them as the product of his own mental life."

He describes kinesthetic perceptions and relates that kind of perception to the size, shape, etc. of one's body.

> "Perceptions are sensations and changes in one's body, of size, and shape, and of the myriad distinctive changes triggered by psychological and physical activities or chemicals. ... During intense physical activity, one's body and the tangible environment occupy all of one's awareness. Intensity of feeling increases, and background awareness fades."

Regarding the concept of "time" and the coding of "time" and time-lines, he writes that the "Attributes of time are: past, present, future, timeless." Similarly, for space: "Attributes of space are: inside one's body, outside one's body, spaceless."

> "The foregoing lists to not exhaust the possible ways in which one may describe the contents of one's own awareness in any particular state of consciousness. Our language lacks precise terms for describing some of the most strongly felt experiences."

How Wilheim Wundt Almost Invented NLP

When I read the history of psychology in the nineteenth and twentieth centuries, I realized that it was only a matter of time before somebody would have stumbled upon what we call NLP, it was also a question of *who* would put it together in its current form.

For example, the very father of modern psychology, *Wilheim Wundt*, came very close to creating NLP. As NLP made "the structure of subjectivity" its focus, Wundt made *consciousness* the object of his psychology. He spent his time investigating consciousness—its elements, structure, and nature.

> "The first step in the investigation of a fact must therefore be a description of the individual ... elements of which it consists..."
> "Wundt's point of view emphasized that conscious experience could be reduced to its component sensory of imaginal elements. ... All experience is comprised of sensations or images." (p. 108)

Wundt began with the presupposition that consciousness plays an active role in its own organization. He called this *Voluntarism*. (That term probably contributed to killing his ideas!) Voluntarism referred to the power of volition to act or will, and to thereby organize *mind* into higher level thought processes. This corresponds to the NLP idea of "running your own brain."

Wundt, however, took a different turn from NLP due to the fact that *empiricism* governed philosophy, epistemology, and methodology. He attempted to identify the basic components of consciousness—to develop "a periodic table of the mind" (Marx and Hillix, 1979, p. 67). The objectivism and positivism of that day lead him to want to create a periodic table of the mind modeled after that of chemistry.

In the end, however, he failed. He did not succeed in discovering *a periodic table of the mental elements*. Why not? Because he also failed to develop a vocabulary of consciousness. Along with other philosophers and empiricists of that day, he was not able to develop an effective language for describing what he and his researchers found in consciousness as they used the tool of introspection. As a result, description become messy, imprecise, vague, and confused. This sabotaged the research. In this way, empiricism constricted his attempts to identify the "laws" by which *mind* worked and functioned.

Also the constructions he came up with were both rigid and primitive. For example, Wundt settled on the words *mediate* and *immediate* experiences to distinguish levels of experience. He said that in *mediate* experience we say, "The flower is red." Here consciousness focuses on the *content* of the flower. In *immediate* experience, we focus not so much on the content, but on the *structure*. In this case, "redness" which we now know does not occur outside of our skin, but within our skins, at the level of the sense receptors.

Then, using an either-or format, Wundt decided that psychologists should be concerned with the study of immediate experience rather than mediate experience. Today we describe this awareness as the distinction between content and structure (or process).

Nor did Wundt have the ability to distinguish between the modalities of consciousness and their features. That could have possibly lead him to his "periodic table of the mind." Wundt had a three-fold goal for his psychology:

1) to analyze conscious processes into their basic elements, 2) to discover how these elements are synthesized or organized, and 3) to determine the laws of connection governing their organization.

These correspond closely to what we do in NLP and Neuro-Semantics. In the first, we analyze conscious processes and identify their basic elements: modalities with their cinematic features, meta-programs, language distinctions, and meta-states. Then we use these elements to specify the processes by which we can use them to create new patterns. We discover the laws of connection governing their organization via strategies, TOTE, meta-state interfaces and the Matrix model.

The following quote from psychology historian, Schultz (1992) indicates that Wundt almost invented NLP when "he classified sensations according to *sense modalities* (vision, hearing, and so on), intensity, and duration" (p. 88). The problem with his arrangement was how he mixed and confused modalities (visual, auditory) with the features and qualities of the modalities (intensity, duration). In this he came so close.

Wundt had several problematic presuppositions that prevented him from moving his psychology as far as the modern Cognitive-Behavioral models. First, he "recognized no fundamental difference between sensations and images, because images are also associated with cortical excitation." In other words, when he came across a V→K synesthesia ["images (V) are associated with cortical excitation" (K)], he did not know what to do with such or how to read it. He concluded that images (V) and sensations (K) were not different.

2) Second, in Wundt's system, he operated primarily from a mind-body dualism and so did not think about mind-body as a system. "He regarded the mind and the body as parallel, but not interacting systems." This prevented him from recognizing how the mind-body-emotion system interacted to create its states. Third, he also operated from a strong distaste (as did so many in that age) from practical applications.

> "His psychology was a pure academic science and intended to be only that; Wundt had no interest in attempting to apply his psychology to practical concerns." (p. 93)

NLP Systemic Model

With *four* meta-domains, NLP now has four avenues and redundant systems for describing any subjective experience.

The First Meta-Domain
Bandler and Grinder's (1975) Meta-Model of language gave NLP a model that applies to all forms of communications—personal, family, business, therapy, and relationships. With that model (and its inverse, the Milton Model) a ferocious and passionate intensity to model excellence everywhere was initiated. Having specified *the structure of magic*, they began exploring all kinds of experiences —hypnosis, communication expertise, getting over the past, inventing compelling futures, etc.

The Second Meta-Domain
The next domain apparently arose when Leslie Cameron-Bandler, practicing "Classic NLP," found that some of the processes did not always work. This provided "a rare and unprecedented opportunity" for her and Richard Bandler to identify the higher level sorting mechanisms which interfered. From that they specified the first *perceptual filters* that operated at a higher "logical level," *meta* to the primary level processing of information. As higher levels govern and modulate lower levels, these meta-programs as unconscious sorting mechanisms could validate or invalidate the lower level experiences.

The Third Meta-Domain
While meta-levels, meta-parts, and meta-positions were mentioned early in NLP, and while Woodsmall even mentioned meta-states in a list of possible meta-programs (1988), it wasn't until 1994 that the Meta-States model was developed. This arose from both Korzybski regarding his *levels of abstraction* model in General Semantics and Bateson (1972, 1979) regarding his numerous meta-level analysis of learning, schizophrenia (double-bind theory), aesthetics, etc.

Meta-States arose from a modeling project around the subject of *The Strategy of Resilience*. Out of the research, the realization dawned that people not only experience first-level, *primary states*, but also states-*about*-states, states-*upon*-states, what Korzybski called "second-order abstractions," or meta-states.

The fourth meta-Domain: Meta-Modalities or Cinematic Frames / Features
What has been called "sub-modalities" is now recognized as actually making up another meta-domain. This was hidden and masked under the prefix *"sub"* that falsely labeled the cinematic features of our mental movies. This gives us the meta-editorial frames that adds textures to the movies of our mind.

Four Avenues to the Same Thing
These four *meta-domains* relate to each other by providing us four different lenses for viewing the structure of experience. With the Meta-Model we have *the language route* to experience. We can use this model to sort and separate the linguistic structures that create the person's magical world. We can hear primary level, sensory-based language that we can immediately track over to a audio-video representation. We can tell when

a person jumps "logical levels" and begins speaking evaluatively using non-sensory based language. This cues us into recognizing the person's meta-maps about reality, the person's *meaning constructions* in terms of beliefs, values, decisions, etc.

Using the *language route* to experience gives us several choices. We can deframe neuro-linguistic reality by pulling apart the semantic constructions. We do this by meta-modeling. This invites the person to move down from the evaluative world of meaning, identity, rules, values, etc. and to provide behavioral equivalents in see-hear-feel language. The reductionistic nature of the Meta-Model shifts a person from a higher "logical level" to a lower, enabling one to reality test the mapping, enrich the maps by observing when and where and in what circumstances the person created such mapping, and run an ecology check to see if such mapping still serves them very well.

The *language route* to experience does more than deframes a person's mental maps. We can just as easily use the Meta-Model to *construct* new generalizations, nominalizations, cause-effect relations, complex equivalences, etc. We can use the Meta-Model and our understanding of both the structure and the secrets of magic to powerfully enrich a person's impoverished maps. I noted this in *The Secrets of Magic* (1998, now *Communication Magic,* 2001). Many Meta-Model questions and processes invite a person to move up "logical levels." "And how do you feel about that feeling?"

The Perception Avenue
As the Meta-Model gives a "yellow brick road" of language for traveling to the Oz of human experience (both expertise and pathology), so Meta-Programs gives us the avenue of *perception.* With the Meta-Model we ask about indications of *ill-formedness and well-formedness* (to use the transformational language of Grinder). But now we ask about the indicators of perceptual filters or meta-programs. In some contexts we may keep this to a minimum of nine meta-programs as Shelly Rose Charvet did in her business applications, or to a more exhaustive list like the 51 that Dr. Bodenhamer and I put in *Figuring Out People.* Either way, the meta-programs give us another "royal road" to subjective experience—the person's way of sorting and paying attention to information.

Cognitive Behavioral psychology describes these perceptual filters as *thinking patterns.* In other words, the thinking patterns developed and used by Ellis and Beck relate to the NLP model as additional meta-programs (see *The Sourcebook of Magic,* 2004). This suggests that we can model and design engineer excellence by paying attention to the meta-level filters that a person uses.

If both the Meta-Model and the Meta-Programs models speak about the same thing, then *how* do they relate to each other? One focuses more on linguistic expressions, the other on perceptual viewpoint. One thinks more about the internal *languaging* that has created the person's reality structures, the other thinks more about the higher level "programs" that have become habitual in what and the way that the person pays attention to things. Meta-Programs do show up in language. We can find and specify various *linguistic markers* that indicate meta-programs. Woodsmall and James (1988) specified many of these. Conversely, within meta-programs we can hear and identify many Meta-Model distinctions.

Where do meta-programs come from? They arise as meta-states become habituated and solidified. Meta-Programs arise from the coalescing of meta-stating processes.

The State Avenue

As distinctions that arise from the Meta-Model and Meta-Programs relate to the same thing, so does the distinctions and features within the Meta-States model. Here we do not so much focus on linguistic distinctions or perceptual filters (although they obviously play a significant role in meta-states). Instead, we focus primarily on the person's *state*, his or her mind-body-emotion state and the "logical level" at which the person experiences that state.

Self-reflexivity is the central and primary mechanism that drives meta-states. This refers to the systemic property of mind (thought, emotion, kinesthetic awareness) *reflecting back onto itself.* When this happens, the very products and experiences of our states *feed back* into the experience itself to create a system—a system of interactive parts. Then out of that *emerges* new and unique configurations that do not exist at the lower levels. Korzybski described this as "second and third order abstractions." Bateson described it using cybernetic terms and system language, hence his introduction of the word "meta" itself into NLP.

Reflexivity initiates our higher level skills of meta-communicating, meta-feeling, meta-thinking, etc. While animals have some capacity for thinking-and-feeling at meta-levels (Bateson studied this in dogs and dolphins), they eventually stop reflecting back at some level (two or three levels up). Yet Korzybski noted that we never stop. The process goes on continually and infinitely. We can always say or think something else about whatever we thought or said. We do this via our ability to use *symbolics* and so designated us a symbolic class of life. Animals, by contrast, live in a world of *signals*, but do not use *symbols* as such.

This provides us a third "royal road" to experience. We can sort for "logical level" and neurological states. This gives us the ability to distinguish between primary and meta-states. They differ radically. The higher meta-states actually speak about conceptual and semantic states and so operate in a more layered and complex way from primary states. In the primary states, we experience *primary emotions* that show up very strongly in kinesthetic experience. So when we ask, "Where do you feel ...?" and supply a primary emotion (i.e. fear, anger, relaxed, calm, joy, displeasure, disgust, aversion, attraction, etc.), most people can immediately and quickly identify the corresponding somatic location.

But ask a person about *a meta-feeling.* "Where do you feel ... dumb, like a jerk, out-of-sorts, weird, low self-esteem, resilience, forgiveness, etc.?" Typically, the person will not be able to point to a specific location kinesthetically. Such pseudo-emotions share more in the nature of a judgment of the mind, rather than a pure and direct kinesthetic state.

"I feel like a failure" speaks of an evaluative level about an experience and the feelings of that experience (sadness, upset, tension, fear, anger, etc.). So we meta-model that language. "What did you fail at specifically?" "When?" "Where?" "Under what circumstances?" "Based upon what set of values, criteria, and standards?" "In whose eyes?"

This gets us back down to the primary sensory-based level. It enables us to deframe the old mapping of the nominalization ("failure"). The meta-state of "failure" arise from the person's mapping processes and when habituated can become the person's meta-program (pessimism, negative self-referencing) for looking out onto the world.

Four Meta-Domains
The meta-domains of NLP reference the same thing through different lenses:

Language — The meta-representation system involving words, linguistics systems, mathematics, etc.

Perception — The thinking and sorting patterns for viewing the world, our perceptual filters.

States — The mind-body-emotion states from which we operate and can layer repeatedly using reflexivity.

Cinematic frames — The qualities and features of our movies.

For example, a global or gestalt thinking style (as a meta-program) will show up in the over-use of generalization patterns (in the Meta-Model, nominalizations, universal quantifiers, lost performative) and in inducing one into a global frame of mind (as a meta-state) and will appear as a movie that has a panoramic point of view.

Meta-Domains as a Developmental Model
As we have inquired about the relationship between the Meta-Model and Meta-Programs, or between the Meta-Model and Meta-States, etc., now we can ask about the inter-relationships between these meta-domains. If they all describe *experience* or *subjectivity*, how can we use them together?

As a theoretical model of mind, emotion, and personality, the meta-domains of NLP provide us a way of thinking about the multi-layered and multi-leveled nature of "personality" as it emerges from simply primary states to ever more complex structures. The following developmental stages offers just a sketch of this from *The Structure of Personality: Ordering and Disordering Using NLP and Neuro-Semantics* (2001).

Stage 1. *VAK or Movie representations of the world.*
Consciousness begins as we use our sense receptors to encounter the energy manifestations "out there." First a child has to learn to "see" (perceive), to form and construct *a perceptual map.* After that comes *the representational map,* a construct based on our perceptions. As we construct our *perceptual maps* of what occurs out there, we eventually use such to construct our *representational maps,* namely our sensory representations. A little child around (six to twelve months) will begin the process of developing "constancy of representation." In doing this, the child can then "hold in mind" images, sounds, and sensations *not* present. Prior to this development, peek-a-boo operates as a really thrilling game. After such re-presentational skill, peek-a-boo loses its excitement.

Stage 2. *Meta-representation of the representational Map.*
The period of *pure* sensory representational maps only lasts a year or so. Before long, we begin to learn a meta-skill. We learn to attach sounds (words) to the sensory-based representations. We label the strawberry with the word "strawberry" and so add *language* to our primary state and experience. But we don't stop there. We develop words about those words. *Fruit* becomes a meta-word, a word *about* other words. And so we *go meta* very early, jump logical levels, and classify our classifications.

Stage 3. *Habituating thinking styles create Meta-Programs.*
By the habituation of our thinking-and-feeling, our sensory and linguistic maps collapse

into the primary level so that our way of thinking (matching or mismatching, toward or away from, global or specific, etc.) becomes a "program" itself, a *Meta*-Program for paying attention to the world and people. In this way, our predispositions and training in running our attention solidifies into higher level perceptual filters, which in turn, affect our perceptions.

Stage 4. *First level Meta-Stating and Meta-States.*
With more growth, we begin to reflect back on our thoughts-and-emotions with other thoughts-and-emotions. We go meta. And as we do, we create a state-*upon*-a-state structure. This initiates a new gestalt—a systemic configuration of layered consciousness, a "second-order abstraction." In a recent training, a young father described his eighteen month infant. The child had recently suffered constipation for a few days (primary state of physical discomfort) and who then became *afraid* of "going potty" (a meta-state). In fact, the child had *decided* to *refuse* to go potty! Such meta-levels and meta-states then *set a frame-of-reference* that can become a belief.

Stage 5. *Then the Meta-Levels Coalesce*
Via continual habituation of the meta-states, our higher frames-of-references of our thinking and feeling coalesce into our primary state, texturing and qualifying them. This means that the layering and embeddedness of state-upon-state merges to become indistinguishable. As a result, we qualify our state. This gives us "*joyful* learning," "*compassionate* anger," "*guilting* fear," "*fear* of fear," etc. As we do this, it frees consciousness to create even more meta-state structures—the Matrix.

Stage 6. *And so the process continues.*
The ever-reflecting back onto itself nature of mind means that with every thought or feeling we then have thoughts and feelings about those. In this dynamic, systemic *flow* of consciousness, we develop various *domains of knowledge* or frames-of-reference which we use to navigate life. In this way we construct the Matrix that we live in.

In the end we have a layered and complex "personality" structure that operates with various *attractors* to continually fulfill themselves in the world. Like the theory of memes, these *neuro-linguistic attractors* set the frame for everything that occurs within this system of thoughts-emotions-and somatic states. And what makes up these "energy systems" within "personality?" Simply our higher level thoughts as beliefs, values, identifications, visions, paradigms, understandings, etc. Of course, none of this is real, it's just a model, just a way of talking about things so that we can take more effective action.

Applying the Meta-Domains to "Personality"
The Meta-Model informs us that "personality" (a nominalization) is *not* a thing, it is not a fixed or stable *thing*. We rather refer to an ever-moving, changing, and reorganizing thinking-and-feeling human being. What we call "personality" emerges systemically from the ongoing interplay of a great many factors in the human neuro-linguistic system. While this enables us to appreciate avoiding setting a frame of determinism about persons, it also introduces a lot of complexity.

To handle this dynamic complexity, the *meta-domains* specify numerous leverage points in the system for intervening and creating generative transformations. Where do these leverage point lie? In the meta-domains of language, perception, state, "logical levels," and movie editing.

Because higher levels drive and modulate lower levels, the meta-domains point us in the direction of reframing and outframing. It points us to *setting new frames of references* at higher levels. Further, since we know that habituating thoughts-and-emotions send such constructs upward where they become meta-programs and meta-states, we effectively resist the delusion that these are *things*. They are not things or entities, but mental constructs—mappings.

We can so easily get caught up in *content* and lose awareness of meta-levels because meta-level phenomena operate outside of consciousness as our meta frames-of-reference. This means that we inevitably live our lives *embedded* in those frames and *governed* by those frames without awareness. To wake up to our Matrix, the meta-domains gives us multiple ways to become aware of our frames and a four-fold way to analyze our Matrix.

Every *state* (primary or meta) involves something dynamic, moving, alive—a fully energized somatic and neurological state. The *Molecules of Emotion* (1997) as described by Pert and others sets up actual forces and energies in the body (the soma). This mind-body connection is the neuro-linguistic interface that describes how beliefs, values, decisions, etc. create physiological effects in us. Cognitive linguistics speak of *embodiment* in the meaning-making process—as beings in the kind of bodies we have, our neurological "abstracting" from the energy manifestations "out there" become transduced into the nervous system as another kind of energy. *Embodied states* have real correlates in the body.

Appendix E

THE FACETS OF A MODEL

What is required for a full *model*? There needs to be four key factors: a theory of principles and conceptual ideas, a set of variables or elements, a set of guidelines for working with and a set of patterns that result from the model.

1) An explanatory theory or hypothesis of the model.

A theory describes our understandings (beliefs, values, guesses) about how an experience or process works. A theory enables us to make educated guesses about what we can expect in using a model. When we test a theory through experiments, we can refine the hypothesis and thereby make it even more useful in predicting responses and mapping the future. This provides the theoretical basis and foundation upon which the model operates and answers the questions of epistemology (the *why* questions).

2) A set of variables and elements of the model.

Every model has pieces and parts that make up its components.

These variables answer the *what* questions: *what* is the model, *what* elements are absolutely necessary and sufficient for the model, *what* mechanisms and processes are involved?

3) A formula or set of guidelines for using the model.

A formula or set of guidelines gives us some kind of structure for the model, a practical way to think about it. This make take the form of a diagram, a flow chart, a list of items, a matrix, etc. In this we can collect all of elements and variables to guide our actions and inform us about what to do next, and how to read feedback. As a working model guidelines give us practical, step-by-step instructions. They give us guiding principles that informs us about what to do, when, where, in what context and circumstances, in what way, how, etc.

4) The technologies and patterns of the model.

Finally a model will have specific applications which will appear as patterns, processes, or what we might call human technologies. These allow us to use the model to achieve something. These answer the *how to* questions. For example, *How* do you reframe meaning?

BIBLIOGRAPHY

Andreas, Steve; Faulkner, Charles (1994). *NLP: The new technology of achievement.* NY: William Marrow and Company.

Andreas, Steve; Andreas Connirae. (1987). *Change your mind and keep the change: Advanced NLP "submodalities" interventions.* Moab, UT: Real People Press.

Bandler, Richard and Grinder, John. (1976). *The structure of magic, Volume II.* Palo Alto, CA: Science & Behavior Books.

Bandler, Richard and Grinder, John. (1979). *Frogs into princes: Neuro-linguistic programming.* Moab, UT: Real People Press.

Bandler, Richard. (1984). *Magic in action.* CA: Meta Publications.

Bateson, Gregory. (1972). *Steps to an ecology of mind.* New York: Ballatine.

Bandler, Richard and Grinder, John. (1982). *Reframing: Neuro-linguistic programming and the transformation of meaning.* Ut: Real People Press.

Bandler, Richard. (1985). *Using your brain for a change.* (Ed. Connirae and Steve Andreas). Moab, UT: Real People Press.

Bandler, Richard; LaValle, John. (1996). *Persuasion engineering: Sales and business, language and behavior.* Capitola, CA: Meta Publications.

Bateson, Gregory. (1972). *Steps to an ecology of mind.* NY; Ballantine Books.

Bodenhamer, Bob. (1995). <u>Taking a Bitter Root To Jesus</u>. Salt Lake City:

Anchor Point. April. 1995 (pages 20-24).

Bodenhamer, Bobby G.; Hall, L. Michael. (1997). *Time-Lining: Patterns for adventuring in time.* Wales, United Kingdom: Anglo-American Books.

Bodenhamer, Bobby G.; Hall. L. Michael. (1999). *The user's manual for the brain: A comprehensive manual for neuro-linguistic programming practitioner certification.* United Kingdom: Crown House Publishers.

Corsetty, Kathy; Pearson, Judith. (1999). *Healthy habits: Total conditioning for a healthy mind and body.* UK: Crown House Publications.

Dilts, Robert; Grinder, John; Bandler, Richard; DeLozier, Judith. (1980). *Neuro-linguistic programming, Volume I: The study of the structure of subjective experience.* Cupertino. CA.: Meta Publications.

Dilts, R.B. (1990). *Changing beliefs systems with NLP.* Cupertino, CA: Meta Publications.

Dilts, Robert B. (1994). *Strategies of Genius, Volume I. Aristotle, Sherlock Homes, Walt Disney, Wolfgang Amadeus Mozart./* Capitola, CA: Meta Publications.

Dilts, Robert B. (1994). *Strategies of Genius, Volume II. Einstein.* Capitola, CA: Meta Publications.

Dilts, Robert B. (1995). *Strategies of Genius, Volume III. Freud, Mozart,* Capitola, CA: Meta Publications.

Chomsky, Noam. (1957). *Syntactic*

structures. The Hague: Mouton Publishers.

Chomsky, Noam. (1965). *Aspects of the theory of syntax.* Cambridge, MA: MIT Press.

Corsetty, Kathy; Pearson, Judith. (1999). *Healthy habits: Total conditioning for a healthy mind and body.* (In press).

Faulkner (1998). Meta-Patterns, Metaphors, & Models. Workshop at the ANLP Conference, London, England, Nov. 1998.

Gardner, Howard. (198). *Frames of mind: The theory of multiple intelligenc*es. NY: BasicBooks.

Gardner, Howard. (1991). *The unschooled mind: How children think and how schools should teach.* NY: HarperCollins.

Gardner, Howard. (1993). *Multiple intelligences: The theory in practice..* NY: BasicBooks.

Gilliland, Burl E.; James, Richard K.; Bowman, James T. (1989). *Theories and strategies in counseling and psychotherapy.* (2nd. ed.). Englewood Cliffs, NJ: Prentice Hall.

Grinder, John; and DeLozier, Judith. (1987). *Turtles all the way down: Prerequisites to personal genius.* Scotts Valley, CA: Grinder & Associates.

Hall, Michael. (2000). *Meta-states: Reflexivity and higher States of mind.* Clifton CO: Neuro-Semantic Publications.

Hall, L. Michael. (1996). *The Spirit of NLP: The process, meaning, and criteria for mastering NLP.* Carmarthen, Wales, England. Anglo-American Book Company Ltd.

Hall, Michael (1997, 1998) *Recognizing the Meta-Levels of Beliefs* series. *Anchor Point*, Nov. and Dec. 1997, Jan. and Feb. 1998. Salt Lake City: Anchor Point Associates.

Hall, L. Michael; Bodenhamer, Bobby G. (2002). *Mind-lines: Lines for changing minds.* (4th edition) Grand Jct. CO: E.T. Publications.

Hall, Michael. (2000). *Communication Magic.* Carmarthen, Wales: Crown House Publications.

Hall, Michael, L. (1998). Changing Beliefs Using Meta-States. (*Anchor Point*, Nov., Dec. 1997, Jan, Feb. 1998). Salt Lake City: UT. Anchor Point Associates.

Hall, Michael; Bodenhamer, Bob. (2005, 2nd edition). *Figuring out people: Design engineering using meta-programs.* Wales, UK: Crown House Publications.

Hall, Michael; Belnap; Barbara. (2004). *The source book of magic: A comprehensive guide to the technology of NLP.* UK: Crown House Publishers.

Huxley, Aldous (1954). *The doors of perception and heaven and hell.* NY: Harper & Row.

Korzybski, Alfred. (1933/ 1994). *Science and sanity: An introduction to non-Aristotelian systems and general semantics,* (5th. ed.). Concord, CA: International Society For General Semantics.

Lakoff, George; Johnson, Mark. (1980). *Metaphors we live by.* Chicago: University of Chicago Press.

Langacker, Ronald. (1987). *Foundations of cognitive grammar,*

Vol. 1. Stanford, CA: Stanford University Press.

Langacker, Ronald W. (1991). *Concept, image and symbol: The cognitive basis of grammar.* New York: Mouton de Gruyter.

Lostere, Kim; Malatesta, Linda. (1989). *Getting the Results You Want* Portand, OR: Metamorphous Press.

Major, David (1996). "A Critical Examination of the Place of 'Belief' in NLP." *NLP World.* The Intercultural Journal on the Theory & Practice of Neuro-Linguistic Programming, Vol. 3, No. 3 (Nov, 1996, pages 21-34).

MacDonald, Will; Bandler, Richard;(1988). *An insider's guide to sub-modalities.* Capitola, CA: Meta Publications.

Miller, George A; Galanter, Eugene; and Pribram, Karl H. (1960). *Plans and the structure of behavior.* NY: Holt, Rinehart and Winston Co.

O'Connor, Josephy; Seymour, John. (1990). *Introducing neuro-linguistic programming: The new psychology of personal excellence.* Great Britain: Crucible,

Overdurf, John; Silverthorn, Julie (1995).*Beyond Words: Languaging Change Through the Quantum Field.* Audio-Cassette set. PA: Neuro-Energetics.

Pert, Candice B. (1997). *Molecules of emotion: Why you feel the way you feel.* NY: Scribner.

Robbie, Eric. (1987). "Sub-Modality Eye Accessing Cues." (pages 15-24). *Journal of NLP International.* Vol. I. #1. Indian Rocks Beach, FL. NLP International.

Roberts, Martin. (1998, 1999). Modelling: Magic, Myth, or Mirage., Part I, II, III. *Rapport: Journal of NLP.* #42, #43, #44. London. ANLP Association.

Schultz, Duane P. (1992). *A history of modern psychology.* Fort Worth, TX: Harcourt Brace Jovanovich College Publishers.

Watzlawick, Paul; Weakland, John; Fisch, Richard. (1974). Change: Principles of problem formation and problem resolution. NY: W.W. Norton & Co.

Watzlawick, Paul. (1978). *The language of change: Elements of therapeutic communication.* NY: Basic Books, Inc.

Watzlawick, Paul. (1984) (Ed). *The invented reality: How do we know what we believe we know?* NY: W.W. Norton & Co.

Woodsmall, Wyatt; James, Tad. (1988). *Time line therapy and the basis of personality.* Cupertino, CA: Meta Publ.

Yeager, Joseph (1985). *Thinking about thinking with NLP.* CA: Meta Publications.

Zinberg, Norman E.. (Ed.) (1977). *Altered states of consciousness.* New York: The Free Press, Division of Macmillan Publishing.

GLOSSARY

As-If Frame: Using a pretend or possibility frame of mind to pretend that some event is real or actually happened and to step into that frame of thinking-and-feeling. "As if" thinking encourages creative problem-solving by going beyond apparent obstacles.

Analogue: A variable that occurs at various degrees between certain limits, like a dimmer switch for a light. An analogue "sub-modality" may vary like from light to dark, while a digital cinematic feature will operate in either the on or off position, as a snapshot or a movie.

Anchoring. An user-friendly version of classical conditioning derived from Pavlovian stimulus-response reaction. Pavlov's bell became the stimulus or anchor cuing the dogs to salivate as the meat powder had. When we link or connect a stimulus (external or internal) to a response, the sight, sound, sensation, smell, or word triggers a response or state.

Association: Imagining ourselves *inside* of an experience or movie, *stepping in* to associate into it. Mentally seeing, hearing, and feeling from inside. We *step into* a state or experience to associate and we *step out* to dissociate.

Beliefs: A gestalt resulting from confirming a thought, the thought now treated as real. When we believe, we hold a generalization about causality, meaning, self, others, behaviors, identity, etc. as true. Beliefs occur at higher "logical levels" to thoughts. As frames, beliefs guide us in perceiving and interpreting reality.

Calibration: Tuning-in to another's state via reading non-verbal signals previously observed and calibrated to the person's style of expression.

Content: The specifics and details of an event, answers *what* and *why?* Contrasts with process or structure.

Context: The setting, frame or process in which events occur and provides meaning for content.

Digital: Off or on as when the light switch is on or off. A digital cinematic feature presents the on/off choice: a "sub-modality" shift from coded as in color or in black-and-white (see analogue).

Dissociation: *Stepping out* of a thought, representation, mental movie, or state and no longer *inside* it or associated. Seeing or hearing things from outside as from a spectator's point of view. Association and dissociation are relative terms, whenever we step out of one state, we are always stepping into another state.

Downtime: Moving from an uptime state to going "down" inside one's mind to see, hear, and feel thoughts and memories. A light trance state with attention focused inward.

Ecology: The dynamic balance of elements in a system that produce health, well-being, and balance, in larger contexts and relationships. The ecology question asks about how a belief, state, decision, or experience fits with one's overall set of relationships and its effect on one's health, business, values, etc.

Elicitation: Evoking a state by word, behavior, gesture, or any stimuli, gathering information by direct observation of non-verbal signals or by asking meta-model questions.

Empowerment: Adding vitality, energy, and new powerful resources to a person; vitality at the neurological level.

Epistemology: The study of how we know what we know, NLP epistemology is based upon "the map is not the territory" distinction.

First Position: Perceiving the world from your own point of view, associated, one of the three perceptual positions.

Frame: Context, environment, meta-level, a way of perceiving something (as in Outcome Frame, "As If" Frame, Backtrack Frame, etc.).

Future Pace: Process of mentally practicing (rehearsing) an event before it happens, a key process for ensuring the permanency of an outcome, a key ingredient in most NLP interventions.

Gestalt: A German term for something that is "more than the sum of the parts." A gestalt state occurs when new emergent properties arise from texturing or meta-stating.

Incongruence: An inner state of conflict between beliefs, emotions, meanings, hopes, dreams, fears, etc., the lack of total commitment to an outcome expressed in incongruent messages, signals, lack of alignment or matching between word and behavior.

Installation: The process for incorporating a new mental strategy (way of doing things) within our mind-body system so it operates automatically. We install through anchoring, metaphors, parables, reframing, future pacing, quality control questions, etc.

Internal representations: All of the sights, sounds, sensations, smells, and tastes that play out on the theater of our mind as snapshots and movies.

Kinesthetic: Sensations, feelings, tactile sensations on surface of skin, proprioceptive sensations inside the body, includes vestibular system or sense of balance.

Logical levels or types: Two nominalizations that describe how we layer level upon level of thoughts-and-feelings so that one is about another and so classifies or types the lower as a member of that class. Meta-levels drive and modulate the levels embedded within them.

Loops: A circle, cycle, a story, metaphor or representation that goes back to its own beginning, so that it loops back (feeds back) onto itself. An open loop: a story left unfinished. A closed loop: finishing a story. In strategies: looping refers to going through a set of procedures that have no exit.

Map: A model of the world, an unique representation of the world built within our brain by abstracting from experiences, involving a neurological and a linguistic map. Internal representations encoding our movie and the frames about it.

Meta: Greek for "above, beyond, and about," thinking about a thought is a meta-thought, a higher "logical level."

Meta-Model: A model with 21 linguistic distinctions that identifies language patterns that obscure meaning via distortion, deletion, and generalization. Each distinction suggests questions that we can use to challenge and clarify imprecise language (called *ill-formedness*). This reconnects one to sensory experience and brings one out of trance. Developed in 1975 by Richard Bandler and John Grinder.

Meta-Programs: The perceptual filters we use as we pay attention to things. The perceptual glasses that govern what and how we see.

Meta-States: A state about a state, applying one state of mind-body (fear, anger, joy, learning) to another state to set it as a higher "logical level." Meta-states result from self-reflexive consciousness. Developed by L. Michael Hall.

Model: A description of how something works, a generalized, deleted or distorted copy of an original, a template for how to think or act. A complete model has a theory, set of variables, guidelines for using them, and patterns or technologies that result from it.

Modeling: A process of observing and replicating the successful actions and behaviors of others. Modeling involves identifying the variables make up an experience, discerning the sequence of internal representations and behaviors, and presenting as a way to accelerate learning an expertise.

Multiple description: The process of describing the same thing from different viewpoints using different models or perspectives.

Neuro-Linguistic Programming: A communication model, a model of modeling excellence, how people structure experience.

Nominalization: A linguistic distinction in the Meta-Model describing a hypnotic pattern, a process or verb turned into a noun, a process frozen in time by *naming* (nominalizing) the process.

Pacing: Matching one's reality, gaining and maintaining rapport with another by joining their model of the world by saying that fits with and matches their language, beliefs, values, current experience, etc., crucial to rapport building.

Perceptual filters: Experience, ideas, beliefs, values, decisions, memories that shape and color the way we see and experience the world, our meta-programs.

Perceptual position: A point of view or perspective. First Position: associated within one's own eyes. Second Position: seeing from the listener's perspective. Third Position: seeing from a meta-position outside self and other, a neural observer. Fourth Position: seeing from the viewpoint of the group, system, or organization. Fifth Position: incorporating all four perceptual positions, the "God" or universe viewpoint.

Predicates: What we assert or predicate about a subject, sensory based words indicating a particular representation system (VAK).

Rapport: A sense of connection with another, a feeling of mutuality, a sense of trust, created by pacing, mirroring and matching, a state of empathy or second position.

Reframing: Altering a frame-of-reference so it looks different, presenting an event or idea from a different point of view or frame so it has a different meaning; we can reframe content or context.

Representation: A *presentation* in our mind of what we have already seen, an idea, thought, sensory-based information or evaluation.

Second position: Perceiving the world from another's point of view or sense of reality.

Sensory-based description: Information directly observable and verifiable by the senses, see-hear-feel language that we can test empirically, in contrast to evaluative descriptions.

"Sleight of Mouth" patterns: The reframing patterns that allow us to alter meaning conversationally. Similar to "sleight of hand" patterns, we shift to a more enhancing frame-of-reference without the listener noticing. Re-modeled as *Mind-Lines* by Hall and Bodenhamer.

State: A mind-body-emotion state, the sum total of all neurological and physical processes in a person at any moment in time, a holistic phenomenon, mood.

Strategy: A sequencing of thinking-behaving to obtain an outcome or create an experience, the structure of subjectivity ordered in a linear model of the TOTE.

"Sub-modality:" The cinematic features or distinctions within each representation system designating the qualities of our internal movies.

Synesthesia: An automatic link from one representation system to another, a V-K synesthesia involves seeing→feeling without a moment of consciousness to think about it, automatic program.

Third position: Perceiving things from the viewpoint of an observer, one of the three perceptual positions, a meta-position for observing both self and other.

Time-line: A metaphor describing how we represent and store sights, sounds and sensations of memories and imagines that codes the construct of "time."

T.O.T.E. A flow-chart model developed by George Miller and associates (Galanter and Pribram) to explain the sequential processes that generate a response. **T**est-**O**perate-**T**est-**E**xit updated the Stimulus—>**R**esponse model of behaviorism, NLP updated by adding representation systems.

Unconscious: Everything *not* in conscious awareness, our experience of our minor representation system.

Uptime: The state where our attention and senses are directed outward to immediate environment, all sensory channels open and alert.

VAK: A short-hand for the sensory representation systems of **V**isual, **A**uditory, and **K**inesthetic. K includes smells (**O**lfactory) and tastes (**G**ustatory).

Value: A nominalization describing a belief about what we deem as important. Valuing a person, idea, experience, etc. creates motivation

L. Michael Hall, Ph.D.
ISNS — International Society of Neuro-Semantics®
P.O. Box 8
Clifton, Colorado 81520—0008   USA
(970) 523-7877

www.runyourownbrain.com
www.neurosemantics.com

Dr. Hall is executive director of the *International Society of Neuro-Semantics* (ISNS) having co-founded it with his business partner, Dr. Bob Bodenhamer in 1996. Prior to finding NLP in 1987 and studying with NLP co-founder Richard Bandler, Michael was a licensed psychotherapist in the state of Colorado with graduate degrees in Business, Literature, and Clinical Counseling. He did his doctoral studies in Cognitive Behavioral Psychology and included NLP in his dissertation at Union Institute University in Cincinnati, Ohio.

Upon the discovery of Meta-States in 1994 during a modeling project on resilience, Meta-States won recognition as "the most significant contribution to NLP in 1995" by the International NLP Trainers Association. From there Michael began developing pattern after pattern using meta-states. That, in turn, led him and associates to apply meta-states to facets of NLP itself and finding all kinds of new rich treasures. It was translated to time-lines, "sub-modalities," the sleight of mouth patterns, meta-programs and more. From this came two dozen practical training applications in sales, persuasion, defusing hotheads, leadership, coaching, relationships, wealth creation, etc.

Today Dr. Hall is involved as a Meta-Analyst or Conversation Coach and an entrepreneur in several businesses (real estate, publishing, etc.). He lives part of the year in the Colorado Rocky Mountains and trains internationally the rest of the time. He is a prolific writer and researcher with more than 30 books to his name.

Books:
1) Meta-States: Mastering the higher levels of your mind (2000).
2) Dragon Slaying: Dragons to Princes (2000).
3) The Spirit of NLP: Mastering NLP. (1999).
4) Languaging: The Linguistics of Psychotherapy (1996).
5) Becoming More Ferocious as a Presenter (1996).
6) Patterns For "Renewing the Mind" (w. Bodenhamer) (1997).
7) Time-Lining: Advance Time-Line Processes (w. Bodenhamer) (1997).
8) NLP: Going Meta—Advance Modeling Using Meta-Levels (1997/2001).
9) Figuring Out People: Design Engineering With Meta-Programs (w. Bodenhamer) (1999).
10) A Sourcebook of Magic (1997/2003).
11) Mind-Lines: Lines For Changing Minds (w. Bodenhamer) (2001).

12) The Secrets of Magic: Communication Excellence (1998). Retitled: *Communication Magic* (2000).
13) Meta-State Magic (2002).
14) Structure of Excellence: Unmasking "Sub-modalities" (w Bodenhamer, 1999).
15) Instant Relaxation (1999, Lederer and Hall).
16) The Structure of Personality: Modeling "Personality Using NLP and Neuro-Semantics (Hall , Bodenhamer, Bolstad, Harmblett, 2001).
17) The Secrets of Personal Mastery (2000).
18 Frame Games: Persuasion Elegance (2000).
19) Games Fit and Slim People Play (2001).

20) Games for Mastering Fear (2001, with Bodenhamer).
21) Games Business Experts Play (2001).
22) The Matrix Model (2002/ 2003).
23) User's Manual of the Brain: Practitioner course, Volume I (1999).
24) User's Manual of the Brain: Master Practitioner Course, Volume II (2002).
25) MovieMind (2002).
26) The Bateson Report (2002).
27) Make it So! (2002).
28) Source Book of Magic, Volume II, Neuro-Semantic Patterns (2003).
29) Propulsion Systems (2003).

30)Games Great Lovers Play (2004).
31) Coaching Conversations (2004, with Michelle Duval).
32) Meta-Coaching: Coaching Change, Vol I. (2004, with Michelle Duval).

To order these Books, contact:

NSP: Neuro-Semantics Publications
P.O. Box 8
Clifton CO. 81520—0008 USA

Crown House Publishers
Crown Buildings, Bancyfelin, Carmarthen, SA33 5ND   U.K.
+44 (0) 1267 211880
Fax: +44 (0) 1267 211882
books@anglo-american.co.uk
www.crownhouse.co.uk

Bobby G. Bodenhamer, D.Min.

1516 Cecelia Dr.
Gastonia, NC 28054
(704) 864-3585
bbodenhammer@carolina.rr.com
www.neurosemantics.com

Dr. Bodenhamer first trained for the ministry, earned a doctorate in Ministry, and served several churches as pastor. He began NLP training in 1990, studying with Dr. Tad James and receiving Master Practitioner and Trainer Certifications. Since then, he has taught and certified NLP trainings at Gastona College.

Beginning in 1996, Dr. Bodenhamer began studying the Meta-States model and then teamed up with Michael to begin co-authoring several books. Since then he has turned out many works as he and Michael have applied the NLP and Meta-States Models to various facets of human experience.

In 1996 also, Dr. Bodenhamer with Michael co-founded the Society of Neuro-Semantics. This has taken his work to a new level, taken him into International Trainings, and set in motion many Institutes of Neuro-Semantics around the world.

Books:
1) Patterns For "Renewing the Mind" (w. Hall, 1997)
2) Time-Lining: Advance Time-Line Processes (w. Hall, 1997)
3) Figuring Out People: Design Engineering With Meta-Programs (w. Hall, 1997)
4) Mind Lines: Lines For Changing Minds (w. Hall, 1997, 2000 3rd edition)
5) The Structure of Excellence: Unmasking the Meta-Levels of Submodalities (w. Hall, 1999)
6) The User's Manual of the Brain (1999, w. Hall)
7) Hypnotic Language (2000, w. Burton)
8) The Structure of Personality: Modeling "Personality" Using NLP and Neuro-Semantics. (Hall , Bodenhamer, Bolstad, Harmblett, 2001)
9) Games for Mastering Fears (2001, with Hall)
10) User's Manual for the Brain, Volume II. (2002, with Hall)